ROWENA

The Life and Collected Works of
ROWENA GRANICE STEELE
California Pioneer
Actress – Author – Newspaper Publisher
By Priscilla Stone Sharp

Dedicated to the memory of my stepmother
Clara Monson Stone
1929-2018

She reminds me so much of Rowena. Both serious-minded, forthright, very intelligent, self-educated, with solid character, high morals and principles, and strong religious faith. They might be distantly related—the Monson and Granniss families both trace their American roots to Colonial era New Haven, Connecticut.

Rowena – The Life and Collected Works of Rowena Granice Steele
© Copyright 2024 by Priscilla Stone Sharp
Cover and illustration by Joe Klimek
Production and promotion by Nazarea Andrews –
www.InkslingerPR.com
ISBN: 979-8-9911038-7-9 (Hard Cover)
ISBN: 979-8-218-45011-3 (Soft Cover)
ISBN: 979-8-9911038-0-0 (EBook)
www.rowenagranicesteele.org

ROWENA

The Life and Collected Works of
ROWENA GRANICE STEELE
California Pioneer
Actress – Author – Newspaper Publisher

Volume I
Biography

by
PRISCILLA STONE SHARP

Table of Contents

Introduction

I first happened upon the name "Rowena Granice Steele" in 2001 (the 100th anniversary of her death) as I was doing research in the *San Joaquin Valley Argus* newspaper, published in Merced, California, by Rowena and her husband, Robert Johnson Steele. I was interested in everything I could learn about life in Merced preparatory to writing a book about my second-great-grand uncle, Mahlon Stone, a pioneer in 1847 to California who lived in Merced from 1850 until his death in 1880.

To be honest, at first I was somewhat put off by Rowena. For one thing, writing in the vernacular of that Victorian era, she almost always referred to herself in the first person plural "we," which to twenty-first century ears can come across as haughty and imperious.

Then I read that in December 1874, her son, Harry Granice, murdered the rival newspaper editor, seemingly in cold blood on a public street in Merced, supposedly in defense or retaliation for some slur upon his mother's honor. That gave the impression of a rather tyrannical attitude of her, if not the whole family, on Merced.

I am thankful I did not stop there while holding those initial impressions because they were soon to change. Over the months that followed, as I continued reading, there was always some little piece that would reach out and grab my attention and warm my heart – an article about orphans or a poor, sickly widow; a long, loving obituary for someone who was not necessarily prominent in the community or well-to-do, very often a child; a praise for some long-ago friend; a "don't despair" piece to cheer up readers; patriotic tributes to America for the Fourth of July; a description of the beauty and wonder of nature. I learned that nearly every social, charitable, health, educational, and welfare organization in Merced began with Rowena's inspiration or was championed in her newspaper columns. These began gradually to reveal to me the true character of this lady.

Slowly over the months, I became enamored with Rowena and began gathering as much information about her as I could. This was not an easy task, since much of what little there is available that was written about her is obscured and some negatively slanted. I learned that she had been an actress in the 1850s in San Francisco and in traveling companies that visited mining towns throughout California; a novelist – in fact, she has the distinction of being California's first female novelist; and finally a newspaper publisher and columnist in Merced for close to forty years.

She wrote, according to her own count, over sixty stories ranging in length from one-page short stories to three or four novel-length works. I have located and transcribed only half of them; sadly, we have to presume the others are lost to posterity. I have gathered over six hundred pages of typewritten research notes, including most of the hundreds of columns Rowena wrote for the paper over the years.

Sometimes I imagine myself going to visit Rowena to interview her at the "Coterie Cottage" on Main Street in Merced. In my daydream, I get off the southbound "puffer belly" steam train at the little depot just beyond the large, elegant El Capitan Hotel. To reach Main Street, I would walk northwest through the picturesque El Capitan Park with its magnificent fountain, erected in 1888 by Charles Henry Huffman and named by the townsfolk in honor of his wife, Laura. In a few short blocks I would soon be at the door of the neat and pretty rose-covered house. As I wait for the bell to be answered, I glance around the grounds and try to picture some of the many parties and ice cream socials held there over the years, and my eye would be drawn to the beautiful, colorful garden of next-door neighbor John Reed that Rowena admired and wrote about often.

The house inside, although called a "cottage," is quite large and very clean and tidy except for the piles of newspapers beside the rocking chair. Everywhere I look, my eyes see a multitude of mementoes and photographs – over forty pictures by Rowena's estimation – covering almost every square inch of the piano, tables, mantle and walls. The many scents, all of them pleasant, that tickle my nose consist of alternating and commingling perfume, cherry-scented pipe tobacco, fireplace residue, fresh bread, and a roast slow-cooking in the oven.

Then I picture Rowena. She is tall and thin, brusque and authoritative, and I must remind myself constantly that the outer "crust" is not, in this case at least, a true reflection of the inner person. She is wearing a dignified, long black dress with full sleeves and a high collar, with a white ruffle and small pin at the neck, a gold chain and dainty, dangling round gold earrings. Her neat and clean hair, just slightly gray, is piled in tight curls at the top of her head. Her unlined face and clear, dark gray eyes belie her sixty-plus years. She and I are sitting at the dining table; she is talking and I am taking notes in shorthand. She looks down and smiles and remarks that it is "quite amusing to look at the odd jumble of crooked little characters."

I would have to visit before January 1890 when her husband passed away. I can picture him sitting in a large sturdy rocking chair in the parlor reading some of the many newspapers, reciprocal subscriptions with journals all over the country. He is completely bald on the top of his head, with a full, luxuriant gray beard and moustache. A man of few verbal words, albeit copious editorials, he seldom speaks. Every once in a while he will take his well-worn pipe out of his mouth to make a comment or suggestion, spoken with a slow Southern drawl.

"Be sure to tell her about the railroad subsidy, Mrs. Steele."

Or, "You are too modest, my dear. History won't remember if you don't tell them."

It's a visit I will imagine often over the years. It is a never-failing pleasant experience, like remembering a visit to a dear friend or relative.

Sometimes I try to get inside Rowena's mind and think about what life must have been like for her – a woman born in the early 1800s who was at least a century ahead of her time in learning, understanding, social insights, awareness, and activism, who was thrust into the wild and violent life of early Gold Rush California. She was an advocate of education, careers and votes for women nearly eighty years before female suffrage was finally achieved in America. She was an actress in P.T. Barnum's American Museum and Theater on Broadway in New York and stages in California in the days when that word was widely used by "polite society" as a euphemism for "prostitute." She was a loyal wife and loving mother who sincerely cared about the welfare of everyone in her view.

She was not perfect. She made some bad decisions in life – most notably, the choice of first husband – and learned some stiff lessons in the process; hopefully, her experiences can impart some wisdom to us, her "spiritual descendants." And, like in the old saying, "If someone truly loves you, you can't do anything wrong, or at least nothing that can't be forgiven," I can forgive her little transgressions, biases and prejudices, or at least look at them in the context of America in the nineteenth century.

Here's the story as I think she would have told it to me. I have tried to let Rowena describe her life as much as possible, through her prolific stories, novels, and columns.

I hope you enjoy learning about Rowena Granice Steele and how she persevered for over half a century, through extreme hardship and ordeals, to enlighten and uplift her readers and contribute to an advancing civilization.

Priscilla Stone Sharp
State College, PA
2024

Chapter I

> I oft in fancy seem to roam
> Back to my old brown cottage home,
> I often wish, though wish in vain,
> That I could be a child again.[1]

Early Family and Home Life

In passing the quiet rural homes of my neighbors, my heart and thoughts go back to a long ago. Again I am in the little brown cottage with its snow-white walls, its large fireplace, bright red brick hearth, white-washed jambs, the quaint old andirons crossed, a large jar filled with greens and variegated with peonies, snow-balls, and the sweet, sweet lilac; the large sweet clover fields where Betsy and I would steal in upon forbidden ground and hunt strawberries; the waving fields of grain. Oh! all these dear old scenes come back to me and are as an oasis in the desert of a long professional life.[2]

I was born in the country, brought up in an old farm house, consisting of a parlor, a sitting room, three sleeping rooms, a kitchen and garret. Oh! that garret! how I should like to tell you about that dear old garret. Oh! happy! happy! remembrance springs up all around me at the recollection of the hours spent in childish sport in that old garret. In or near the centre a rope is made fast to the rafters for a swing; I can even now imagine that I hear the rain as it came patter, patter, down upon the moss-covered shingles—then was the playhouse ornamented with

rows of gaudy pieces of broken china; a little of
everything was to be found in that dear old never-to-
be-forgotten rainy day playhouse; the accumulation
of years was stored away up there, and yet how clean
everything looked.[3]

Through this picturesque description, Rowena Granice
Steele tells us about her childhood home in Goshen, New York
State, where she was born on June 20, 1824, the fourth of five
children of Henry ('Harry') and Julia Daines Granniss[i]. In the
family were John, born in 1815, Joel in 1819, Mary in 1820,
Rowena, and, three years later, little sister Frances — "Fanny" as
she was called.

It must have been a nearly idyllic early childhood. Still
rural in the twenty-first century, Goshen was then a remote
farming community in Orange County, about twenty miles west of
West Point, famous for its "Goshen butter." Rowena gives us to
understand the family was "genteel poor," meaning they were
refined, not rich in a fiscal sense but in all the natural aspects — in
the beauty of their natural surroundings; good, wholesome
nourishment for their bodies; learning and intelligence for their
minds; religious training, character, manners and comportment for
their souls.

Mr. Granniss was apparently a prosperous and frugal
farmer who was able to provide plenty of food for the family. In a
column about a typical Thanksgiving feast in those days, Rowena
later wrote: "The day previous the large brick ovens were heated,
and oven after oven full of mince pies, pumpkin pies, cranberry
tarts, and light bread were baked, while turkeys, chickens, ducks,
pigs, and spare ribs were prepared, and early on the morning of

---

[i] The spelling of the family name changes over the years, sometimes "Granis,"
"Grannis," "Graness," "Graniss," "Granise," and finally, for Rowena,
"Granice." Likewise, many different spellings of Daines, including "Dains" and
"Danes" have survived through the years.

Thanksgiving the oven was heated and these meats, with a good-sized Indian pudding, were put in to bake."[4]

Another favorite holiday memory for her was Christmas. In an article of 1876 (in which she decried the use of public or "community" Christmas trees as a new tradition because of the inherent unfairness of some children of wealthier families receiving more and better presents than the poor children of the community), she described what the celebration was like for her family in the 1820s:

> It is a country home. The ground is covered with snow. Little bright faces are at the window — the sound of jingle, JINGLE, JINGLE, and, then, as the handsome turnout approaches, the upper part of the window is filled with older faces, expressive of determination to know who's coming; then follows a variety of opinions of who they are and where they are going. All unconscious the sleigh-load of happy hearts glides by. In a few moments a similar sound is heard, not so joyous, not so full of mirthful music, a sort of a tinkle, TINKLE, for a dear old couple seated in an old-fashioned, high-backed, green-painted sleigh, with one horse and a single strap of bells, which only repeat chink, CHINK, a little louder as the old dappled gray trots along the slippery road. He's going to take these dear old folks to spend Christmas with some of the younger branches, and he must go slow and sure and safe. So the sleighs one after another pass and re-pass all day, while mother is in the kitchen giving orders or preparing the work herself of picking raisins, getting the turkey ready, boiling doughnuts, brightening up the spoons and getting the dishes ready for the Christmas dinner.

All through this day there has been a little veil of
mystery thrown over others' actions, a little by-talk
whenever a neighbor came in or mother and some
older and wiser member of the family have been seen
to come very softly out of the front room after
carefully and noiselessly pushing a bureau drawer to
its place.

Night comes on — the fire burns cheerfully and
throws its bright shadow on the red hearth. The
stockings are laid out and after a kiss and a promise
from mother that the stockings shall be put on those
very nails as soon as the fire goes down a little, the
night-capped heads filled with pleasant thoughts of
full stockings and Merry Christmas sink down upon
the soft white pillows of the trundle bed and the
young mind roars off to dreamland.

There are no sighs of disappointed hopes escaping
their red lips, but a bright smile of hope and sweet
expectation lights up each little face, for their hearts
tell them that they will have all in their stockings that
mother deems good for them. They have been taught
to look for nothing which is not within her means to
give. They have gone to sleep with clean faces, dry
feet, and happy hearts.[5]

Very little is known about Rowena's parents and no
pictures of them survive. We can glean from her stories an idea of
the character of some of those near and dear to her. For example,
in "The Old Shoe," one of several short Christmas stories in the
Argus, she describes a character who was most likely patterned
after her own mother: "A plain, refined, well-educated lady, who
received but little fashionable company."[6] She wrote often
throughout her career about other women, using the passage from
the Bible, "Her children arise and call her blessed" (Proverbs

31:28), and one gets the impression she used it often in describing Julia. Unfortunately, no apt descriptions of Harry Granniss survive.

She remembered her maternal grandfather, Harry Daines, a Revolutionary War veteran, as "one of the old 'Dutch Continentals who, in ragged regimentals, faltered not.' He was a holy man. He it was who filled our baby ears with tales of trials, sufferings and privations, and the reward of true heroism. He it was who taught our lisping tongue to thank God for freedom, and about 'Hurrah for Washington!'"[7] Probably because of these memories of her dear grandfather, Rowena was a passionate patriot her entire life. Among her favorite holidays was always the "Grand and Glorious Fourth of July," and almost every year beginning in May the columns of the *Argus* were filled with exhortations for her readers to fittingly celebrate the nation's natal day.

Another fond childhood memory of grandparents was lifted up in association with calico fabric when she wrote: "The word calico has always been associated with the kitchen, and drudgery; but, surely, after the display of neat, delicate cotton cloth prints of [the Calico Ball in Merced on] Monday evening, it shall, at the mention of the word, send my thoughts through a pretty flower garden in early springtime, and the violets, the blue-bells, the roses (from pale pink to deepest tints of red), buttercups, dear little daisies, and Joseph's coat of many colors, which grew down in my good old grandfather's garden … in all their brightest hues."[8]

According to Sydney S. Granniss, a distant cousin of Rowena who wrote a genealogy of the Granniss family in 1901, her father's people came from Connecticut in the earliest times. Mr. Granniss traced the lineage back to Edward (called "Edward Granest" in the Colonial records), who was in New Haven as early as 1650.[9] Harry's father, Rowena's paternal grandfather, Eldad Granniss, died in 1802 when Harry and his sisters, Florinda and

Rowena, were quite young. They also had an older half-brother, Bezaleel, by Eldad's first marriage, who was taken to Pennsylvania to live with his mother's people after her death. According to Rowena, her father never saw his brother again, and presumably Bezaleel never knew that he had a half-brother and sisters.[10]

According to Frederick Augustus Strong, who authored a genealogy of the Grannis family in 1927, grandfather Eldad Granniss also fought in the American Revolution in the Sixth Company of Wadsworth's Brigade with his cousin Capt. Nathaniel Bunnell, and Rowena's great-grandfather Caleb Granniss served in the French and Indian War in 1759.[11] They were deceased long before Rowena was born.

In about 1810, Rowena's aunt Rowena Granniss became the second wife of Nathaniel Hawley Hinman, Sr., and moved to Catskill, New York, along the Hudson River in the beautiful Catskill Mountain area. The passing away of the wife of her cousin, Nathaniel H. Hinman, Jr., in 1886 brought back "pleasant reminiscences of the happy days spent in the pleasant village of Catskill"[12] sixty years before. She also reunited in California in later life with Helen Walter Brown (wife of steamer Captain John K. Brown of Alameda) and wrote, "her sainted mother and myself were playmates in the village of Catskill many years ago, and the mantle of sweet, confiding friendship which bound the mother to my girlish heart seems to have fallen upon the daughter, who is well-known in literary circles as a gifted descriptive writer."[13]

In Rowena's youth, there was still an extensive Granniss family in Connecticut, and presumably Harry would have taken the children up to visit the old family homestead in Cheshire. From New York City, where they were living in the 1830s, they would have gone by steamship across Long Island Sound and up the Connecticut River or by coach along the old Boston Post Road, crossing several wide rivers by ferry. It would be at least a decade (1848) before the rails would be installed between New

York and New Haven. In that context, it is amazing to think that Rowena was living in Merced in 1900 when the first "horseless carriage" was brought there, and when she was a girl transportation was yet so primitive there were not even trains connecting New York with New England.

One wonders what she would have thought passing the New Haven commons (called "The Green"), seeing the stately churches lined up around it and most especially the magnificent buildings of Yale University. Would she have been struck by the fact that no girls of her day would ever be allowed to matriculate in such a school? While Rowena, as a child, attended public school in a day when it was not fashionable for girls to be formally educated, it was probably never with a view that she would be anything other than a housewife and mother. Above all, the most important things girls were to learn were the "domestic arts"—sewing, cooking, preserving, cleaning, and laundry. It was a widely held belief that the brain of a female was not large enough to contain facts about housework and family skills in addition to art and literature, let alone languages and sciences such as medicine. Yet, Rowena continued to write about and advocate the importance of education for women, so that, by the time her granddaughter, Cecelia "Celie" Granice, attended college at Berkeley in 1900, Rowena and other pioneer female professionals had begun to prove their worth, and there were wealthy benefactresses such as Phoebe Hearst endowing women's programs in colleges all over the country.

Some small Quaker colleges were enrolling girls in the mid-eighteen hundreds, but it would take another thirty years before women were allowed to study at Yale and other such hallowed halls of learning. And, while her sister females were content being housewives and mothers — or, if it was absolutely necessary that they work, shop girls, nurses, maids, or primary school teachers — it is obvious that Rowena early on became determined to excel in every aspect of life toward which she set her path, domestic and professional. Throughout her life, she showed firmness and resolve under the most trying and tragic circumstances, seemingly that whenever anyone said, "You cannot," it made her even more determined to say, "I will so!" Unfortunately, that attitude in Victorian-era women only made them greater targets for critics and cruel oppressors, male and female alike, who thought women should be taught to "keep their place."

Move to New York City and Education

Sometime after 1830, Harry sold the homestead in Orange County, most likely because of failing health and inability to run the farm, and moved the family into New York City to a home in the neighborhood of Charlton, King, Varick and Grove Streets near what is now the Greenwich Village area (at that time as remote from the city as Oakland is from San Francisco). She describes the neighborhood in a visit home in 1889 (her only trip back to New York from the time she left in 1856):

> The school house on the corner of Grove and Hudson although somewhat improved, looks much as it did sixty years ago when as a five year old lisping child, I muttered the words Baker, Briar, Friar, etc., and strange as it may seem with all of the gigantic strides improvement has made in the great city of New York I found little change in the streets I have mentioned. The same houses for blocks and blocks. There [at Charlton and Hudson] stood the building in which the Hon. David C. Broderick[ii] kept his

---

[ii] This is the same Senator David C. Broderick who was the loser in the duel with ex-California Supreme Court Justice David S. Terry in September 1859 near Lake Merced in San Francisco. Judge Terry then later became chief defense counsel for Rowena's son, Harry, in the murder trials of 1875-1877 and was himself murdered in 1889.

saloon for many years, looking just as it did forty years ago, with the exception of the red curtains then fashionable for windows and glass doors of a Porter House as saloons were then called. I am informed that the cause of this standstill in the way of improvement in this part of the city is owing to the fact that the property is owned by the Trinity Church and the Astors and was leased by the owners of the buildings for one hundred years. Of course, the time has nearly expired, and the lessees do not wish to make any new improvements.

In 1830 a man by the name of Berrian put up a small, one-story house on a leased lot on Varick street, near King, and opened what was then known as a Victualling House and had a large sign painted upon which was the following: *Our own house, on our own plan and I can sell as cheap as any man and my name is Sam Berrian.* This was repeated daily in a loud voice by the urchins of the neighborhood as they passed by. That house with its broad sign is still standing although the lettering is obliterated either by the brush or by time.[14]

In a lengthy, but very insightful and interesting serialized article in the *Argus*, beginning on January 19, 1878, Rowena gives a detailed account of early childhood education in the city of New York in the early 1800s:

Among the finest and most commodious of the public school buildings in the city of New York forty-seven years ago was one situated on Grand between Thompson and Laurance streets. It was a large two-story and basement brick structure standing in the center of four lots. On either side was

a yard used as entrance to the back door of each
department, through which the pupils passed. These
yards were fenced in by high board fences and used
for playgrounds. The gates were closed and locked at
nine o'clock each morning, and the tardy child was
obliged to ask admission at the front door, where he
or she had to explain the cause of being late by a
note from parent or guardian. The exterior of the
building was neat but elegant compared with the
buildings of that day. Facing on the street was what
we New Yorkers call a stoop, with broad steps
running up on the right and left. Two large front
doors opened in from the stoop. These doors were
used for the admission of teachers, school officers
and visitors. ...

We shall now undertake to give a brief, but correct,
description of the juvenile and infantile suite of
rooms, and the manner of teaching and training. The
juvenile and infantile rooms were separated by large
sliding doors. The juvenile was the front room,
lighted by twelve large windows. Beneath these
windows was a bench of comfortable height from
the floor. In front of this bench was a desk extending
the entire length of the bench. In front of each
scholar was a place underneath the desk large enough
to hold a slate and a lunch. Just in front of this desk
is another bench not quite as high as the one behind
it. These benches seated two hundred children. The
floor, which was scrubbed once a month regularly,
fresh sanded once a week, and drawn over every
night after the school was dismissed, was laid with
black lines about two or three inches in width, in
straight and circular form; the straight lines extending
lengthwise and across the room within four or five
feet from the wall. Upon this line the children

marched and countermarched to their seats, singing the following quaint little childish verse:

We go to our places with smiles on our faces,
And say all our lessons distinctly and slow,
For if we don't do it, we surely will rue it,
As we will be found useless wherever we go,

each foot keeping time with the sweet, earnest little voice. The black circles were used by classes for spelling and reading. Six pupils, with toes turned out and heels turned in, and hands behind, occupied each circle while reciting their lessons. At the same time the little ones left upon the benches are engaged in making letters in sand, which has been sprinkled upon the desk for that purpose, and which is afterwards swept off by monitors.

When the recitations were finished, the pupils stepped out upon the straight line and were joined by the little sand writers. Then came the order from one of the teachers: "Face front! Face front! March!" and the line of two hundred file out into the yard for a recess where they are met by two hundred from the infant room.

We forgot to make mention of the regulations for opening the school in the morning. We will now take occasion to speak of the interesting ceremony. When the pupils were quietly seated in both rooms of the basement department, the sliding doors were drawn open and a beautiful picture was presented. In the center of the front room, seated upon a large, well-furnished platform, sat the two principal teachers, Mrs. Heart and Mrs. Clark. By the side of each sat an assistant teacher, Miss Agnes Angis and Miss Sally Ann Heart.

* * *

In front of the railing, with their hands resting upon
the desk, stand two young girls, the head monitors of
that room. In the back room, upon a small platform,
sits the principal teacher of the infant class. By her
side stand two girls about twelve years of age. As the
sound of the moving doors dies away, silence reigns
for a moment. Then the clear, sweet voice of Mrs.
Heart is heard as she reads a chapter from the Bible.
Again all is still, and every little hand moves up to the
face. The nose rests upon the tips of the fingers,
while the thumbs are folded beneath the chin, and
every little bright eye closed. Then Mrs. Clark rises to
her feet and utters in a clear voice the morning
prayer.

As the word "Amen" is pronounced, eight hundred
little hands are held up for inspection. Clean or
unclean? That is the question, and although it was
very seldom that a dirty hand was found among
them, still the rigid examination was repeated every
morning — five mornings in the week.

After the hand inspection, the sliding doors were
closed, and the day's instruction commenced, which
consisted of reading, spelling, sand and slate writing,
practice lessons in geography demonstrated by
charts; reciting all the tables in arithmetic, including
the table of Roman notation, interspersed with
marching, singing and gesturing.

There were many little ones in the infant class not
over two years of age. "Why were these babies sent
to school?" exclaim some of our readers. Why, gentle
reader, the public school system was organized
originally for the express benefit of the poor, and
many mothers, who were obliged to support a large
family by their labor, had the privilege of sending the
little two-year-old with the larger children to the

school, with a certain knowledge that her little one
would be under the care of a kind teacher who had
been instructed by the trustees that the care of the
infants was an important part of her duty.

* * *

Speaking in our last chapter of the extreme youth of
some of the children who attended the public school
forty-seven years ago, we could tell many interesting
anecdotes. But having a purpose in view in writing
these chapters, we will not digress — suffice it that
these little ones were not intruders as will be seen by
the preparations made for their comfort and
accommodation. On one side of the room used for
the instruction of the infant class was a room about
fourteen feet square fitted up with the conveniences
of a first-class stateroom: Wash-stands, basins,
towels, sponges, soap, also combs and brushes.

Upon the carpeted floor was spread several little
pallets, and upon the long summer afternoons half a
dozen or more of the rosy-cheeked youngsters could
be found sleeping in this room as sweetly and
soundly as though they were at home in their own
little beds. It was the business of one of the under
teachers to attend to the requirements of the helpless
ones. And as each one awoke, the face and hands
were washed, the hair combed, and with a kiss upon
the cherry lips, they were sent or taken to the
classroom. These little ones repeated twice each day
the multiplication table, with quaint and fantastic
gestures, changing the gesture at the beginning of
each column, and we will venture to say that there
was not a child four years of age in the building who
could not recite that table correctly, even backwards

and skipping about, that is, if they had attended the school two months.

They also recited pages of the child's first geography and understood what the sciences taught. The little songs they sang were lessons which helped to form their future characters. There were also several recitation rooms, where the monitors and older pupils recited their lessons either to Mrs. Heart or Mrs. Clark.

Many of these girls were going through the rudiments preparatory to higher branches, with a view to fit themselves for public school teachers. For, at that time, it was thought that in order to be a proficient public school teacher, the education and ability to teach should be gained through a public school experience, and those pupils who evinced a superior talent in the government of a class and in imparting instruction to the children entrusted to their care, never escaped the eye of these watchful teachers, Mrs. Heart and Mrs. Clark. It made no difference how coarse or scant their attire, they received a just and unprejudiced attention from their superior teachers, and no pains were spared to cultivate and improve the germ implanted by nature in these children of poverty.

We have no doubt but that hundreds of the good, model grandmothers, and honorable men of today look back and bless the memory of those sweet, gentle women, Mrs. Heart and Mrs. Clark. To our young imagination they were as grand as queens, so dignified and yet so kind and simple. Mrs. Heart was about forty years of age. She always dressed in black, either silk, merino, or thin barege, or Canton crepe, according to the season. A large and very fine lace collar reached nearly to the armhole of her dress; it was fastened at the throat with a small, pearl-headed pin. She also wore an ample cap of lace with five or six yards of a pleated border. Several bows of white satin ribbon decorated the top of the cap. Her high, broad forehead was adorned with six small glossy jet puffs on either side. Her large, intelligent black eyes beamed kindness upon the most belligerent little imp who was sent to her desk for corporeal punishment.

Both of these lady teachers were married, and their husbands frequently visited the schoolroom. They were gentlemen of means, and seemed to take quite an interest in school affairs. Of course, in that large city we knew but little of the home life of our schoolteachers, but we have always been impressed with the idea that these ladies had been among the most prominent of the first movers in the great public school system. And that they, with many other highly educated ladies of ample means, had left their homes of ease and comfort and entered the schoolroom as teachers, for the sole purpose of establishing a system that should prove a benefit to the generations who should come after them.

* * *

We will now leave the infant or primary departments and introduce the reader to Mrs. Winans, the principal instructress of the girls' high school. Mrs. W. was a dignified middle-aged lady, possessing a full knowledge of the classics in addition to a highly cultivated mind. At nine in the morning she took her seat upon a large platform, and after the classes were all in their proper places, a chapter was read from the Bible, a morning hymn sung, and a prayer uttered, which closed the opening exercises.

Attached to the main room of the girl's high school room was an anteroom, used for a clothes room, where neatly starched sunbonnets, cloaks, shawls, and other garments belonging to the children were hung up previous to entering the schoolroom. There were also three large recitation rooms which were used for classes of advanced pupils. This was a very judicious arrangement. In these neat, quiet rooms were charts, maps and globes for the use of the higher classes in geography; also, blackboards, pointers, chalk and sponges, adapted to the working out of sums and problems. This was, indeed, an excellent idea, as it obviated the confusion necessarily occasioned by blackboard exercises being practiced in the main room. In this department there were five paid teachers and some eight or ten monitors.

No studying [in class] was allowed; all lessons must be learned at home. This improved the memory and made it more retentive. The discipline and rules were so rigidly enforced, and so implicitly obeyed, that school life in those days seemed to have but little connection with the doings of the outside world. The desks in this department ran across the room like the pews in a church, with center, middle, and side aisles, each pupil occupying a round stool of comfortable height, and when their hands were not employed with slate and pencil they were folded upon their backs.

There were no stoop-shouldered girls in the public schools forty-five years ago. One of the prominent branches taught was good manners and a healthful and graceful carriage. When marking in line for exercise, right foot, left foot, they moved with the regularity of a body of well-drilled soldiers.

Lessons in penmanship were given three times a week. And, as another proof that the public school system was organized for the special benefit of the poor, needlework in all its branches was taught, and three afternoons of each week an hour was devoted in gaining knowledge in this useful acquirement. On sewing day, in the afternoon at 3 o'clock, a monitor took her position at the head of each class with a splint workbasket in her hand containing a piece of work, thread, needle and thimble for each girl in her class, and at the word, "Distribute," the work was handed out.

This piece of work was a small bit of unbleached cotton cloth, and the work to be performed upon it was seam-felling, over-handing, hemming, stitching, and button-hole making. When, according to the capacity of the pupil, all the work that could be done upon it was finished, the scraps were thrown into the ragbag and sold for paper rags at six cents a pound.

When a girl had passed through all the grades of plain sewing, and was pronounced a good seamstress, she could bring her own sewing to school and work upon it while the others were learning; or, if she had a taste for fancy work, she was promoted to the marking and sample class, where she was taught silk, worsted, and linen floss embroidery. And many a young girl whose father was quite well to do would, after leaving school, earn her own support by the beautiful art of embroidery. Others, of a poorer class, could without losing time to learn a trade, make a good living by plain hand sewing.

These old-time New York public schools frequently sent forth a girl fourteen years old, with a good English education and well prepared to go out into the world and make an honest and respectable living from the instructions she had received through those competent, well-qualified teachers.

There was another and still stronger proof of the magnanimous principles of the public school system in its early history. It was that every article used in the school was supplied from the school fund. Books, slates, pencils, writing material, in fact, everything appertaining to the requirements of the schoolroom was furnished free of charge to the pupils to use during school hours, or to take home for the purpose of studying. As any careless act in regard to soiling or damaging the books was considered deserving of punishment, great care was taken to keep them in good order, so that each set of books passed through the hands of several pupils.[15]

Father's Death – Marriages of Siblings – Life in the Jersey Countryside

Harry Granniss died sometime between 1834 and 1836; where he is buried is not known. By that time, John was working in Troy Hills, New Jersey, where he met his future wife, and it is quite probable that Joel was already apprenticing away from home as a shoemaker, leaving Julia with the three girls, Mary aged about 15, Rowena, 12, and Fanny, 8. For Rowena, it seems apparent that her father's death marked the end of a wonderful childhood and the beginning of huge personal losses she was to suffer over the coming years—deaths of so many near and dear to her, including her own son, and the inevitable betrayals by mean-spirited and small-minded people that scarcely any human being can escape. Like most everyone else, she tried to bear them and said later that she always endeavored to cling to the comforting words of the old hymn, "Our troubles and our trials here will only make us richer there."[16]

With the boys well on their way professionally, it is reasonable to assume that, after her husband's death, Julia would have redoubled her efforts at getting the girls educated and suitably married. Perhaps she took in embroidering or sewing or washing and ironing to supplement whatever support Mr. Granniss had left for her and the children. In that regard, Rowena could have been speaking from experience when she described the efforts of the heroine in her novel *Leonnie St. James; Or, The Suicide's Curse* to search for work in the city.

> She had wandered the city over, seeking for something to do that would enable her to earn a scanty subsistence. She thought that she might make shirts. She one day called at a Jew's shop, the proprietor of which had advertised for five hundred hands.
>
> "Yah, I vill give you vork, but you must leave one tollar deposit on a bundle—dat ish two shirts—for security," was his answer.
>
> "A dollar!" said Leonnie in surprise. "I have not got a shilling in the world. But I will tell you where I live, and you shall have them all safe day after tomorrow."
>
> "Oh, dat ish very goot shtory, but ish no shuit me. You leave one tollar, und ven you pring te shirts pack, I pays you fifty cents; tat ish te price of te making. I keeps te tollar as long as you vorks for me, und ten you gets te tollar pack."[17]

Conceivably, by this method, a woman looking to support herself in the 1830s in New York would have to sew three shirts a week to make a meager $1.50, and this all by hand stitching; the sewing machine was not widely available until 1857. Otherwise, if she was uneducated, the only other source of income would be working as a domestic or, as a last resort, relegated to the many

factories or "sweat shops" as they were called, where she would
work alongside other women and often little children, usually
closed up in a windowless, unsanitary, and unsafe workshop, ten
hours a day, six days a week, to earn the barest subsistence.

In the introduction to *Leonnie*, a tragic story of a young
schoolgirl in New York seduced by a heartless wretch and
abandoned with a small child, Rowena gives us a glimpse into her
own home life and her early attempts at making a living and how,
in her later writing, she tried to draw her characters from those she
had heard about or knew in real life.

> When very young, I acted as tract distributor in the
> great city of New York. To me this occupation was a
> most pleasing one, for, being naturally of a commun-
> icative disposition, I imparted freely the history of
> my own life and was often repaid by that of the
> listener in return. I also draw many truths and
> conclusions from my own checkered and eventful
> life; especially when speaking of home — of a kind,
> loving mother, and pure, gentle, affectionate,
> confiding sisters — trials and struggles with pride
> and poverty; these are old, familiar scenes, and cling
> to me through all the vicissitudes of life.[18]

In this, as in all of her stories, she "endeavored ... to bring a moral
to bear upon it."[19] One gets the general impression after reading
all of her extant novels and stories that it was her aim to illustrate
the virtues, or strength of character, that human beings are
hopefully striving to attain. Her stories are replete with rewards
for positive qualities such as abiding love, faith in God, kindness,
patience, charity, chastity, honor, perseverance, and courage;
whereas the ne'er-do-wells are always appropriately punished.
Even seeming "innocents," such as Leonnie St. James and Dell

Dart, who simply make poor behavior judgments or put too much trust in fiendish men, do not escape the inevitable tragic end.

Rowena also gives a glimpse of life for a young girl trying to make a living in New York City in the 1830s in "The Old Shoe":

> I learned a trade, one which made it necessary for me to go to a shop every morning and work unceasingly, ten hours a day, summer and winter, for a small pittance, just sufficient to pay a dollar and a half a week for my board, fifty cents for my washing, and clothe me in the plainest garments, scarcely suited to the inclemency of these severe Northern winters. For two years I had started each weekday morning from the upper part of Varick street, and walked down to Chamber, through Chamber street to Broadway, along Broadway to Liberty with a little basket of lunch in my hand, and a thick green veil drawn closely over my face; not that I was ashamed to see or be seen by honest people, but to avoid the impudent stares of the throng of heartless libertines who are ever on the alert to entice the poor, virtuous working girl from the paths of purity.[20]

In this paragraph, Rowena also provides further insights about life for women in New York City in the 1830s. If brother Joel was still at home when their father died, it is highly probable that he would have been placed in charge of the family — even though only a boy of fifteen or sixteen. Women had very few independent rights at that time and, unless possessed of a separate, substantial means of support, needed a male guardian or protector — a father, uncle, brother or son. It was not wise for a girl to be alone on the streets, especially in certain neighborhoods of the city. In her novella *Dell Dart; Or, Within the Meshes*, Rowena creates a vivid picture of the downfall, disgrace, and eventual tragic finish of a young orphan girl in Boston who is seduced and kidnapped by a gambler.

If Joel was left with the burden of being "man of the house," it was undoubtedly too great a responsibility for a teenager. In such cases it is not uncommon for the young fellow, in order to exert his authority, to become somewhat of a tyrant, and for Rowena, without doubt a highly spirited, determined child, it would have inevitably caused a strain in their relationship. This, or some other similar problem, may explain something of a mystery in her life that, while she has written numerous glowing articles and tributes about everyone else in the family, there is not one sentence about her brother Joel or his family anywhere to be found.

The next major event in the family was brother John's marriage to Rachel DeHart on May 24, 1836, in the New Jersey countryside for which Rowena was to grow so fond over the next two decades. ("Dear old Jersey home, although not our native State, still the sweetest, brightest, and sunniest part of our happy girlhood was spent within call of [sister Mary Granniss Keeler's] orchard...."[21]). John and Rachel began married life in the same small town in Morris County where lived Rachel's father and mother, Daniel DeHart and Martha Quimby, both from very old and prominent Colonial New Jersey families, then eventually settled nearby in Orange County.

In describing John, Frederick Strong said that, "[t]hough of a quiet, retiring nature, he was of resolute purpose and forceful in expression and action."[22] Over the years, he was called upon for greater community responsibilities and was eventually elected to several posts including first Marshall of West Orange, New Jersey, Committeeman, Town Clerk and Assessor.[23] In writing about her brother, Rowena noted that he was "honest, just and true" and continued in a tribute to him, "There will be no fraud where and while you hold an office of public trust."[24] John and Rachel were the parents of Mary Elizabeth, born in 1837, who died in infancy; Laura Frances, 1838; Martha Ann, 1842; Mary Caroline, 1844; and Daniel D., 1848. On their fiftieth wedding anniversary, Rowena had occasion to note, "we doubt if ever a couple lived together fifty years who have enjoyed more true matrimonial bliss than Mr. and Mrs. John Granniss. In all those years this couple have not been separated one week, and their home has been in the State of New Jersey."[25]

Sister Mary was the next to fall in love and leave the family nest. In May 1840 she married Thaddeus (sometimes spelled Thaddus) Keeler, a superintendent of buildings and later a broker. He worked for a while in the City and sometime after 1850 they, too, left the city and moved out to Parsippany, New Jersey, where he followed the path of gentleman farmer. In a loving obituary written after Mary Granniss Keeler's death in April 1890, Rowena remembered her sister: "Mrs. Keeler was a poet and in her younger years was a brilliant society woman, noted among her friends for possessing the happy gift of entertaining large assemblages at her home."[26] It was important for Rowena to keep the early memories of her elder sister because, when she went home for a visit in 1889, she was heartbroken to find her sister had become a helpless invalid who did not recognize her.

Mary and her husband apparently named their first-born child after Rowena. She died in childhood — undoubtedly another great sadness in Rowena's young life. Mary and Mr. Keeler had three other children who lived to adulthood: Frank, born in 1842; Virginia, 1844; and William S., 1848. William became a prominent physician in the City. Virginia married William Schenck and had two children when she died, at only twenty-five years of age, in 1869. Mary and her husband helped care for the grandchildren until Mr. Schenck remarried and moved to Pennsylvania. One of those children, Augusta "Gussie" Schenck eventually joined her Aunt Rowena in Merced, California, served for a time as governess at the Griffith Ranch and married George Anderson in Modesto in 1890.

Rowena apparently spent most of her teenage and young womanhood years in New Jersey with brother John, and later sisters Mary and Fanny and their families, and, from her reminiscences we understand that it was a wonderful time in her life. Not only was it a healthier environment than the city, but also society in the country in the 1800s was not so formal and rigid; for example, since there was not a great many people there, all the young people of the village were regularly invited to balls and parties, even at the wealthiest homes. She must have had many occasions to practice Mrs. Winans' lessons in manners, carriage, and deportment that she had learned during her few years at the high school in the City.

One of her friends in those early years in New Jersey was John Alonzo "Lon" Quimby, who went to California in 1849, was a representative to the State Legislature and later Mayor of San Jose for eight years. He retired from public life in the 1870s and ran a large lumber business in San Jose. He and his brother Eugene were among the boys and girls with whom Rowena associated in those days in New Jersey. Over the years, she would remember fondly how they "used to leap five rail fences, ride on horseback, go to apple cuts, quilting and kissing bees, and played 'Old Sledge' for who should 'go down cellar after cider'."[27] (It's odd to think about young people in the nineteenth century playing kissing and courting games; none of us can imagine our parents, let alone grandparents, indulging in such sport.)

A walk down the streets of Merced one morning in November 1887 brought back childhood memories of the game of quoits (horseshoes): "This old game seems as new and as enjoyable today as it was sixty years ago when we sat on the old door stone of the old brown house down the lane in Orange county, N.J., and watched with childish glee the men and boys pitch the horseshoes that were kept, as a general thing, under the house for luck."[28]

One particularly amusing experience she had in the country that never left her memory was as a girl about fourteen years of age when she was called to help an invalid lady for a few days:

The apartment which the lady occupied during the day was a large front room with two doors, one opening out upon the porch and the other into the kitchen.

As the family kept no servant except a small boy to do chores, I found it necessary to go to the kitchen to set things to rights as soon as I arrived, but I had not anticipated having such work to perform and I did not come prepared with a proper dress. Not expecting to remain from home more than two or three days, I took nothing but what I wore, a light print dress and white apron.

"Put on one of my old dresses," said Mrs. Holcomb, the lady of the house, and in spite of the pain she was suffering she laughed; for her weight was at least two hundred and fifty pounds, while I was extremely tall and slender and did not weigh over one hundred and ten. However, by wrapping it around me and pinning it over the back and front of the waist, and fastening the skirt up and tying a coarse apron about me, I managed to stay in the extensive garment. After placing my clean print and white apron upon the back of a large chair, I rolled up my sleeves and entered heart and hands into the culinary duties.

Dick, the [hired] boy, laughed at the comic appearance I made and brought one of the old lady's wide frilled caps and large iron-bound specs, and motioned in pantomime for me to put them on and complete the rig. We both tittered and tee-hee-ed. With the help of Dick, we at last got started to work, and soon dishes, pans, pots and kettles were shining in their respective places.

Mr. Holcomb with a young hired man was working in a distant field. I told Dick to keep a lookout and tell me if he saw them coming so that I could run and get out of sight. I also asked Mrs. Holcomb to keep a little watch upon the lane and give me warning of the approach of visitors. There was a long lane leading from the main road to the garden gate, and an unobstructed view to the end, so one would have ample time to make considerable preparation for the reception of guests before they got to the front door.

Just as I had the large dinner pot about half washed Mrs. Holcomb called out, "Company coming!" I dropped the pot and ran to look out of the window and there, behold! was a company of four ladies and two gentlemen, mounted upon horses and dressed in a most stylish manner. Long green, blue and black riding habits almost swept the ground, plumes of every hue danced with the breeze. It was a gay party, and all were strangers to me.

"From the city!" I exclaimed.

I looked back into the room, good gracious, what confusion! The articles which Mrs. Holcomb had ordered Dick to bring to her lay scattered all over the floor, a basket of old rags with half of them outside, three huge bandboxes with old-fashioned bonnets lying beside them. I flew around in nervous excitement. I must get all these things out of sight, and then snatch my dress and make my escape through the kitchen door to some other apartment. I shoved one thing after another under the high, old-fashioned bedstead. Oh! how the perspiration ran down my face, as nearer, nearer came the dashing equestrians. I could hear the sweet, silvery voices of the ladies and the gay retorts of the gentlemen, and the tramping hooves of the horses.

The things were all stowed away under the bed, the footsteps of the visitors were upon the porch. I snatched my dress and flew to the kitchen door, and oh, horror! Dick, the young rogue, had fastened it on the other side! There I stood pounding and shaking. The front door opened and in rushed the young girls and gentlemen, nieces and nephews of Aunt Holcomb's who had come to see her because she was sick.

And there I stood with that old-fashioned cap with the great iron-framed specs standing just above the frill, in my hurry and flurry my thin arm had slipped out of one of the enormous sleeves and left the arm and shoulder entirely bare. I became faint and dizzy. I made an effort to scream. I tried to spring forward and pass them, and in the struggle I awoke.

It was only a dream!

Down in that easy chair I had fallen asleep. I had passed through all that ridiculous scene in the short space of ten minutes. When I got up and went out into the kitchen I found the potpie and pudding ready for the table, everything still in its place.[29]

In 1842, Joel married Cornelia Boker in Orange County, New York. They lived in Middletown for a while then moved to Parsippany, New Jersey, later in the 1850s. Both apparently were beset with physical ailments. Joel died in 1856 in Parsippany, and Cornelia followed him to the grave just six months later. Known children were three sons, Henry, born in 1843, Frank, 1845, and

John, 1847, and baby daughter Anna Augusta, who died in infancy
in 1849. The boys went to live with their Boker grandparents in
Orange County, New York, for a time. When the Civil War broke
out all three, the youngest being only fifteen, joined a New York
regiment, and the two eldest were killed at the Battle of Malvern
Hill in Pennsylvania in July of 1862. Young John apparently never
went home again, but wandered west to Iowa.[30]

How heartbreaking that must have been for Rowena to
hear that terrible news after the war, and it was especially tragic
considering at the time she was married to Robert J. Steele, who
was a "dyed-and-true" Confederate from Mississippi, and, trying
to be a loyal wife to an otherwise decent, devoted, honest man,
one can imagine how her emotions were torn for her loved ones
on the side of the Union.

In 1845, Fanny married William K. Gray. They stayed in
the City for several years, and by 1852 they, too, had moved to a
home in East Orange, New Jersey, very near Mary and John and
eventually Joel. Mr. Gray was an interesting man. He had gone
out to sea on a whaling boat when he was a young boy, then
became a tailor in New York, a teacher in New Jersey, and eventually graduating medical school as a mature married man. They
had six children — one girl, Mary, who married a dentist, Dr.
Roderick Sanger, and five boys, William K. Jr., Richardson,
Henry, Edward, and Thomas Neptune Claughley Gray (born in
1854 and named after Rowena's first husband, Thomas N.
Claughley). Thomas, Richardson and William all became eminent
physicians. Richardson was also an ordained clergyman in the
Methodist-Episcopal Church who was called to missionary work
in Pithoragarh, India, and wrote home interesting letters about his
experiences, several of which Rowena published in the *San
Joaquin Valley Argus* in the 1870s.

Rowena was very attached especially to this sister and her
husband. In several of her stories the character of physician was
named "Dr. Gray."

Chapter II

Our hopes are flown—yet parted hours
Still in the depths of memory lie,
Like night gems in the silent blue
Of summer's deep and brilliant sky.[1]

New York City in the Early 1800s

NEW YORK! busy, bustling New York! What a variety
is found within thy limits. The emporium of fashion,
amusement, beauty and gaiety—of want, beggary and
misery! The dashing belle and the squalid mendicant
walk side by side; the millionaire and rag-picker ride
in the same 'bus, and pull the same string to stop the
vehicle; the one to enter his luxurious mansion on
Fifth Avenue, the other his garret or cellar on one of
the by-streets, where dwell the poor of all nations.
Such is life in New York![2]

While she obviously loved the New Jersey countryside,
Rowena spent a great deal of time in the City in those years of her
young womanhood. In a story about the famous singer and
Temperance speaker, James M. Brown, she describes some scenes
of those days:

Ah, well does the writer of this remember the
winter of '43, a bevy of rosy-cheeked, bright-eyed
girls would rush pell-mell into the quiet domicile of
our widowed mother and exclaim: "Oh, guess who is
going to speak tonight at the Lady Hudson Hall?"

Although we knew well enough just by the way in which we were interrogated, still not wishing to deprive them of the pleasure of making the announcement we would, with an enquiring look (feigned) ask: "Who?"

"Brown of Yonkers! Come, hurry, or we will be late."

What cared we for wind, frost, snow or slippery sidewalks? With a warm pair of woolen yarn stockings drawn over our shoes we could defy old sidewalk, and enveloped in a thick cloth cloak with quilted lining, a little quilted hood and fur collar, we could place our blue noses within the clasp of a comfortable mitten and laugh at old Boreas, and bid defiance to the howling Storm King. The sweet singing, and eloquent, truthful speaking of "Brown of Yonkers" would soon warm us and give us courage to brave the homeward trip.[3]

A typical department store shopping trip was charmingly rendered in *Eudolia Dudley*, the story of a young, uneducated orphan who was separated from her sisters early in life.

At ten the conveyance was at the door. Eudolia was dressed in simple white, with a pretty, blue scarf ornamented with white embroidered roses thrown lightly over her shoulders. A delicate, plain, crepe bonnet and gloves to match completed her toilet for a day's pleasure ride over the smooth paved Bloomingdale Road. Mrs. Hurley, neatly attired, followed her, and soon they were rattling along toward Broadway, near Chamber Street. On that ever busy thoroughfare stood the store of the now prince merchant of the marble palace. Although both the building and the store would, at the present day, be considered rather humble to outward appearance, still the finest, best and most reliable goods could be obtained at the counters of Stewart's store. At this establishment, Mrs. Hurley had ordered the driver to stop.[4]

Holidays presented exciting opportunities for celebration in the City, as this 1884 account of New Year's traditions in the 1840s indicates:

In New York City forty years ago on these occasions, the streets presented a lively and beautiful sight. Ladies of that day dressed in gay colors, wore large bonnets with immense long, graceful feathers of every shade, and on the 2d of January when making calls, each tried to outdo the other in elegance of costume. Bonnets were then worn of pink, green, blue, yellow, purple, white silk and velvet, and also the dresses and cloaks were of bright gay colors. If the ground was covered with snow, as it frequently was in those days, the scene was one of wild delight with the fine horses plunging through the snow, jingling bells, magnificent sleighs, smiling faces, merry voices, rosy cheeks and bright eyes. On those occasions Broadway and Canal streets presented a scene never to be forgotten by those who had the pleasure to be an eyewitness.

But the ladies did not leave their mirth outside; they took it in their merry glad hearts into the elegant parlors, and many a bachelor brother or uncle on this day lost his heart and broke his resolve to live single, and soon thereafter would become a happy benedict.[5]

Marriage to Thomas Claughley — Births of Harry and George

Julia Daines Granniss passed away on August 26, 1849, and was buried at Greenwood Cemetery in Brooklyn, New York. Sometime between 1844 and 1849, Rowena married Thomas Neptune Claughley[6], who, according to Rowena, writing some years later, was born in County Armagh, Ireland[7] in about 1816 (he was listed as being 44 years old at his death in 1860). No other fact is known of Claughley's background or parentage. It may be that he was the son of or otherwise related to Irish merchant James Claughley who died aged 58 in 1845, the victim of a violent assault when he was pushed off a car of the Harlem railroad by William Galvin, also Irish, employed as a porter in the store of George E. Waring. Next-of-kin was reported as being a son, Samuel W. Claughley.[8]

In the 1829-'30 New York City Directory appears grocer James Claughley on Hester Street at the corner of Mulberry. A "James Claughley" again appears in 1839-'40 as a grocer at 155 Grand, corner of Orange, and Thomas appears for the first time that year as a dealer in sofas at 3 Howard, with a home address of 155 Grand. That they are related somehow is apparent by the common address. This is within one mile of the neighborhood where the Granniss family lived.

Some researchers have put Rowena's marriage to Claughley in 1844.[9] This is a problem for several reasons. First and most important, taking into context the culture, social conditions, and prejudices of the day, it is very doubtful that Mrs. Granniss would have ever approved of her young daughter marrying an uneducated Irish immigrant workingman, even if he was a merchant. This was at a time in New York City when bands such as the "Five Points Gangs" were beginning to reach the zenith of their power. The Irish in particular were associating themselves with the ruthless and corrupt political bosses at Tammany Hall, and there was a great deal of prejudice in genteel society against the immigrants, particularly the Irish, crowding into New York by the thousands.

If Thomas Claughley and his brother James associated with the same men in New York that they were known to be connected with later in San Francisco, that would include the infamous "Dutch Charley" Duane who was to come to nefarious prominence along with David Broderick in San Francisco in the 1850s. Born in Tipperary, Ireland, in December 1827, Charles Patrick Duane emigrated to Albany, New York when he was nine years old. At fifteen, he left home and apprenticed himself to a wagon maker in New York City, joined a local fire company and made a name for himself as a boxer and enthusiastic member of a gang of vicious rapists, extortionists and bullies. Such is the saddening blemish on the origins of the heroic firefighting companies in New York that in those early days they were made up of these young urban street gangs, who drank, gambled, "bare-knuckle" boxed, whored, and strutted their way into the notice of Tammany Hall political bosses. In fact, it has been noted that no man could get elected to an office in New York who did not have the support of these "volunteer fire companies." These gangs quickly became notorious in the election process as "shoulder-strikers"[iii] who gathered at polling places and bullied voters and came up with ever more ingenious methods to stuff ballot boxes to guarantee the outcome of elections.[10]

The second concern about the possibility of an 1844 marriage arises from a coroner's inquiry into the death of fourteen-month-old Margaret Eliza Claughley on March 20, 1846. This little girl, who died of convulsions, was identified as the daughter of Thomas and Eliza Jane Claughley, born in New York. No record of this marriage or its conclusion can be found, but if it

---

[iii] The term "shoulder-striker" came about to describe the way these hired bullies walked up and down the row of men lined up to vote, "strike" against their shoulders violently, and loudly whisper "Vote for - -!" The term became synonymous with political corruption, particularly in San Francisco.

is the same Thomas Claughley, this means there could not have been a marriage to Rowena before 1847 at the earliest.

It is widely assumed that Rowena's tale "The Two Wives," one of the stories gathered in her first book, *The Family Gem*, published in Sacramento in 1857, was loosely based on the story of her marriage to Thomas Claughley. In it she describes the heroine's elopement from her aunt's home in Baltimore to Philadelphia with "a young gentleman whose visits were disagreeable to the family."[11] The couple went to New York where the husband then entered into business. Rowena may have chosen Baltimore for a good reason. In no other cities except Baltimore and New York were there any Claughleys found living in the early 1800s. If we assume they were married in 1847 or 1848, before Mrs. Granniss died in Aug 1849, this elopement may be a truer description than previously suspected, albeit from her mother's home in New York, not an aunt's home in Baltimore.

Regardless of when it occurred, Thomas and Rowena were definitely married by December 3, 1849, when Henry Hale ('Harry') Claughley, the eldest of their two sons, was born. According to Rowena, they were living on Ninth Avenue between Eighteenth and Nineteenth streets, and Thomas was the "proprietor of the extensive Furniture Warerooms on the corner of Bowery and Bond Streets."[12] That address is within the boundaries of the 16th Ward of New York City, where Thomas and Rowena were listed on the August 6, 1850, Census:

Clawley [*sic*], Thomas, 34, Male, Upholsterer, born NY
— , Rowena, 26, Female, born NY
— , Henry, 8 Months, Male, born NY
Bentley, Ellen, 60, Female, born Ireland, Cannot read or write
Rudden, Mary, 25, Female, born Ireland, Cannot read or write
Collins, Hannah, 30, Female, born Ireland
Toll, Alice, 20, Female, born Ireland
Riley, Margaret, 19, Female, born Ireland
Gillhooley, John, 30, Male, Baker, born Ireland
O'Brien, James, 20, Male, Driver, born Ireland[13]

Living in the same building in a separate apartment were Rowena's sister, Fanny, her husband, William K. Gray, and their baby, William Jr., born in April of that year.

The presence of so many apparently unrelated Irish immigrants in the same apartment is a curious thing and should be examined a little more closely. That they were not servants is indicated by two things: First, on other pages of the 1850 census servants or "domestics" are clearly identified as such, and here they are not; second, this is a multi-family dwelling, as indicated by the multiple "visits" of the census worker at the same address, and it would be near impossible for a couple living in an apartment to have so many servants. More likely, Thomas sought to offset his living expenses by subletting rooms in their apartment to recent Irish immigrants.

It is simply inconceivable to imagine how Rowena, a recently-wed mother, raised in a close-knit, cultured, and nurturing Yankee family, accustomed to attending balls and parties at the most fashionable houses in the City and New Jersey countryside, could have coped with suddenly being thrust into close living quarters with so many unrelated immigrants, young and old, obviously poor, some of them illiterate. Did Thomas also expect her to cook and wash and clean up after these people? One's immediate reaction is to murmur, "Thank Heaven her sister Fanny was close by." This may also help to understand why she and Fanny, of all the other brothers and sister, were so close and ardently loyal for the remainder of their lives.

Whatever the situation, to Rowena's credit, she never once maligned her husband's name or complained in writing about him or their living conditions. Indeed, as seen above, in her 1875 recollection, she turned the "upholsterer" of the 1850 census into a "proprietor of extensive Furniture Warerooms" (or was this her attempt to retroactively lift the disgrace of an unwise, unsuitable marriage that would haunt her for the rest of her life?). If one is to believe the story of "The Two Wives" is a description of her own marriage, in it she states they enjoyed "[t]hree years of unalloyed happiness," that her husband was kind and affectionate, provided liberally for her wants, and she had no cause to regret the elopement.[14] Unfortunately, taking into consideration the realities of domestic life for most women of the day, it strikes the reader as being more wishful thinking than factual account.

Thomas Leaves for California

However happy she may or may not have been, the most fateful blow to the stability of their life together was delivered in early 1853, when she was in late-term pregnancy with her second son, George Law Claughley (born, according to the family Bible, on May 1, 1853). Thomas sailed for California. She describes the scene when he informed her he was leaving in "The Two Wives," although in her story the babe was already born; how much more heartbreaking must it have been for Rowena who was still pregnant and would not deliver George until at least a week after her husband left. It is also interesting to note that there was a steamship named the GEORGE LAW plying the Atlantic in the early 1850s, and it may be that the little boy was rather

melodramatically given the name of the vessel that carried his
father away.

My eldest boy was about two years old, the
youngest three months, when one day their father
came home and said to me, "Augusta, I must leave
you for a while; I am going to California, and as soon
as I make money enough, I will return or send for
you." (Those words are familiar to the ears of many a
heartbroken wife.)

I threw my arms about his neck and burst into tears;
they were the first bitter tears I had ever shed. "Oh,
you will not leave me, dear Charles — what will
become of me if I am left without your protection?
Have I not forsaken every friend for you? Have you
not been my only companion for three years, and
you will not forsake me now? Oh! take me with you.
I will go in the capacity of a servant to some family,
anything rather than be left behind."

I called his attention to the children. He took the
babe; held it to his bosom, and the tears flowed
down his manly cheeks.

"I never saw you weep before, dear Charles. Why
will you bring so much unhappiness upon us?"

"Augusta," he said, "it must be so. I have had an
excellent offer, and one that will prove profitable to
both. I shall not be absent more than one year. I will
either return or send for you in that time."

I found all entreaties in vain, so I said no more, but
set silently, though sorrowfully, to work to make
preparations for his journey.

The day arrived for the sailing of the ship that was
to bear my husband to a strange land. All the
morning my tears would flow in spite of all my

efforts to suppress them. Charles saw the depth of my grief, and I knew his heart repented the step he had taken, for he loved me. Yes, I believe he loved me truly and sincerely.

The hour for parting came, but I will pass it over; it was too sacred, too sorrowful to dwell upon — 'twas passed and I was left alone.[15]

In Thomas' case the "excellent offer" undoubtedly came from his brother, James, who had preceded him to California in 1850, presumably in association with David Broderick, New York saloon-keeper, fire company commander, and Tammany Hall Democrat who went to California with several others to take control of the party in that new state.

Thomas arrived in San Francisco on the Pacific steamer "Columbus" about midnight on Friday, May 20, 1853, along with 215 other passengers after a twenty-day journey from the western shore of Panama (apparently this was an unusually long journey owing, in part, to the poor quality of coal used). At first, according to "The Two Wives," letters and support arrived regularly. "Each mail brought letters and frequently money. In all his letters he told me how much more he loved me than he had ever thought he could love any woman."[16]

Eventually, however, the letters became infrequent and cold in tone; financial assistance stopped, as eventually did all communication. According to the story, Rowena reached out for him several times. "I wrote him by every steamer begging him to come home — called to his mind his promises to send for me, appealed to him through our children, but all to no purpose. I could get no answer. Sometimes I thought that perhaps he had died, and the thought almost drove me to madness."[17]

Perhaps in one of those letters, she also told him of the birth of her sister's son, Thomas Neptune Claughley Gray, on March 10, 1854, at Liberty Corner, in Somerset County, New

Jersey, where the family had settled and William K. Gray was working as a schoolteacher. One can imagine how she called out to her husband to come home and assume a place in the family that would justify this honor and how heartrending was his refusal to return.

But she had no time to sit crushed and broken; Rowena had herself and two baby sons to support.

"America's Greatest Showman" — Phineas T. Barnum

> [Advertisement.]
> FOURTH OF JULY AT BARNUM'S MUSEUM.—
> Cool, quiet and interesting. Performances nearly
> every hour. The great $500 prize Drama! Farces,
> Songs, Dances &c. The feats of the monkeys, the feats
> of the lady in the lion's den, the living skeleton, the
> dwarf lady, living sea tigers, &c. Only two shillings to
> see everything. (New York Daily News)

Rowena has written very little about her early years with P.T. Barnum's American Museum and Theater at the corner of Broadway and Ann Street in New York City. Nor do we know when or how she met him.

Phineas Taylor Barnum was born July 5, 1810, in Bethel, Fairfield County, Connecticut, to Philo Barnum and his second wife, Irene Taylor. He began his working career in sales in Brooklyn and by managing a boardinghouse, and in 1835 entered into the "show" business when he bought and exhibited an old slave, Joice Heth, who claimed she was over one hundred years old and had been a nursemaid for George Washington. His next major acquisition was the diminutive "General Tom Thumb" in 1842, with whom he subsequently made a triumphant, financially successful tour of Europe.

He had purchased the Museum in 1841 and set about creating what would become the classic example of sensational or "side-show" type displays combined with educational and cultural exhibits, historical paintings, wax figures, along with dramatic works, vignettes, and lectures centered on American history, wholesome family life, antislavery, and Temperance. Through his American Museum, Barnum was the first to combine sensational entertainment and gaudy display with instruction and moral uplift.[18]

Barnum was an ardent "teetotaler" and Temperance worker who shrewdly knew that in order for his museum and theater to be a success, he must appeal to all strata of society—male and female, immigrant and native-born, poor, middle and upper classes, and especially family members of all ages. According to the excellent City University of New York website on Barnum's Museum:

> He welcomed the middle-class women who would never have attended a performance in the city's rowdy theaters. Barnum reassured respectable women that inside his establishment they would never meet the "vulgarisms and immorality ... sometimes permitted" on stages in places like the Bowery Theater down the street. Barnum's museum was something altogether different from the boisterous male world of the theater and tavern where the only unescorted women were the prostitutes in the third tier. In fact, Barnum promised to keep out "females of known bad character."
>
> * * *
>
> Barnum took advantage of the large cultural shift that brought middle-class values of home and family to the center of American public life. Salaried workers and retail clerks replaced artisans and farmers as the dominant figures on the American cultural scene. It was women who engineered this cultural shift, promoting what historians have called the "cult of domesticity." Although they could not

vote, women, particularly middle-class white women, exercised influence in more subtle ways. They directed the social and cultural resources of new middle-class families, presiding over their homes while their husbands went out to work. They instructed their families in the tenets of Christianity and brought up sons to be industrious, good, and honest clerks. They joined together in Protestant revivals and reform organizations, working together to promote temperance, abolish slavery, curb prostitution, and extend women's rights. They read and wrote for periodicals that ran stories, celebrating feelings and detailing the sentimental connections of the heart.

Barnum understood that women with such middle-class aspirations might lead their families to his museum if it too could be made to seem a part of this respectable world. He addressed his patrons as "Ladies" and flattered them for their good taste and cultural knowledge. To keep his audience happy and reassure them of their propriety, he presented entertainments that celebrated Christianity, domesticity, and sobriety. He staged Biblical melodramas and opened his Lecture Room to religious services. ...

* * *

For a few years, he staged enormously popular baby contests pretending to honor the sanctity of domesticity and motherhood. Yet as some critics noticed that the success of the shows undermined the very intimacy and privacy on which true domesticity was based. And amid the moral talk and edifying exhibits, attractions such as the Circassian Beauty — with her plunging neckline and story of

white slavery — still offered Museum visitors a taste
of the Bowery.[19]

Rowena was certainly aware of Barnum in 1850 when he
brought the famous Swedish singer Jenny Lind to America, whose
appearance here caused such a stir and was so successful it is
estimated that overall ticket sales for her tour brought Barnum
almost three quarters of a million dollars, an astronomical amount
in those days. In an article in 1887, Rowena reminisced about the
arrival of Ms. Lind, the "Angel of Music," in New York:

> Well do we remember the feverish excitement
> which filled the heads and hearts of the great
> multitude of people in the city of New York during
> the spring and summer of 1850. The articles which
> appeared in the daily papers were of a most
> sensational character and were calculated to enthuse
> the minds of the lovers of music and the votaries of
> fashion.
>
> For many weeks previous to the arrival of the
> musical phenomena, the large dry goods stores, such
> as Stewart's, Arnolds & Hern's, Lord & Taylor's and
> others were crowded with lady customers selecting
> rich laces, silks, satins and other dress material.
> Alexander kid gloves went off by the thousands of
> boxes. The millinery shops were raked for flowers
> and magnificent headdresses. Dressmakers were
> rushed. It was indeed a harvest for the working
> business people. Old carriages were repainted and
> brought into use. Jenny Lind was the talk at table, in
> parlors, and at all times and on all occasions.
>
> At length the day looked for arrived, and with it
> Jenny Lind. It unfortunately happened to be on a
> Sunday, and about seven in the evening, but the news

spread through an extra called out by the little noisy carriers, and New York arose as one, and soon the old City Hall park was filled to its utmost capacity with people eager and anxious to catch a glimpse of the figure or hear the sound of the voice of the Angel of Music. Thousands stood upon the sidewalks and filled the middle of Broadway in the neighborhood of the Irving House.

About eight o'clock p.m., as near as we can recollect, a shout went up, and the murmur of voices was like the roaring of a mighty sea as the carriage containing P.T. Barnum, Jenny Lind and others came dashing up Broadway. A rich carpet was spread from the curbstone to the entrance of the hotel. Then came the call for Jenny Lind. Mr. Barnum stepped out of one of the second story windows, upon the little porch, enclosed by iron railings and said a few words to the vast throng. He asked to have the lady excused, as she was much fatigued by the journey, but the crowd had come to see and welcome Jenny Lind, and they were not to be put off. Mr. Barnum, seeing that there was no use of trying to satisfy the people by excuses, rushed back and soon returned with a lady. The night was dark, and nothing but the outline of a lady's figure could be seen, but the people cheered and Mr. Barnum holding the lady by the hand, introduced her as the "Swedish nightingale," and when the people cheered, the lady bowed and gracefully acknowledged the honors heaped upon her on a foreign shore.

The lady retired, and the people went away satisfied, while Barnum and a few friends laughed over the joke, for instead of the lady who so gracefully acknowledged the honors as being Jenny Lind, it was

one of the chambermaids of the hotel, who was paid
to represent, in dumb show, the great singer.[20]

By her own acknowledgement, Rowena was associating
and traveling with theater people as early as 1851, and decidedly
not in the capacity of servant, as the following recollection shows,
apparently sparked by a letter written by Olive Logan, the actress
turned fiery feminist author and lecturer, which was published in
the *San Francisco Call* in 1878:

> During the summer of 1851, we were journeying
> with old John Green and his excellent lady wife on
> our way from New York to Nashville, Tennessee.
> When we arrived at Cincinnati we were informed
> that the Cumberland River was so low that our party
> would be compelled to travel through from
> Louisville to Nashville by stage.
>
> "Then we will remain here and take a good rest,
> Ann," said the jocund John.
>
> "Very well," responded the acquiescent lady.
>
> The above suggestion, together with the ready
> assent on the part of Mrs. Green filled our heart with
> joy. We loved sightseeing, and we knew that that
> wealthy, indulgent, childless old couple, who were
> jocularly introducing us as their daughter, would
> leave nothing undone to gratify our penchant.
>
> On the day of our arrival, the firemen of Cincinnati
> were having a celebration, and companies from
> several of the neighboring cities had joined in the
> long and imposing procession. A "Triumphal Arch,"
> composed of evergreens, spanned one of the
> principal streets, and the procession, as it was about
> to pass under it, paused, every hat was removed, and
> a loud, clear voice exclaimed — "Three cheers for

the Star of the West." We were then informed that
the life-sized portrait placed in the center of the arch
was a likeness of Miss Eliza Logan, and that the
rivalry between her and Julia Dean [Ed. Note:
Another famous and popular 19th century actress]
caused the friends of the former to style her the "Star
of the West."

On the following morning we were invited by Mr.
and Mrs. Green to accompany them to the residence
of the far-famed John [*sic*, Cornelius?] Logan. The
visit we shall never forget. Neither shall we forget the
many pleasant hours subsequently spent by us with
this talented and entertaining family during our brief
stay in Cincinnati. But most vividly impressed upon
our mind of all that transpired during these visits was
the remark we alluded to at the beginning of this
article.

"You must be very proud of your family, Mr.
Logan," we said.

"I am, Madam, very proud of my girls, but that girl,
Olive, who just passed out of the room: — that girl,
Madam, will make Rome howl!"[21]

And indeed she did. Before she died in 1906, Olive Logan made
the entire "civilized" world "howl" in response to what were for
that time outrageous social beliefs and teachings.

Rowena also later reminisced with pleasure about when
she attended the grand openings of three of America's famous
"palace hotels": The Barnett in Cincinnati, and the Metropolitan
and St. Nicholas in New York,[22] the latter of which was
considered to be the most luxurious hotel in New York when it
opened in 1853.

The earliest we learn of Rowena's obviously happy
association with Barnum was the summer of 1853 when she was a

member of the traveling drama company that went to Cleveland (apparently toddler Harry and infant George were welcomed as part of the group as well):

> This wonderful man, Mr. P.T. Barnum, is just as generous as he is witty. In the years gone by we have laughed until the tears ran down our cheeks at his merry jokes. We have also felt the briny dew welling up from our hearts at the many tales of his kind and charitable acts, not from his own lips, but from the lips of those who had been the recipients of his noble and generous acts.
>
> But with all of his great fund of joke and wit and humor, we once saw Mr. P.T. Barnum nonplussed. In the summer of 1853 Mr. Barnum found it to his interest to take his New York museum dramatic company to Cleveland, Ohio, for a season for two weeks — and a right merry trip it was. We were one of the number. We took the cars at Jersey City at an early hour, and during all of that tedious day of heat and dust, and cross babies, Mr. Barnum kept everyone in a good humor. The car was crowded, and the day passed off pleasantly; and we felt thankful to the great showman for the enjoyment that had been thrown into that day's journey.
>
> Just at night the train stopped at a town for a few moments, and in rushed a little newsboy, crying out, "Have a copy of Barnum's Pictorial? Here's Ballou's and Barnum's Pictorials! Only 25 cents! Barnum's! Ballou's!"
>
> There had been considerable competition, we might say opposition, between the two magazines for several months. The passengers all turned to look at Mr. Barnum as the little boy approached his seat. The little fellow still kept up the cry — "Ballou's!

Barnum's! Have one, sir?" he exclaimed, seeing Mr. Barnum's big, good-natured face covered with smiles.

"Well, let me look at them. Which is the best, my son?" asked the joker, with a sly twinkle.

"Oh! I guess Barnum's is, sir, for he's the biggest humbug."

A roar of laughter followed. The next instant we heard the boy call out — "Oh! sir, this is a two and a half piece."

"That's all right," laughed Barnum, "it's worth two and a half to hear old Barnum called a humbug."

And as the boy passed out he said, in a loud tone of voice, "Golly, I guess that must be old Ballou himself!"[23]

The first proof positive we have of Rowena actually appearing on Barnum's stage is a November 1853 playbill in which "Rowena Granice" is shown as the actress playing the role of "Aunty Vermont" in a production of *Uncle Tom's Cabin*. "A perfect crowd of humanity, of all ages and sexes, witnessed this astonishingly-gotten-up American moral drama. ... Every scene was cheered enthusiastically. Every speech awoke the wildest shouts of delight," proclaimed an advertisement on November 8, 1853[24]. According to another ad, Rowena was one of a cast of over forty actors, "the most talented in New York," the production was "full of lively incidents, and overflowing with life, spirit, genuine pathos, and irresistible humor," the "scenery is the best, most varied, and perfect ever witnessed upon the stage.... The play itself winds up in the happiest manner, making Virtue triumphant and Vice detestable, instead of permitting wickedness to prosper, and goodness to suffer, and thus leaving an untoward impression of the justice of Providence on the minds of the audience."[25] (Here we see evidence of Barnum's appeal to ladies and families, combined with his antislavery attitude.)

It is interesting to highlight here the fact that Rowena's entire stage life in New York and California was conducted as "Rowena Granice," although her name technically was "Rowena Granniss Claughley." There is no doubt — regardless of Barnum's struggles to maintain a wholesome and virtuous environment for both his patrons and his staff, there was still a tremendous amount of prejudice in the mid-1800s, first, towards married women (and more especially mothers) entering employment of any kind, and, second, any woman working as an "actress," which was almost synonymous with "prostitute." Doubtless Thomas would have been mortified that Rowena caused him, what would have been for a mid-nineteenth century Catholic immigrant merchant, an excruciating embarrassment.

One can almost hear the Irishman roar with indignation, "I'll not have it, I tell ye! I'll not see me wife flauntin' herself in front of the public in this shameless manner. Have ye no morals, woman? Ye're no better'n a common guttersnipe in me own eye. Faith 'n heaven, will the saints preserve us!" Indeed, it is not unreasonable to assume that his wife working on the stage may even have been one of the catalysts for his removal to California.

Rowena must have suffered the same reaction from her Granniss relations, probably one or both of her brothers, thereby giving an explanation of why she changed the spelling of her maiden name, rendering it so different from any other Granniss at that or any other period in history. Yet, examining the choices — housework, cooking, sewing, washing diapers and piles of laundry in a dingy, run-down tenement crowded with low-class immigrants and not enough money to put decent clothes on yourself or your babies –or– traveling and associating with glamorous, refined, well-dressed, articulate people and oneself performing in a dramatic company before crowds of appreciative people and receiving a decent wage in the process; there is probably not a woman alive in the twentieth or twenty-first century who would choose the former. Simply put, Rowena was born one hundred years ahead of her time.

Financially independent, happily engaged in a fulfilling career in the exciting theater milieu of New York City, wearing beautiful dresses and attending plays, operas, parties and balls in the most luxurious theaters and hotels in town, it was doubtful that Rowena would have missed the histrionics and bitter arguments with a hotheaded Irish husband of known inebriate habits. Yet, she was still a married woman who had little control over her personal life, and absolutely no rights as far as possession of money or custody of children.

In addition, she was still a "little fish in the big sea" of the New York theater, and Barnum's was far from considered "legitimate" among the theater glitterati of the day. For an actress to further her career and become a success, it was necessary to go on tour, if not to Europe, preferably to California and even as far as the Sandwich Islands (Hawaii) and Australia, and to make sure glowing reviews and reports of acting triumphs were sent back to the New York papers.

Barnum's financial reversals due to substantial, unsuccessful investments in Bridgeport, Connecticut, his bankruptcy and eventual loss of the Museum probably clinched Rowena's decision. Sometime in the early spring of 1856, Rowena placed Harry and George, just six and three years old, in a safe, secure home, kissed their sweet little faces goodbye, and promising they would not be separated long, boarded an Atlantic steamship bound for Panama.

As she left New York, the following appeared in the *New York Sun Times*, no doubt through the influence and assistance of her venerated and magnanimous employer, Phineas T. Barnum.

> Mrs. Granice—This lady, so well known for her popular readings of the drama, as well as for the remarkable versatility of talent as an actress,

performing as she has done, Lady MacBeth and lively
Yankee characters with equal class and success,
leaves in the next steamer, we understand, for San
Francisco. Her genius will win her a warm welcome
wherever she may find herself.[26]

Chapter III

San Francisco

... [F]rom the outer telegraph station at Point Lobos, a telegram announces in San Francisco that "the mail steamer — is in sight, — miles outside the heads." To almost all "expectation is on tip-toe," and the welcome intelligence is rapidly passed from lip to lip, and recorded on the various bulletin boards of the city, that the "—steamer is telegraphed."After an hour or more of suspense, the loud boom-oom-oom-o-o-o-o-o-m of the steamer's gun reverberates through the city, and announces that she is passing between Alcatraz Island and Telegraph Hill, and will soon be at her berth alongside the wharf....[1]

We can only imagine the astonishment Rowena experienced as she walked down the gangplank of the "Golden Age" on March 14, 1856 and saw San Francisco for the first time. In one of her short stories written fourteen years later, she described the day:

We arrived in San Francisco on the fourteenth of March. 'Twas a dark, gloomy day, and very muddy; all was strange—strange faces all around me. Oh, wretched, wretched were those days I spent all alone, away up in one corner on the third floor of the Railroad House, on Long Wharf.... I used to stand at the window and read the signs. I could not see many people passing, for I was so high up, and the awning hid them from view.[2]

In the Bay were dozens of sailing vessels of every kind and description, including the largest ferryboat in the world plying the waters between San Francisco and Oakland. Off in a large area of the Bay could still be seen the jumble of rotting masts poking at all angles out of the water — skeletons of sailing vessels abandoned by their crews years before for the siren-like enticement of riches awaiting them in the inland gold fields to the east. Perhaps most impressive, the huge "Long Wharf" built over the decaying carcasses of many of the boats, with its multi-storied wooden buildings forming a kind of floating city.

Downtown, several substantial stone and brick buildings had gone up, and some very fine mansions built with the riches pouring out of the mines and flowing through San Francisco. Surrounding these buildings, looking almost like a dingy halo, thousands of rough-hewn wooden houses lined up and down the steep, treeless, often fog-enshrouded hills, from the top of Telegraph Hill down to the Bay and up Tiburon Hill and on and on, as far as the eye could see. Some unpaved, unplanked streets so thick with mud in the wet season she would sink to her ankles trying to get from one side to the other even as she tried to keep her long dress out of the animal waste and trash. Vehicles, wagons and conveyances of all kinds, horses and mules, workmen, traders, businessmen, gamblers, "sharpers," seamen, "professional ladies," immigrants and passers-through from almost every continent in the world crowded the streets and byways. The cacophonous sounds emanating from all of the above throbbed in her ears, interspersed with the little "noisy carriers" standing on the street corners peddling their papers — "Extree! Extree! Read all about it!"

Everywhere she looked, things in this city of between thirty and fifty thousand residents were booming:

Laborers of various kinds are still hewing down the
rocky hills, excavating the streets, grading and
planking them; they are levelling building lots, and
rearing mammoth hotels, hospitals, stores, and other
edifices; they are piling and capping water lots, and
raising a new town upon the deep; gas and water
works are forming; sand hills are being continually
shifted, and cast, piecemeal, into the bay. The
wharves are constantly lined with clipper and other
ships, the discharge of whose cargoes gives employment to an army of sailors and boatmen, stevedores
and longshoremen.[3]

Rowena herself gave a humorous account of another
arrival at the San Francisco docks some sixteen years later that
gives us an apt description of what the traveler experienced upon
embarkation at that port:

At last we arrived at the wharf at San Francisco,
amid the dirt, din of hackmen and dilapidated
houses. Such a din of tongues! If ever the organ of
combativeness gets the better of me, it is when I find
myself beleaguered by a disgusting set of hackmen.
"Wish a carriage, ma'am?"
"Yes," was my reply, "to the Grand Hotel."
"Come right along," said the officious runner at the
same time snatching my basket and shawl. I had to
follow and almost run to keep up with him, and
before I could realize where I was, amid the
confusion, I found myself on the Brooklyn Hotel
coach, stuffed in with six green, dirty-looking
foreigners. I could see half a dozen ragged urchins
with their thumbs to their "turnip" noses grinning
and hissing — "Greeny!"

After taking a trip all over the city with my six
companions from the Faderland, I was set down at
the Grand Hotel; and while I was settling the fare the
officious, meddling driver gently suggested the idea,
in plain words, that he thought that I had better have
gone to a second-class house. I gave him to
understand by tapping my open purse, that I had yet
a few spare twenties, and told him that I always put
up at a first-class house. He went on his way looking
as though he would like to say, "The more fool
you."[4]

The helter-skelter scramble of the Argonauts of '49 to grab
their fortunes from this golden land, and the veritable flood of
human parasites who were determined to just as quickly "mine the
miners" and relieve them of that fortune, were slowly being
replaced by the civilizing influences of respectable women and
families who were beginning to take hold of the town. Honest,
good people of faith — Christians and Jews alike — sought to make
this beautiful state, with its verdant land and temperate climate, a
life-long home where they could nurture and educate their
children in peace and safety, and for the first time, "decent"
women outnumbered prostitutes in San Francisco.[5] But for now,
and for a while to come, mayhem yet prevailed. And often that
was confused with "law and order" in the form of the various
vigilante organizations that demanded from the state and city
officials — and frequently usurped — the power to maintain peace
and civility.

Three newspapermen who experienced San Francisco in
this unstable time of transition described the conditions just three
years before Rowena's arrival:

For the honest, industrious and peaceable man, San
Francisco is now as safe a residence as he can find in

any other large city. For the rowdy and "shoulder-striker," the drunkard, the insolent, foulmouthed speaker, the quarrelsome, desperate politician and calumnious writer, the gambler, the daring speculator in strange ways of business, it is a dangerous place to dwell in. There are many of such characters here, and it is principally their excesses and quarrels that make our sad daily record of murders, duels, and suicides.[6]

Who were these shoulder-strikers and "the quarrelsome, desperate politician"? None other than David C. Broderick and dozens of his New York cronies, including Dutch Charley Duane and, no doubt, Messrs. James and Thomas Claughley. The Vigilance Committee? The bankers, physicians, merchants, mechanics, and skilled laborers of the City, most of them husbands and family men.

To give an example of the social and political conditions of the town at the time Rowena arrived, here is an abbreviated chronology of some of the mind-spinning, incredible events going on in San Francisco just two months to the day after Rowena arrived:

May 14, 1856 — In a climax to a long-running feud, James King of William[iv], crusading reformer/editor of *The Evening Bulletin*, publishes an article concerning James P. Casey, county supervisor, rival newspaperman (*Sunday Times*), and foreman of Crescent Engine Co. No. 10, exposing Casey's criminal history in New York and stay at Sing-Sing Prison. (King was the avowed enemy of the almost unbelievably corrupt political machine headed by Broderick.) The May 14 issue of the *Bulletin* appears on

---

[iv] Since there were apparently several men by the name of "James King" in the city, this was a name adopted by King to denote himself as the son "of William" King.

the streets at 3 p.m.; between 4 and 5 p.m., King is accosted on the street and shot by Casey, who is immediately arrested and imprisoned. In the same jail is Charles Cora, an Italian gambler, who is awaiting retrial for the 1855 murder of U.S. Marshall Gen. William H. Richardson in response to his public insult to Cora's long-time mistress, prostitute Corabella "Belle" Ryan. By 6:30 there is an excited crowd around the jail, which the mayor tries to disperse. Excitement continues all that evening, with marches and public speeches.

May 15, 1856 — A Vigilance Committee is organized, and the Executive Committee begins secret meetings. Many wives and mothers of San Francisco give support over the ensuing months by remonstrating against prostitution and political corruption in letters to newspapers.[7]

May 16, 1856 — A call for recruits for the Vigilance Committee goes out, over six thousand men are enrolled, mostly European-American merchants, businessmen and skilled workers, with the notable exception of the Irish who are specifically excluded. Drilling of members begins on a large scale. Sheriff Scannell calls for a posse to defend the prison. Governor J. Neely Johnson arrives from Sacramento, interviews Vigilance leaders and permits a small guard of vigilantes to encamp within the prison walls.

May 17, 1856 — The Vigilance Committee removes to its permanent quarters on Sacramento Street ("Fort "Gunnybags," so named because of the perimeter of gunnysacks lined up around the front of the building); the Vigilance guard withdraws from the prison.

May 18, 1856 — In an effort to enlist a strong guard for the jail, Sheriff Scannell goes into the streets and serves upon every man he meets an order to report to the jail and assist in repelling the attack that he knows the Vigilance

Committee is planning. He succeeds in getting only fifty to respond, most of them criminal lawyers and "heelers" of Broderick's political machine, one of whom is Dutch Charley. The Sheriff sensibly offers no resistance when twenty-six hundred well-armed men surround the jail; Casey and Cora are placed into carriages and removed to Fort Gunnybags, followed by almost the entire population of San Francisco howling for their immediate lynching.

May 20, 1856 — King dies of his wound at about 1:30 p.m. Casey is tried for "premeditated and unjustifiable murder" before the Executive Committee, convicted and sentenced to hang.

May 22, 1856 — King's funeral is held before an immense crowd. At the Vigilance headquarters, Casey is ministered to by Archbishop Alemany and Cora is allowed to marry Belle. Casey and Cora are strung up and hung from scaffolding erected from the second-story windows of Fort Gunnybags. Before plunging to his death, Casey calls out to God and his "aged mother" telling the assembled crowd below: "I am not guilty of any crime. ... I only acted as I was taught – according to my early education – to avenge an insult."[v]

May - July 1856 — The Committee begins arresting several persons and investigating cases of "political crimes" (election fraud, bullying, ballot-stuffing, trick ballot boxes with false bottoms, and similar offenses), and in the process conducts illegal searches, suspends civil rights, confiscates federal arms, and undermines state and local militias. Two prisoners — alleged murderers Joseph Hetherington and Philander Brace — are executed, and some two dozen others are banished from the state, mostly

---

[v] After Cora's death, Belle sold her house of prostitution and became widely known for charitable works. She died on February 17, 1862.

Irish Catholic Democrats (alleged shoulder-strikers), including Dutch Charley Duane and "policeman" James Claughley, Rowena's brother-in-law.[8]

May 31, 1856 — Former U.S. heavyweight champion James "Yankee Jim" Sullivan, one of Broderick's thugs, dies in the Vigilance prison supposedly in a fit of *delirium tremens*. Vigilantes claim it was suicide, but an inquiry by the Catholic Church finds that Sullivan was murdered and allows him to be buried at Mission Dolores Cemetery.

June 3 – 4, 1856 — Governor Johnson issues a proclamation declaring San Francisco "in a state of insurrection," appoints then banker and future General William Tecumseh Sherman as leader of a militia to bring order to the City, and forwards a request to General Wool for arms for the militia from the arsenal at Benicia. At San Francisco, members of a "conciliation committee" carry communications between Sherman and the Vigilance Committee, hoping to bring about a peaceable settlement.

June 5 - 9, 1856 — General Wool replies that he has no authority to grant the Governor's request, the Governor repeats his demand upon General Wool for arms, making a formal and urgent requisition at Benicia. On the same day, he meets Sherman and the "conciliation" delegates from San Francisco. The peace negotiations fail, and Sherman resigns his commission as major-general of the militia. General Wool refuses to aid the Governor against the Committee.

June 19, 1856 — The Governor writes to the President, asking for federal assistance in suppressing the Committee.

June 21, 1856 — California Supreme Court Justice David S. Terry and other members of the "Law and Order Party" organized in opposition to the Vigilance Committee confront Vigilance policeman Sterling A. Hopkins, the hangman of Casey. Hopkins attacks Terry with a pistol and, in the ensuing struggle, Hopkins is stabbed by Terry, who is then chased to the Law and Order armory and arrested. He is held captive for nearly a month.

July 19, 1856 — The President writes from Washington declining, on grounds of constitutional law, to assist in the suppression of the Vigilance Committee.

August 7, 1856 — Hopkins survives his wounds, and Judge Terry is released by the Committee.

August 18, 1856 — Final parade of the Vigilance Committee.

November 3, 1856 — The Vigilance Committee is officially disbanded, and Governor Johnson revokes his proclamation.[9]

Not until three years later would it become known that the chief supporter of the Law and Order Party in its efforts to rid the city of the Vigilance Committee was Broderick, who, while maintaining a supposedly neutral demeanor, was funneling thousands of dollars to politicians and newspapers in an eventually successful effort to turn the tide of public opinion against the vigilantes. Broderick and his henchmen, while a little calmer and temporarily subdued as a result of the vigilantes' actions of the summer, would maintain his vice-like control over the City and he and Justice Terry would be political associates — for a couple of years at least.

This was the dizzying turmoil into which Rowena stepped when she walked down the wharf, passed through the throng of workmen, "hawkers" and hangers-on, and climbed into a carriage for the short ride to a hotel, perhaps the Railroad House Hotel, which boasted an impressive menu of meals, a "cupola and town clock, which are visible from all parts of the city, and from the balcony of which a more beautiful view of the city, bay and surrounding country can always be obtained."[10]

She immediately set about visiting newspapers, and the following announcement appeared in the *Daily Alta California* two days later:

> **Mrs. Rowena Granice**—This lady, who is not
> unknown to fame on the Atlantic side as an
> accomplished actress and delineator of the Yankee
> character, has arrived in San Francisco by the *Golden
> Age* and will soon appear upon our theatrical
> boards.[11]

It is very likely she was referred by one of the editors to English
tragedienne Mrs. Goddard and her actor/manager husband, John
Caple, who, along with actress Mrs. Woodward, had rented the
Union Theater on Commercial Street between Kearny and Dupont
Streets for the spring season (apparently not to be confused with
the "Bella Union," at Washington and Kearny Streets, which was
mainly a gambling and booze hall and melodeon). She was
booked at the Union on April 7 and her San Francisco debut
appearance elicited a splendid review in the *Alta*:

> Union Theatre—Miss Granice made her debut at the
> Union last evening and appeared in the "Dumb Girl
> of Oran" and in the "Yankee Housemaid," in which
> she sustained the Yankee character of "Jemima
> Sunflower" very admirably. This is the line of
> character in which she excels and which will secure
> her in San Francisco crowded houses.[12]

Unfortunately, this review was not enough to sustain a long run.
As San Francisco theater historian J.H. McCabe noted in his
journal for April 8, 1856: "2nd & last night engagement Miss
Rowena Granice — Union."[13]

According to Galloway, "following her successful
engagement in San Francisco," Rowena left almost immediately
for Sacramento where she "opened at the Sacramento Theater on
May 7, and played to well-filled houses for eight performances.
She took a benefit for herself on May 10, and on her last two

appearances she was on the same program with the famous Edwin Booth[vi]. Her performances were described as 'sprightly' and they 'drew forth many hearty laughs.' In 'Old Folks at Home,' another anonymously authored play, performed in Sacramento on May 10, 1856, she sang as well as acted."[14]

Relationship With Mr. Claughley and his Family

Where was Thomas all this time? It is quite conceivable that he was waiting for Rowena at the dock on March 14 when she alighted from the boat. He certainly would have known she was coming, either by letter or telegram; in any event, he most definitely learned of her arrival shortly after the article appeared on March 16 in the *Alta* and in the advertisements for her first night's performance at the Union.

Rowena has never written anything more about Thomas, but if we are to accept "The Two Wives" as an approximate account of their relationship, we learn that her husband had married an actress and was in Sacramento, where she followed immediately.

> Next morning [the proprietor of the San Francisco hotel] called at my door and informed me that the Charles Webb who had married the actress was then stopping in the city of Sacramento and added that he would advise me to take the boat that evening, go up to Sacramento and satisfy myself whether it was my husband or not. I acted upon his advice and arrived there early the next morning. ...
>
> I visited the hotel where I had been informed he was stopping. I took a seat in the parlor and awaited the return of the servant who had gone to his room to tell him that a lady wished to see him. I was not

---

[vi] Brother of John Wilkes Booth, assassin of President Abraham Lincoln in April 1865.

long kept in suspense, for in a few moments Charles
Webb stood before me. My first impulse was to
grasp him by the throat and never let go my hold
until he had ceased to breathe. But when he said,
"Why, Gussy," the voice seemed so familiar, so kind,
that it changed all feeling of revenge. The old
affection which I had cherished for years, sprang up
afresh. I fell upon his bosom and wept like a child.
The trial had been too much for me — I fainted.

When I awoke a slender form was bending over me,
and a sweet face smiled as I gazed upon it. A soft,
white hand smoothed my aching brow. Charles was
standing near the sofa upon which I reclined.... I
looked for some moments, first at one and then the
other. The silence seemed painful to all. The young
woman was the first to speak.

"Dear Charles," she said, in the most tender and
loving tones, "who is this lady? Is she your sister?"

"Sister! Sister!" cried I, "no, not his sister, but his
wife — the mother of his boys — and if he has dared
to wrong me, let him tremble!"

Charles looked as though a thunderbolt had
descended from heaven and struck him. It was the
first time he had ever witnessed in me the slightest
display of angry passion.

"Yes," I continued, "let him tremble, for by the
heaven above us, he shall not live — his lifeblood
alone shall pay the forfeit!" And as I uttered these
words, I sprang from the sofa and caught the girl by
the arm, who stood pale and trembling like a
frightened fawn.

"Who are you, and why are you here with this
man?"

"That man!" repeated she and pointing toward
Charles, "Why, he is my husband. Oh! Do not harm

him," said she, falling upon her knees. "Oh! Spare him. I will give him up, I will quit him, never see him again, but for the love of heaven do not kill him. He is not to blame; it was all my fault. I loved him so deeply, so madly! Oh, let fall your vengeance upon me, but for God's sake do not injure him!"

All this was spoken with so much earnestness, so much real feeling, that I was at once convinced of her innocence and his guilt. Her appeal had awakened all the sympathies of my nature, and I pitied her from my heart. Yes, I pitied her and hated him. I took the fair girl gently by the hand and raised her. For a few moments I gazed upon her; she was fair and beautiful, and seemingly about eighteen years of age. Such beauty — such innocence — to be so basely betrayed!

And as I stood thus gazing upon her, I felt that all the love I had ever cherished for Charles Webb had turned to hate. I thought of him with loathing and disgust. Then, turning again to her, I said, "Take him and be happy while you can, for the time will come when you will find him unworthy the deep love you now evince for him. Remember my words, and let them be a warning."

Then, advancing towards him, I thus addressed him: "Charles Webb, you are at liberty to go where you please, do as you please. I will never molest or annoy you. You are now beneath my revenge — fallen so low in my estimation within the last hour that you have become unworthy even of my hate, and the only feeling I now entertain for you is contempt. Take it — it is all I have to offer you. We part forever. I have but two requests to make: the first is that you treat this girl with kindness — love

her, cherish her with tender regard, and protect her. I
believe she is every way worthy of a better fate than
that which has so unluckily befallen her, and as you
value your happiness here and your soul's safety
hereafter, do not abuse or forsake her. The second
request I have to make is that you will never mention
my name, or those of my children."

He made no reply; what his feelings were I could
not even guess nor will I attempt to describe my
own. I gave one look of pity to the poor, deluded
creature who was clinging to him and murmured to
myself, "Oh, may you never feel the pang that rends
my disturbed bosom!"[15]

From there the story of Augusta Webb totally departs from
that of Rowena Granice Claughley, for while in the story Augusta
went immediately to a lawyer and procured a divorce from the
immoral and repulsive Charles, there is no record of Rowena ever
obtaining a divorce from Thomas; in fact, just a year later, in late
1857 or early 1858, Thomas showed up in Sacramento, where
Rowena was then living with the children, Harry and George, and
published a notice that Rowena was still his wife.

Likewise, there is no record of Thomas Claughley
marrying another woman in San Francisco or Sacramento
(although good records were not kept in those days and that is no
proof it did not happen). Almost certainly, he was not thrilled that
Rowena had shown up in San Francisco, but he very likely
dutifully escorted his wife around town and pretended for a while
to be the loving, honorable husband, as he tried in vain to keep
from her the intelligence about his mistress, who was, indeed,
probably an actress.

The assertion that he was found *flagrante delicto*, that he
"had taken up with another woman and she never had anything
more to do with him," has been passed down to us from Rowena's

granddaughter, Constance Steele Cook, who reported the same to R. Dean Galloway in 1968.[16] According to Soulé, et al., however, divorces were easily obtainable and were frequently done in those tumultuous times in California. Why, then, did Rowena not avail herself of the simple legal procedure? It may have had a great deal to do with the general attitude of the public in San Francisco toward women in general and divorcées, in particular:

> It is difficult for any woman, however pure, to preserve an unblemished reputation in a community like San Francisco, where there is so great a majority of men, and where so many are unprincipled in mind and debauchees by inclination. Not all women are unchaste whom voluptuaries and scandal-mongers may wish to think such. The wives and daughters of respectable citizens must be held pure and worthy. Their presence here confers inestimable blessings upon society. There are known mistresses and common prostitutes enough left to bring disgrace upon the place. By the laws of California divorces are readily obtainable by both husband and wife, one of whom may think him or herself injured by the unfaithful or cruel conduct of the other, and who, perhaps, disliking his or her mate, or loving another, may wish to break the bonds of wedlock. Divorces are accordingly growing very numerous here, and have helped to raise a general calumny against the sex.[17]

To bolster our analysis of Rowena's state of mind in this regard we can also turn back to "The Two Wives," in which Augusta Webb later laments her treatment as a divorcée: "California can boast of more cold-hearted, hardened and selfish women than the world combined. They pretend to look with holy horror upon a woman who sues for a divorce when they themselves, perhaps, have been divorced and married in better circumstances."[18]

On the other hand, it may simply have been a convenience for Rowena to be a married woman, which conferred some measure of respectability and protection — regardless of the reputation of the drunken profligate to whom she was attached — and she probably told Mr. Claughley in terms certain and clear, "Get out of my life! Stay out of my life! Do not let your presence darken my door!" (to no avail, alas, since Mr. Claughley continued to show up from time to time for four more years). The children were thenceforth and evermore known as Harry Hale Granice and George Law Granice, even before Thomas died in 1860. Rowena has never told us fully, and rather mysteriously left it to our imagination, what heinous things Thomas Claughley did to warrant having his name removed from his children, especially sons who would be the ones to carry on the family identity.

In the meantime, there was a curious situation of another actress married to a Claughley in San Francisco at the same time, and this presented an interesting dilemma. Thomas' brother, James A. Claughley, was married to an actress of rather worthy note named Mary A. Claughley (née Mary Jane Stephens, according to Rowena[19], born in 1827 in New York). Nothing is known of Mary's early life. She made her theatrical debut in San Francisco in June 1852 at the First American Theater.[20] In October of that year she performed with the Willow Company in San Francisco. From January through June of the next year she went on tour to Marysville, where she became known as the "reigning star" with the Bingham Company, receiving leading roles from that point forward. In 1854, she was in Marysville again in March with the Chapman Company appearing in several plays in which she was pronounced "excellent," back to Sacramento and San Francisco in May and June in several of Shakespeare's plays, ending up the year with the Laura Keene

Company in "Faint Heart Ne'er Won Fair Lady" and with the Neafie Company in "King John."[21]

On March 24, 1856, just one week after Rowena arrived in the city, Mary was performing at the Metropolitan Theatre, Montgomery Street near Jackson, with "the talented and accomplished actress, M'lle Marie Duret (who has been engaged for a limited number of nights)."[22] On Saturday evening, May 24, 1856 (while, presumably, Rowena was in Sacramento), Mary appeared in San Francisco in "John Brougham's five-act Comedy of the GAME OF LOVE! — A glorious Farce, Ethiopian Delineations, an Original Fireman's Address, Singing, Dancing, Tableaux &c."[23] And on the 20th of June, while her husband James was apparently being put on trial and eventually banished from the State by the Vigilance Committee, Mary was appearing as "Hermione" in the play "Damon and Pythias" at the Union Theatre, Commercial Street, with Mr. J.B. Booth[vii] as "Damon."[24] On 23 June 1856 she again appeared with Mr. Booth, this night at the Union in "Stage Struck Barber."[25] Sometime in 1856 she appeared with the company of the famous Julia Dean Hayne, where she played in the tragedy of "Griselda," and "was regarded as a deserving actress, who … heightened the enthusiasm of the audience by her excellent acting."[26]

According to Gold Rush stage historian Helene Koon, by 1858 Mary's career had begun to take a decided downturn. In March of that year she appeared in "Winter's Tale" where the critic considered her "poor" and she was described as having a "monotonous voice," and in a new production of "King John" where her performance was cruelly dubbed "stupid." In September of 1863 she played a "Greek matron" in the play "Ingomar, the Barbarian," in Virginia City, with the Maguire Stock Company; the performance was reviewed by Mark Twain.[27] She died of

---

[vii] Junius Brutus Booth, Jr., brother of Edwin and John Wilkes Booth.

typhus on August 21 (or 22), 1864, in San Francisco, and was referred to as "an actress of much merit and an estimable lady."[28]

We do not know what became of James after the 1856 banishment by the Executive Committee of the vigilantes, but he was apparently back in San Francisco by 1860 (as were many of the other exiles, including Dutch Charley Duane). James was shown in the 1858 City Directory (p. 91), "on Filbert btw. Mason and Taylor," and Thomas is listed as a manufacturer-upholsterer at 19 Sacramento. In the 1860-'61 San Francisco City Directory (p.94), James and Mary received separate listings at the same address:

> Claughley, James, dwl N s Filbert nr Taylor (*i.e.*,
> north side of Filbert near Taylor)
> Claughley, Mary, Mrs., actress, dwl N s Filbert nr Taylor

According to the 1860 Federal census[29], James, 46, a "packer," and wife Mary, 32, lived with children James A., Jr., 14, born in New York (most probably a child of a former marriage of James), Marietta C., 4, Lizzie S., 3, and baby David C. Broderick Claughley, born in 1859 and named in posthumous honor of political boss Broderick who died in a pistol duel with Supreme Court Justice David Terry in September of that year. (Another daughter named Marietta Stillman Claughley, born in San Francisco about 20 October 1854, died four months later and was buried at Lone Mountain Cemetery.)

Was it possible that Mary really was the "other wife" in Thomas' life — the actress Rowena wrote about confronting in "The Two Wives" — and that she was in a feigned marriage, "in name only," to James because Thomas was already wed and unable to divorce his wife in New York? Carrying the theory further, does it mean that the children, all born in San Francisco — Marietta S., in 1854, Marietta C., in 1856, Lizzie (1857), and David — were then the children of Thomas? And could that be what really brought Rowena to San Francisco in 1856, because gossip was brought back to New York that Thomas was attached to a woman — an actress, no less — in San Francisco who had a child who died and was expecting another? We may never know, but until refutation is obtained, the possibility cannot be entirely dismissed.

At a minimum, these children were the cousins of Harry and George, yet no mention is ever made of them from the pen of Rowena or any other member of the family. James was apparently deceased by 1864, since Mary's obituary described her as "wife of the late Jas. Claughley."[30] Of the surviving children, the fate of Lizzie is unknown. James Jr. turned up as a soldier at Fort Warren in Boston in the 1880 Federal Census; Marietta C. married Harlan P. McGuire in San Francisco in 1876 and moved to Portland, Oregon; and David C.B. Claughley was listed on the 1880 Census living with the William Quinn family in San Jose, Santa Clara County. He apparently never married. In 1920 he was living in Sacramento and working for an oil company; he was listed as "single."

If it were true that it was Thomas, not James, who was coupled with Mary, then of a certainty all of the men in San Francisco — and especially the "theater crowd," politicians, firemen and shoulder-strikers prominent among them — would have known. They, including Broderick's close friend and powerful theater impresario, Tom Maguire, would no doubt have tried to "blackball" Rowena (meaning, then, that it was acceptable for a mistress to be working on stage, but not a wife?). Perhaps that explains why Rowena was so well received in Sacramento and in the theaters of the mining towns, but after the spring of 1857 generally confined to the melodeons or "bit theaters" in San Francisco, and why she was never on the same stage or in the same traveling company with Mary Claughley.

Rowena would be confused in the public's minds with Mary Claughley for several years, including when Mary died in 1864, when it was reported:

> MRS. CLOUGHLEY [Rowena Granice Steele], actress, died, on Monday evening last, in San Francisco.[31]

Chapter IV

California Theater Experience — Beginning of Writing Career

In the summer of 1856, another "star" was to ascend over San Francisco who was to almost overshadow Rowena: The great Lola Montez—the Countess of Landsfeldt and mistress of Ludwig I of Bavaria—came home after an absence from California of a little over a year in Honolulu. Soon she was appearing at the American Theatre in "petite comedies" and was again an object of curiosity and tittle-tattle. For one thing, from the far islands she brought a collection of fantastic birds, one of which, a white, talking cockatoo, she carried about on her shoulder. Most importantly, though, was the story of her manager/agent, Mr. Folland, who fell overboard and drowned on the return voyage — Were they lovers? Was it suicide? The talk of the town, if not about the lynchings and the Vigilance Committee's goings-on, was all about the great Lola Montez.

Then Lola began auctioning her jewelry—according to the *Alta California* an astonishing quantity of magnificent pieces, said to have a value of from fifteen to twenty thousand dollars—for the benefit of Folland's two children.[1] That put a damper on the gossip for a while. Lola left just a year later for the East, where she died in January 1861.

In a compassionate tribute written by Rowena, she informs us that she only knew Ms. Montez by her reputation for acts of generosity, charity, and kindness, and pointed out what almost might have been an autobiographical note for her own early life on the stage: "At a tender age, alone and friendless, she launched her frail bark upon the broad ocean of public opinion, and without counting upon adverse winds, she thought to steer clear of shoals and quick-sands. There were many ways before her, and if, through lack of experience, she chose the wrong one, there perhaps was no kind voice to call her back, but thousands of brainless, heartless ones to cheer her on to ruin for the mere satisfaction of witnessing the wreck which they had helped to make." Noting that, "Of the absent and the dead, [we should] speak nothing but good," a philosophy that would guide Rowena for the rest of her life, she summed up by speaking directly to women, pointing out important, timeless truths of nurturing children: "Dear lady readers, speak only of her good qualities, for had she, like many of you, been surrounded by kindly influences, her young mind trained to moral worth, her ambition checked by the gentle and loving voice of a mother; had brothers and sisters and kind friends gathered around the fireside of her early home and watched her into womanhood, with her lofty and towering talent, she might have been the brightest ornament of the present age."[2]

Another trend that was developing in the California theater at about the time Rowena arrived, which would adversely impact the future of her stage career, was pointed out by the *Fireman's Journal* on August 23, 1856:

> At no time since the advent of the drama in California has such general apathy been manifested by the community towards nearly all kinds of amusements than the present. The "legitimate" seems to be thrown aside for "clap trap" shows and "gewgaw" entertainments, not only in this city, but also throughout the interior of the state, and people patronize and give them countenance by their presence. The heroes of the "sock and buskin" recite their parts to empty houses, and the halls of Thespis no more resound with the loud acclamations of the "gods" and "groundlings," as they yelled with delight in times gone by at a stirring passage from Shakespeare. Opera, Comedy, and Tragedy have had

their day. The curtain has fallen, and the farce is about to commence. In consequence of this dull state of affairs we have but little to chronicle in the way of amusements. The Metropolitan is closed and likely to remain so, until some new "star" visits the country and shines forth upon its boards getting one half of the clear receipts of the house for the gratification of showing himself off — speaking a few words and going through a few pantomimic gyrations to the delight of the dilettanti in the boxes, while the stock actors, to whom he owes most of her [*sic*, his?] success in life, go supperless to bed and starve until another star makes his appearance, when the same scenes are to be gone through with over again.

Fancy entertainments at present seem all the rage, and will remain so, until the public know how to appreciate good legitimate theatrical amusements. We don't mean by this what is known as the "blood and thunder" style, nor the highfaluting mode of declamation, that should call forth public approval, on the contrary, it might be condemned for all the benefit it confers on those who witness that kind of representation. We mean those sterling old English and American comedies, brilliant with wit and sentiment and elegant plays, replete with beautiful and classical language. Let them be taken form the dusty shelves where they have laid so long and be substituted in the place of the old hum-drum, namby-pamby trash, which has lately taken possession of the stage, and let us have good stock companies to play the characters, and not your conceited "stars," whose egregious egotism, and self-esteem is to be pitied, while the public are to blame for fostering these theatrical ulcers in their midst.

The manager of the Metropolitan might well exclaim, like the swarthy moor, "My occupation's gone," for its vestibules, seats, and corridors have been deserted; but we hope only for a short season, and when it again opens, may the public come forward and sustain it, or else we will soon find out that we have not a decent company in the State, and for neglecting to support a good leading theatre, may find it hard to induce stock actors of merit to visit us hereafter.[3]

After Sacramento, Rowena was soon off on tour in mining camps and towns. Over the years Rowena would find the most appreciative audiences were at the mines, as these grizzled, unkempt, lonely miners would flock to see and were always appreciative of the soft, gentle, refined and perfumed ladies.

On July 4, 1856, she appeared at Frisbie's Theatre in Nevada City, Nevada County, with the company formed by Mr. and Mrs. Conner.

A new attraction has been added in the person of Miss Rowena Granice, from the New York Theatres, in Yankee characters. She was greeted approvingly on Monday evening, her first appearance, and on the succeeding night. Heavy tragedy—especially in warm weather, if run too long, is apt to produce a languor and monotony—which such an actress as Miss Granice, is sure to dispel. The fun-loving portion of an audience have found a great additional source of amusement in Miss Granice.

Our people are liberal in the bestowment of favors on talent and merit, and we bespeak for Miss G. a liberal share of patronage.[4]

On August 17, 1856, she appeared with Dan Virgil 'D.V.' Gates at the Tower Theatre in Weaverville, Trinity County, where "the hills echoed with the thundering applause of a male audience, in admiration of her popular hits."[5]

She then commenced a tour with the Risley Troup. In Placerville, El Dorado County, a fire on July 6, 1856, had destroyed both the Empire and Placer Theaters. A new theater with seating for 1,500 (a huge accomplishment for a rough mining town in those days and indicative of the appeal of the miners for entertainment) was built on the site of the former Empire and opened on October 30, 1856, with a special address composed for the occasion and read by Rowena.[6]

From February through March 1857, she was back in San Francisco with the McDonough Company appearing as a leading lady in an impressive group of plays: "Pizarro," as Desdemona in "Othello," "Rival Pages," "Putnam," and "Ichabod's Come."[7] In March she and Julia Hudson gave a benefit performance at the Metropolitan[8] (presumably they were the beneficiaries, a common practice in those days).

Then in early spring 1857, sons Harry and George, eight and almost four years old, arrived in San Francisco. How her mother's heart must have sung with joy at the reunion with her little boys! It was a long, dangerous, harrowing voyage for adults, let alone for children traveling without their mother. And this offers us some additional proof that it was not her original intention to stay in California, since a loving and caring mother like she always was would never have left her children behind unless she intended to come back. No doubt, Rowena was smitten with this beautiful new land and determined to make it her home. For the next forty years she consistently wrote in hundreds of articles glowing praises about her travel destinations, from the San Francisco Bay to the incredible, majestic Yosemite mountains, from the northern mines to the Los Angeles orange groves, from the vast, productive farmland of the San Joaquin Valley to the beautiful, glistening waters and shorelines of the Pacific, and everywhere in between.

Harry and George stayed in San Francisco for a few months where they attended public schools.[9] It was no doubt soon apparent to Rowena, however, that San Francisco, especially with Claughley hanging about, was no place for the children. Sacramento–the City of the Plains-was the place to go, to the beautiful green spot at the confluence of the American and Sacramento Rivers, the state Capitol created just three years before where, to outward appearances at least, a more refined crowd of people were gathered, most of them well-educated elected representatives to the State Legislature. Among them were Col. William S. Long, "one of the most brilliant and promising young lawyers of the state," and his wife, Sarah Rutherford Long, of whom Rowena was to write thirty years later: "At the time the writer first knew this worthy woman, she was the most elegant lady in the City of the Plains, occupying, with her husband, a fine suite of rooms at the Orleans Hotel. Well do we remember this kind, gentle, lovely lady, bending over our burning, aching head, while [we were] suffering with brain fever. The soft white hand, the gentle voice, the low tones of sympathy gave hope of recovery, even though the opinion of the wise and eminent attending physician had decided otherwise."[10]

Rowena enrolled Harry and George in a private boarding school on 7th Street and set up a home for herself nearby in a "neat little cottage" on N Street between 3rd and 4th Streets. This "cottage" was probably a two-story house with living room (or parlor), dining room, and kitchen on the first floor, three or four bedrooms above, with a porch off the parlor and balcony off the front-facing bedroom. During the fall and winter months Rowena says she "employ[ed] her time in writing sketches and domestic stories for literary papers and magazines."[11] "It was there that parties of half-starved, gaunt literary and theatrical women of refined manners and slim purses used to meet and each contribute their mite towards a good fat chicken and all would join in preparing a dinner which, when served, would be fit for a queen or a number of queens."[12] Some of these theater people, for whom she was to form a lifelong affection, included costumer Susan Paullin, her husband, James R. Paullin, and their children, all actors—Sue Robinson; "Miss Albertine" Manchester; and Caroline Moreton.

It was in this cottage, she tells us later, that she wrote "Dora Fielding; Or, The Actress' Debut," her first story of fourteen columns for the *California Spirit of the Times* (formerly *The Fireman's Journal*), and it was here that she collected the short stories that would make up the first novel, *The Family Gem*, published by Aspell in 1858, several of which had already appeared in journals such as the *Golden Era* and the *Yreka Union*. Rowena alludes to her troubles with Claughley in the introduction to this book where she writes that the stories "were written, most of them, many months ago amidst the duties of the stage and the tearful realities of domestic desolation — of which it behooves me not to speak."

And it was in this house that she found a great measure of happiness and personal satisfaction, as she tells us in *Dell Dart; Or, Within the Meshes* published in 1874 (which book, as it turns out, was the catalyst for the publication of what has become known as "the Fatal Slander" that caused her son Harry to shoot and kill Edward Madden in Merced in December 1874 – more later).

> Most of the little parlors in that neighborhood opened out upon the front porch, and through the green blind doors the shadows of the branches and leaves of the trees and vines came in and leaped and capered about among the bright colors of the carpet, and peeped coquettishly in and out among the lace curtains, each fantastic leaper bringing in a puff of

fragrance from the millions of roses climbing over the neighboring cottages, and scattering the sweets mingled with the fresh, bracing air into every nook and corner of the well-swept, well-dusted households.

I love to dwell upon the beauties of that particular morning ... as I stood upon the upper piazza gathering a bouquet. My thoughts were busy with my first triumph in my literary attempts. Say what you will, great writers, you know that no after-triumphs, no world-spread fame has ever brought back that nervous, self-admiration with which you viewed your first effort in print. 'Tis like the feeling of a mother toward her first-born is that first child of the brain. It is such a shy, modest pride! A pride that would blush at its own daring. A pride hid away down in the heart.

"Well, what has your pleasant emotions on that particular morning to do with the victim who has been so unfortunate as to get entangled in the meshes?" whispers an inquisitive little elf.

Nothing. I only wanted to say that I was in a very pleasant frame of mind and sort of half in love with myself and everybody and everything around me. One don't have many such gold-tinted, heart-satisfied moments in life, and they are worth cherishing. They help to lighten the darker, heavier burdens of our checkered lives....[13]

The Family Gem is also the first opportunity we get to see a picture of Rowena. On the inside front cover is a portrait made from a woodcut. One might first assume it is a copy of a daguerreotype, and by the style of dress, we can estimate it was done earlier in the 1850s, however the hairstyle, which seems to be short with back-flowing, soft curls, is completely out of character of the severe, Victorian styles so common in that day. Also, Rowena is seen with one elbow on a table with her hand resting jauntily against the side of her head, and that is completely atypical from the usual stiff poses necessitated by the time the shutter had to be open. Another incongruity is that she is looking straight at us, "into the camera," whereas most portraits of that day have the subject gazing off to the side.

Physically, her face shows a sweet softness, with an almost Mona Lisa smile, yet there is a certain flash in the eyes that hint at a great reservoir of will and determination. It will forever remain a dichotomy for us how this very pretty lady could have been called "old and faded" and a "flamboyant fright" just two years later.

In the Spring of 1857, an odd occurrence took place, according to a *Bee* article:

LOCAL NEWS.
--

WOMAN'S RIGHTS.—A slight personal difficulty occurred yesterday on K street between Dr. Justis Gates and Miss Rowena Granice, a well-known actress. The affair as stated to us was about as follows: The lady in question, who has been connected with [Dan Virgil] Gates theatrically, is in the habit of frequenting the [apothecary] store of Dr. Gates oftener than he considered necessary, which was a source of annoyance to him, and yesterday morning he requested her not to call again. In a few minutes after the request was made, she entered the store armed with a small cow skin whip, and raised her arm to strike the Doctor, who instantly caught her by the wrist and took from her the unfeminine implement, and ordered her from the store; in the meanwhile a considerable crowd collected around the

store to whom the facts were explained, and they
retired with a knowledge of the affair similar to this
statement, which we have good reason to believe to
be correct.[14]

We can only surmise as to what provocation Rowena was
reacting to, whether Dr. Gates said something or physically
accosted her while insisting she leave the premises; however, we
know that she always took particular umbrage with personal
insults and gossip and slander. In all her writings, those were the
only instances in which she advocated violence, specifically
whipping, as an appropriate response.

The next day Rowena apparently published a card
"expressing regret at nothing except that she did not 'succeed in
the undertaking.'"[15] In June it was reported that she had been
fined $20 and costs for "disturbing the peace."[16] It is not clear
whether this legal proceeding was the result of the Gates kerfuffle.

Then, the next day appeared an article about an attempted
theft from Rowena by a fellow actress:

> A female member of the histrionic profession,
> answering to the name of Brown, was arraigned at
> the instance of Miss Rowena Granice, from whom
> said Madame Brown had attempted to take certain
> articles of ladies' wearing apparel. Miss Granice
> discovered Mrs. Brown in her room with the articles
> in question strewn upon the floor, when they should
> have properly been in a trunk. Mrs. B. was found
> guilty, and Miss Granice, with true womanly feeling
> and tenderness, deposited her own watch as security
> for the defendant's appearance on Monday
> morning.[17]

Giving more color to the incident, Rowena wrote a letter to the editor of the Sacramento paper which was reprinted in the Chico paper.

SACRAMENTO, June 9, 1857.

EDS. SACRAMENTO AGE:—I perceive by your columns that your reporter has committed a great error in stating that Mrs. Brown was fined twenty dollars for stealing my *shirt*. Now, I want to say to the young gentleman (for I suppose he must be young) that Miss Rowena Granice don't wear shirts, and he ought to be ashamed to circulate such a falsehood. I detest shirts!—with their long sleeves and stiff standing collars, buttoned up to the throat—*ugh*! I'd choke to death in one of them. I wonder if he ever saw me, and if so, if he thinks I look like a woman that would wear a shirt. No, indeed! if I had one of the masculine articles I soon would show it the door. Wear a shirt? indeed! Why I don't even aspire to wear the breeches! Please tell him—do—for me, and oblige your humble servant,

ROWENA GRANICE.[18]

From newspaper clippings and the playbill collection at the California Historical Society in San Francisco, we learn that Rowena spent an incredibly busy Spring and Summer in this cottage in 1857 taking care of her boys, writing stories and overseeing and starring in the production of a hectic theater calendar.

In April 1857, she appeared with D.V. Gates at a benefit for the Oroville Fire Department, "greeted by a crowded house. The performance throughout gave general satisfaction to all present. These talented artists will appear tonight in a new bill of attraction, full of fun and variety. And, in addition, will give a Cotillion Party, aided by a *Good Band of Music*."[19]

June 17 at the National Theater (K Street near 5th) ("a great novelty local comedy" by Hugh F. McDermott, Esq., entitled "Fashion's Folly; or, Life in California," starring Rowena as Mrs. Olix, a grass widow, the performance to commence with the new Yankee farce in one act entitled "Ichabod's Come")

June 24, one night at the Forrest Theatre ("Our Gal" starring Rowena, as Mahetable, and Caroline Moreton; also featuring the Highland Fling with Miss Louisa Paullin, to be followed by "the laughable farce" of "The Rival Pages," concluding with "the new and laughable farce" of "The Yankee Housemaid; Or, Jerusha Sunflower in Mexico")

August 10, Rowena leased the Sacramento Theater for a season, opening with "Old Folks at Home." "She intends to have a succession of novelties that will please and gratify her patrons. New pieces, new farces; new songs, new dances, etc., will be presented. We wish her success."[20]

August 24 back at the National for the rest of the summer ("Margaret Catchpole: The Heroine of Humble Life; or, The Female Horse Thief," a great historical drama in three acts, starring Miss Albertine)

August 26 - "Jack Sheppard; or, The House-Breaker of the Last Century," starring Miss Albertine, adapted from a novel by William Harrison Ainsworth, "to conclude with the laughable farce" of "The Illustrious Stranger"

August 28 - "a drama of intense interest" called "The Ocean Child," starring Miss Albertine and Miss Paullin, to conclude with "The Cobbler's Wife"

August 29 - "the admirable comedy" of "The Merry Monarch: Charles II of England," starring Rowena, Mary Copp, and

Miss Albertine, "with an admired song" by Miss Paullin, after which Miss Albertine's own version of an "admirable burletta" called "The Stage-Struck Chambermaid," to conclude with "Buried Alive"

August 31 - "Therese, The Orphan of Geneva," starring Rowena as Therese; featured song "Give Me a Cot," concluding with the comedy "Slasher and Crasher" starring Miss Paullin

September 3 - Dickens' domestic drama "Nicholas Nickleby," starring Rowena as Smike, a favorite dance, and concluding with the farce of "The Swiss Cottage" starring Miss Louisa Paullin; and closing on

September 4 - "George Barnwell; or, The London Apprentice," the great moral tragedy, featuring "Negro Dance" by Mr. Sheppard and to conclude with "Ichabod's Come!" featuring Rowena as Jerusha and Ichabod[21]

Missing from this list is a June 27, 1857 complimentary for McDermott, where, it turned out, the ticket sales were insufficient to cover the theater costs leading to a rather comical string of events.

Ignominious Flight of an Author.—H.F. McDermott, the author-actor, was to receive a complimentary benefit at Sacramento on Saturday night, and his own piece, "Fashion's Folly," was to be produced. The amount of cash received at the box office not being sufficient to satisfy the clamorous demands of the music, etc., he was forced to dismiss the audience and send them to the treasurer to get their money refunded. In the meantime, however, the gas bill (some $20) had been paid, so that there was not sufficient *dinero* to give each his dollar back. The audience were vociferous in their demands, and a friend of Mac's intimated to him if he did not retreat he would be tarred and feathered. The only egress was through a door which was blocked up with gaping creditors, so Mac consented to don a disguise. He was quickly robed in a character dress of Rowena Granice, and wigged and bonneted in a Yankee costume, and made his escape. The crowd having "got wind" of the matter, gave chase. After a chapter of accidents and hair breadth escapes, Mac reached his hotel, entered his room, barred the door and remained there until he thought he might safely venture out again. In the *Item* of Sunday, Mac comes out in a card, and informs his patrons that their money will be refunded on application at the box office.

Hard is the "Fate of Genius!"—*S.F. Call.*[22]

On September 8 it was reported that the National Theater, "which, for the past two weeks, has been under the direction of Rowena Granice, closed last evening for want of patronage, and the few who were present had their money returned to them. The play announced was 'The Exile,' a dramatized story of Ned McGowan, and the few persons who were present to witness it, shows that it was not a subject of much interest to the community generally."[23]

That very day, a story was published claiming that Thomas Claughley had appeared uninvited at Rowena's Sacramento home the Sunday before and allegedly had caught Rowena *in flagrante delicto* with another man.

A DOMESTIC SCENE. At an early hour on Sunday morning, soon after the San Francisco boat arrived, a gentleman might have been seen rapping at the door of a neat little cottage not far from the corner of

Third and a street the name of which is a letter found
not far from the middle of the alphabet. Soon a
window was raised from the inside, and a nightcap,
encircling a head that was neither fair nor forty, but
nevertheless quite good looking, was visible, and a
melodious voice interrogated, "Who's there making
such a noise at this unseemly hour?" "It is your own
dear husband, love," replied the gentleman in a
gentle tone, "won't you hasten to let me in?" "Go
away, you brute!" exclaimed the "soft" one, "I am a
poor, lone woman, and my husband is in San
Francisco, and if you don't depart instantly I will
raise the neighborhood." The man being convinced
that the woman was his wife, and feeling satisfied
that he was recognized, made arrangements to enter
the house forcibly, and suspecting that the sooner he
got in the more he would see, effected a rapid
entrance through the window just in time to observe
by moonlight, the short, stout form of a young
Sacramento lawyer disappearing through the back
door. Upon ascending to his wife's chamber he
discovered a pair of boots not the size usually worn
by himself, and also found other unmistakable
evidence that she had not been utterly without
consolation during his brief absence below. As the
bird had flown, the injured husband thought there
was no use in making much ado about what had
happened, but quietly remained in town till Monday,
when, in the absence of his faithless wife, he
removed his two children and placed them in what
he considered better keeping, and transported the
furniture to one of the San Francisco steamers,
intending to take it to that city, but the woman
returned just in season to have it replevined as the

property of a friend who held a bill of sale of it, and succeeded in having her husband arrested on a charge, we believe, of disturbing the peace. He, however, gave bail for his appearance, and will probably be discharged upon examination. Thus closes act first, scene first, in this domestic drama, which would give the renowned McDermott, were he here, an opportunity of adding another spectacle to his play of "Fashion's Folly."

Truly, "all the world's a stage," etc.[24]

Though no names were given, it was eminently obvious because of the address, the insinuations to the theater, and the "two children," as to whom the article is referencing. As if to dispel any lingering doubt, Thomas posted a letter two days later.

More about the "Domestic Scene"—Reply from a Husband.

The following card, presented us by Mr. T.N. Claughley, the husband of Rowena Granice, we publish as a reply to an article that appeared in the BEE of Tuesday, headed "A Domestic Scene," Mr. C. believing that the article was designed for him. We cannot perceive how he or his wife should take it as personal, if there was no truth to it, as no names were mentioned. The language used in his card is rather strong, and smacks slightly of the stage, but there is nothing particularly wrong about it, *provided* it is true:

A CARD.

SACRAMENTO, Sept. 9th, 1857.

MESSRS. EDITORS:—My attention has been directed to an infamous article that appeared in yesterday's issue headed "A Domestic Scene," reflecting dishonor, in no unmeasurable terms, upon the reputation of my wife; and although no names are mentioned, the programme of the pantomime is too transparent not to be plainly understood by hundreds in this city. As an act of justice to my wife and family, the painful necessity devolved upon me not to permit the scurrilous, slanderous and filthy article to pass unnoticed. I take this occasion to pronounce it false—false in its inception, malicious in its motives, and wicked in its designs and consequences as ever the ingenuity of man conceived or the "wagging tongue" of slander thundered forth, and can only be equaled by his corrupt and lying heart.

It is true that I came from the Bay on Friday morning—not Sunday, as the article sets forth, doubtless with no other view than that of giving plausibility to its base and malicious intents. For had the author stated the fact, that I came up on Friday morning, the article would have been a lie on its face, and no one would have believed it. My wife was well aware of my intended visit, and was expecting me on the morning that I came, and had been waiting up past the usual hour at which the steamers are expected; but the boat having been detained about two hours beyond her time, it was about four o'clock when I reached the house. I saw from the outside a light burning in her chamber, and knocked at the door. Receiving no answer, nor hearing no movements within, I went around to the back door and knocked with the view of awaking the children without disturbing the mother. After knocking several times, and the deathlike stillness still prevailing throughout the house, I concluded to make an attempt to enter and find my way to the sofa; but, being unacquainted with the interior of the house, and it being so dark at the time that nothing could be discernable, I returned and knocked again. Presently, I heard my little boy calling to his mother that someone was knocking. After the lapse of a few moments she came down and opened the door; and, in going to my wife's chamber, I discovered no "boots' or any other article that could possibly excite the suspicion of the most credulous; nor yet did I see the form of any human being "disappearing through the back door."

The villain who could thus basely manufacture such scandalous and malicious falsehoods, "a whip should be placed in the hands of every honest man to lash the rascal through the world."

So far as concerns the removal of my household furniture, and disposal of the children, it originated from no suspicion of her chastity whatever, but from considerations wholly of a different character, which can in no manner be either interesting, entertaining or instructive to the public. In what I made an ineffectual attempt to do, was designed for her benefit, rather than from any advantage to myself; although I consulted my own as well as her personal interest, comfort and happiness—having already sacrificed too much on account of her professional enterprise, which I have been exciting myself to induce her to abandon, as it has already ruined her health, and retire for some time at least from the arduous and exciting labors of her profession until her health should be fully restored. But, unfortunately, her ambition outruns her judgment, hence the cause of our unpleasant affair.

And now, in conclusion, I would say that the base and craven-hearted wretch who would thus falsely and maliciously magnify a slight personal domestic affair, to pander to the morbid tastes and appetites of the depraved and vicious, to the disgrace of a devoted wife and mother, the mortification of a husband and father, and to the reproach of unoffending, innocent children, is deserving of the execration of all mankind.[25]

Later that month, after making sure the boys were well cared for at their home in Sacramento, Rowena began a fall tour through the mining district with the D.V. Gates Company. According to Koon, "[s]he charmed audiences from the beginning, and wherever she went she was given special marks of favor. Miners threw bags of gold to her, and Oroville gave her a belt with a gold buckle."[26] But it was also on this tour that she had a frightening encounter with the infamous Honey Lake Tribe of Indians:

ATTACKED BY INDIANS.
An Adventurous Trip in Northern California.

———

Exciting Termination of a Traveling Theatrical Venture—Pursued by the Honey Lake Indians

———

Written for The Sunday Call.

———

Late in the summer of 1857 a party of ladies and gentlemen, members of the theatrical professions, left San Francisco for a trip through the northern mines with a view of giving parlor entertainments. Among the company were genial Jake Thomas and wife, Jimmy Griffith, Mortimer, Miss Lulu and others. The company had been selected with care, as the object of the manager was mainly to give his wife, who was in delicate health, the benefit of the mountain air and a change of scene. A strong, easy carriage and four fine, safe horses and an experienced driver had been secured. This kind, considerate husband and manager was the possessor of ample means to pay all expenses, even if the company should fail to draw paying houses. This information was imparted to each of the company previous to starting upon the trip so that it was no great wonder, with this very important bit of knowledge and the prospect of six or eight weeks' travel through the mountains during the charming California autumn months,

That all hearts were light,

And eyes were bright,

as we bade adieu to the restless waters of the bay and the busy scenes of the city of hills. The company had been well advertised by an advance agent and the performers had the satisfaction of playing to crowded houses and being greeted by enthusiastic audiences each evening as they journeyed on from town to town. And after the performance was over each one, with pleasant memories and the sound of rapturous applause still ringing in their ears, sought the couch of rest and awakened in the early morning refreshed by sleep, to feel the soft, cool mountain air as it wafted the fragrance of wildwood flowers through the open casement. These lovely flowers, so profuse in the mountains, seemed to have retained all of their spring sweetness for autumn exhalation. The

days passed pleasantly and the nights proved
profitable, and we found nothing to mar our
pleasure. Each day brought with it some pleasant
episode to change the monotony of "here to-day,
there to-morrow" sort of life.

SUMMONED HOME.

Now, as all the pleasant and unpleasant things in life
must come to an end, so with this pleasant
journeying. We had arrived at the town of Yreka, and
after performing there three nights with satisfactory
success, the question arose should we proceed to the
town of Jacksonville, Oregon, or should we return to
San Francisco. While trying to settle the question, the
clerk of the house stepped into the parlor where the
manager and the leading people of the company were
seated and handed the writer a letter. This letter
settled the question as far as Miss Lulu and myself
were concerned. It told me that important business
made it necessary for me to return to San Francisco
immediately, and as Miss Lulu had been placed in my
charge by her mother, with instructions not to leave
her daughter should the company separate at any
time, I felt it an imperative duty devolving upon me
to take Lulu back with me. The company had
decided to go into Oregon for an extended trip and
were fortunate in securing the services of two young
lady actresses who were stopping at Yreka. All was
satisfactorily arranged, and Lulu and myself would
leave Yreka on the stage which left at midnight.

During the afternoon, while all were in the parlor
enjoying a parting chat, Jimmy rushed in and in an
excited tone of voice said, "Mrs. G, you and Lulu
had better not go over that Shasta trail; it is full of
Injuns. I just saw an account in the paper," he

continued, "of the return to this county of the Honey Lake tribe."

"Bring up the paper," exclaimed Mortimer. Jimmy ran off to obey the order.

"Honey Lake Indians," said Mr. B. "Why, I don't remember to have ever heard of their exodus. I wonder if it took place before the flood."

This jocund remark brought forth a peal of laughter from all save Lulu and myself. Lulu looked serious from a natural youthful timidity of everything at the slightest hint of danger. Not so with me — I had never been afraid of anything except dogs and Indians.

SERIOUS PROSPECTS.

Lulu noticed the look of seriousness which had crept over my face and said to me, "If you are afraid, I won't go one step."

"I certainly shall not knowingly lead you into danger, Lulu," I replied. "I shall look into the matter though before deciding what course I shall take. If the Indians are on the trail and there is danger, Wells Fargo's expressman, who rides ahead with the treasure, will surely know it and will not endanger the lives of women by allowing them to follow in."

Just then Jimmy came in with the paper containing the article. We found it something of a sensational character and concluded not to worry about it until I had a talk with the expressman. This worthy gentleman, true to the interest of the company by which he was employed, scouted the idea of there being Indians anywhere near the trail over which the passengers for Shasta would have to pass. He laughed quite heartily at Lulu and told her that some romancer must have gotten up the report. This killed her fears and quelled my apprehensions.

About 9 o'clock Lulu and I bade our friends good-by, and retired to get a little rest. We would be called to take the stage at midnight and should continue to keep our seats in this vehicle, with the exception of leaving them at the breakfast station for 30 minutes, until we arrived at the station for dinner. At one o'clock we would take saddle horses and travel over a narrow trail until we arrived at a station where we would again take the stage for Shasta and Sacramento. The expressman informed us that we would arrive at this station about sundown and remain there until midnight. After mounting our horses and just before we started, the expressman brought a nice-looking old gentleman to where Lulu and I were and introduced him as Mr. Gage, and then remarked, "This gentleman will ride behind you, ladies, and see that you are all safe going up and down these steep places. Your animals are safe," he added and with a pleasant bow left us, jumping into his saddle gave the word, and the train of about twelve passengers moved on.

A PLEASANT JOURNEY.

For at least two hours we rode along enjoying the scenery and talking over the pleasant incidents of our trip from San Francisco to Yreka and occasionally hearing a few words from our companion, Mr. Gage. We had lost sight of the train, and Lulu asked Mr. Gage if we had not better hurry on and overtake the men. His reply was that he thought we were making pretty good time.

I being ahead of Lulu, she said, "Mr. Gage, when you wish me to hurry along faster, just let me know and I will whip up."

"You're doing nicely," he said. "It is always better to save the animals for the last four or five miles."

A few moments after, Mr. Gage called out to Lulu, "Miss, just stop a moment, I believe your saddle is getting loose."

Lulu and I both stopped our mules, and Mr. Gage got down first, tied his animal and assisted Lulu to dismount. I saw the gentleman fuss a little with the buckle and then he remarked, "It's safe enough now," and after assisting Lulu to remount he climbed slowly into his saddle and still seemed to be fixing the straps and buckles. All at once the sound of the firing of a heavy gun from a distance rumbled through the woods.

Lulu screamed. "Oh! was that from the Indians?"

Mr. Gage looked up with a smile and said, "No, what made you think of Indians?"

"Oh, we heard that there were Indians on this trail while we were in Yreka."

"You did?" he said with a laugh. "Well, I guess you don't know much about Indians. When you hear from them it won't be from the firing of a gun. The kind of Indians we have here fight with the still, sure arrows, but there are no Indians on this trail, nor have there been any near here for several years. That was a signal gun of safety that the expressman fires off when he has timid, nervous ladies in the train. Now we can travel on slow or fast. It will be a beautiful moonlight night, and if we don't get to the station until 7 o'clock we can get a good supper without being too tired to enjoy it."

After this assuring speech, Lulu began to sing, and we talked and laughed and began to truly enjoy the ride, one moment upon a hilltop, the next down in a shady dell.

"How far is it to the station?" I asked a half hour after we had heard the report of the gun.

"Only about four miles," was Mr. Gage's reply.

A BEAUTIFUL SUNSET.

With this cheering information, I settled myself to enjoy the beautiful scenery. The sun had just disappeared behind the purple mist which hung like a royal robe over the high, far-away mountains. The western sky was a lovely picture — one of those magnificent sunsets which enraptures the soul of the lover of the beautiful. Cerulean tints blended with pink, amber and purple, lit up by a blaze of golden light.

"How lovely!" I exclaimed.

"Perfectly magnificent!" responded Lulu and as we journeyed on a feeling of sweet content stole into my heart. I seemed to be in a pleasant dream. Lulu, too, seemed absorbed in pleasant thoughts.

Turning a point in the trail, I caught a glimpse of her fair young face. A bright smile played about her cherry red lips. She was intent upon watching the lovely sky picture. The sun was entirely out of sight and the shade of the early evening was creeping over the earth. "This reminds me of the lines from Byron's 'Lara,'" I said, looking back at Lulu.

"Oh, repeat them," she said.

Of course, I could not refuse.

All was so still, so soft in earth and air
You scarce would start to meet a spirit there;
Secure that naught of evil could delight
To walk in such a scene on such a night.

Scarce had the last word left my lips when Lulu screamed out in a voice of terror, "Oh! look there!"

I turned, and the sight which met my eyes seemed to freeze my blood and stop the beating of my heart. I saw Mr. Gage urging his animal to pass poor little Lulu.

"Coward!" I called out. "Stay behind and protect us!" What was it I saw? I saw at least twenty Indians with gay feathers and painted faces and not more than 600 feet from the trail. The only advantage we had was that the savages had to climb up a steep, rocky hill. They were in a little valley and had laid aside their weapons. I saw them picking up their bows and arrows and saw them start toward us. My mule was going at a rapid rate and Lulu's was close behind. I called out, "Lulu, don't get frightened! Throw down your rein and hold on with your arms." She obeyed me and I dropped my rein. The mules were as much frightened as we were and sped on through the brush and trees to which our clothing caught and ripped and tore.

PURSUED BY THE INDIANS.

On, on we went, with the Indians in hot pursuit. We could hear the arrows strike the trees. I called back to Lulu several times to have courage, that we would soon get to the station. I began to feel very weak, and when next I attempted to speak I could not use my tongue. It was fastened to the roof of my mouth. Then I knew no more until I felt myself being gently taken from the saddle. I could hear kindly voices all around me, but I could not speak. I was taken to a room and placed upon a bed. I was in my full senses, but still my tongue clove to the roof of my mouth. At length I saw a lady leaning over me with a glass, which she put to my mouth, but I could not swallow.

"Oh, doctor!" she called out, "come quick!" The doctor came and was not long in discovering my condition and in a few moments gave me relief. As soon as I could speak I asked for Lulu.

"She is very weak," said the doctor. "Her nervous system has received a terrible shock."

Being naturally strong and healthy, I soon recovered and went in to my poor little friend. We remained at the station two days waiting for Lulu to recover sufficiently to travel, and while there we heard a gentleman tell the following story: "You see, ladies, the expressman had been a little shaky about them Indians for several days. There was one spot on the trail where he felt certain the Indians would make the attack if they were really back and in that neighborhood, and it was from that point that the gun you heard was fired. The expressman told Gage to hold you and the girl back on pretense of the saddle being loose. If there was danger he would send a man back to let Gage know. If there was no danger he would fire off the gun. He got to the place and hunted around, but could find no signs of the savages, and thinking all was safe, he fired and we galloped on. But when it got so late we all began to get uneasy and every man about the place was just about to start when you got here. I tell you what, you had a narrow escape. Three of the arrows struck Mr. Gage and made three mighty big holes in his coat. They must have been some kind of crosswise, as they just grazed the coat and didn't strike the flesh."

As soon as Lulu could bear the journey, we started and reached Sacramento in safety. The next day we took the steamer Antelope for San Francisco.

All who read the newspapers of those days will
remember the frightful death of Curley, the popular
stage driver who was murdered by these Honey Lake
Indians, and also the terrible murder of an old man
and his wife and many others. Poor Lulu died several
years after of consumption. Of the other
professionals who started out on that pleasant trip
many have passed away, but the memory of the
pleasant weeks and also the recollection of the night
we were chased by the Indians is just as fresh as
though they were occurrences of yesterday.[27]

According to Koon, Rowena went back to San Francisco
in the fall of 1857, and from February through March of 1858, she
toured the mines with J.P. "Yankee" Addams.[28] Addams, who was
"[a]lways ready for anything and equal to anything ... with a
black cloak and a black wig [or] with a black cloak and a red wig,
he was ready for any tragedy or comedy part at ten minutes
notice,"[29] had arrived from the East on October 22, 1857 and
played at the American Theater in San Francisco from the 25th
through November 7 when he took a second benefit.[30] From there,
Koon says, he toured the mines with his own company with
"mediocre success" from November 1857 through March 1858,[31]
although McCabe states he was at the Lyceum in San Francisco
from January 8-10, 1858.[32] It was in Sacramento in March of that
year that a most curious event is purported to have taken place
between Addams and Rowena:

Singular Theatrical Marriage.

From a certificate of marriage exhibited to several
parties we learn that on Friday, March 5, Rev. J.A.
Benton united in marriage in this city J.P. Addams,
the well-known Yankee comedian, and Rowena
Granice. An attempt has been made to keep the

matter private, but the showing of the marriage certificate let it out. What strikes us as singular about it is, that a few weeks ago we published a notice signed "N. Claughley" forbidding anyone to credit his wife Rowena Granice, on his account, and a few months [September 1857] since we published a card written by Mr. Claughley under the diction of Miss Granice wherein she was claimed as his wife.

Queer country, this.[33]

Was this some sort of cruel joke or revenge by Thomas? A publicity stunt by Addams? Did other actors perhaps impersonate Rowena and Addams? Or, as Rowena alludes to in the article on actresses in *The Family Gem*, did some envious party plant the article to "blacken the reputation" of one who "possesses talent of a higher order, or a more charming personal appearance than some of the older members of the profession"?[34] Rowena never referred to Mr. Addams for the rest of her life, let alone let us in on the true nature of their relationship. Yet, Galloway confirmed that the marriage license was on file in Sacramento, "though no record of a divorce from Claughley nor an annulment of the marriage to Addams can be found."[35] The supposed marriage shadowed Rowena in several newspaper articles through the rest of 1858 and into early 1859, and she continued suffering a tumultuous relationship with Thomas for another two years.

The Gaieties Theatre; Or, Temple of Mirth and Song

Although the exact date cannot be documented, it is well established that sometime in the summer of 1856 Rowena leased the space known as No. 77 Long Wharf and kept it running until at least December 1859. Originally built over many of the old rotting ships that were abandoned by their crews, much of Long Wharf had been nearly destroyed in a huge fire in 1851. Rebuilt in 1852, No. 77 became Charles P. Kimball's "Noisy Carrier's Book and Stationery Company." In October 1852 Kimball married Isabel Dunn, daughter of a ship's blacksmith who had a shop down the Wharf, and moved his wife into an apartment he had built over the store.[36]

In just a few years, with hard work and perseverance, Kimball, a prim and formal Yankee in tall silk hat and long-tailed coat, built the business from the confinement of a long narrow stall to a store that encompassed the entire first floor of No. 77. By 1855 he was so successful that he had to move "Noisy Carrier's" to larger quarters at No. 64-66 Long Wharf, leaving No. 77 vacant. The Kimball family, by then composed of Charles and Isabel, and children James, John, Booth and Rebecca, remained in the upstairs apartment.[37]

The cavernous first floor was leased out to Rowena Granice, manageress, who named the melodeon or "bit theater" "The Gaieties – Temple of Mirth and Song."

Evidently, according to Kimball's journals, which author Dolores Waldorf Bryant had in her possession when in 1942 she wrote an article about No. 77 Long Wharf for the California Historical Society Journal, Thomas Claughley was involved hands-on in the rental and operation, if not disposition of liquor stock, of the bar and theater,

> ... where once the ardent Son of Temperance, Charles Kimball, had sold books, extension pens, ink and ledgers. Rowena circulated among the patrons, managed the shows put on in the long back room (which apparently ran parallel to the Wharf), saw to it that the boys had their meals and schooling, kept Tom from imbibing too freely of the stock in trade, wrote short stories and essays, and played the leads in all the plays. Rowena was not a clinging vine.[38]

At some point, probably on tour in the mining country in 1856, Rowena made the acquaintance of Charlotte "Little Lotta" Crabtree, a pretty eight-year-old singer and dancer. Charlotte Mignon Crabtree, born November 10, 1847 in New York, was the daughter of John Ashworth Crabtree and Mary Ann Livesey Crabtree, both immigrants from England. Rowena may even have known them in New York; for a few years before coming to California they had a bookstore off Broadway. John came to the gold fields first to seek his fortune in 1851 and, just like Rowena was abandoned by her husband, Mary Ann and Little Lotta, left behind in New York, soon packed up their bags and came to find him. From that point on, John's presence in their lives was infrequent and then ceased when Mary Ann finally "sent him packing" back to England with some of the profits from Little Lotta's lucrative stage career.

The appreciative miners were soon throwing gold nuggets and coins at the lovely little child with her bouncing blonde curls as she danced and sang her heart out for their amusement, and Mary Ann would scramble around the stage picking up the loot. As it got too much to carry, she shrewdly began investing in property wherever they went (as apparently did Rowena through-out the years, albeit of much less value), building Lotta's fortune to over four million dollars in real estate by the time she died, unmarried, in Boston in 1924.

Rowena may have "discovered" Lotta and encouraged the development of her early career on stages in front of the miners, but it was the famous Lola Montez who took the child under her wing and introduced her to the higher class of San Francisco entertainment that, by that time, was heading towards the variety and minstrel show formula. Lotta was the perfect little trouper in the right place at the optimum period in the evolution of California theater. According to McCabe, "La Petite" Lotta's first appearance in San Francisco was on November 20, 1857 (the same day Lola Montez left for the East).[39] Over the years she became a huge success nationwide. In 1867, the *New York Times* described her as having "[t]he face of a beautiful doll and the ways of a playful kitten," and said "her natural smartness needs but to be cultivated to make her the most sparkling actress of her age."[40] In between time, sometime between 1856 and 1859, Lotta danced and warbled at Rowena's humble melodeon, The Temple of Mirth and Song, on at least two occasions.

A visitor to the Gaieties who chronicled one of those appearances in great detail was Thaddeus Stevens Kenderdine of Solebury Township, Bucks County, Pennsylvania.[*] Born in 1836, son of lumber dealer John Kenderdine and his wife Martha Quinby, John had tramped about the country in his younger days, ending up in San Francisco in 1858. He combined his reminiscences into a book published in 1888.

> SAN FRANCISCO is a city of theatres. With but a sixth part of the population (in 1858) of Philadelphia, it can boast of almost as many places of amusement. From Maguire's Opera House down, through intermediate grades to the lowest cafe chantant, are a series of entertainments from which fastidious to lax can select a place of evening resort. Occupying a middle rank among these are the "Bit Theatres," so termed from the price of admission, a "bit," or shilling. These are generally conducted by broken-down professionals, and their assistants are amateurs; their patrons being a medley of those who cannot afford higher priced places of diversion, or who go out of curiosity.

---

[*] Coincidentally, members of the Kenderdine family are pivotal characters in this author's first book, *Langhorn and Mary—A 19th Century American Love Story* (Amber Books, 2003). A historical novel set in Bucks County in the mid-1800s, it draws all of its characters from real people who actually lived there, including Thaddeus, his father, John, and brother, Robert.

In my walks about the city my attention had often been drawn toward those abodes of the minor drama through the mediums of glaring posters. These, after describing the features of the coming entertainment, short dramas, acrobatic feats, singing and dancing, conspicuously remarked that the best liquor could be had for twelve and a half cents; thus putting the professions of the stage and bar on an equal footing.

In 1858 the part of the city, covering what once had been the bay, had so extended that a view parallel with the front and taking in the upper town made San Francisco resemble a recumbent giantess, a little tipsy, or rather "half Seas over," with her feet in the water, and with the contents of her wide-spreading lap in danger of dropping through the fragile apron. Beneath the flat, where now were filth and mud, and the swash of waves as they climbed and fell back from the slimy wharf timbers, once ships were moored, and here, deserted by their gold-greedy crews, some lay rotting, until enclosed by wharf and street they became absorbed in the growing town. The architecture of this built-over portion was shabby enough, and consisted mainly of warehouses, offices connected with shipping, junk shops, Jew clothing stores, Chinese laundries and low groggeries. The hollow square, which these buildings surrounded, was the dumping place for superfluous material from the high ground overlooking the bay, as well as for the odds and ends which communities generally surreptitiously throw into such places. On the planked streets, after the arrival of States' steamers and other craft, drays thundered back and forth, confidence men played their little games on incoming passengers, hotel runners did their work, and bootblacks left their shining marks.

One day in my saunterings over this portion of the city I came across one of the places of amusement heading this chapter. It was of no greater pretension than scores of the rickety buildings surrounding it, except that it was of two stories. The bar-room was as prominent a part of the premises as the liquor announcement was of the posters, as the audience was forced to pass through it to get to the "auditorium."

The manager was Miss Rowena Granice, whether an assumed or real name I don't know. I saw her in the trying light of day standing—leaning from a sort of inside balcony above the bar-room—like another Juliet, or rather like the grandmother of that interesting young woman, although on her face paint, powder and paste had done their work, until she looked like a flamboyant fright: an exemplification of the conflict we are warring with time, and of the fact that we may apply pigment and dye, we may pad and bewig, and wrap our forms in the gay robes of youth, only to see what we are trying to fend off come back like a pent-up flood, and, washing off cosmetic and color, and obliterating our other shams, deliver the human humbug to Old Age's grim follower. The Romeo who played to this Juliet was a rotund German, who, from his position on the bar-room floor, invited her to step down from her perch and take a drink with him; a request she coyly agreed to.

Miss Rowena, in spite of this uncomplimentary introduction, seemed like one who had been the possessor of good looks and an actress of note, but who, on account of loss of personal attractions rather than of professional ability, had been obliged to leave more aristocratic boards for this humble theatre. Enterprising, if old and faded, she had managed her "Gaieties" until it was at the head of its class.

Facilis decencus averni and easy of access was the "Bit Theatre." Passing through the purgatorial bar-room, a place reeking with the fumes of tobacco and liquor, I gave the "open sesame" of a "bit" to a willing recipient, and was ushered into the room adjoining. On entering through a vista of smoke I saw a row of "tallow dips," and behind them the mimic stage. In front of these, on a floor some ten yards square, were rows of tables, around which were the theatrical as well as the vinous guests of the "Gaieties." Before these were placed by attentive waiters the wished-for liquids from the adjoining room. Around three sides of the building was a gallery; the whole building seating about three hundred people.

The view on entering was unique. Enveloped in dense fumes of tobacco, the audience was drinking and talking. It was a mélange of rough miners, fresh from the mountains and now on their way home to the States, and conspicuous for their shaggy beards and weapons; inoffensive looking gamblers seeking whom they might devour, and curious sight-seers. Mingled among them were a number of boys of various ages and sizes to match.

I secured a seat near the stage. For companion I had a specimen of the genus small boy, the lad who gets familiar and ends by getting impudent. I found him throughout the evening a source of entertainment and general information. As a theatrical critic he was good for his age. He was well acquainted with the three minor actors, who were young like himself. As there was no way from the Street to the stage except through the auditorium, the players were obliged to make ingress among the audience. As they passed us my little friend addressed them in quite a familiar way, though, to do him justice, more from a desire to show me his acquaintance with them than from any lack of respect. Not so with some of his fellows. These spoke to them in words neither becoming nor complimentary. The young actors bore these pin thrusts into their dignity with the nonchalance of veteran tragedians when receiving sentient attention from a demonstrative lobby. Disappearing through a side door they left the audience anxiously expecting their reappearance.

At length the bell announcing the rising of the curtain was heard, and simultaneous with its ringing there was a hush in the ubiquitous conversation and clink of glasses, and soon commenced the performance of "Brigham Young; or, The Prophet's Dream." This was a mixture of comedy and tragedy, the former preponderating. The Prophet was represented by a celebrated acrobat, whose main forte was in tying himself up in bow-knots, but who, in a pinch, could figure in the drama. His Sultana was the ripe-aged Miss Rowena, his other wives being represented by three juvenile actors, arrayed in female garments, and who created a great amount of amusement by their efforts to adapt themselves to their parts. The only efforts made to carry dignity into the play were by the two leading characters, and, to do them justice, they did well under trying circumstances; but, alas! their efforts were not appreciated by their listeners, who would loudly laugh at and guy them during affecting scenes.

Unasked-for advice and unseemly remarks would discompose the Sultana while in heroic attitude she prepared to slay the faithless Prophet, while the high-tragedy voice and action of the latter were turned into ridicule. Especially were assaults made on the dignity of poor Brigham when, after performing in an affecting scene, he came in front of the curtain in the role of a "supe," to extinguish the footlights, in order that the room might be darkened to the proper consistency while he indulged in his dream. In the face of a battery of uncomplimentary remarks he accomplished his humble mission, and then retired to reappear in his remarkable vision, in which the ghost of his murdered wife was to awaken him to consciousness, remorse and penitence. The only appreciated acting was done by the young actors in female rig, who, at last ignoring the characters in which they were designed to act, seemed only posses-sed with a desire to amuse the audience; and this they did until the clouds of tobacco swayed to and fro with the shocks of convulsive laughter underlying them.

During the performance of this play my friend, the small boy, rendered me great service. Entertaining me with critiques on the actors and their style, he told me the names of his friends as they came upon the scene. My small boy was of the dignified pattern, and did not join his fellows in their ridicule of the actors, but confined his remarks to me, as also the smoke of a large cigar he was puffing.

Following the play was a series of acrobatic feats by the late Brigham, and then a dance by one of the boys. Next came a song by a little girl of twelve years, who, on account of the homeliness of her last name, was simply known as "Miss Lottie" on the bills. The dance was accomplished to the entire satisfaction of the audience, but, owing to hoarseness, Lottie broke down amid the "Shells of the Ocean." Thrice she essayed the effort and as often failed. The miners, many of whom had known her when among the mountains on a professional tour, sympathized with her condition as much as they wanted to hear her sing, and it was amusing to listen to them in their rough but kind tones encouraging her to go on.

At last, getting into a pet at her failure, she ran off the stage amid the applause of her friends. I did not know I would ever hear of this girl again. She became a popular actress; generally, on account of her small stature taking juvenile parts, which she still continues, although over forty years old. Her mother still accompanies her on her tours. Her success has been great, and her fortune is in the hundred thousands. She is called Lotta, and her name of Crabtree is still kept subdued. A beautiful fountain bearing her name—her first name, remember—ornaments the city where she made her successful start in life; a gift from her to the city whence she made her start to fame, if her questionable notoriety can be so called.

The performance was over, and by this time the lights in the vitiated air were burning blue. Odors at variance with those of "Araby the Blest" filled the air from the floor to the ceiling. The attentions of the waiters on their guests had had their natural effect. The drinking part of the audience was getting uproarious. Omens of a continuation of the evening performances were making themselves manifest, and, thinking a bed in a hotel preferable to a muss in a place like this, I left the "Gaieties," and, passing through the thronged bar-room, emerged to the silent and gloomy world without."[41]

Kenderdine was a Quaker, and the strict beliefs of that sect should be held in perspective regarding his disdain for the drinking and carousing he is describing. At the same time we must appreciate that he either had an incredible memory or pieced the book together from letters written home at the time or notes in a journal. In any event, he manages to paint for us the most descriptive word picture of the wharf and the theater, its environs, patrons, and performers that has yet to be uncovered.

But, who is this "Rowena Granice" he is describing? An "old and faded," "flamboyant fright," painted up "grandmother"? That is most certainly not the Rowena we saw in the portrait in 1858 in *The Family Gem* nor the lady who was described in 1881, at fifty-seven years of age, as "a tall, brown-haired woman, with sweet, gently molded face."[42]

In the book "Golden Footlights," a biography of Lotta Crabtree, author Phyllis Wynn Jackson says of Rowena, "[t]he only redeeming feature of the Gaieties was its actress-manager, Rowena Granice. She was a handsome but somewhat battered woman of uncertain age, who habitually wore make-up and had dyed her hair an unlovely shade of red. Yet she was warm-hearted and intelligent, with a distinguished air of having seen better days." Describing a visit with Lotta and her mother some three years later, the author states by that time, "Rowena was wearing a silk dress, and her hair dye was much more successful."[43]

It will forever remain an enigma for me, and every admirer of Rowena's who has preceded me, how it was that she, who seemingly in her youth and definitely in her older years firmly and enthusiastically embraced the principles of the Temperance movement, who was renowned thirty years later for her personal comeliness, and who was phenomenal in her abilities to manage a home, children, publishing and writing career, lecture and stage profession all at the same time, would stoop to this. Jackson's use of the word "battered" is telling. Was this perhaps a Rowena who had been temporarily beaten down, psychologically if not physically, by a drunken husband, not to mention the mass of evil gossips and snipes always waiting for an opportunity to destroy anyone they perceive as weak? Was the garish make-up necessary to hide bruises?

Possibly Kenderdine and Jackson were giving us a description of a nineteenth century woman who was in the throes of clinical depression. Though the term was unknown then, Rowena often wrote about its victims, and how they were able to wrench themselves from its suffocating grip, as if she herself had lived it and knew what it was like.

On the Honolulu Stage

We learn from newspaper articles that Rowena made her way to and stayed briefly in Honolulu, Hawaii, in January 1859.

> TO THE KANAKAS.—Miss Rowena Granice, or properly Mrs. Yankee Addams, has left San Francisco for a professional tour in the Sandwich Islands.[44]

> A NEW ACTRESS.—Miss Rowena Granice, from the Theaters of San Francisco came passenger in the *Yankee*, and will, we learn, make a stay of a few weeks here. Miss Granice's particular line, as we are informed, is low comedy, in which she is said to be perfectly irresistible. A new company has been formed at the Royal, for the purpose of bringing forward light pieces, playing in connection with the Minstrels, the whole under the management of Mr. Lew Rattler. They will undoubtedly meet with success. The performances last evening were extremely mirth-provoking. They play again this evening. We are indebted to the fair actress for a neatly printed pamphlet, entitled the "Family Gem,"

containing a number of interesting tales. From a cursory perusal of several of them, we judge her to be also an authoress of sparkling talents.[45]

THEATER.—Miss Rowena Granice, who is a "host within herself," since she assumed the management of the theater, it appears has met with but indifferent success. True, the season is very much against her; but then it is really astonishing that when such pieces as the "Dumb Girl of Oran," "Old Folks at Home," and other very interesting novelties are put forth for the amusement of the theater-going public of Honolulu—her exertions to please are untiring. She not only plays her own parts remarkably well, but frequently acts as prompter to those who, through negligence or other causes require her watchfulness and aid. As May Westfield in "Old Folks at Home," on last Saturday night, Miss G. really took the audience by storm, and plaudit followed plaudit until the fair actress must have felt some compensation in the enthusiasm manifested by those present, for the paltry meagerness of the house…. We learn that Miss G. proposes giving another entertainment on Saturday night next, if she can procure the theater on terms sufficiently fair to justify the probable receipt of expenses.[46]

Royal Hawaiian Theatre.

On Wednesday evening Miss Granice took a benefit before a numerous audience. The comedy of "The Rough Diamond" was the first piece produced, in which Miss Granice took the character of *Margery*, which she sustained throughout with great credit, and elicited frequent and rapturous applause…. The

"Maniac Scene" by Miss Granice evidently showed
that she is as familiar with tragedy as she is with low
comedy. In the "Combat Scene" of "Macbeth," Miss
Granice surprised all who were present, and the
common remark was, "That can't be the Yankee gal!"
That Miss Granice possesses great histrionic talent
no one will doubt after witnessing her three nights'
performances, and we trust during his stay here, she
will meet with that support which she justly merits.

                                        ***

Since writing the above we are informed that it is
the intention of Miss Granice to remain on the island
for some time, to take the Theatre, and to form a
company to amuse the Honolulu folks during the
dull season. "The Exile," a piece written by Miss
Granice, will shortly be produced; and we find in a
California paper the following remarks relative to the
same: "'The Exile' possesses merit, and the
authoress, Miss Granice, should be made to feel that
the public appreciate her talent."[47]

THEATER.—We believe the theater is to be closed
for a time. Miss Granice, the energetic manageress
and versatile actress, finds it don't pay to play to
empty houses. The season is very much against her,
besides we have been surfeited with theatricals for a
long time past. When the spring fleet arrives the
manageress may hope for better success. We are
sorry to learn, too, that she is suffering from ill-
health.[48]

According to *The Polynesian* of February 19, 1859, Rowena
returned to San Francisco on February 17 aboard the "Frances
Palmer." On March 26, 1859, it was reported that she was in the

process of organizing a new company and would soon begin touring the mountain towns.

> Miss Granice has obtained considerable celebrity as a writer as well as a theatrical artist, and the Honolulu papers, whence she has just returned, are loud in her praise. If she secures the services of a good company, she will probably meet with success; but with a namby-pamby class, such as too often are brought to the mountains, it will hardly pay. It is a great mistake that managers are too apt to fall into, that the citizens of our mining towns cannot appreciate good playing and that anything—no matter now poor, will do for them. Give us good playing, and they will be supported handsomely. We shall be pleased to see Miss Granice with a good company.[49]

Whatever the trouble that had precipitated her travel to Hawaii, it seems Rowena was back in control of her life and the Gaieties by mid-1859, as noted in McCabe's journal for August 9, 1859: "In operation at this date on Long Wharf under direction of Miss Rowena Granice, Gaieties."[50] She was also coming to final terms with Thomas:

> A "scene" occurred at the Gaieties Theatre today. Miss Rowena Granice, the sole lessee and proprietor, was in peaceable possession. Mr. Thomas Claughley last night closed and nailed it up. Miss Rowena Granice this morning opened it. Mr. Claughley closed it a second time and Miss Rowena Granice opened it a second time, and kept it open, and declares that she will keep it open. During the above play of "dead open and shut," Mr. Claughley and Miss Granice were arrested, at each other's complaint, for

malicious mischief; and the chorus was performed by the crowd, who shouted, "Hurrah for crinoline!" Miss Granice seems to be persecuted by Claughley; but if she be left alone, she will soon get the better of him.[51]

NOW AT THE GAIETIES.—Miss Rowena Granice, wife of Thomas Claughly [*sic*], and that personage, have been indulging in a bit of a row. It appears that Claughly bought the "Gaieties" for $900, and promised to give Miss Granice a bill of sale for the place as soon as she should have paid for it. She claims to have done so, and that he has not given her the bill of sale, while Claughly claims that the place is his. Yesterday, Claughly locked it up, and Miss Granice knocked it open with a hatchet. He had her arrested, and while she was at the police station giving bail, he locked it up again. She went back, found it locked, and again burst it open with a hatchet, and declares she will keep it open.[52]

ROWENA GRANICE has published a communication in a San Francisco paper stating that she was locked out of the Gaieties Theatre by Mr. Claughley. She says:

> "I fought bravely for what I considered my rights for two days, but found the parties had the advantage of me in numbers—six vulgar men against one woman was more than I could stand—and having no money to fee a lawyer, I concluded to give them possession. So good bye to the Gaieties! I have a fair prospect of doing better, if those

who profess to be my friends will
stand by me."[53]

Rowena eventually regained control of the theater,
renamed it as "The Varieties" and began advertising in earnest,
but that was not enough to keep it going. By that time the entire
Wharf was "fast becoming a street of second-hand clothing shops
and vacant stores."[54] On the 23rd or 24th of December 1859, Little
Lotta gave a final benefit performance of Topsy in "Uncle Tom's
Cabin,"[55] and the short-lived theatrical life of the
Gaieties/Varieties Theater was over.

Meanwhile, on the morning of September 13, 1859, near
Lake Merced in what is now Daly City, just as the sun was
coming up over the far eastern hills, another event unfolded that
was to impact California and Rowena in particular for the rest of
her life: Senator David C. Broderick and Ex-Supreme Court
Justice David S. Terry met on the "field of honor" for what was to
be the last reported pistol duel in California. Broderick was the
loser; he died at 9:20 in the morning three days later.

Precipitating the duel, Terry had resigned his position on
the bench the day after the September election and sent the
challenge to Broderick. Broderick was advised by his friends and
associates not to accept the challenge, as Terry was known to be a
better shot, but Terry urged it on knowing that "the chances were
many to one that his coolness and marksmanship would rid
politics of a hated leader,"[56] and Broderick was unable to
gracefully back out of the archaic "code duello." In the process,
Terry (a Southern "States' Rights" Democrat) unwittingly made
Broderick (a Douglas Democrat who had broken with the party on
the slavery question) a martyr for the antislavery cause. His dying
words were reportedly: "They have killed me because I was
opposed to slavery and a corrupt administration."[57]

While thousands of people filed past the coffin at the
Union Hotel, and an estimated thirty thousand turned out to hear

the effusive funeral eulogies, Terry was arrested and brought to Marin County for trial, but the case was dismissed because the witnesses' boat was delayed and they were unable to appear and testify at the time set. Terry immediately fled to Texas where he joined the Confederate army three years later. After the war, he went to Mexico briefly and eventually returned to California where he settled into a law practice in Stockton. He was able to put off his own violent end for another twenty years. In the meantime, he would become pivotal in Rowena's life as lead defense counsel in young Harry's murder trials.

Rowena left the stage and turned to writing in earnest. She placed the boys with George Bookmaster, age 34, a master mariner born in New York, and his wife,[58] ensconced herself in her house on the east side of Dupont Street near Green in San Francisco and proceeded to write *Victims of Fate,* which she later told reporters was a fictionalized account of Broderick's life.

> "VICTIMS OF FATE."—A neatly printed novelette bearing this title has been placed on our table by Rowena Granice, the authoress, and whilom actress, etc. It is founded on local incidents and the principal personage is declared to have had a counterpart in a distinguished politician of California, now deceased.[59]

> "THE VICTIMS OF FATE." –This is the title of a novelette of forty pages, written by Rowena Granice, author of the Family Gem, and other stories, printed in San Francisco. It is said to have special reference to the late Hon. D.C. Broderick, and indeed he appears to be the hero of the tale, for the author's preface contains the following:
> "Some of the incidents of this little story (although mingled with fiction) are real facts. I had the honor of being acquainted with the hero, from my earliest

childhood. First as a lad of little promise, although to
use a quaint expression, King-Bee among his boy
companions. After, as a young, enterprising aspirant
for political fame. Last, as the finished gentleman and
a nation's pride."[60]

Purportedly, over six thousand copies were printed and sold; none
has been found to this date.

By the following Summer 1860, Rowena was a widow and
Claughley would bother her no more. His dissipated body gave up
its earthly existence on June 22, 1860, Galloway says from
"consumption."[61] He was buried at Lone Mountain Cemetery, in
Grave 4, Tier 72 on the Ridge. This cemetery was severely
damaged during the 1906 earthquake. Sometime after 1937, all of
the bodies were removed to Colma, south of San Francisco, to
make way for expansion, and the headstones were used to build up
the breakers in the bay.

Chapter V

"I know I am in education and position your inferior, but in honesty and principle I own no superior. You are alone, without a protector. I love you deeply, devotedly; I could be your slave, and what I lack in worldly wealth, I will make up in truth and affection. … I will do all that a man can do to endeavor to make you happy. My heart and head, and hands, shall each and all be devoted to your peace and happiness."[1]

Robert Johnson 'R.J.' Steele

On Thursday, June 13, 1861, before Justice of the Peace Berry in Salmon Falls, El Dorado County, California, thirty-six-year-old widow Rowena Granice Claughley, with sons Harry and George Granice, eleven and eight, standing by her side, was married to Robert Johnson Steele, thirty-eight.[2] At the time, R.J. was owner and editor of the *Democratic Signal* in Auburn, Placer County, where the family settled after the wedding.

How they met is not known, but it was most likely in one of the mountain mining towns when Rowena was performing in traveling troupes or, more likely, selling her books, since she always made a point of visiting the newspaper office first thing in every town where she traveled. There is a clue contained in an surprising September 1860 article:

> ROWENA GRANICE.—Miss Rowena Granice appears in the *Placer Courier* in a communication of a column and a half in length in defense of the rightfulness and expediency of slavery.[3]

At the time, R.J. was owner-editor of the *Placer Courier*, and he being a firm Democrat and Southern sympathizer, it can be reasonably surmised that he hired Rowena to write the article for him. Rowena never wrote about slavery again or expressed her views in that regard, although it is claimed by others that she conducted public readings and skits in support of the Confederacy during the War. Another article in the *Sacramento Bee* announced that "'The Beautiful Kanaka Girl; Or, The Withered Garland,' a novelette, written by Rowena Granice, will shortly be commenced in the *Placer Courier*."[4]

To the best of our knowledge, R.J. had never married, like a great many of the early pioneers to California, probably due to the scarcity of marriageable women. One can imagine how dozens of men would have been smitten with Rowena as she gave dramatic readings in these mining towns or smiled sweetly and conversed pleasantly with them while they bought her books. She was always a commanding figure and had learned to carry herself as a lady of breeding, education and self-sufficiency. She was, by far and away, unique—as different from the prostitutes, fandango girls, and washwomen, who populated these mining towns in the early years, as from the plain and stern ranch wives. Out of all those prospective husbands, some of whom were quite wealthy, she chose R.J. Steele.

R.J. was born on October 22, 1822, in Rockingham, Richmond County, North Carolina, the firstborn of William Graves and Mary B. Steele (his mother being of the Wade family of Virginia). He was named after his grandfather, who, according to family lore, came to America as a British soldier during the Revolution, was wounded in battle and deserted by his fellow soldiers, befriended by some of the settlers and nursed back to health. But, those stories should be taken with a "grain of salt." We do know that the elder Robert Johnson Steele married twice, his two wives being Eliza Pickerel and, after her death, Martha

Graves, and that he settled near Little River in the area that later became Steele Township.

William and Mary Steele moved first to Hardeman County, Tennessee for a short time and then to Mississippi, to "the place where Ripley is now located was a forest."[5] Over the years they were the parents of nine children: R.J., Daniel Webster Steele (about 1825), Martha Ann Steele (1826), John Calhoun Steele (about 1830), Andrew Jackson Steele (1833), Napoleon Bonaparte Steele (1836), Mary Victoria Steele (1838), Henry Clay Steele (1842), and the ninth child unknown who probably died young.

The fates of brothers Daniel and John are not known; R.J. never mentioned them in the *Argus*. Andrew Jackson Steele married a girl from Massachusetts by the name of Maggie Ann. Maggie died on January 16, 1869, along with an infant son, William, and Andrew died November 12, 1871, leaving two daughters, one of whom — Laura — came to live with R.J. and Rowena in Merced in the 1870s (this was a very sad case and could possibly have provided the story line for one of Rowena's tragedies).

R.J.'s sister Martha married Josiah Flint Lewis and moved to Monticello, Minnesota, where she was the mother of seven children and grandmother to many. She and R.J. remained close throughout their lives, and he was very happy to see her again when she came to California to visit in 1886. "The brother and sister had not seen each other for thirty-four years. The meeting was a joyful one though a little shower of tears mingled with the kisses."[6] It was their last meeting; Martha Lewis died in June 1888.

Mary Victoria married, first, E.E. Alexander, who died, and then a newspaperman, Benjamin Fielding C. Brooks, and with him had five children, at least two of whom died young. They settled in Nashville, Tennessee, where he published *The National Flag* and she edited the literary department. Rowena and her sister-in-law traded compliments on occasion — "Mrs. Brooks is a lady of culture and possesses considerable literary ability. She also has a large share of that which is so necessary to newspaper work, industry and a laudable ambition."[7] — and the *National Flag* printed a few of Rowena's short stories and articles. In the summer of 1888, a year and a half before he died, R.J. was able to visit the family of his recently deceased sister Martha in Minnesota and his sister Mary Victoria in Tennessee, a trip made much more stressful owing to his health problems.

Brother Napoleon ('N.B.') Steele died on March 20, 1872 near Mound City, Arkansas; apparently he never married and no children were mentioned. R.J. talked about his "unspeakable sorrow" at losing his brother and adapted a poem by Fitz-Greene Halleck in his honor:

> Green be the turf above thee,
> Brother-friend of my better days;
> None knew thee but to love thee,
> Nor named thee but to praise.[8]

Perhaps the most poignant of all the sibling losses for Robert was the death of his brother Henry Clay Steele on September 10, 1876, at the home of their sister, Martha Lewis, in Minnesota. It was Rowena who wrote the obituary, pointing out that Henry was "born in Mississippi, but at the time the Civil War broke out he was residing in Minnesota. There he joined the ranks of the Union army, while two other brothers, now deceased, were battling for the Southern Confederacy." Although, as far as we know, R.J. did not join the fighting in the war, he was definitely a staunch Confederate.

R.J. left Jackson, Mississippi, in May 1846 immediately after war against Mexico was declared, with Company E, State Fencibles, under Captain Louis McManus. He was mustered into service at Vicksburg in the First Mississippi Rifles, commanded by then-Col. Jefferson Davis, West Point graduate and recently elected to the U.S. House of Representatives from Mississippi. The regiment sailed from New Orleans to Brazos, Santiago, and subsequently saw fierce fighting at the battles of Monterey in December 1846 and Buena Vista in February of the next year. According to one website, at Monterey the regiment had the most battle deaths of any volunteer regiment and the second most of any regiment that fought in the war, second only to the Eighth Infantry.[9]

When his term of service was over in May 1847, he returned home to Mississippi, then crossed the country twice in 1849 with wagon trains. Two companions on those trips were Col. Thomas A. Falconer, of Holly Springs, Mississippi, who later started up the *Columbia Gazette* with R.J.'s help, and James Bell, of Lounds County, Mississippi, who, like Steele, eventually settled in Merced.

Sometime in '49 R.J. joined the crowd of men picking and panning for gold northeast of Sacramento. One of his companions, "Deacon" Edwin Moore, later became County Recorder of Mariposa County. R.J. reminisced about their days together when they were reunited in 1868: "We recognize the gentleman as an old mining partner, with whom we rolled rocks and shoveled and washed auriferous sand many days in '49 and '50 on the American river, but whom we had not seen for eighteen years. He is a pleasant, genial companion, an unwavering friend and an honest man."[10] Another miner was George J. Hobson, a native of St. Joseph, Missouri, who died in San Jose in January 1890 (just two weeks before R.J.). In an obituary for Hobson, R.J. shared information about their mining days in the winter of 1849:

> [Hobson] again sallied forth with a small party intending to work during the winter in the rich mines of Oregon Canyon, near Georgetown, El Dorado County, at which place the writer met him and we formed a party of seven and built a log cabin in a little grove at the north end of the embryo town for winter quarters. Not finding diggings to suit, during a

dry spell of weather in December, five of our party
were persuaded by [Hobson] to move to Stony Bar,
on Rector's Creek (North Fork of the Middle Fork
of the American), where we spent the winter mining,
our lodgings being a low log cabin roofed with thin
canvas. The weather during the winter months being
excessively stormy, but little work other than
crevicing along the banks of the river could be done,
yet all the party enjoyed good health and added
largely to the store of precious metal in their
purses....[11]

According to family history, Steele was so successful at
mining that sometime after 1850 he went home to Tippah County,
Mississippi, where his mother and father were still living, with
"several thousand dollars" in his pocket, returning to California in
1853 where he began mining a claim on Pierson's Hill and later
Columbia Flat in Columbia, Tuolumne County.[12] He invested
some of his profits with his old friend Falconer in the *Columbia
Gazette* and soon became involved in the operation and editing of
the paper, which had under its title the slogan, "Where shall the
PRESS the PEOPLE'S RIGHTS maintain, unawed by influence, and
unbribed by GAIN."[13] On August 19, 1854, he began a partnership
with John C. Duchow to publish the *Gazette* and manage the
printing office. Within months the *Gazette* became the *Gazette
and Southern Mines Advertiser*, and the partnership changed to
Steele and Thomas N. Cazneau. By August 1856, Duchow
returned to ownership of the paper along with a Mr. Carder, with
Steele "proposing to engage in other pursuits more congenial to
his feelings."[14] Their differences must have been worked out,
since Galloway says R.J. remained in ownership of the *Gazette*
until 1857. One wonders if this back and forth flow of ownership
could also be indicative of wins and losses in high-stakes card
games, so common in those pioneer days of California.

He was still in Columbia as of Spring 1858 when he was arrested and sent to Tuolumne County jail from May 4 to June 15 for assault with a deadly weapon. This is the only incidence of violence connected to R.J. Steele personally, although Rowena did make a couple of veiled, somewhat teasing, allusions to his temper over the years.

The next newspaper venture was the *Placer Courier* at Yankee Jim's, Placer County, one of the most prosperous gold mining areas in California, founded in 1849 by a man named Robinson who was not so fortunate as his namesake town. He was hanged in San Diego in 1852 for stealing a rowboat. In April 1859 R.J. moved the *Courier* to nearby Forest Hill, where he was shown living on the 1860 census with printers J.C. Parks, 28, and George Haskett, 22, both born in New York. According to the census, R.J. possessed $500 in real estate and $900 in personal property.[15]

On December 29, 1860, R.J. sold the *Courier* to Philip Lynch and bought the *Democratic Signal* in Auburn. Just before he and Rowena married he had changed the name of the paper to the *States Rights Journal* as a show of support for the Confederate cause, but that paper very shortly ceased publication, and the *Union Advocate* took its place.[16]

We can't help but wonder what induced Rowena, a Yankee actress and writer with Republican tendencies, to marry Robert when she probably could have had her pick of all the eligible men in California — and there were thousands. For one thing, his intellect probably more closely matched her own. He had started publishing and editing newspapers in California at about the same time Rowena had begun acting and writing. He was not rich, but he offered a comfortable living and, most importantly, protection and security for her and her sons. He was a tall, handsome, distinguished-looking man, a classic antebellum Southern gentleman who was probably extraordinarily polite and chivalrous, and she no doubt recognized that he would cherish and respect her above everything and everyone. Indeed, in the years to come, he would prove to be loyal, steadfast, and honest (sometimes too honest, i.e., "dead right"). And here, finally, was a man who would fully appreciate her intellectual capabilities, for, best of all, he provided a ready-made outlet for that talent for the rest of her life — writing and publishing. She was able to overlook, indeed, enthusiastically embrace for a while, his zealous political penchant.

They began their marital and business partnership immediately by publishing *Leonnie St. James; Or, The Suicide's Curse* at the printing office in Auburn in 1862. Rowena and the boys went door to door throughout the area's mining towns selling the little books, and she later told her grandchildren that they also prepared and sold lunches to the miners on occasion.[17] They also apparently teamed up together to give performances.

> Entertainment at the Empire.—Mrs. Rowena Granice Steele, assisted by her sons Masters Harry and George, give a chaste and promiscuous performance at the Empire Hotel this evening. The programme is a good one, and should draw a good audience.[18]

In the introduction to *Leonnie*, Rowena makes her first published argument that it is quite feasible for a married woman to have an occupation or avocation in addition to her marital responsibilities:

> I have frequently heard the remarks that "an authoress," or "blue-stocking," as they sometimes call us, "should be shunned as a wife; that they are, as a general thing, slovenly and idle in their habits." But this is a mistaken notion; I have had the pleasure of meeting Miss Grace Greenwood, Miss Jane Porter,

> Fanny Fern and a number of other authoresses of
> greater or less celebrity, and I found them plain, neat,
> tidy, unpretending women, pleasing and lady-like in
> conversation, and entirely free from what is called
> "strong mindedness" in women. As for myself, every
> piece I have written (and they number about sixty)
> was composed while engaged in domestic affairs. I
> have often laid down the dish-towel to take up my
> pen for the purpose of noting down an idea; and at
> my leisure would gather up these disconnected ideas;
> and then, summoning my real characters around me,
> weave them together as we do the different colored
> flowers, when forming them into a bouquet.[19]

That was a theme she would revisit often in the years to come in
advocating the importance of education for women and even
going so far as to suggest that married women could handle jobs
outside the home.

Snelling – Act I – The Merced Banner

In June of 1862 the family moved to Snelling, the seat of
the new Merced County formed in 1855 out of Mariposa County.
The area took the name of the river flowing out of Yosemite given
in 1806 by Mexican soldiers who, when they finally came upon
water after walking through the dry, dusty plain from the west,
exclaimed, "El rio de los Mercedes!"

In 1862 most of the settlement was still along the river.
Many years later, Rowena recalled what the area looked like when
they first arrived:

> ... [T]he main part of Merced county was a wild,
> barren, desolate waste. The only sound then heard ...
> was the doleful howl of the hungry coyote, the
> dismal lowing of wild cattle, or the hooting of the

night owl, mingled with the dirge-like sound of the moaning turtledove. No grateful shade trees, no cool, clear water to refresh the weary traveler. During the stormy season the black mud, dangerous bogs, and quicksand prevented stockmen from hunting their herds, so the cattle and horses were let to roam over the man-forsaken plains with the deer and other wild animals. At certain times during the summer of each year hundreds of men and boys, mounted upon their caballo bronchos, followed by some enterprising individual with a hotel and barroom on wheels, would spend many days and nights on the plains hunting and branding stock. This *modus operandi* was called a rodeo.[20]

R.J. Steele was to remain friends with these stockmen as long as he supported the open range, but as soon as the farmers started moving in and planting vast areas in grain and other crops he gradually switched his support to the fencing in of stock, thus incurring the life-long enmity of sheep and cattle ranchers. One of them, N.B. Stoneroad, along with his brothers, George W. and Thomas, and his brother-in-law, William Dickensen, took their 10,000 sheep to New Mexico in 1876.[21]

In an article entitled "History of Snelling" in the *Argus* in June 1870, the history of the establishment of the little town of Snelling for the twenty previous years was described:

Snelling, the county seat of Merced county, is situated on the north bank of the Merced river and within about six miles of the head of Merced valley proper. The land lying between the bluffs enclosing the valley (as it were with two walls) is in a high state of cultivation, interspersed here and there with beautiful gardens, orchards, vineyards and handsome dwellings, rendering it almost a paradise, and presenting to the view of the weary traveler as he approaches from the highlands from either the north or south, a scene unparalleled for beauty throughout the entire country bordering on the Pacific Coast. The valley being a part of, and the largest tributary to the San Joaquin Valley, is of more than average fertility, producing a greater variety of products than any other portion of the great valley of which it forms an integral part.

The site of the town was first settled upon and the land taken up by Dr. David Wallace Lewis, John M. Montgomery, and Samuel Scott who, seeing the eligibility of the place for a hotel, built a large house and opened a house of entertainment early in the spring of 1851, which was kept by Dr. Lewis, who first opened business in a brush tent, which answered the purpose until the large wooden structure, afterwards known as Snelling's Hotel, was completed.

The Snelling family, from whom the town derives its name, arrived at the place early in the Fall of 1851, purchased the property and continued its possessor for a number of years thereafter.

In the month of May, 1855, the county of Merced was organized, and the county seat was established at George Turner's ranch, on Mariposa Creek. The first court held in the county was the County Court and Court of Sessions, and was held in the open air under a large open tree. Dr. J.W. Fitzhugh, County Judge, presided, and the officers of the Court were J.W. Smith, District Attorney, E.G. Rector, Clerk, Chas. F. Bludworth, Sheriff, and George Turner, Deputy Sheriff.

In 1856 the town of Snelling was laid off and permanently established as the county seat, and in the following two years the court-house and jail and a number of business houses and dwellings were erected, and it became a flourishing and growing town.

In the winter of 1861-62 the old Snelling hotel, Judge Fitzhugh's residence and orchard, and some other buildings were destroyed by the memorable flood of that time which, together with the instability of the titles to lots and the land surrounding the town, checked the growth of the place for several months. But in July Mr. Prince completed and opened a hotel, and the MERCED BANNER, the pioneer newspaper of the county was issued from the press with R.J. Steele and wife as editors. These enterprises gave quite an impetus to improvement, and several new buildings were erected, and several new business houses were established.

On the 12th of September, 1862, almost the entire business portion of the town was destroyed by fire, making the second great calamity for that year. The citizens commenced to rebuild immediately, and in a short time the town presented an appearance indicative of thrift—Prince's Hotel was rebuilt, the Galt House was removed from LaGrange and erected by A.B. Anderson, and considerable accessions were made to the population.[22]

By the time the Granice-Steele family arrived at Snelling in 1862, North and South were firmly clenched in the bloody conflagration — the Civil War — over a thousand miles to the east. Perhaps R.J. chose Snelling, at that time a rather remote, sparsely populated town on the Merced River, because the majority of the citizens were Southerners, among them fellow Mississippians James Wood Robertson and John W. Bost; Arkansans Stoneroad;

Kentuckians James Bush Sensabaugh, Eleazer T. Givens, Samuel
Scott (builder of the fabulous mansion in Snelling), John M.
Montgomery, and Archibald Stevinson; Alabamans William A.
McCreary (Lee Steele's future father-in-law) and W.L. Means;
and Missourian William C. Turner. Most shared Steele's
Democratic principles, so much so that Merced was called "the
South Carolina of California." One lone loyal voice was New
Yorker Harvey J. Ostrander, who proudly hoisted the Union colors
on a pole in front of his home and let it be known that he was
prepared to stand guard with arms if necessary.[23]

As an example of the sometimes dizzying ebb and flow of
personal and political alliances over the years, it is ironic to note
that Robertson, fellow Democrat Peter Dinwiddie "P.D."
Wigginton, and the Stoneroads would become the most prominent
among the Steeles' avowed enemies within ten years, precipitating
with their vitriol and backstabbing the horrible events of 1874;
and Ostrander and fellow Northerner Dr. Joshua Griffith were to
become two of the Steele family's staunchest supporters in their
darkest hours in 1875 and '76 when Harry was on trial for murder
and George died suddenly.

Recalling Snelling ten years later, Rowena wrote wistfully
of the "good old days" at the beginning of their residence there:

> [In 1862] Snelling was an unpretending little burg,
> containing within its limits a neat, substantial court
> house and jail combined, enclosed within a plain,
> board fence; two stores—small, wooden structures—
> where the customer could purchase on credit or for
> cash everything required for family use; one hotel,
> two saloons, one livery stable, one blacksmith shop,
> one or two wheelwright establishments, and one
> printing office. At that period the men, women and
> children dressed plainly. On Sunday when there was
> preaching at the court house, more than half the

ladies appeared in sun-bonnets, shakers, or just a
green veil thrown over their plainly arranged hair.
The children who attended the little schoolhouse
were all clean, but exceedingly plain in their attire.
The balls and parties were then pleasant, social
reunions; the most aristocratic venturing on nothing
more costly than delaines, lawns or tarlatans, the
latter material sometimes so sweetly and simply
trimmed as to cause the youthful wearers to look like
young angels. Several bright, joyous, young faces
come up before me as I write. People slept with their
doors unfastened or left them merely latched when
going off on a visit. There was no diamonds, gold or
silver ware. No point lace or costly furs to tempt or
reward the burglar.[24]

To the present day, the courthouse is still there, almost one
hundred and fifty years later, although the county court moved to
Merced in 1873. R.J. and Rowena and the boys probably attended
Southern Methodist or Presbyterian services there, although it is
difficult to tell what their religious affiliation was; throughout the
years, they would include many items in the columns of the
Weekly Merced Herald and its later incarnation, the *Argus,* from
and about all the churches in Merced County, even the sizable
Jewish population. When she died in 1901, Rowena was buried
from the First Presbyterian Church in Merced. We also know they
attended a Presbyterian Thanksgiving service in Stockton on
November 26, 1868, because on December 5, R.J. printed a full-
length, two-column-width denouncement of the pastor, Rev.
James A. Daly, with the headline: "A Ministerial Falsifier—Quack
Doctor of Divinity—Mistaking the Pulpit for the Rostrum on
Thanksgiving Day," apparently because the good reverend chose
the occasion to lambaste slavery and preach on the importance of
educating the freed slaves to assume suffrage.

Calling the new paper the *Merced Banner*, it was R.J.'s intention to set up a Southern Democrat organ in an area where he thought, mistakenly as it turned out, he would be free to express his political opinions. Rowena took over the role of "editress" of the literary and society departments. She recalled many years later how the printing press, purchased from the *Stanislaus Index* at Knight's Ferry in Stanislaus County, was brought south and across the river by oxen team:

> Mr. Peter Fee, Sr., a highly respectable Norwegian gentleman, who lived two miles from the town of Snelling, stepped forward and offered to bring it over with his ox-team. His offer was gladly accepted, and on the twenty-fifth of June 1862, a large number of people gathered in the little town and with nervous expectation watched the coming of the bovine procession. They were not kept long in suspense, for before the sun sank on that bright June day, the horns of the oxen were seen, then the whole team and wagon, with its precious freight and brave driver, came winding down the bluff, and as the procession neared the town shouts loud and strong went up, and their sound mingled with the dust, and the cheering was kept up until the tired oxen stopped in front of the office. Strong men volunteered to lift and carry, and in a short time everything belonging to a country printing office was safely landed inside the door. Then of course they all adjourned to the hotel to celebrate.
>
> The next day Mr. Steele, with his little stepsons, Harry and George Granice, aged respectively nine and twelve years, set to work in good earnest to get out the first issue. Mr. Steele had promised the people that they should have the *Banner* the morning

after the glorious Fourth. So with his little typesetter and roller-boy he divided his time between the type and his pen, while Mrs. Steele plied the pen and scissors in the interest of her department. And true to promise, the paper went forth on the fifth of July, 1862. Copies of the paper were sent gratuitously to one or more post offices in all the Western and Southern states.[25]

There is but one issue of the first two years' printings of the *Banner* extant (November 21, 1863), and items from it have been reprinted in the *History of Merced County*. Rowena must have kept some, since she reprinted one of the articles from the first issue in a recollection in 1879:

[T]he first newspaper ... office was at Snelling, in what is now known as the old Bludworth house. The title of the paper was *"The Merced Banner,"* Editor and Proprietor, ROBERT J. STEELE; Associate Editor, ROWENA GRANICE STEELE. On the 4th of July, 1862, which was Friday, there was a large ball given in the town of Snelling at Prince's Hotel. The hotel stood upon the ground where now stands Mayers' Hall. The supper was set in a temporary house, covered with green bushes. For the benefit of the matrons, who were then young ladies, of Merced county, we publish the report of the ball, which we wrote on the following morning, between five and six o'clock after dancing all night!

BALL AT SNELLING.

We had the pleasure of attending a ball at the new hotel in this place on the evening of the 4th inst., given by the *Prince* of landlords, a noble-hearted man, and one who "knows how to keep a hotel."

We are informed that about one hundred tickets were sold, and that it was by far the largest ball ever given in Merced county. At an early hour in the day carriages containing ladies and their escorts were seen flying in all directions, and soon the streets were full of men, and the Hotel and private houses were crowded with hoops and dimity.

During the afternoon we took a peep into the kitchen and counted no less than six good-sized pigs, ten turkeys and forty chickens, besides "lots of chicken fixin's". The whole of the culinary department was under the management of Mrs. Prince, the estimable landlady who is unquestionably without a rival in the management of such affairs.

At nine o'clock the band struck up a lively air summoning the worshipers at the shrine of Terpsichore to the brilliantly lighted saloon where they "tripped the light fantastic toe" until broad daylight, and many of them didn't go home in the morning.

Among the large number who attended we will make mention of the few to whom we had the pleasure of being introduced. Mrs. Judge Fitzhugh, the most dignified and brilliant lady of the company, dress—white tarlatan, six flounces, trimmed with broad black ribbon; head dress, black ostrich feathers, and jet jewelry. Mrs. Belle Davis, of La Grange, a tall, graceful blonde, with Grecian feathers, attracted much admiration; dress white tarlatan trimmed with groups of narrow ruffles ornamented with small bows of white satin ribbon; hair arranged in broad braids and looped up with white Japonicas; and as she moved with the stately bearing of a queen, through the dance, was pronounced the belle of the evening. Miss Malinda Brown looked pretty and fascinating; dress white tarlatan, several tucks trimmed with white satin ribbon. Miss Mary Fitzhugh looked and moved like a sylph. Her roguish eyes and silvery laugh made more than one of the opposite sex sigh and inwardly wish that he was the chosen one of her heart. Mrs. Croseu, a charming and vivacious brunette, drew a large crowd of admirers in her train; dress white tarlatan trimmed with cherry colored ribbon. Mrs. McPherson, of New Year's Diggings, an attractive lady, dressed in pink and white satin brocade, overdress of pink illusion. Mrs. Farrell of Coulterville, an amiable and graceful lady, dress, pure white, three flounces elegantly embroidered. Mrs. Peck, of Dickerson's Ferry, dress pink tarlatan double skirt looped up at the sides with wreaths of variegated flowers, looked graceful and danced with ease.

It would be impossible for us to mention all who were present, but among the most prominent of those not mentioned above were the Misses Ruddle, Magie, Mitchel, Hatty McDonald, Miss Anderson, Miss Woodcock, Miss Hathaway, Mrs. Peck, Miss Latour and Mrs. Howard. All seemed to enjoy themselves and were undoubtedly well pleased with the arrangements.[26]

Of those ladies, Laura Benson Fitzhugh, wife of County judge Dr. John William ('J.W.') Fitzhugh, was to become Rowena's "heart's best friend." Laura was born about 1826 in Boone County, Missouri, of a wealthy and influential family. Her mother died when she was young, and she was placed in a boarding school until the age of sixteen when she married Dr.

Fitzhugh, a widower almost eighteen years her senior with two
infant sons, Thomas and John W. Jr. (His first wife was his
cousin, Anna Thornton, granddaughter of President William
Henry Harrison.) The doctor and Laura lived for a time on a farm
in Henry County, Missouri, with their children, Henry ('Hale'),
Mary, and Cole, where he divided his attention between farming
and medicine, and served as representative to the State
Legislature. In 1849, he joined thousands of other men afflicted
with "gold fever" and came to California for the first time. In 1852
he returned home, gathered up his wife and children from their
home of comfort and luxury and brought them to what then was
the wilderness of Merced County, bringing along several slaves
and other servants.

The family settled first on Mariposa Creek about three
miles above Plainsburg, then in Snelling, where the youngest
children, Rose and Gordon were born, and another little son,
Frank Knox Fitzhugh, who died in October 1864 at seven months.
Dr. Fitzhugh continued to work his mining investments in
California and Nevada at the same time practicing medicine, both
in Merced County and in the mining country, and serving for a
time as Merced County's first judge.[27] Unfortunately, he lost his
wife's considerable wealth in a bad speculation, but never gave up
hope over the years that he would be able to recoup the loss. And
she, apparently, was ever loyal even in the face of financial ruin.
Rowena tells of a time when she was visiting Mrs. Fitzhugh, and a
letter was handed to her by Cole.

"Oh! It's from the Doctor." We watched the
glowing tender expression of her countenance until
we saw the silent tears glistening in her eyes.

She then looked up and, smiling through the crystal
drops, said, "Just listen!" And again the tear-dimmed
orbs sought the page, and she read aloud: "My dear, I
feel that a fortune is within my grasp. Be patient a

few short months and your brightest hopes and
aspirations will, I trust, be gratified. I have given my
claim a name which I for years have loved above all
other names. I call it the 'Laura'."

In February 1877, when Dr. Fitzhugh died suddenly from
pneumonia while treating the miners in the mountains of Mono
County, Rowena wrote:

The grief-stricken family had lost a devoted husband,
a tender and affectionate father. He had been a truth-
worthy public officer, a warm, true and unselfish
friend; a polite, courteous, gentle-mannered,
hospitable gentleman; a strictly moral man; a
consistent Christian, a Master Mason, an Odd Fellow
in good standing, the angel of the sickroom, and a
physician of great merit. He studied more than mere
books, and used at times in his profession that which
was more potent than drugs. He studied human
nature, and ministered to minds diseased as well as
bodies.[28]

Rowena admired Mrs. Fitzhugh greatly and enjoyed being
in her company. She was a "delicate lady, who had never known
aught but a life of ease and refinement," but came willingly to the
frontier with her husband, "and, after arriving, although almost
constantly surrounded by the coarse, rough, and vulgar, she not
only retained all the refinement that nature and education had
given her, but by her elegance and gracefulness of manner she
assisted in cultivation those with whom she associated." No doubt
it was Laura who helped Rowena define her initial bias toward the
South as regards slavery and "States' Rights." One can almost
hear her repeating the rhetoric so often heard in those days in
defense of the pernicious practice: "Why, we have always been

kind to our slaves. They are ignorant heathens, and it is our duty to protect them." Eventually, Rowena's racist attitudes changed drastically as she came in contact with freed slaves and freeborn African-Americans.

Rowena was heart stricken when "delicate, fragile blossom" Laura Fitzhugh passed away on June 5, 1877, just a few months after her husband. She wrote lengthy, loving obituaries and tributes for each, and for years she valued their last gifts — from Laura a bouquet of orange blossoms, which, though dry and faded, were still fragrant, and from Dr. Fitzhugh a gold-flecked rock specimen. "Oh! How the heart swells, and aches, and throbs when the truth flashes o'er us that we shall never meet this well-beloved and dearly-cherished friend on earth again."[29]

Birth of Lee Richmond Steele; Confederate Sympathies in Merced County

In addition to her household duties and journalism responsibilities, Rowena endeavored to keep alive her stage presence, as well, as is evidenced by an ad in the paper just one month after they arrived in 1862:

> On Saturday evening, August 3, Mrs. Steele proposes to give one of her chaste and versatile Dramatic Entertainments at Prince's Hotel, Snelling, assisted by Masters Harry and George Granice, consisting of Readings, Recitations, Songs, Funny Scenes and Dances. Admission one dollar. For program, see handbills.[30]

No copies of the handbill survived, so we do not know what items she read and sang; however, it is doubtful her Yankee "Jemima Sunflower" routines of old would have gone over very well in this Southern Democrat-leaning society.

On May 18, 1863, Lee Richmond Steele was born in Snelling. His name gives further indication of the Steeles' Southern allegiance. In fact, according to an item in the *Golden Era* of May 24, 1863, Lee's full name was actually "Jefferson Davis Lee Stonewall Jackson Steele" and, should there be any further question about the political stance of his parents, the *Era* facetiously suggested that "Southern Confederacy" should be added to the baby's name.[31] The same issue of the paper carried a poem sent in by a Copperhead, wherein the first letters of each line formed the vertical words "Hurrah for the South." But the paper caught the sneak and changed the letters so that it read "North" instead. "Bad luck this time, Johnny Rebel. Try again," the paper sneered.

There is another story that when news was received at Snelling of one of the Union defeats at Bull Run in Manassas Junction, Virginia, with many thousand federal soldiers killed (July 1861 and August 1862), there was firing of cannons and general rejoicing. It is also said that Wigginton was going about the country giving campaign speeches for secession candidates, accompanied by Jim Wilson, who sang songs with violin accompaniment, among them "We'll Hang Abe Lincoln from a [Sour Apple] Tree" and "We'll Drive the Bloody Tyrant [Lincoln] From Our Dear Native Soil."[32]

During Harry's troubles in the 1870s, one newspaper sniped at Rowena that it was not surprising her son would turn to violence ...

> ... owing to the false course of tutelage imposed upon young Granice by a too chivalrous mother who, perhaps fails, even now, to recognize in this calamity the error of her earlier teaching. When the southern rebellion had been fully inaugurated, and was looking everywhere for assistance we hear that the mother of young Granice was traveling through

this part of the State on a lecturing tour, to fire the
Southern heart and involve the early settlers in
antagonism to the Federal Government. It is within
the remembrance of many, no doubt, that the same
boy, then a youth of about ten years, was placed
upon the platform on his knees and sworn, in the
most theatrical style, to vindicate the secession
principles of the mother, even to the taking of
human life.[33]

Is this the June 1862 appearance in Auburn or another? If this
report was true, it was probably George, not Harry, who
accompanied Rowena. Harry would have been a teenager at the
time and would no doubt have stayed back in Snelling working for
his stepfather at the *Banner*. At the age of fifteen, according to
Rowena, he was employed at the Mariposa *Free Press*, which was
published by James Lawrence. "While working there the foreman
was taken ill," she wrote, "and Master Harry succeeded in getting
out the paper for two weeks without the least assistance from older
or wiser heads."[34]

According to Galloway, the sole copy of the *Banner* that
he was able to find was almost entirely devoted to editorials and
news items that gave encouragement and sympathy to the South in
the Civil War. In the first three columns of the front page was
printed a letter from W.C. Rives, a Southerner. It was headlined
by R.J. Steele: "NO CAUSE FOR DESPONDENCY. The weak nerved,
faint-hearted friends of the South, in her struggle for liberty and
independence, will receive an encouragement from the letter...."
Galloway continues, "The remainder of the page, most of page
two and two columns of page three present articles, news stories
and editorials opposing the war, conscription, and infringements
on states' rights."

Other material in the issue includes a long editorial in
opposition to a proposed law requiring cattlemen to fence their

land. "The editor states that the farmers should plant hedges around their land to keep out the cattle!"[35] Steele later changed position and advocated that the voters of each county should regulate the fence issue and called upon the people of Merced to follow the example of Paradise Valley where "the pursuit of the people has been changed from exclusively pastoral to agricultural without detriment to the interests of any...."[36]

That the *Banner* was Democrat is undisputed; in fact, Rowena states that at one point, "it was not Democratic enough" to suit some of the residents of Merced County, perhaps owing in part to her Northern birth. Her name was withdrawn from the masthead of the paper, but she continued to write domestic stories and articles about local happenings.[37] And, while the *Banner* claimed several times to be loyal, as demonstrated in a resolution printed in 1862, the editor was continuously critical of the military.[38] On the other hand, Galloway found, although there was a tremendous Confederacy sentiment in Merced County and many of those pro-Southern citizens were personally embittered, a military report in 1862 concluded no one had declined to pay his taxes, and there was no indication of an armed organization among them.[39] But that was not enough to forestall disaster for the little *Banner* office.

One issue of the *Banner* during the war claimed "the United States officers will go to any length to sustain their master, Abe Lincoln, whose cringing slaves they are."[40] It was inflammatory items like this that undoubtedly proved to be the "final straw" for members of the 2d Cavalry, California Volunteers, under the command of Captain Starr, in February 1864. The troop had started out from Benecia on their way to Visalia, but the soldiers had become so unruly that Starr requested they be exchanged for a company of Infantry. He turned them back to Benecia; they had reached Hill's Ferry, when they proposed to cross over to Snelling and "bust up the *Banner* office." According to the troopers, "articles reflecting upon them as soldiers had appeared in the

Banner, and they would have their revenge." Captain Starr tried to order them away, but they refused, and being alone and defenseless opposite twenty-eight armed men, he could not detain them.

Rowena described what happened next for the 1881 *History of Merced County*:

> [A]t about eight o'clock, while Mr. Steele was engaged in printing cards, the office door was thrown open and he found himself surrounded by a band of men dressed in blue and armed to the teeth. Four of them leveled their guns and requested him to step out into the street. "What is your business, gentlemen?" he said. "We have come to destroy this press and type," was the reply. Mr. Steele walked out, and then commenced the destruction. Mrs. Steele, who was busy preparing breakfast in a back room, hearing the terrible noise, caught up her infant son and ran to the office door, but was ordered back. The scene was one of terror and confusion for about ten minutes, then the work was done; the type was scattered, the press broken in pieces and the stove, which was full of fire, was upset, and the office was in a blaze. The brave fellows(?) twenty-eight in number, then rode off, calling out, "We are a band of brothers on our own hook."
>
> The fire was extinguished by Mrs. Steele and her little sons. Hundreds of men gathered in town as the news spread of the destruction, and by noon the Court House yard was filled with excited people. But like many other things the excitement died away, and no one was injured save Mr. Steele and his family. But even with this dark prospect Mr. Steele soon picked up the type and got the press mended and went on with the paper. So with the aid of half a dozen little boys who volunteered, the type was all

put into pans and Harry and George Granice commenced distributing. Mr. Steele, with the assistance of some friendly neighbors, got the press up on a wooden leg, and the week following a very small *Banner* came out of the chaos.[41]

One of the members of that unit was Frederick Hoffman, a native of Germany, who came to this country as a young man and joined the Cavalry in 1862. He died in Mariposa in 1917 at the age of eighty-seven.[42]

The Steeles managed to get out a few more, abbreviated issues when, "[a] few weeks later," Rowena writes, "a man by the name of Pierce came to Snelling, and by his bland manners and smooth tongue induced a wealthy gentleman, a resident of the county, to advance him the money to purchase the good-will and remnants of the office." According to Galloway, this man was actually Lovick Pierce Hall, a Copperhead newspaperman, who was using the aliases of William Hall or William Pierce at the time. He had been arrested in January 1863 for disloyal practices as co-editor and co-publisher of the *Visalia Equal Rights Expositor*. Hall published only a few issues of the renamed *Merced Democrat* during the month of July before being arrested again on July 24, 1864 for treasonable acts. He was apparently promptly released upon signing an oath of loyalty and posting a bond, but the newspaper was defunct.[43]

R.J. and Rowena, unable either to get back the newspaper or get up a new one, packed up the boys and left Merced sometime in the Fall of 1864. It would be almost four years before they returned to Merced County for good, and it marked the last time that any Granice or Steele did not stand and face the struggle head on.

Chapter VI

Four Years Wandering Around California and Nevada

From the fall of 1864, when they left Snelling, until summer of 1865 nothing is known of the whereabouts of R.J., Rowena and the boys. Galloway's research shows that R.J. claimed he was refused jobs in Aurora, Genoa and other towns in Nevada and California on account of his reputation for disloyalty, if not outright treason[1], and R.J. later said that he "became an itinerant type-picker and occasional editor in other portions of the state."[2]

Back in Snelling, in May of 1865, Democrat lawyers and Southern sympathizers P.D. Wigginton and J.W. Robertson revitalized the old printing press and inaugurated the *Weekly Merced Herald* to take the place of the defunct *Banner*. "Despite repeated failures to permanently establish a newspaper in Merced County," they wrote in the inaugural issue, "we have undertaken the publication of the *Weekly Merced Herald*. Measuring our prospect for success by that of those who have preceded us in this County, we have little to induce us to the undertaking. But we have ever believed that a newspaper properly conducted could be made to live in Snelling." In an obvious reference to the trashing of the Banner office in February 1864, the publishers stated, "[W]e hope to conduct the *Herald* in such a manner as to avoid the wrath of mobocracy or the interference of the military authorities, and escape a fate now so common to Democratic journals."

It is in the *Herald* in June of 1865 that we have the first indication of Rowena's activities in El Dorado Camp (now known as Mountain Ranch) in Calaveras County:

> Mrs. Rowena G. Steele is giving Readings and
> Entertainments in this county. She favored us with a
> call on her way to El Dorado Camp.—*San Andreas
> Register*
> Where is Sir Charles?—Ed.[3]

The editor's question regarding the whereabouts of "Sir Charles"
is, we assume, a reference to R.J. Steele. That question was
answered within a month:

> ROBERT STEELE, formerly editor of the *Merced
> Banner*, and Mrs. RO[W]ENA GRANICE, his wife and
> editress of the same paper, paid us a visit on
> Wednesday last. The little Steeles were along, and all
> were en route to Aurora, Esmeralda county, Nevada,
> where, Bob says, he has bought a printing office, and
> is going to take charge of a Black Republican
> newspaper. Anything for "grub" we suppose is his
> motto.[4]

The next time we hear about them is in September, when
the *Herald* makes this brief notation:

> MRS. ROWENA GRANICE STEELE.—The Alpine
> *Chronicle* says: Mrs. Rowena Granice Steele will give
> an entertainment, consisting of Shakespearean
> readings, singing, etc., at Bodie's Hotel, this evening.
> On tomorrow and Monday evenings she will give an
> entertainment at Silver Mountain.[5]

Silver Mountain is now a ghost town. It was originally called
"Köngsberg" or "Konigsberg" when it was founded in the late
1850s-early 1860s by Scandinavian miners prospecting for silver.
By 1863, the name was changed to Silver Mountain City; in 1866

the town had a population of 3,000. It was the county seat of Alpine County, located in Northern California near Lake Tahoe, from its creation in 1864 to 1875.

In October of 1865 Rowena visited Mariposa, which is very near Snelling, and the following, rather compassionate article, was reported in the *Gazette* there:

> We understand that Mrs. Rowena Granice Steele intends to visit Mariposa about the 22nd inst. for the purpose of giving one of those pleasing parlor entertainments for which she is so justly celebrated.... This lady has suffered many trials and misfortunes in the last few years, and with failing health and a young family entirely dependent upon her exertions we sincerely hope that her reception will be a sympathetic and substantial one.[6]

It could be that she was also visiting Harry at his work at the *Mariposa Free Press* at this time. Galloway was struck with the commiseration evident in the *Gazette* editor, who, he said, "did not often speak kindly of Democrats."[7] Some other items interesting to us that are imbedded in this little article are Rowena's "failing health" and the fact that she had "a young family entirely dependent upon her exertions." By this time, she had just entered her forties and was perhaps even suffering the symptoms of menopause, let alone diminished energy of middle age. And, most importantly, was the apparent absence of R.J. in their lives.

A year later, December 1866, finds Rowena and the boys, Harry included, still without R.J., living at Deadman's Bar in Tuolumne County, when a terrible tragedy struck the already beleaguered family:

INCENDIARY.—The *Amador Dispatch* learns that the house of Mrs. Rowena G. Steele, situated on Deadman's Bar, in Tuolumne County, was burned on the morning of the ninth inst. Mrs. Steele was sick in bed at the time, and only made her escape by the presence of mind and heroism of her oldest son, a lad of about seventeen summers, who carried his mother from the burning flames to a place of safety. The rest of the persons in the house, consisting of a hired man and three children, escaped as the timbers of the burning building [were] falling. It will be remembered that Mrs. Steele and her little son had during the past summer been engaged in giving theatrical entertainments, from which she realized a sufficiency to purchase a home for herself and children. The fire is supposed to have been the work of an incendiary.[8]

How terrifying this must have been for Rowena! This also provides us a greater understanding of the closeness that developed between mother and sons over the years. She says later, when describing her relationship with Harry and George, "Being so constantly with their mother they became her constant companions and confidants and shared with her her joys and her griefs. There ever was a deep, tender and affectionate love binding these three together."[9] It is no wonder that they would be even more attached now that her life had been saved by her son's bravery.

Again the absence of R.J. during this troubling time is conspicuous. It may be that he was working in another county, or it could even have been that he went to Hawaii (Sandwich Islands). There was a great deal of travel between California and Hawaii at that time. Rowena, in her book *Dell Dart*, recalled having done so herself in 1859: "Shortly after these circumstances had occurred [meeting Dell by chance at a roadside inn in Northern California], I sailed from California to the Sandwich Islands, and amid new excitements and scenes and cares I seldom thought of poor Dell."[10] In "The Victim of the Reef," a story serialized for the *Argus* in May 1876, about a young man who is enticed to Hawaii by a rival suitor for his fiancée, drugged and imprisoned, Rowena describes Honolulu of the late 1850s:

> Honolulu! Bright, beautiful Honolulu! Sister of the Polynesias and Queen of the Cluster! Memory goes back amid a glow of happy — yes, sad and happy — thoughts to the days and moonlit nights when alone I wandered o'er your greensward and inhaled the fragrance wafted on the gentle breeze from your magnificent orange groves. I have been filled with awe and wonder as I sat beneath the star-studded sky, meditating on the secrets of nature. Those beautiful islands, lying away out in mid-ocean, as though the Great Unknown Architect had formed them from the many shaped clouds, which float so lazily over the broad expanse, and dropped them down into that archipelago for a resting place for weary, storm-tossed mariners! For hours I have been spellbound, surrounded by all that was grand, wonderful and sublime, simple, sweet and lovely.
>
> There was the crater, lying in its gray, grim silence. A feeling of nervous wonder would steal over me as my imagination pictured it in its grand but terrible beauty, when, after low, subterraneous mutterings of many days, it burst forth in its magnificent fury, emitting lurid flames and casting up its ashes and huge rocks, and vomiting streams of molten lava, which went rushing and roaring and hissing, as though mad with pain and eager to reach the dashing

waves and therein seek the cooling balm of nature. The scenes of confusion, the wild and terrified natives, flying from the wrath of Luna, the only power their dark, untutored minds have ever learned to love, worship or fear. The millions of dead fishes floating upon the broad, turbulent, angry waters.

It was difficult for the mind to realize the fact that such sense of terror had been enacted there, where all was now so divinely, sweetly, so soul-soothingly quiet — there, where the silvery moonbeams frolicked and sported in delicate shadows through the leaves of the tall coconut trees, and toyed with the grim old fury-spent monster with as much confidence as the infant playingly draws its rosy fingers over the blue veins of the snowy breast of its mother.

Again, I exclaim, as my thoughts go back to the lovely scenes: Sweet Honolulu! Bright little city of the sea! Well may the weary, but life and health seeking, invalid look to thee for the restoring balm. Health lurks in the fresh and luscious fruit; it is mingled with the pure sea breeze, whose breath is laden with odors of the pineapple, the orange blossom and banana. The air, the sky, and the very earth upon which you tread is pure and clear from mud or dust. Is this a little heaven? you ask. Sitting with my face towards the old crater, and listening to the monotonous sighing and soughing of the restless sea, I should be inclined to think that such I would have as my heaven, if I could just have the society of the angels and could see and know the Great Master.[11]

Perhaps, too, the asthma and heart trouble that would plague R.J. for the rest of his life were beginning to bother him. In

"The Little Gold Cross," a charming Christmas story published in the *Argus* in December 1871, the main character, "Aunt Eloise," relates a family situation almost identical to the Steeles' own trials and predicaments in the latter half of the 1860s:

Some twelve years ago your uncle became embarrassed in business, thro' the carelessness and dishonesty of those in whom he most confided; in a few months after the crash came. My poor husband was a ruined man financially. He had struggled manfully; he had summoned all the strength and energy of his indomitable nature; and when the blow came he fell, with his fortune honestly earned.

For weeks he lay upon his bed with brain fever; when, at length, he was able to sit up for a few hours each day, the doctor whispered to me not to hope too much.

"I think," he said, "his lungs are affected; and, with that cough, he cannot last long."

"Oh, Doctor!" I cried, "Is there no preventive, no cure?"

"I have no hope of affecting a cure with medicine; his mind is too much diseased. A change of scenery and climate might have the power to bring about a change."

From that moment there was a will and determination in my every act. Your noble, earnest uncle should have the benefit of the last hope; he should visit the beautiful, verdant islands; he should look upon the glorious sunsets which shine so radiantly upon the cluster, away out in the sea; he should inhale the fragrant odors of the orange blossoms, and the cool, sweet breezes of the healthful air of the Polynesias. After much persuasion, and many assurances that I could get along and live comfortably, he started, with the intention of remaining six months.

I need not tell you of the grief of parting; which, though bitter, very bitter, was cheered in a measure by the sweet hope of a meeting. My residence at the time of my husband's departure was in Stockton. I remained there three months, struggling with pride and poverty. At the expiration of that time I was induced to try my fortunes in a mining town in the interior. A few relics of former elegance were disposed of for a mere trifle; with a small sum of money, and my two darling little ones, I started.

I was well and strong and willing to work; true, I had never performed menial labor, but times had changed with me as they had with thousands of others. The soft, white hands of the doctor, the lawyer, the merchant, and even the divine had become brown and hardened by honest labor, and I was determined not to spare mine. If I could not find employment as teacher or seamstress, I must accept the first lucrative situation offered.[12]

R.J. Steele was again in the household by February 24, 1868, apparently restored to full physical fitness. He became foreman of the *Tuolumne City News* in Tuolumne County from February until August 1868 when they moved back to Merced County, where they would stay for the remainder of their lives. According to Galloway, R.J. left Tuolumne City with the good wishes of his employer, Democrat crusading editor and publisher, J.D. Spencer, who said that R.J. "got out a good-looking paper and could be relied upon to work without supervision," thereby allowing Spencer the freedom to travel for the purposes of politicking and soliciting business.

Galloway also noted the intriguing lack of any mention of Rowena in the Tuolumne City paper in that six-month period.[13]

Snelling, Act II — The Weekly Merced Herald and San Joaquin Valley Argus

In August of 1868 R.J. and Rowena were back in Snelling and in control of the publication and editorship of the *Weekly Merced Herald*, eventually, one year later, to become the *San Joaquin Valley Argus*, "to still further extend its circulation and thereby make it more advantageous to advertisers."[14] From 1865 on, thanks to the stewardship of Wigginton, Robertson, then Lyttleton W. 'L.W.' Talbott, and finally Steele, up through the establishment of other newspapers in the 1870s and '80s such as the *Tribune*, which later became the *Express,* and then the *Sun,* there is preserved on microfilm an almost unbroken historical record of Merced County.

Galloway states that the return of the Steeles to Snelling and their purchase of the *Herald* was difficult. In a lively exchange of charges, Talbott claimed that R.J. deliberately misled him and the subscribers into thinking that the *Herald* was to be continued and, indeed, in the August 14 issue of the *Herald*, R.J. alluded to its continuation. Talbott later charged that Steele had promised to start a newspaper in the new town of Dover on the San Joaquin River at the expiration of his contract and said, further, that he had done a favor to R.J. by bringing him back to Snelling in 1868, that he had turned over the largest subscription list that had ever been known in Merced County but that half of the subscribers refused to take the *Herald* when they found out that Steele was to be the editor. R.J. subsequently lost an election to Talbott for Justice of the Peace in Snelling by a vote of 123 to 28. "Nevertheless, the *Argus* prospered," Galloway wrote. "Its subscription list increased from about 400 in 1869 to 650 in 1870, which was said to be the largest circulation of any newspaper in the Valley south of Stockton."[15]

Eventually in full control, R.J. immediately renamed the paper the *Merced Herald* and promised the readers ...

> [O]ur energies and the modicum of ability which we possess will be devoted to the promotion of the interests of Merced county, and that whatever publications we may make will be done with an eye single to their advancement; and we appeal to the people in the various sections of the county, together with the settlements in other counties adjacent, to aid us with such facts as will enable us to lay before the public such information as will be beneficial to them. Politically we will adhere to the doctrines and tenets of the Democratic party, and will ever be found fighting in the ranks for the preservation of the form of government handed down to us by our fathers of the Revolution, taking the Constitution as our guide with the commentaries and explanations of those who figured so conspicuously in framing that time-honored instrument as to be denominated by the great men of the past generation as the "Fathers of the Constitution".... [16]

R.J. was still every ounce a Southern Democrat. In this crucial period following the victory of the North in the War Between the States, those "doctrines and tenets" consisted of:

> [S]trictest economy in the administration of the Government and the reduction of the expenditures.... The immediate restoration of the states of the South to their original status in the Union ... and a general amnesty for all political offenses.
> The equalization of taxation ...

> Abrogate the useless offices established by the now
> dominant party during the war, reduce the military to
> obedience to the civil laws of the country, and
> abolish the Freedman's Bureau and the despotic
> system of military government established over the
> people of the Southern States.[17]

Needless to say, he was not in favor of the abolition of slavery or
extending suffrage to Blacks or women.

> While we despair of ever seeing a healthy public
> sentiment again prevail in regard to the political *status*
> of the races in these States, we yet hold to the
> opinion that the white is the superior and should be
> the governing race … we have an abiding faith that
> our children will witness that happy state of affairs
> … though a sea of negro and white blood may have
> to be waded through to accomplish it."[18]

Some of the other members of the Democratic party in the
County were James Robertson, by then County Judge; P.D.
Wigginton, partner in a real estate brokerage with Mark Howell;
Samuel H.P. Ross; A.B. ('Andy') Anderson; C.M. Blair; and J.B.
Sensabaugh.

Anderson and his wife, Hannah, came to Snelling from
Stanislaus County in 1862, the same year as the Steeles originally
arrived, and became the proprietors of the Galt House Hotel in
Snelling. Andy moved to Fresno to open a new hotel in 1878
while Hannah continued to run the hotel in Snelling for many
years thereafter, and Rowena always made it a point to stop and
see her whenever she came near Snelling. In April 1888, the
Journal of Commerce noted that the "Galt House is recognized
throughout the [San Joaquin] valley as one where a first-class
meal and a comfortable bed can always be had. Mrs. Anderson, an

old but cheerful lady, is the proprietress. She is the pioneer hotelkeeper of the town and has a host of friends among those who travel though the valley. Mrs. Anderson resided here before Merced was made a county by itself and has kept the hotel since 1864."[19] Their son, A.B. Jr. ('Boney'), was George Granice's best friend. He died tragically in March 1878 by accidental shooting while hunting in Fresno County. In a long, heart-rending obituary, so very typical of all her tributes, Rowena noted that he was twenty-two years old and had just begun to learn telegraphy.

Samuel H.P. Ross, who died on June 26, 1873, at his residence near Hopeton, was a '49er who turned to teaching school and ranching at Hopeton, where he married the widow of James Ruddle. He passed the bar and became a lawyer in about 1855, was three times elected District Attorney and, just before his death, County Superintendent of Schools.

Charles M. Blair was County Clerk in Merced County in the late 1860s, also a merchant in Snelling and later Merced. The family moved to San Francisco in the late 1870s where the daughters, Josie, Sallie, and Susie became, according to Rowena who wrote frequently about them, "well and favorably known as the gifted Blair Family of musical fame."[20]

Sensabaugh also died young, at forty, from heart disease on September 4, 1875, leaving a wife and four small children. The paper noted that he was "kind, genial, loving" and "was stamped with unquestionable honesty."[21] One of the children, Wade, who was close in age to Lee Steele, became the telegraph messenger in Merced.

With the old days of the melodeons and "bit theaters" in San Francisco and Sacramento now long behind Rowena, the Steeles were free to openly express their anti-alcohol position, and what a quandary it presented! Wine was already becoming one of the staple products of Merced County. In October 1868, R.J. noted that vineyard owner J.B. Cocanour brought a bottle of wine to the *Herald* office, "which, being tasted by a number of visitors, was pronounced by some who claim to be judges, equal to the best quality produced in Sonoma and Los Angeles." The issue of Temperance vis-à-vis wine was then deftly sidestepped with the notation, "As an article of commerce, we desire to see the production of wine fostered and encouraged in our State, but we do not desire to witness its consumption among our people. But hereafter it will become an important item in the list of articles exported from this county."[22]

Calico Balls and Masquerades

Although they lived in Snelling for only five years (1868 to 1873), this period was one of the happiest and busiest chapters of Rowena's life. For years afterward she would revisit Snelling, in person and in memories with a melancholy longing for the wonderful days spent there. She gradually began writing short stories, the first two being "The Old Shoe" in December 1868 and "Aunt Abby and the Village Gossip," February 1869, in which Aunt Abby finds a rather unique and questionable method of silencing the gossip — by thrashing her soundly with a riding whip across the back and shoulders and then making her ingest wine.[viii]

The first column under the pseudonym of "Vacuna" (a goddess of agriculture in Roman mythology) in January 1869 began what would become a portfolio of hundreds of columns on social issues and happenings in Merced County:

> MR. EDITOR.—Could any of the old settlers of Snelling, who are quietly sleeping the sleep that knows no waking on yonder lonely hillside, have revisited the town almost any day or night during the last three weeks, they would have thrown up their

---

[viii] This is one of only three instances, in all of Rowena's writings, of aggressive behavior on the part of a heroine or even remotely suggesting revenge or violence. Usually she wrote about bad things happening to good people and how, with fortitude and other positive character traits, one could survive and triumph.

fleshless hands in wonder and exclaimed: "*O! tempora, Oh, mores!*" The general cry of old and young, rich and poor, saint and sinner has been—

"On with the dance! Let joy be unconfined."

It has been an unbroken spell of gayety and pleasure, mingled with dancing, visiting, confectionary, toys, smiles, music, songs, laughter, turkeys, mince pies, frost cake, lectures, presentations, trees, happy hearts, lovely faces, coquettish glances, rich dresses, sparkling jewelry, heavenly forms, conquests, stolen kisses, weddings, sudden recoveries, unrumpled pillow cases, fire crackers, hand organs, serenades, tramp of steeds, rattling wheels, merry jests, hearty hand shaking, children in want of bits, well seasoned with the sound of miniature musical instruments.[23]

Week after week, Rowena listed off the names of townspeople who attended balls, suppers, dramatic readings, musical fests, weddings and parties. She described the costumes and dresses of the ladies in the same way the society pages in New York papers had been doing for years. But, alas, not everyone in town was appreciative of her or the notice they received from her pen, as evidenced by this facetious little article about a calico ball at Mayer's Hall in Snelling in 1870:

I should like to make mention of some of the ladies and their tasteful dresses, but I understand that some of the ladies took offense at having their name mentioned after the last grand ball. I must remain content with making mention of the very becoming costumes of a few gentlemen—I know they won't object."

* * *

> Mr. Anthony Meany wore a calico vest which
> showed just a little beneath his well-fitting cloth coat;
> there was a sly twinkle in his roguish eye which said,
> "It's all my wife would let me sport."[24]

Meany, then a building contractor who erected the Scott mansion in Snelling, among other buildings, was later the sheriff of Merced and a principal member of the "County Clique" that later persecuted and harassed the Steeles and Harry Granice. But, obviously, this calico ball was at a time, short though it was, when they were all still friends.

The *Herald* and later the *Argus* continuously published articles about the new settlers arriving and the new towns and settlements that were forming in the County, as well as the condition of the soil, the water situation over the years preceding the construction of the vast canal systems, and the health of the various crops season after season. The editors made it a point to travel around the County as often as possible and present a wide coverage. Through the columns of the paper one can thus track the growth of all the villages and towns over the years, some of them in areas adjoining Merced County.

The *Argus* seems to have been thriving in Snelling, as evidenced by this article from October 1869.

> R.J. Steele, Esq., editor of the San Joaquin Valley
> *Argus*, has recently treated himself to a new press,
> type, &c. He has his two sons, George and Henry
> with him. They do all the type setting and strike off
> the paper. Both are intelligent youths. We call in at
> the *Argus* office but the editor was absent. His sons
> gave us a couple copies of the last issue which they
> were then striking off. Steele is making money. Few
> editors now-a-days can say as much. The people

down this way are extremely liberal and patronize
their county paper well.[25]

In April 1871, the *Argus* was referred to as "an extensively
circulated, highly entertaining and exceedingly influential sheet
published at Snelling, Merced county, in this state...."[26]

In Snelling and later in Merced, Rowena would constantly
encourage the townsfolk to clean up the town and spruce up their
houses and complimented those who did:

> In perambulating about your town I find many
> improvements since I left here four years ago, among
> the most prominent of which is the pretty cottage
> residences of Messrs. Wigginton, Ward, Breen,
> Sensabaugh and Blair. Neat houses and bright flower
> gardens give signs of domestic happiness. Your
> business house and hotels appear in a flourishing
> state. Your blacksmiths, wagon-makers, carpenters,
> and mechanics of all branches appear to be
> prospering. Your lawyers, doctors, and other profess-
> ional men are all well dressed, and wear upon their
> happy faces a showing of prosperity. Your variety
> and fancy stores give token that sugar plums and
> tobacco are appreciated. Your barber looks as well
> satisfied as a bank note shaver; your bonifaces look
> as pleasant as if board was up and butter down.[27]

However, in the late 1860s, the most prominent thing the town
lacked, in her opinion, was a proper schoolhouse for the children.
In this article, as in hundreds of others, she followed the old
principle of "praise before criticism," and even then tried to make
that criticism in the form of a suggestion. "Fathers, mothers and
bachelors, bestir yourselves, think seriously and act promptly
upon this subject. Think, besides the advantage it would be to the

children already here, what an inducement it would be for families to come and settle among you."[28] Apparently, her appeal fell on willing hearts and hands; by 1871 she would proudly write of the new improvements in town, "grandest of all, is our school house, where daily nearly one hundred girls and boys—our future men and women—gather to receive such instructions, examples and educations as will fit them to fill the different spheres of life which nature intends them."[29]

It was shortly after this article in 1869 that Rowena began writing in earnest and often on what would be two of her favorite themes — the importance of girls receiving a good education and, most shocking of all for some, married women working outside the home.

> The following [an article on women employed in government offices in Washington] should prove an encouragement to parents to persevere and even make some sacrifices to educate their daughters. It should prove an incentive to girls to go on and improve in all the useful branches of learning, and prepare themselves to be useful in after life. There will be no necessity for you to wear out a miserable existence in some "shoddy's" nursery or kitchen. Useful education will fit you to meet and mingle with the greatest women and men of all nations. Leave all the superfluous branches until you become perfect mistress of the useful. Study, if you can, the foreign languages. Any little gypsy can play the piano, but it requires a woman of sound mind and a thorough, practical education to serve as clerk at Washington. Girls of Merced, in all your boasted beauty of face and form, in all your intelligence and brilliancy of mind, arouse! Wake up your slumbering ambition;

apply yourselves to the study of useful knowledge, to
go forth independent and face the coming years.[30]

In 1870, when Rosa Fitzhugh graduated from the Oakland
Institute, Rowena wrote, "I hope to live to panegyrize many of the
bright, intelligent girls of our county; we have plenty of them. Be
industrious, little ones. Study with a zeal becoming your intellects
and inscribe your names upon the tablet of true womanly
nobleness."[31]

African-Americans, Chinese, Mexicans, and Indians

The paper printed week after week for nearly thirty years
announcements of every wedding, birth, death, moving, passing
through town, and coming and going that came to the attention of
the editors, especially the many summer visitors to Yosemite (or
"Yo Semite," as it was printed in those days). In the case of
African-Americans, Indians, Mexicans and Chinese, however, the
article was usually brief, devoid of full names and almost always
included something derogatory and negative about the people as a
whole:

> CHINAMAN KILLED.—On Monday night last a
> Chinaman was stabbed and almost instantly killed in
> this town by one of "his docile and inoffensive"
> countrymen. The murderer and his victim were each
> employed as cooks in different families but slept
> together, and it was in their bedroom that the
> difficulty occurred. The murderer has not been
> arrested.[32]

> JUSTIFIABLE HOMICIDE.—A case of justifiable
> homicide recently transpired near Hopeton, in this
> county. It seems that an Indian, called Joe, in the
> employ of James A. Neill, had for a few days been on

a drunken spree with some companions, and returned to the ranch in a state of intoxication. His supply of liquor having run out, he demanded more of Neill, who, he knew, generally kept the article about the place for private use. Neill refused to give it to him, and Joe attacked Neill in a furious manner. Neill picked up a hoe-handle and broke it over Joe's head, but without sufficient force to do any good. Joe then commenced striking Neill, who drew a clasp knife and stabbed Joe, the blade entering the body a little above and to the right of the left nipple. He walked a few steps and fell and soon expired....[33]

The notable exception was the August 18, 1868 Christian wedding at the Galt House in Snelling of Ah Lang Anderson (was this perhaps the adopted son of J.B. and Hannah?) and Miss Ah Chow of Knight's Ferry ("Canton and Ho-Ep-Ton papers please copy.")[34]

To twenty-first century enlightened minds with liberal ideals, this attitude is justifiably shocking, but in those days it was, unfortunately, the common perception of anyone who was not European or American Caucasian. On the other hand, it is interesting to watch the more positive evolution of Rowena's racial attitudes over the years from her personal contacts with the people. Foremost among these was the large African-American family of Snelling barber and musician A.E. Talley and his wife, Elizabeth. Talley's "tonsorial saloon and bathhouse" was located adjoining the *Argus* office in Snelling, and for several years he placed large advertisements in the *Herald* and *Argus*, which no doubt pleased R.J. and Rowena.

A.E. was born in Virginia; Elizabeth was from Louisiana. They came to Snelling in about 1859 where they were married and became the parents of twelve children, eight of whom reached adulthood, one of them handicapped for life. Lizzie's aged mother, Harriett Russell, also lived with them. In Snelling A.E. formed a band with Theodore Taubert and over the years they would delight the citizens of Merced County with their musical skills at balls, parties, plays, weddings, and holiday celebrations.

In addition to his music, A.E. and Lizzie knew instinctively the way to win forever the good will and affection of the editors of the *Argus*:

> ICE CREAM.—Talley, the indefatigable barber and musician, chose an hour in the afternoon of Thursday last, when the mercury was at 106° in the shade, to compliment this office and its attaches with ice cream, which reduced the temperature at least ten degrees. Talley will henceforth, until the close of hot weather, have ice cream prepared in his tonsorial saloon every day and evening, and solicits the patronage of our citizens who indulge in such luxuries.[35]

Rowena tells us through the columns of the *Argus* over the years about the many times that Talley brought strawberries and other fruit or played at a party, and she reported with obvious happiness that the Talleys had moved to Merced to "a neat little shop on 17th street near Washington Hall" in December 1878 and that A.E. had begun playing more often to the delight of Mercedites: "Our old neighbor, A.E. Talley, took the house by storm with his quaint banjo solo. We think that Talley improves with age."[36]

A.E. died on December 12, 1879. For some reason, despite all of her affectionate notes about him over the years, Rowena did not write an obituary. Perhaps she was out of town or maybe it was because "Marcus," the reporter for the rival paper *Merced Express* "scooped" her with a glowing, and surprisingly liberal, piece:

Yes, friend Talley is dead; farewell for a little while,
good old friend; by and by the Master will call for
me, too, and then I trust to go and clasp hands with
you, and hear your shout of welcome home "old
boy," and we will wear our crowns together, for there
is no distinction of persons with God, and certainly
there should be none with us.[37]

Lizzie married Jesse Neill in October 1883 and was
widowed again just thirteen months later. When A.E. and Lizzie's
son James, "a bright, intelligent boy," died in a terrible hunting
accident in November 1885, Rowena wrote an obituary which was
more a sympathetic and loving column for Lizzie than it was a
memorial for James.[38] Somewhat surprising, in none of these
articles was the word "colored" ever mentioned, as was the
practice then in newspapers to distinguish African-Americans.

Is it a coincidence that, having A.E. and Lizzie Talley and
their large family as close neighbors, R.J. ceased writing articles
about the "superior white race" and a premonition of a "sea of
negro and white blood"? He even began writing items
condemning outrages and violence aimed at the Blacks in the
South, then advocated that they should be placed on reservations
"for their own protection." He never turned around completely his
theory that the African- and European-Americans could never live
in peace together, except to note, somewhat grudgingly, on his
visit to Tennessee in 1888 that in "Nashville, a city of from
125,000 to 150,000 population, ... the blacks and whites are so
sandwiched together that it is hard to tell which is most
numerous."[39]

Rowena wrote a telling little piece in September 1870
about events that caught her attention while walking about the
town one evening:

On Tuesday evening, feeling the need of a little exercise I sauntered towards town, and seeing Mayer's Hall lighted up, I called at the door and was politely invited to enter by Mr. Locke, who informed me that he had opened a writing school. I spent a few moments in pleasant conversation with his amiable lady, then bid good night to the worthy pair and also the pupils and returned to retrace my steps towards home, when my attention was attracted to a light; yes, many lights, in the Court House. Although possessed of very little curiosity, I do believe that little spirit induced me to take a peep. A little cripple who was standing at my side offered to accompany me. We slipped softly through the door which was ajar, glided noiselessly into a dark corner, and I then felt like saying with Paul Pry: "Just popped in; hope I don't intrude," when the mysterious whispering from the far end of the room sent a thrill through me. My little cripple companion whispered "Ku-Klux," and the next instant we glided out as noiselessly as we entered. We came to the conclusion that that kind of "dead-heading" wouldn't do.[40]

Clearly, she had no use for the radical racism of that organization, and it doesn't seem that the Klan thereafter maintained a noticeable presence in Merced County — at least nothing reported in the papers.

For the Chinese — the "pagan hordes that are now flocking … from China, Japan and the Pacific Islands"[41] — it would take many years for Rowena and the Nation to come around to an acceptance that the thousands of workers, imported by the railroads and mines ostensibly for temporary labor, were here to stay. It would have to reach a crescendo of hysteria, with anti-Chinese laws, speeches, banners, and rallies in the 1880s, in which

R.J. Steele was a leader, before attitudes would turn around even moderately.

The American Indians, on the other hand, would never receive sympathy or acceptance from the Steeles or America in the 1800s. Memory was too fresh, and resentment too deep, of the oftentimes horrific ways with which some of the Indian tribes had fought off the invasion of their land, the annihilation of their basic food source, the buffalo, and the murder of their people through starvation, disease and massacre. Sadly, R.J. gave in to the general sentiment, and possibly incited further terrible behavior, in his editorials: "The murderous foe should be treated as wolves and coyotes, and soldiers should be paid a bounty for scalps taken, and no prisoners should be taken except when the savages come unarmed into the camp of our army."[42]

It is interesting to note that the Steele family's prejudices of the nineteenth century were not carried over into the twentieth: In 1910 their son Lee married Eloisa Castro, a young lady of mixed Indian and Mexican heritage, and had with her four children.

Chapter VII

More Grand Calico Balls and Masquerades

During their five years in Snelling, while R.J. became more deeply involved in the political issues and scandals of the day as an active member of the Democrat party, Rowena began traveling and forming her own political and social platforms, at the same time continuing her demanding labors as a Victorian-era housewife and mother, along with the "brain work" of weekly columnist, author and lecturer. By this time, in addition to the three boys living in the household, R.J.'s orphaned niece Laura Steele had joined the family, and it was also quite common at any given time to have one or more young printer's apprentices in residence at the home.

In November 1872, thanks to a small public disagreement Rowena had with Dr. Carrie Young, a physician, magazine editor and visiting lecturer, about sanitary conditions around the Steele house in Snelling and how best to care for her family, Rowena gave us a glimpse of her incredibly busy daily life:

> Mrs. S[teele, referring to herself in the third person] is far advanced upon the shady side of forty, and no longer possesses the bodily strength and vigor of youth, still she cooks, washes, irons, makes and mends for seven in the family, and does more brain work in seven days (in every week) than Mrs. Y[oung] does in as many weeks. Had the lady have looked just a little to the right of the puddle she could have seen one hundred boxes of flowers, all planted and reared by the hands of Mrs. S. Had she had looked into the storeroom she could have found, in large quantity and great variety, preserves and canned fruit, put up for family use by the hands of

Mrs. S. Had she have inspected the clothes-presses
and bureau drawers, she would have seen dozens of
articles of clothing, fashioned and finished by the
hands of Mrs. S. Had she have visited the bedrooms
she would not have found a particle of bedding,
except the blankets, but what had been made by Mrs.
S. She could also, if curiosity had prompted her, have
found a roll of rag carpet containing forty yards,
every rag cut and sewed by Mrs. S. Had she have
visited the printing office in the town which Mrs. S.
resides and looked over the files of papers, she could
have found columns and columns of original reading
matter written by Mrs. S.

I make mention of these things to show that Mrs. S.
is not an idle, slovenly woman, indifferent to bad
smells and filth, and that a mud-hole such as Mrs. Y.
mentions would be fully as offensive to Mrs. S. as to
Mrs. Y.[1]

We do know of at least one household appliance that made
her life somewhat easier, and that was in November 1870 when
Houston's Automaton Washing Machines were introduced to
Snelling. "We have tried the article at our house," wrote the
Steeles, "and find that they greatly reduce the labor of the
household in this particular and has a very happy effect in keeping
peace in the family on wash days, doing away entirely with the
necessity of a cold dinner...."[2]

Added to that already hectic schedule was a myriad of
social and church activities, among Rowena's favorites being the
calico balls and masquerades. Many of the costumes for these
events were supplied by her old friend Susan Vickers Paullin
(wife of J.R. and mother of Louisa, James and Edgar — all actors
who appeared with Rowena in the old theater days in San
Francisco and Sacramento). Since her husband suffered an

incapacitating accident in 1859, Mrs. Paullin had become a successful costumer in San Francisco in order to support her family.

Apparently there was quite a bit of opposition to these activities, however, especially the expense of professional costumers such as Mrs. Paullin, on the part of the men of Snelling, in addition to considerable gossip in the town, as evidenced by this article in 1871. Rowena prefaced the column with suggestions for making inexpensive costumes, easily put together out of everyday fabrics, such as a nun, "Quakeress," European peasant, and Roman and Greek characters, and continued:

> Snelling is far behind every town of its size in variety of amusements. We have never had a festival, never had a ladies fair. Charades, tableaux, and dramatic associations have been looked upon with horror. Still there are half a dozen saloons, which are nightly crowded, and these moral husbands seem to have a lively, pleasant time, if one may judge from the ringing of glasses, the rattling of billiard balls, and the peels of loud, merry laughter which are heard in passing, but the quiet wife sits home with the babes, and patiently awaits his coming....
>
> We have ladies of talent in our town who are willing to enter in and assist in getting up such innocent amusements as would greatly advance the intelligence, add to the intellectual and social condition of society, check in a measure the progress of that slimy, serpent-like reptile, which has crept in and taken up its abode in our midst: I mean that foul and loathsome enemy to the peace and happiness of homes, that monster which makes hundreds of bleeding hearts cry out in their pent-up grief— Slander.

"Curse the tongue—
Thence the slanderous rumour,
Like the adder's drop
Fills her venom, withering friendship's faith,
Turning love's favour."

Husbands, fathers, brothers, you have it in your power to drive this monster from among us. How, you ask? My answer is: When your wife, daughter or sister wishes to assist in setting up an innocent amusement, which will add to her happiness, encourage her, go with her, do not object to her joining in because this one or that one is engaged in it; if your wife is pure and good, her purity and goodness will be to the others—

"Like the stained web which whitens in the sun
Grown pure by being purely shown upon."

I hope the Masquerade will prove a success, and will be conducted in such manner that the ladies and gentlemen of Snelling will feel like encouraging the repetition of masquerades and other innocent amusement.[3]

Evidently her appeals were heard and heeded, as reported in the next week's paper and in many articles over the ensuing several years:

The grand ball which took place at Mayer's Hall on Friday night, March 17th, under the management of Joseph Leeson, John C. Breen, Anthony Meany, Joseph Coulter and J.S. Williams, proved a most pleasant and brilliant success. Too much praise cannot be accorded the above-named gentlemen for the very efficient manner in which the affair was conducted.

The supper served by Mr. J.M. Strong at the Coulter Hotel was gotten up in a most sumptuous and tasteful style, at which about a hundred and twenty-five ladies and gentlemen proved themselves epicures of the first order by the ample justice they did to the substantial viands, delicious pastry and the ornate and varied confectionery.

The music under the management of [Theodore F.] Taubert and [A.E.] Talley rang out in soul stirring strains and gave a charm which music alone can give on such occasions.

The pleasant Hall was neatly fitted up and brilliantly lighted, which brought out to perfection the gay colors of the costumes and the glitter of the gold and silver trimmings. It would be impossible for the most gifted descriptive writer to express in words the joyousness, satisfaction and general good cheer. The whole atmosphere seemed filled with smiling faces, happy hearts, congenial feelings and exclamations of Oh! wasn't it a grand and perfect success![4]

She went on to describe with obvious delight some of the dozens of costumes, including Mrs. May Anderson "in the superb character of 'Jupiter in Exile'"; Mrs. Nettie McPherson as "Minne-Ha-Ha"; Mrs. Belle Robertson as "Zingara" "flitted about light and fairy-like as the sunbeams of her own fair Italy"; Mrs. Fanny Kendrick as "Queen of Hearts"; Mrs. Russ Ward, as an "Italian Prima-Donna," "looked a perfect little birdling about to trill out in sweet notes of gladness"; Mrs. Linie Skelton, as "Evening Star," "looked to perfection that bright, clear queen among the azure blue clouds and silver streaks"; Mrs. Belle Davis as "Morning Star"; Mrs. Ada Williams as a "Spanish Bolero" "looked every inch a man in the jaunty suit of black velvet and silver"; Mrs. Eugenie Halstead, as the "Peasant Girl"; and many more.

Several men participated, as well: Mr. Simon, as the "English Jockey," "looked a true son of the turf"; Mr. Brooks as "Solon Shingle"; Mr. James Halstead, as the "Turbaned Turk," "looked as happy as though he had just parted from the prettiest nymph of the harem"; Henry Latour as the "Wild Irishman"; the Hon. Russ Ward "disconnected himself from his high office and played the humble 'Peanut Girl,' much to the amusement of the ladies"; Mr. Anthony Meany as "Lord Bacon"; Mr. A.B. Anderson, proprietor of the Galt House, in his true character of an old-style Kentucky gentleman — six foot six"; Mr. Sam Bates, of Hornitos, as an "Italian Brigand"; "Young Harry Bludworth — six feet two in height — personated the bold 'General Lom' with an air *a la militaire*"; Peter Fee, Jr. "as the 'Lady in Black,' was a splendid make-up,"[5] and dozens more.

This was to begin a tradition of many years' duration of grand balls, masquerades and parties in Merced County that were faithfully advertised and reported in the columns of the *Argus*, although after the murder and trial from December 1874 on, Rowena's personal *joie de vivre* was understandably drastically dampened.

Fires, Fevers and Agues

One of the omnipresent dangers of living in predominantly wooden buildings in the seasonally hot, dry and dusty San Joaquin Valley was the dreaded monster: Fire! According to the History of Snelling written by Rowena in 1870, on September 12, 1862, "almost the entire business portion of the town was destroyed by fire, making the second great calamity for that year [the first being a flood in the winter of 1861-'62]. The citizens commenced to rebuild immediately, and in a short time the town presented an appearance indicative of thrift — Prince's Hotel was rebuilt, the Galt House was removed from LaGrange and erected by A.B.

Anderson, and considerable accessions were made to the population."[6]

On Saturday, July 22, 1871, another terrible inferno nearly destroyed little Snelling. Following is a portion of the article in which R.J. described the events, including the heroic actions on the part of nanny Belle Mann, who saved her little charges but was scarred for life as a result, and a Mr. Martin, "the brave stranger, who, although he had not one dime at stake, worked, led and encouraged with true fireman's zeal the equally brave men and boys of Snelling"[7]:

A Destructive Fire—Accidents and Incidents.

About 10 o'clock on Saturday night last, 22d inst., our usually quiet town was thrown into an alarming excitement by the cry of Fire! Fire! Fire! In an instant the streets were filled with people rushing frantically to the scene of the conflagration. We were among the first who reached the fire, and, as there was no fire organization—no ladders of much account and very little water immediately at hand, the fire gained considerable headway before anything could be brought to bear to encourage the slightest hope of saving a single building in the main portion of the town. Fortunately, however, the windmills, of which there are a number, together with a number of small hand pumps—all in good working order—were put into operation, supplying a sufficient quantity of water to keep at least one hundred buckets and vessels of every description capable of holding even one quart of water in constant use. The lift and force pump of Andrew Casaccia's with plenty of good hose, and being well manned, furnished stream enough to prevent Mr. Casaccia's saloon from taking

fire. Mr. Martin, who remained with the hose on top
of the saloon until everything was safe, deserves
special mention; he stood his ground manfully,
though at times it did seem he, and some others, in
about the same dilemma, must perish if they did not
abandon their posts, but they never flinched.

With all our experience in fire duty we have never
witnessed such concert of action and determination
to master the fiery element as on this occasion. All
were apparently quiet —no extraordinary excitement,
and all seemed to work as if they had taken a contract
job which *must* be finished in a few minutes—and the
job was finished (so that danger of the town burning
was past) in less than one hour. Too much praise
cannot be awarded to the entire community—
strangers and residents—for their timely and untiring
exertions in saving our town from total destruction.

ORIGIN OF THE FIRE.

The origin of the fire, as nigh as it can be
ascertained, was as follows: Mr. Geo. W. Halstead
and wife were attending dancing school, leaving at
home a young lady by the name of Belle Mann
(about 15 years of age) and three children, one an
infant. The children all went to bed, leaving the lamp
(a new patent fluid tube lamp) burning on the
bureau. This was the second time the lamp had been
lighted. The infant was sleeping in a cradle in the
room where the lamp stood. Miss Mann and the
other two children were in another room on the
opposite side of the house—all asleep. Miss Mann
says the screams of the child in the cradle awoke her.
Springing instantly from the bed she darted into the
room where the child lay, the cradle entirely
enveloped in flames, seized the child and took it to
the porch; returning, seized the second and thrust it

through the window and told it to run for life, then snatching up the third made her escape before anyone could reach her, but not without being severely, though not fatally, burned. Her right arm to the shoulder was terribly burned while in the act of rescuing the infant from the cradle, as also were her shoulder and some other portions of her body. The infant was very severely burnt, and for a time supposed to be fatal; but, as we are writing, intelligence is brought us that they are both convalescent.

Everything being so dry and heated, it required but a few minutes for the fire to spread over the entire district which was consumed. The losses, as correctly as can be ascertained, are as follows:

Geo. W. Halstead, Jr., dwelling house, furniture, clothing, etc., $800, no insurance.

Shaver & Halstead, blacksmith shop, tools, damage to stock, etc., $2,000, no insurance.

N. Breen[ix], wagon-maker's shop, stock and tools, $1,400, insured for $1,000.

A.J. Meany, carpenter's shop and four other buildings, stock, tools, etc., $3,000, no insurance.

Marsh & Brook, Painters, stock and tools, loss not ascertained, no insurance.

A.B. Anderson, agricultural implements, $1,000, no insurance.

Twenty buildings in Chinatown, of which number three were stores, one butcher's shop and two restaurants, loss $10,000, no insurance.[8]

[ix] This is the same Nick Breen who would save Harry Granice from being taken by a lynch mob in December 1874.

Coincidentally, there was a great fire in San Francisco on the same night that destroyed Mechanics' Mill causing $260,000 in damages and putting over one hundred men out of work. It is also a sad commentary to note that obviously the full brunt of the fire in Snelling that night was felt in the Chinese quarter, yet, judging by the great amount of damages, little effort, if any, was put forth to save those buildings.

As an immediate result of this fire, on August 14, a committee was appointed for the purpose of organizing a fire department composed of A.B. Anderson, Chairman, and R.J. Steele, Secretary, and another committee to enquire into the costs of building a tank, windmill and laying pipes, its members being A.J. Meany, C.M. Blair, L.P. Wilson, L.W. Talbott, and William H. Turner. Under her usual pseudonym of "Vacuna," Rowena wrote an enthusiastic response, which was to set the tone for fire company benefits for decades to come: "What say you, ladies and gentlemen, to having a fireman's ball, the proceeds to be given toward the organization of a hook and ladder company? Let the ladies furnish the supper, the musicians volunteer, the printer ditto, and let all our brave lads, each and every one, wear on the lapel of his coat a blue badge with the words inscribed thereon, 'Snelling H.&L. Co., No. 1.'"[9]

Another problem that marred an otherwise almost idyllic life in Snelling was the seemingly constant "fevers and agues," as reported over an almost three-year period:

February 1870 — "Mrs. John Ivett will please accept our most sincere thanks for the generous supply of delicacies sent to the sick of our family last week."[10]

June 1871 — "Owing to sickness of Mrs. Steele, the performance [of the Snelling Temperance Dramatic Troupe] heretofore announced for Monday evening next, was unavoidably postponed."[11]

August 1871 — "[M]uch sickness is reported throughout the country. Fevers, though of not very malignant type prevail through the plains and foothills, keeping our doctors busily employed. Unless a change takes place soon, we fear there will be a great deal of suffering among the people."[12] And, "Owing to the severe indisposition of several members of our family, including two of our regular compositors, we are a little behind with our paper this week."[13]

September 1871 — "Mr. Editor:—Partially, maybe wishing to be in the fashion, but more positively, in my opinion, I became an invalid, and by the advice of my most excellent physicians, Drs. Fitzhugh and McLean, I started on a trip to San Francisco, hoping that the sea breeze, pleasant scenes and mingling with old friends might restore me to health."[14]

August 1872 — "There has not been as much sickness in the whole of Merced during the past eight years as there has been in Snelling for four months back. I doubt if there is one family, for miles around, where there is not from one to six of its inmates down with fever or just recovering. Your readers at a distance will doubtless be surprised to learn that there has not been a single death within the limits of the town for over three months."[15] And, "Our editor, having been confined to his bed for several days with fever...."[16]

December 1872 — "Ague and Fever.... 'Mrs. S. and all her family are sick again.' ... 'Yes, it's chills and fevers, fevers and chills, all the time.'..."[17]

On a return visit to Snelling in 1875, Rowena noted sadly, "Dear old Snelling, with all its malaria and miasma, and chills and fever, I love thee still...."[18]

These "fevers and agues" seem to have been endemic in Snelling alone since, after removing to Merced in 1873, Rowena did not complain or remark on it again, and it does not seem to be related to George's death in 1876 unless it was an slow-acting disease that he contracted while living there.

One interesting idea Rowena put forth to help prevent the occurrence of fever and ague, especially during the dry, hot summer, was carpeting:

> Now, don't laugh at the idea of a rag carpet, or any other carpet being an important subject, for I do most truly believe, after giving the matter most serious consideration, that if all the slightly laid floors of California were comfortably covered with good, stout rag carpets, fever and ague and many other diseases incident to the six months of dry, hot summer seasons might in great part be prevented. It may be a new and perhaps erroneous idea, but everyone has a right to an opinion, and I will have mine, simple though it may appear. The foul air which must necessarily arise from the decaying vegetation on our unwatered plains sweeps under our lightly built houses. Take all new settled countries where people have invested their little all for the better, does not chills and fever most prevail? Take any town or city where the houses are kept well carpeted, and you find but little complaint of those maladies. Therefore, I trust you will not think lightly of my rag carpet idea.[19]

She may have had a valid point, since we now know that some serious illnesses, such as Valley Fever, are carried into our bodies by inhaling spores and dust. She also advocated for the convenience and health of the townspeople the idea of a market where fresh meats, fruits, fish and produce could be obtained.

What is most needed of all things, for the comfort and convenience of the residents of our town, is a domestic market, from which families could be supplied daily and hourly with fresh butter, eggs, cheese, ham, smoked beef, fruit, vegetables, chickens and all kinds of poultry and game, also fresh fish. Two enterprising men, with a small cash capital and team to run out into the country, would, in a short time, with judicious management, do a first-rate paying business. A milk depot would do well in connection with the market.

Although I have entertained this idea for many months past, while our population has been so rapidly increasing, it was brought with double force to my mind a few days since, while purchasing strawberries from a peddler. The idea of delicious, luscious, delightfully flavored strawberries in a horrid cigar box, shook up and jostled together until the perfume of the choice Havana and the fragrance of the delicious strawberry are so mixed and mingled that the natural flavor of both are lost, or, at least, one so tainted with the other that one is at a loss to know whether it is to be eaten or inhaled. Old smokers and chewers may perhaps relish the mixture, but to the delicate taste, unused to the pernicious weed, the compound is extremely unpalatable. ...

How much nicer and fresher fruit, vegetables, eggs, butter, milk and all such edibles would taste, and how much healthier if carried direct to market at an early hour in the morning, and placed in a cool place, kept crisp and cool with shade and water than they are now, peddled about in an open wagon in the hot sun, wind and dust; and, then, it would be more profitable to the producers, for often when the vender of the

> perishable articles calls at a house the mistress is not
> at home or has not made up her mind what she will
> have for the next meal—perhaps a half dozen
> visitors come an hour or so after the butter, milk, or
> vegetable man has left. If these articles were in the
> market she could send at any time, and three times
> the quantity of such produce would be consumed if it
> could be obtained just when it was wanted.[20]

She was apparently successful; within a few months a Mr.
Hathaway opened just such a shop, and one or more grocery stores
were in evidence in Snelling and Merced City from that point
onward.

"California's Pilgrim in the Cause of Temperance"

In addition to the columns under the pseudonym "Vacuna"
throughout these years in Snelling that chronicled the weekly
happenings in town, Rowena flowed from her hand a steady
stream of short stories and novelettes. Among them during these
years in Snelling were "Deserted" (July 24, 1869), about a man
whose wife leaves him and their daughter for her former fiancé;
"Aunt and I" (November 6, 1869), an interesting piece about
courting and romance customs in New York in the mid-nineteenth
century; "Auntie's Christmas Story" (December 24, 1870), about
an actress on Barnum's stage whose fiancé returns to find she has
married another after hearing he had died in California;
"Columbia Louden; Or, Why She Loved Him" (March 12, 1870),
a young woman whose inheritance is squandered by her gambler
husband and who is abandoned in a mining town; "Ruth Ray"
(February 5, 1870), the story of a girl who elopes with a man who
falsely thinks she is from a wealthy family; "The Bachelor's
Choice" (June 4, 1870), a chronicle of the imprudence of some
men to choose a bride not half his own age ("It is unnatural on the
part of the young lady and unwise on the part of the foolish old

gentleman.”); and “Beckie Bell” (August 27, 1870), a humorous piece about a New York society snob whose uncouth country relatives show up for a surprise visit.

As if she didn’t have enough to do, in April 1870, R.J., Rowena and George became founding members of the Snelling Division of the Sons of Temperance, later joined with the International Order of Good Templars (I.O.G.T.). R.J. became “District and Division Deputy Grand Worthy Patriarch.” Other initial officers included John Heath, Mary Hoskins, J.M. Denny, G.E. Jamison, Dennis Rogers, Catharine Marks, J. Perez, Mary Tackett[x], W.L. Jamison, and Frank Halstead. Rowena was elected Recording Secretary.

Rowena quickly set about getting up a Temperance Society Dramatic Troupe, formed in the winter of 1870-’71 with J.C. Breen as Treasurer, Joseph Leeson, Prompter, C. Killmer, Stage Manager, A.E. Talley, Orchestra Leader, J. Perez, Property-man, and George Morton, Artist. Their first production, the “thrilling Moral Drama, entitled THE DRUNKARD! *Or, The Fallen Saved*,” was staged in Mayer’s Hall on Saturday, April 1, 1871, starring Rowena as Mary Wilson and future lawyer and District Attorney, Frank H. Farrar, as Edward Middleton.

> A more appropriate piece could not have been selected by this troop for their first night, as it is a powerful and living picture, and all who may have the good fortune to witness it cannot fail to accord to it—“a true picture.” Should the Company be successful in their efforts to please, amuse and instruct—the legitimate object of the Drama—they will continue their performances, from time to time, with a change of pieces, new dresses, scenery, etc.

---

[x] Mary or “May,” as she was sometimes called, was a teacher and the niece of Judge James W. Robertson. She would later unwittingly figure prominently in the Granice-Madden murder drama.

With the talent and experience of Mrs. R.G. Steele to instruct and encourage, we see no cause for a doubt of ultimate success. The net proceeds are not as has been supposed by many—for individuals—but for Society purposes.[21]

The critic's review of the play, albeit written by the star's husband, was encouraging:

On Saturday evening last this troop gave their first entertainment, when was presented, for the first time here, the moral drama of "The Drunkard," which proved a grand success and gave satisfaction to all who attended. The Hall was densely crowded [about 200 people]; the reserved chairs filled with gaily-attired ladies presented a fine appearance. At precisely eight o'clock the curtain rose. The arrangement of the play is excellent, having the comic scenes follow up the serious ones so rapidly that the tears of sympathy, dropped for the fallen one and the helpless family, mingle with the tear of laughter.

Mary Wilson, as a stage character, possesses but little merit, still Mrs. Steele made all that could be made of the part. Mr. Frank H. Farrar (his first appearance) played Edward Middleton with great effect. Mr. C. Killmer as Lawyer Cribbs could not be excelled by the most experienced stage villain. Mr. James Halstead, as William Dowton, caused much laughter in the comic scenes, and he acted well the part of the simple, honest friend. George L. Granice, as Miss Spindle, the fussy old maid, played the spinster to perfection. Peter Fee, Jr., as Mrs. Wilson, did justice to the part of the poor widow. Mr. John Jeru, as the Landlord, was most excellent. Farmers

Brown and Stevens were well personated by John M. Denny and Charles Combs. Boney Anderson and Henry Latour led off the loafer and barroom scenes in real loafer style and made things very lively. Master Lee [Steele], as Julia, looked and spoke just like the little child of poverty. The piece had been well rehearsed, and all the performers were dead-letter-perfect in their parts.

Mr. Joseph Leeson, as Prompter, managed everything connected with the duties devolving upon that office to perfection, and with the assistance of Jesus Perez as property man, the scenes were changed and properties provided with the smoothness of a well-regulated theater.

Mr. J.C. Breen, "First robber," as old theatricals sometimes call the Treasurer, gave a most excellent account of his stewardship. Much credit is due Mr. Denny for the neat appearance of the stage, etc.

We understand this troop are making preparations to give another entertainment with an entire new programme, and we bespeak for them a full house whenever they appear behind the footlights.[22]

The show was taken on the road to Bear Valley in May of that year. Back in Snelling the next month "the very popular Comedietta" entitled "The Rough Diamond," was added to the program, featuring Rowena as Margery.

The next scheduled staging, in June 1871, of the play by Sheridan entitled "Pizarro, or, the Death of Rolla," in which Rowena played "her celebrated character of 'Elvira'"[23] had to be postponed owing to the illness of Rowena. It was eventually held on July 1st and "was attended by a large number of the ladies and gentlemen of our town and vicinity."[24]

Despite Rowena's appeal about the importance of theater in the town — "Where the legitimate drama is well presented and patronized, ignorance and silly prejudice must and will disappear, the Drama improves and refines the mind; it is a relief from the monotony of everyday life, strengthens and invigorates the businessman, gives our children an idea of the outside world and helps their thoughts to expand"[25] — and the addition of new sets thanks to Mr. H. Brook, of the firm of Marsh & Brook, the life of the Snelling Temperance Dramatic Troupe was short. The terrible fire in July 1871 necessitated the next performance being put off until the first week in September, when Rowena's illness again prevented the show from going on. No more is ever mentioned about the troupe.

It could also be that the railroad subsidy furor and other divisive political troubles that were going on simultaneously were beginning to tear away at the social fabric of the village. In the same issues of the *Argus* that Rowena was writing about drama, education, and health, R.J. Steele was week after week pouring out fiery invectives against the railroads, local politicians, and "courthouse hangers-on." In the ensuing months, people were forced to choose up sides and declare loyalties; without a doubt, anti-Steele gossip was rampant, and Rowena, who rarely expressed any political views, was invariably caught in the middle. The life of Merced County was drastically changing, and the demise of the little Snelling Temperance Dramatic Troupe was simply a harbinger of worse things to come.

Still, it would begin what would become for Rowena a life's work of writing, traveling and lecturing. It is perhaps more for this work, as much for her fiction writing, that Rowena would become well known, especially in California, so that one Oakland newspaper reporter in the 1880s dubbed her "California's pilgrim in the cause of Temperance."[26] Countless articles and stories appeared in the *Argus* and other journals over the years, and she logged thousands of miles on trains, stagecoaches, wagons, carriages, horseback and foot. She spoke in churches, private homes, and large, ornate lecture halls with from a few to thousands of listeners. Her resolve and perseverance were unyielding, her efforts unflagging in this important cause. To her dying day, she never wavered in her disdain for liquor.

Women's Rights and Suffrage

While she had always advocated the importance of educating girls, Rowena had not publicly espoused the women's rights movement until a trip to San Francisco in 1871 to visit Harry, who was attending the Pacific Business College, where her opinions began to coalesce.

VACUNA ON WOMAN'S RIGHTS.

MR. EDITOR:—Until within a few weeks the sentence "Woman's Rights" had a harsh, unwomanly sound upon my ear. It brought out in bold characters to my imagination a troop of obdurate Lady MacBeth's crying:
> "Come, you spirits
>   That tend on mortal thoughts!
> Unsex me here and fill me from
>   The crown to the toe top full
> Of direst cruelty; make thick my blood,
>   Stop up the access and passage to remorse,
> That no compunctious visitings of nature
>   Shake my fell purpose"—

meaning Woman's Suffrage, the ballot box annihilation of dressmakers, milliners and fluting irons. I could see the cheerful homes of towns and cities turned into huge hotels, and all the burden of domestic cares cast upon the shoulders of the moon-eyed heathen. But since my late visit to San Francisco

I have taken a far different view of the matter, or, at least the words "Woman's Rights," have been associated in my mind with a different class of individuals.

One morning I called at the post office for letters, and to my surprise my call was responded to by a sweet voiced, neatly habited lady. "Lady clerks in the post office," I remarked to my companion.

"Oh, yes," was the reply. "Woman's rights are cropping out considerable in this city, and in fact in all the cities of the United States, and the movement is receiving considerable encouragement throughout Europe, and I hope," she continued, "that the day is not far distant when women of talent and genius will be permitted to fill such stations in life as they are capable of filling."

As we passed through Montgomery Street my eye accidentally fell upon a little sign upon which was painted in modest letters, "Women's Co-operative Printing Union."

"More of Woman's Rights," I said, laughing, "and smacks of strong-mindedness and Woman's Suffrage."

"Let us go up," suggested my companion, and as we ascended the stairs leading to the office, I felt certain that I should meet at least a few of my much dreaded Lady MacBeths, or of the more disgusting class of sallow dyspeptics who had been snubbed by the lords of creation and shunned by the more retiring of their own sex.

At the head of the stairs we were met by a pleasant little lad who said, "Do you wish to see Mrs. Richmond?"

Wishing to see someone connected with the establishment and having no knowledge of names or persons we answered, "Yes."

In a few moments we heard the gentle tones of a cultivated voice — it was a woman's; the next moment a charming, dignified, intelligent lady stood before us.

"Mrs. Richmond," I said, rising from my seat. She gave a smiling assent. I then introduced myself and young companion.

In the course of a half hour's conversation, I became convinced that the proprietress of the Women's Co-operative Printing Union was a Lady — a true woman — and fully equal to the task she had so heroically undertaken. The gentle suavity of manners, taste, and extreme neatness of attire, could not fail to command the respect and admiration of the most fastidious anti-woman's rights man or woman.

"I am not working for woman's suffrage," she remarked. "I ask but woman's right to labor in the field according to her mental and physical strength; and her right to demand and receive remuneration according to the labor she performs." She said a great many good things; in fact, all she said was good, true and womanly.

Through her polite invitation we visited the compositors' room. Here we found six ladies engaged in setting type, also several gentlemen and boys.

"Quite an establishment," I remarked, as my eye fell upon the number of presses.

"Yes," said Mrs. R., "we have just as much as we can do and are often obliged to work all night."

I told her that I should like to become acquainted with the true motive of the woman's movement, adding that I considered myself quite ignorant upon the subject.

"Do you not get woman's rights papers?" she asked in a tone of astonishment.

"I do not," I replied. She then kindly made out a list, handing it to me, she said, "Obtain these, read and judge for yourself." I thanked her and bid her good day.

I now read regularly "The Woman's Pacific Coast Journal," edited by Mrs. Carrie Young, "The Pioneer," by Emily Pitt Stevens, and "Woodhull and Claflin's Weekly." In perusing the above ably conducted journals I have gained much useful information and am now convinced that there are thousands of good, true women engaged in this great reform. I know from a painful experience that women have not been properly rewarded for their labor, and thousands of women, older and younger than myself, can testify to this truth. As far as woman's rights go toward elevating woman toward the situation in life her natural gifts and acquired education entitle her, Ladies, I go with you heart and hand.[27]

It would be another two years before Rowena would publicly embrace the Women's Suffrage movement, and when she did so, it was with her usual firm enthusiasm.

I trust that every white woman will respond to its [Suffrage movement's] sentiments in thought, and if they know nothing from personal experience of the purity and charity and nobleness of its object, that they will remember that it is women's efforts to raise women, and give it the benefit of their good wishes at least. And a word to those noble workers for the reform, advancement and elevation of their sister women, let your first great effort be to impress upon the minds of men and convince them that the true woman is man's most faithful, true and firm friend; and that in their efforts to advance the cause of women, she is only a co-worker with good, true and honest men; that she only wishes to place woman in such a position as to become advisor, counselor and sharer in his good work, instead of awaiting dependent upon his pocket. I am convinced that no true wife, mother or sister wishes to deprive her son, husband or brother of one whit of his rights, or power, or greatness. She only asks that a path lay opened by which she can reach and accomplish the great end for which nature has fitted her morally and intellectually.

There is no sensible, honest-hearted man living but what will admit that if intelligence, education, refinement, honesty and industry were the qualifications for suffrage, regardless of sex, that the woman list would far out-number that of men. I do not say this boastfully, for I do honestly and truly believe that if women's lives could be more in confidence and companionship with men, that man instead of becoming her inferior would improve in morals and habits until there would be no place where a respectable man would go that would [not] be equally respectable for women.

Don't get discouraged, ladies, if men do *howl* and *screech* and call names; no great cause was ever won without bitter opposition. It took seven years hard fighting to gain American independence, and no doubt it would have taken seven more if it had not have been for our brave old grandmothers. More than half the glory is due to their generalship, words of advice, consolation and patient endurance.[28]

In this regard she was particularly insulted that the Fifteenth Amendment of the American Constitution granted *all* white men the vote and specifically excluded women: "Which shall have the right of suffrage? The low, vulgar, uneducated hoodlum, the driveling, incoherent drunkard, the barroom, midnight debauchee, the men who stop in their vagrant tramps for thirty days [referring to the requirement of a month's residence to qualify for voting], or the bright, intelligent women, who own their homes and pay taxes—the mothers, wives and sisters of the home circle...."[29]

After the election of 1879 failed to produce the hoped-for enfranchisement of women, the *Argus* remarked: "Women will still be on an equality with Chinamen [*i.e.,* not given the vote]; yes, you need not be proud of your wife, sister or mother, however good, noble and intelligent they may be. The men who are in power now have put them down on a level with the degraded Chinaman. The Portuquee, Negro, the Mexican, the driveling drunkard, the veriest loafer can vote and make laws to govern the high-souled noble mothers of our country. Shame! on our men. Shame! on our fathers, husbands, brothers."[30]

Through the California State Woman Suffrage Association, incorporated on July 27, 1869, Rowena met and formed lifelong friendships with Clara M. Foltz and Laura DeForce Gordon — the first two female lawyers in California; Laura's sister, Gertie DeForce Cluff, who for many years was publisher and editor of the *Valley Review* at Lodi; Maria Hill; Sarah Wallace; Phoebe (Mrs. George) Hearst, and many others. From 1874 on, Rowena attended nearly every State meeting of the Suffrage Association (later California Woman's Suffrage Society).

At a meeting of the Society held in San Francisco on December 14, 1876, Rowena was chosen as a member of the Board of Directors, and Mrs. Gordon was elected President.

In the *History of Woman Suffrage* written in 1886, Rowena was noted as being the most prominent suffrage worker from Merced County: "Merced county, the home of Rowena Granice Steele, the author, and publisher of the *San Joaquin Valley Argus,* has furnished the State with a worthy and capable advocate of woman suffrage, both as a speaker and writer. In her cozy, rose-embowered cottage at Merced, she generously entertains her numerous guests, who always seek out this distinguished and warm-hearted friend of woman."[31]

Even though she toiled in the cause for nearly thirty years, was a highly educated businesswoman who owned property and paid taxes, the sorrow is she never personally benefited by receiving the right to vote in a local, state or national election.

The Railroad Subsidy — The "County Clique" — The Feuds Begin

It wasn't long after the Steeles arrived back in Snelling until the seemingly calm and happy life of the village began to unravel. While Rowena became involved in educational, social and philanthropic activities, R.J. plunged into the political and government arenas, and the deeper he delved the more concerned he became that it manifested the very worst aspects that human nature had to offer — greed, corruption, self-interest — the very opposite of his natural altruistic ideals that mirrored and enhanced Rowena's desire to serve the people around her and to benefit society in general.

Perhaps it all started with the railroad subsidy scandal. It was mid-September 1870 when Mr. William B. Hyde, the "clever [and] genial gentleman" agent of the Central Pacific Railroad Company[32] showed up in town and began talking with the county supervisors, judge, sheriff and other authorities about the need for a subsidy from the people of Merced County as an inducement to ensure the railroad passing through in a timely manner. R.J. immediately "smelled a rat" and set about to investigate for himself the propriety and necessity of the scheme. His stepson, Harry Granice, described what happened in his obituary for R.J. in 1890:

> Mr. Steele was one of the most conscientious of newspapermen and was never known to sacrifice principles for the almighty dollar. In [1870] when the Central Pacific Railroad Company sought to secure a subsidy of $150,000 from Merced County bearing interest at the rate of ten percent per annum, compounded annually, payable in 20 years, he resisted, through the columns of the *San Joaquin Valley Argus*, the voting of the subsidy and defeated the project although the county officials "stood in" with the railroad people. The scheme was killed by his securing from the Secretary of the State's office, which had been recorded there, a copy of an agreement entered into by the Central Pacific Company, the party of the first part, and J. Friedlander, Chapman & Page, Wm. C. Ralston, the Bank of California and other large holders of property in Fresno and Kern Counties, the parties of the second part, whereby the railroad people stipulated and agreed for a certain amount of compensation in land to run their road through the corner of Merced, Fresno and Kern Counties, on or before the spring of 1872, failing in which the Central Pacific was to forfeit a stipulated sum of money—$1,000,000, if we recollect aright.
>
> As the subsidy would have amounted to nearly a million of dollars at the maturity of the bonds

tremendous exertions were made by the company's agents to suppress the publication of the agreement, which would go to prove that the road would be built, subsidy or no subsidy. But old Bob Steele was true to the interests of the taxpayers, and to the personal knowledge of the writer, when he was waited upon and urged for a large monetary consideration to suppress the odious agreement he indignantly spurned the offer and ordered the intruder out of the office. The result was that while he might have made $10,000, or even $20,000 by suppression, the agreement appeared in print the next day, and created such consternation among the advocates of the subsidy that the election, which had been called by published proclamation by the Supervisors, was declared off and never came to a vote.

Merced County got the railroad without one cent of subsidy and was saved nearly $1,000,000 by the timely intervention of Mr. Steele, who was too honest to attain wealth as it is generally attained in these days.[33]

Rowena pointed out later that, by opposing the indebtedness to the railroad and thereby reducing the burden of taxation upon the people, it may have saved the county from almost certain ruin, since it, along with the other expenditures of the county, "would have raised the rates of taxation to a figure so high as to drive capital and enterprise from the county and leave its present beautiful fields a desert."[34]

While R.J. had apparently saved the taxpayers of Merced County upwards of a million dollars, as a negative result he unfortunately generated the enmity of most of the local politicians from that day forward. Chiefly among them were his old

Democrat cronies P.D. Wigginton, Judge James W. Robertson, Sheriff A.J. Meany, and Judge Russ Ward. While Rowena touted the growth and businesses of the growing town and used the society columns of the *Argus* to describe the beautiful gowns worn by the wives of the politicians and businessmen:

> Mrs. Robertson waltzed to perfection, dress of pale lemon tarlatan, deep French flounces beaded, with black velvet, blue silk overskirt trimmed with black lace, which suits her rich olive complexion.... Mrs. Meany, Madonna-like in her appearance, looked sweet in her simple dress of white, black silk over-shirt and bodice; a heavy plait of hair over the forehead gave her face a style of Grecian beauty. Mrs. [Eliza] Ward fully verified the words of the poet, "Beauty unadorned is adored the most," in her rich, but simple attire of white and cherry....[35]

R.J. was weekly exposing their husbands' wrongdoings in the "Items of Local Interest" columns, referring to them often as the "County Clique." Although remaining loyal to the National Democratic party for several more years, he quickly became dis-affected with the local Democrats, and in turn they nominated him for coroner at the new village of Dover. "If elected, we will qualify and serve, and, perhaps our first official act may be to hold an inquest upon the dead body of the Democratic Party," R.J. shot back in the June 17, 1871 issue of the *Argus*.

In the meantime, unrelenting "Progress" was overtaking the little village of Snelling. The "Iron Horse" was approaching, and life would never again be the same for the residents of Merced County.

Chapter VIII

The Railroad Comes to Merced and Snelling is Deserted

On August 26, 1871, R.J. heralded the commencement of the third volume of the *Argus* with plans to enlarge the paper to 32 columns "to keep pace with the increase of population and march of progress and improvement in the San Joaquin Valley." The most important of those improvements was the laying of tracks in Merced County by the Central Pacific Railroad, a subsidiary of the Southern Pacific Railroad. "In a few months at most," R.J. wrote, "the railroad will be completed to the center of this county, which cannot fail to create, or cause to be moved into the county a large amount of property, and bring a great influx of population into the valley."[1]

Due, no doubt, in no small part to the failure of the railroad subsidy proposal, opposition to which was spearheaded by R.J. Steele, the Southern Pacific, through its agent for land acquisition, Charles Henry Huffman, decided on a route away from Snelling directly into the center of the county, through the then small villages of Livingston and Merced, 17 miles southwest. Huffman, now considered to be the "founder" of Merced City, in fact, chose it for his own family home and added many great improvements over the years.

In the fall and winter of 1871-'72 the new town of Merced experienced growth at a dizzying speed, as chronicled by R.J. in January and February 1872:

> THE NEW TOWN.—Merced, the new town on the railroad near the crossing of Bear Creek, we understand is being built up quite rapidly. Mr.

McClenathan, of Modesto, is putting up a large livery stable; McReady & Washburn, of Mariposa, are also erecting a livery stable; the railroad company are erecting a hotel and a depot building, several saloons, two or three eating houses, and two butcher stalls are being put up, all of which are designed to be in readiness for use by the time the sale of lots shall commence. The carpenters and brick masons of this place [Snelling] are all making preparations to move to the new town where they hope to reap a rich harvest the present season. There is no doubt but that Merced will be built up rapidly and in the space of a few months become a large inland town, eclipsing any town now in this section of the State.[2]

THE TOWN OF MERCED.—We were at the new town of Merced on Monday last, and found all astir, every one being busily engaged in building and preparing for the great day to come, Thursday next, when the sale of lots is to take place. The Railroad company having a temporary hotel in operation, and Mr. Charles S. Evans has a restaurant and lodging house, those being the only houses of entertainment at that time open in the place. Messrs. Washburn and McCready were erecting sheds to serve as a livery stable, and Mr. McClenathan, of Modesto, was also putting up at a rapid rate. George Powell, Esq., who used to handle the ribbons so cleverly and make regular trips from Hornitos to Modesto, has opened a neat drinking saloon, and appeared to be master of the situation. An enterprising man has started a meat market, and we were informed that A.M. Hicks would also open a meat market in the place in the course of the week. Besides the buildings above mentioned there were a number of tents and board sheds, put up for the accommodation of carpenters, and other work men, giving the place very much the appearance of new mining camps in early days. The site of the new town is a beautiful level plain, though rather low for wet weather, and when the place is built up with permanent buildings, will make a sightly town, and convenient of access for a great extent of country surrounding it. The land in the immediate vicinity of the town is of the richest quality, making it one of the most desirable places to locate that we know of in the valley. The place is also within a few miles of the geographical center of the county, and already the question of removal of the county seat is being discussed "pro and con" by the people of all sections of the county. It is certainly a handsome site for a town, and when built up and properly established will be entitled to lay claims to become the seat of justice of our prosperous county. We hope, however, that proper time will be given for preparation to be made for so important an event, and that it may not be accomplished before proper arrangements are made for the accommodation of those who might be called there to transact business or attend upon the courts. Here we have a good courthouse, good hotels and livery stables, and everything requisite to make visitors comfortable; therefore, it would not be well to make hurried arrangements for removal, but wait until a court-house and offices can be prepared before it is accomplished. Railroads build up a country through which they are extended, and they likewise revolutionize and change the current of business affairs, breaking down old established towns and building up new ones, and we have no expectation of an exception being made in our case only insofar as the country surrounding Snelling being capable of supporting and maintaining a large local trade which cannot be diverted from it, and which will increase and become more and more important year after year.[3]

MERCED.—Buildings at the new town of Merced are springing up as if by magic. Since the sale of lots, two weeks ago, some fifteen or twenty buildings have been started, some of which are rapidly approaching completion, and yet we hear of a number of others to be commenced as soon as workmen and materials can be obtained. The basement of a large hotel— being erected by the railroad company—is going up rapidly, and in the course of three months the town will be able to boast of one of the largest and finest hotels in the southern part of the State. We are informed that it is to be a four-story building—the basement of brick—and when finished to contain one hundred and seventy-five rooms. As Merced is to be the terminus of railroad travel for Yosemite tourists, a large, well-furnished hotel will be necessary for their accommodation, and the railroad company is not inclined to permit them to lack for suitable accommodations at so important a point on the line of travel.[4]

As R.J. pointed out in January, there had already been a mass exodus from Snelling to Merced during that fall and winter. Rowena was away in San Francisco from September to November 1871, and lamented the dwindling population of her beloved town in her absence in her "Home Correspondence" from Vacuna on January 11, 1872.

Ten years ago Snelling was an unpretending little burg, containing within its limits a neat, substantial court house and jail combined, enclosed within a plain, board fence; two stores—small, wooden structures—where the customer could purchase on credit or for cash everything required for family use; one hotel, two saloons, one livery stable, one blacksmith shop, one or two wheelwright establishments, and one printing office. At that period the men, women and children dressed plainly. On Sunday when there was preaching at the court house, more than half the ladies appeared in sun-bonnets, shakers, or just a green veil thrown over their plainly arranged hair. The children who attended the little schoolhouse were all clean, but exceedingly plain in their attire. The balls and parties were then pleasant, social reunions; the most aristocratic venturing on nothing more costly than delaines, lawns or tarlatans, the latter material sometimes so sweetly and simply trimmed as to cause the youthful wearers to look like young angels. Several bright, joyous, young faces come up before me as I write. People slept with their doors unfastened or left them merely latched when going off on a visit. There was no diamonds, gold or silver ware. No point lace or costly furs to tempt or reward the burglar.

There are many happy memories connected with those quiet, unpretending days. But what a change has come over the reality of those days now, gone, never, never to return. Gone, as some of the dear faces and familiar voices have passed into the vast eternity never more to mingle with us, or share with

us their love, affection, friendship or esteem upon
this side of the grave.

* * *

It has ended, so far as Snelling is concerned. She
has lost the prop which buoyed up her false pride
and insane career. The channel through which the
public money passed, casting fortunes at the feet of
some of her citizens—the county seat—has gone to
make new victims—gone to dazzle a few more
parents into the idea of educating their children into
the ways of idleness, and make them scorn honest
industry; teach their boys to treat with coldness and
disrespect the boys who are independent enough to
earn a living by daily toil, and their daughters to turn
up their noses at the girls who wash dishes, and make
mothers' work light.

Good, thrifty, honest people who are not afraid of
labor, and who wish to see their sons and daughters
grow up men and women of which America will be
proud, can say goodbye to it without a sigh of regret,
for taxpayers of Snelling and vicinity have had no
control over the exorbitant demands of public
servants, even while the business of the county was
transacted before their eyes. So it can make no
difference on that point, and henceforth, instead of
depending upon a floating population, those who
make up their minds to remain and share the future
fortunes of Snelling must honestly and patiently labor
to carve out an independence, and I predict for the
men and women who possess the spirit to do so a
bright, successful and pleasant future.

Of particular interest is an article in February where
Rowena described the social scene in January 1872 as "the gayest
ever known at Snelling. It has passed off in one round of pleasure:

Balls, parties, routs, dinners, suppers, candy-pulling, kissing bees, cards and games. There has been but little sickness, no deaths, no heartaches, no poverty in this home of plenty, *although your humble correspondent has lived in the little end and looked on while rich neighbors reveled in music and the dance* [emphasis added]."[5] It seems the isolation and shunning of the Steeles from Snelling society as a result of the railroad subsidy controversy and other political squabbles had begun. Rowena, who rarely delved into politics, tried valiantly to stay above the fray (indeed, in September 1872 expressed her "disgust for everything connected with politics"), at the same time suffered constant personal affronts and disrespectful treatment from many sides.

By March 1872 the Steeles were resigned to the fact that they needed to have a major presence in Merced town if they were to remain viable as the foremost newspaper family in the County. It was decided that Harry, who had spent the last year in San Francisco studying at the Pacific Business College, would open the *Merced People*. "Though young in years, the editor and publisher of this new candidate for public favor has had some ten years' experience in the printing business, and is well qualified to conduct a paper such as he proposes to make the *Merced People*."[6] In the inaugural issue, Harry specifically claimed the new paper's independence. "Politically, we have neither friends to reward nor enemies to punish.... This paper will be the champion of the people—not the organ of a clique."[7]

Throughout 1870-'72, in addition to her weekly columns by Vacuna, Rowena continued pouring out several short stories, including "A Leaf From Memory," about a tailoress in early 1800s New York City (January 23, 1871); "The Little Gold Cross, a Christmas Story" (December 23, 1871); "Hazelton Kent's Bride," relating the sad life of an orphaned boy from a family brought to financial ruin (January 20, 1872); "Poor Joe, Or, The Secret Disclosed," a tale of tragic love (May 18, 1872); "Eudolia Dudley; Or, Never too Late," the story of an orphan who finds her siblings and true love (September 21, 1872); "Kitty Lynn," about a young man's great love for and attachment to his mother (October 16, 1872).

In addition, there are numerous articles promoting schools, education and exhorting the well-to-do to offer scholarships to the unfortunate, and Rowena was ever watchful of the social problems and human conditions of the day. In August 1872, for example, she took up the cause of humane treatment of the insane, noting:

> [B]ut oh! saddest of all are the cases of the unfortunate insane, who are transferred from their homes to the city prison. Is insanity a crime, that the name of the poor victim should be associated with the repulsive title of prison? Could there not be some small, cheap structure erected and called the hospital for the insane where such could be received and cared for until after the examination had taken place? Only to think of a respectable lady; a wife and mother, being dragged, as it were, to a loathsome cell, and there, amid the demoniac curses of the drunkard, the thief, the wanton and scum of a large city, giving birth to a tender babe, putting the brand upon its innocent brow of being born in a prison. I refer to the following article which appeared in the California Republican of Saturday, August 10th:
>
>> A SAD CASE.—Mrs. Charlotte Blank was today adjudged to be committed to the Insane Asylum at Stockton by the proper authorities. The unfortunate woman was confined this morning in the City Prison, and her ravings were of the most heart-rending description. She was seized with an affection of the brain last

> week while attending on her sick
> family, and now imagines that her
> child has been torn to pieces and
> thrown in a cellar, and that her
> husband's eyes have been torn out.
> This case is one of the saddest which
> has ever come under our observation.

Oh, ye women of San Francisco! why, amid all your charity have you failed to look into this branch of inhumanity? Is it too small an affair for your ambition? Do you only deal in large and costly structures and spacious grounds? ... I am too poor to contribute my mite towards the erection of a place of reception for the insane, I must hope and trust some, as sympathetic as myself, and blessed with a goodly share of wealth will move in the matter.[8]

The County Printing Contract

In December 1872, the rift between R.J. Steele and the "County Clique" was further accelerated and exacerbated when the County Supervisors, consisting of Silas March, Capt. John K. Mears, and Ion Simons, voted down two-to-one (March voting no) a motion to thereafter award the County printing contract to the lowest bidder. In a particularly scathing article, wherein R.J. compares the governance of the County officers to "the management of the affairs of the City of New York by the Tammany Ring — or "Tammany Thieves," R.J. goes on to further excoriate the "corruption":

> We are informed that, when this motion was made, James W. Robertson, County Judge of Merced county, arose and objected to the passage of the motion and offered as reasons therefore that the ARGUS would obtain the contract and that that would

be as bad as giving the public printing of the county to a Republican paper, and stated that Steele had voted for Booth for Governor and also for Grant for President. Although Judge Robertson had no possible means of knowing how we voted upon either occasion, and made his statements regardless of truth, for the sole purpose of preventing honest action by the Board, whereby we would have an opportunity to bid for the county printing, we do not propose to make that a point in our remarks upon the subject at this time, but will come to the principles which seem to be the governing motives which rule county officers in managing the affairs of the county and which seem to be a counterpart of those which governed the management of the affairs of the City of New York by the Tammany Ring — or Tammany Thieves, as that sweet-scented set of officials are called since the people took the affairs of the city in their own hands and exposed the wholesale swindles and thefts of Boss Tweed and company. And here we desire to ask the taxpayers of Merced county a few questions: Is it the duty of an officer of the county to conduct the affairs of the county in the interest of a party or the corrupt clique now holding power here, or would capable, faithful and honest officers conduct the affairs of the county in a manner conducive to the best interests of the whole people, regardless of political bias or partisan predilections? Would not the people regard an officer as a scoundrel and a swindler who would give a Democrat a contract for furnishing wood for the use of the county offices at $10.00 per cord in preference to a Republican who offered as good or a better article at $5.00 per cord? And, was not the argument of Judge Robertson based upon the principle that "to the victors belong the spoils" and that a newspaper belonging to and the slave of the corrupt Ring should have the county printing, even though it cost the taxpayers twice or thrice what the ARGUS has ever charged or would now do the same service for? And, further, does it not appear that the argument of the corrupt partisan judge, who descended from the dignity that ought to attach to the station to become the attorney of a rascally Ring was sufficient to govern the action of a majority of the Board, namely Mears and Simons in their vote upon the motion?

It seems the established rule of the Board of Supervisors as it is now constituted, and in accordance with the advice of the County Judge, that none but members of the Clique shall be permitted to compete for contracts to perform work for the county, especially a newspaper printer or publisher. Will the taxpayers of Merced county continue to submit to such outrages by officials who seem to have no regard whatever for the obligations which they took upon themselves upon assuming office? If so, what has become of those boasted principles of independence and love of fair and honest dealing which heretofore were supposed to be implanted in the bosoms of American freeman?

Can any Republican or Democratic taxpayers, not a member of the Ring, consider his interests safe when controlled by such principles as seem to have actuated Judge Robertson and Supervisors Mears and Simons in opposing the motion of Supervisor March to let the contract to do the county printing to the lowest bidder? We think not![9]

The printing contract was eventually awarded to "the Clique organ," the *Merced Tribune* edited by Edward Madden.

> There is no denying the fact that the county printing for the past six months has cost more than it has ever cost to do the same service for an entire year at any other period in the history of the county, and if the work had been honestly let out by contract to the lowest bidder, it would have been done for a great deal less money than was charged by the Clique organ and paid for by order of the Board of Supervisors.
>
> We know that those wicked men and unfaithful officers will attempt to create sympathy in the minds of the people by pleading that we write in regard to them in a spirit of persecution. But the people should remember that these officers refuse to let investigation take place by failing to call a grand jury from term to term, notwithstanding crimes are known to have been committed in the county, and men accused of crime have been committed to jail to await the action of the grand jury. Let there be a grand jury called and investigation take place.[10]

Move to Merced

In the summer and fall of 1872, talk began in earnest to move the County seat to Merced. The vote was held on December 12, 1872, with the final tally going to Merced by 566 votes, Livingston receiving 236, and Snelling 181. R.J. was disparaging of the outcome and blamed the overwhelming vote on the idea that "many residents of this county are not in possession of the facts necessary to form a correct and satisfactory conclusion in regard to this result."[11] He proceeded to lay out those facts as he saw them:

It is charged that this result is due solely to railroad influence. The railroad company laid out the town of Merced, and owning the surrounding property and a part of the town, undoubtedly caused the members of the company to feel a lively interest in its prosperity, and used their influence for its advancement. But a careful examination of the recent vote with previous ones, and the vote of the whole county considered, clearly shows that colonization had but little to do with the result. There were other and more potent influences than railroad in producing this result, which we will now suggest.

It has long been known that a clique existed here which controlled the affairs of the county and controlled them to the exclusive advantage of such clique. As an evidence of this, Mr. Kendrick was appointed jailor, with a salary of one hundred dollars per month, and notwithstanding the large salary for work not worth one quarter of the amount, prisoners escaped whenever they found it to their advantage to do so, and other prisoners sent to jail as a punishment, or for security, were allowed to roam about the court house yard at their own pleasure, though the people had to pay an extra hundred dollars per month for their care and attention.

The District Attorney had the collection of delinquent taxes, yet he has never reported the amount he has collected, although the law expressly requires him to do so; and although such a thing is a fact which the Board of Supervisors ought to discover in the discharge of their official duty, yet they ignore this official neglect, if not malfeasance, in office. * * *

Again, the law expressly provides that the Clerk of
the Board shall receive two hundred and fifty dollars
a year in full payment for his services as Clerk of
such Board. Yet in open defiance of this law the
Board of Supervisors allowed Mr. Hicks, their Clerk,
one hundred dollars per month, twelve hundred
dollars per year, and that he should draw such salary
from the beginning of his present term.

All jobs of building, repairing or other work for the
county were let at prices greatly above the value of
such work, and, let to none but clique members or
favorites.

The ARGUS always denounced such abuse of power
and squandering of the people's money. This course
did not suit those who were living so sumptuously
off the people's money and so they started a paper of
their own, at Merced, and used all the means in their
power to break this paper down and foster that one.
The Board of Supervisors, prompted by Judge
Robertson and other members of the Clique, refused
to let the county printing to the lowest bidder, and
gave it to the clique organ at exorbitant rates in order
to make that paper live and kill the ARGUS.

Now, in our opinion, all these facts, and more
which we shall give hereafter, caused the people to
believe that there was an unscrupulous nest in
Snelling living and luxuriating on the people's money
and that the hopes of breaking up this nest by a
removal of the county seat was a leading cause of
Snelling receiving such a small part of the popular
vote in the late election.[12]

With no other option before them to ensure the viability of the
paper, the decision was made, and in the same issue, R.J. declared
the impending removal of the *San Joaquin Valley Argus* to

Merced. He promised the paper would continue to improve, grow and prosper in the new surroundings.

> In future, as in the past, the course of the paper will be *fearlessly independent* in the expression of *truth*, condemning the actions of evildoers, regardless of their power and influence, and praising, whenever praise is due, however humble the object whom we may deem deserving of encomiums in its columns. Politically, no change has taken place in the sentiments and opinions of the editor, and none may be expected; therefore, demagogues and political charlatans — the agents and advocates of corrupt rings and cliques — will in the future, as in the past, receive no favors from the paper, and may be expected to continue to make war upon it, in the hope of curtailing its influence and limiting its usefulness. While it will not be the organ of any party, clique, ring, or sect, it will continue to be a disseminator of general and local news, devoted to the true interests of the section of the State in which it is located.[13]

The final move was announced on March 8, 1873, to happen "as soon as the road from here to Merced becomes passable for loaded teams." It was completed sometime before April 1, 1873, when R.J. wrote that the office was "now located in the town of Merced, and we hope in the new location to be able to present to our patrons a better paper, containing a greater variety of interesting local news than was ever before possible."[14] This move absorbed the short-lived *Merced People*, and Harry went back to work on the *Argus*.

In unabated fury, R.J. immediately began railing, in column after column over the ensuing months, against local politicians ("Men filled with trickery such as has ruled in Merced for the past few years...") and the political Clique, complaining about such issues as "illegal conduct of business by the Board of Supervisors, fraudulent contracts, misappropriation of county funds, illegal salaries and perquisites, unethical and illegal awarding of County printing contract, without bid, to the *Tribune*—the "Clique-owned organ." Madden, of the *Tribune*, responded: "[I]t is ... the height of impudence for that journalistic sneak, Bob Steele, to ask the people of the town he so deliberately slandered to support his dirty sheet."[15] Thus began the almost weekly constant barrage of vitriol between the two newspaper editors that would become increasingly personal and vicious over the next eighteen months.

On the domestic side, Rowena chronicled the move in her Home Correspondence of April 1, 1873:

> MERCED, April 1st, 1873.
> MR. EDITOR:—Surely no timid tabby of the feline race ever felt more forcibly the truth of the quaint, old-fashioned adage of "feeling like a cat in a strange garret" than does your tired, weary, bone-aching correspondent. The reality of climbing up stairs and bumping one's head against the rafters destroys all the romance of "Dear old garret, and rain on the roof." But, then, you know, anything to live in a city, especially this inland, un-watered city. I have been singing unconsciously all the morning little snatches of songs such as "Oh give me a cot in the valley I love," but no liberal customer has yet proffered the generous gift. I suppose they are waiting to see whether I really mean it or not. A smiling, pleasant individual said to me a few moments ago: "Permit me to give you a fine lot—I started and stared, and was about to throw my arms about his neck and kiss

him for his mother, when the wretch continued —
"of vegetables." Of course, I didn't feel cheap, nor
streaked, nor like running him off with a broomstick.
I smiled and thanked him and accepted the trash just
as though vegetables were the height of my ambition,
while a tear of regret glistened in my eye as I
pondered upon the benevolence of mankind in
general and vegetable men in particular. But laying all
frivolity aside, I must confess that I feel a trifle
homesick with no trees, no birds, and no flowers. I
miss the little white, the brown, and the cream-
colored cottages, and the pleasant, familiar voices
which greeted me daily from their open doors. But
experience has taught me that we cannot always
linger with the friends and amid the scenes that are
dear to us. Comparatively few in this great, stirring
world spend and end their days in their natal place.
We are all the creatures of circumstances, but much
of our happiness depends upon being reconciled to
fate and looking upon the bright side. To my hopeful
heart, even in this sky parlor, a pretty little cottage, a
flower garden, shade trees with merry sunshine
peeping in and out subject to the gentle zephyrs, a
bay window with hanging baskets, all in the proper
time, gives me a sweet contentment and pleasure
almost equal to the reality.

"I'll gather roses while I lay," and bask in the
sunshine of bright anticipation, hoping to win friends
here in my new home who will cheer and encourage
me in the hour of misfortune and who will enjoy
with me the bright golden joyous days of prosperity.
As home correspondent, I shall consider it a pleasant
duty to give good and pleasing reports of public
gatherings, speak kindly and encouragingly of the

schools and their teachers. I shall, as I have done for
the last twenty years, scrupulously avoid wounding
the feelings of each and every one. If I have nothing
good and agreeable to say, I'll wait for the next train
(of thoughts). In a word, the readers of the Argus will
ever find a friend in   VACUNA.[16]

Rowena continued writing her weekly columns about the weather
(good and bad), local social events (balls, parties, church festivals,
theatrical events, holiday celebrations, picnics in the countryside),
her travels around the county visiting towns and ranches and to the
northern parts of the state giving lectures and readings on
Temperance, and especially announcing and promoting businesses—dry goods stores, millinery and dressmaking shops,
hairdressing saloons, perfumeries and cosmetics, jewelry stores,
shoe shops and booteries. Particularly favored among these was
Mrs. Kate Keogh's new lunch room.

New Refreshment Saloon

17th Street Between K & L.

Mrs. **KATE KEOGH** BEGS LEAVE TO inform the ladies and
gentlemen of Merced and vicinity that she has opened a
Lunch Room
at the above-named place and is prepared to serve most excellent
lunches at all hours on the most Reasonable Terms. Visitors from
the country will find this a quiet place to rest and refresh themselves
with any or all of the following delicacies:
Cakes, Pies, Jellies, and Confectionery,
Coffee, Oysters, Oranges, Tea,
Cold Ham, Lemons, Chocolate,
Bologna Sausage, Pine Apples,
Fresh Rolls, Headcheese, Bananas,

Twist Bread, Pickled Tongue, Ice Cream,
Graham Bread, Corned Beef, Soda Water,
French Crackers, Smoked Beef, Lemonade.
ICE CREAM
Every day and evening during the Summer

———

To the Ladies:
*A FULL ASSORTMENT of CHOICE LADIES TOILET
AND FANCY ARTICLES.*
Merced, April 27th, 1873.

Kate, widow of Richard Keogh, and her children Katie, Edgar and Austin were next-door neighbors to the Steeles on 17th Street, where the family lived in a garret above the printing office for some time. Rowena probably favored Mrs. Keogh because Harry was "sweet on" young Katie. (The two eventually married on 4 May 1879, at the Catholic rectory in San Francisco.) Following Rowena's endorsement, Mrs. Keogh's business increased rapidly, and in July 1873 she moved to a new location at the corner of Front and M Streets, renaming the lunch room as the Delmonico. In October 1873, Kate moved the Delmonico to the upper end of Front Street, nearly opposite the freight depot. By 1874, Kate had apparently given up the restaurant business and was making and selling ice cream from her new home on 19th street. In November 1874, she began offering her services as a nurse for "invalid ladies, either by the week or the month."

Taking up a new cause, in May 1873, Rowena wrote lamenting the poor treatment received by many former prostitutes and advocating for forgiveness, mercy and acceptance into "polite society."

A Hard Case.—A poor erring 'Magdalen', a resident of Virginia City, who has been trying hard to atone for her past errors by present good conduct, was last week excluded from a ballroom in Virginia City, to which she had been admitted in company with her husband. The poor girl took the affair so much to heart that she has been seriously ill ever since, and yesterday her life was despaired of.—*Gold Hill* [Nevada] *News, May 5th*.

The above is not an isolated case. This turning out of ballrooms poor, unfortunate, friendless women has been practiced, particularly in California, for many years by coarse, vulgar, promiscuous crowds which have assembled from time to time in towns, villages and cities. How frail then and uncertain must be the reputation of the man or woman who can be contaminated by one unfortunate, especially one who has repented of the errors of her former life and is striving to rise above the hateful past. No true lady, with pure, refined mind, need fear contamination, nor do they. Thousands of noble, virtuous women in great cities all over the civilized world visit daily the haunts of vice and impurity, and try by kind words and their own pure presence to win the unfortunate from sin and folly. The most pernicious weed cannot rob the sweet, pure rose of one jot of its fragrance. The modest little violet loses none of its natural redolence by close proximity to the most offensive plant or herb. Neither does the lichen detract one iota from the flowery beauty of the kalmia. What think you, gentle reader, would have been the effect upon a portion of the inmates of that ballroom had the recording angel who keeps a record of all the deeds done in the past have appeared among them and in a voice loud and clear bid them, "Hold! hold! while I read to you every act of your lives." Think you that there would not have been some shrinking, some heart-trembling, some efforts made to escape the dreadful revelations? In nine cases out of ten the very ones who are the most loud and urgent in their accusations would be the first to shrink from the recording messenger. To the young and inexperienced who may by association be led into this error we would say that purity and genteel breeding need not fear contamination.[17]

This article may have been the creative seed for Rowena's novel published in 1874, *Dell Dart; Or, Within the Meshes*, which provided the basis for Madden's "fatal slander."

She also espoused the ideals of amity and accord, at least among the religious groups in Merced. In July 1873, when the two main churches in Merced—Catholic and Methodist-Episcopal—chose to hold festivals on the same day, there appeared to Rowena to be a "pernicious spirit" of discontent and feelings of opposition among some in town.

"What an idea," I soliloquized when left alone, "that two Christian denominations cannot each get up a festival in the same town, in the same year, without this contemptible little spirit of envy creeping in with its poisonous fangs, and by throwing a little insinuation here, and a hateful innuendo there, and a shoulder shrug or two thrown in to strengthen the doubt, if any remains." Why is it that people cannot take a sensible view of these things and argue something after this manner: "It takes all kinds of people to make a world," said the quaint old adage. We find in these modern times that it takes a few sorts to make up a town—different people with different tastes, habits, and each and all clinging, more or less to early associations, especially to early religious teachings which grew with their growth. Two denominations in our town have each succeeded in erecting a house of worship, much to their credit be it said, and they both require means to furnish such things as are necessary to their convenience and the public comfort and accommodation.... You all have my best wishes for your success, and what is in my humble power to do, I shall do regardless of sect, for I have good, warm, true friends among you both and know that it is your right to enjoy your religious views unmolested.[18]

Sadly, it is doubtful these feelings of acceptance and camaraderie would have been extended to Merced residents of other races or non-Christian religions, but it is an indication of Rowena's more liberal leanings at least to the Caucasian, Christian residents.

In September 1873, Rowena published "Blue-Eyed Mary; Or, The Heart's Sacrifice," about James M. Brown and the work of the Lodge of Good Templars. She then embarked on six months of travel around the state to call on newspaper offices, visit Temperance groups, inspect schools, and give lectures in churches and hotels, reporting her adventures every week in the Home Correspondence column. Some of the places she visited from Fall 1873 through Summer 1874 were Borden Station (Alabama Settlement), Tulare, Visalia, Portersville, Plano, Turlock, Oakland (twice), San Francisco (three times, including the Woman's Suffrage Convention in July 1874), San Jose, Vallejo, Bridgeport (formerly Cordelia), Suisun, Denverton, Calistoga, St. Helena, Dixon (Solano County), Livermore, Hayward, Stockton, Lodi, Galt, Sacramento, Roseville, Auburn, Colfax, and Truckee, an amazing itinerary considering all of the travel to outlying towns had to be done by stagecoach, wagon, carriage or horseback. These articles are so numerous and so thorough, giving names of many people she met along the way and glimpses into the history of 19th century California settlements, they are worthy of their own separate volume.

In one of these columns, in January 1874, Rowena put forth her idea for a "House for the Stranger"—a public reception and reading room—to be an alternative for young men to the bars and saloons that provided the only entertainment for them in most towns. She wrote that, "I thought what a good chance there was for me to immortalize myself if I were only a millionaire, by erecting a neat, substantial building."

It should be one story high, and above the door on a marble slab the words: House for the Stranger. The interior I would have laid off in four large rooms, with a broad hall in the center, on one side the front and back rooms should communicate with sliding doors, to be used in case of necessity for weddings, funerals, or the reception of distinguished strangers. The front room on the opposite side to be set apart for a library and reading room, furnished with desks and all kinds of writing material; the walls on one side filled with maps. The room next to the library to be used for a gentleman's sitting room, where they could smoke and talk of business. The two first-mentioned rooms to be used as sitting rooms for both ladies and gentlemen of the neighborhood where they could meet and spend an hour in pleasant chat, read newspapers or a book, and get the current news. All parts of the house accessible to strangers who might be passing through, where they might feel themselves properly at home. I would have a bulletin board so that young men or anyone looking for employment could post their notices, families or merchants wishing help could also notify the public through this medium.[19]

She encouraged the ladies of Merced to consider such a project:

> Oh, what a good field is here spread out before the ladies of this town, one from which they may reap a rich harvest in the satisfaction of doing so great, so good, so noble a work. Such an establishment would no doubt in ten years save hundreds of young men from a drunkard's life, and be the means of reforming many who now feel themselves without the pale of good society who would here be a welcome visitor with nothing to pay but his respects to those with whom he met.[20]

This was more than a decade before Scottish-American millionaire philanthropist Andrew Carnegie began building and donating libraries in cities and towns all around the country. We would like to think "a little birdy" planted Rowena's inspiration in his ear.

The Feud Intensifies Dramatically

During all of these months away Rowena was, presumably, unaware of the seriousness of the feud between her husband and Edward Madden, although she was probably sent copies of the *Argus* and kept up with R.J.'s political positions and campaigns, including the "in-your-face" gloating at the Clique and its newspaper, Madden's *Herald*, upon the election of Alexander Deering the *Argus*-approved People's Party candidate for Judge of the 13th District (Mariposa, Tulare, Fresno and Merced Counties). "HURRAH!" the *Argus* trumpets. "Deering's Majority in the District at Least 600!" "The Clique Repudiated!" "[Judge]

Robertson and Madden very mad!" "The County Judge on the Rampage!" "Cliquers Wearing Long Faces!"

> [B]y repeated potations during the day and evening—
> for drowning sorrow, we suppose—the judge
> [Robertson] succeeded in getting on a big-sized mad,
> and indulged in curses loud and deep of Steele and all
> who have had anything to do with the People's Party.
> Madden, the tool of the Clique, whose name is
> placed at the head of the Tribune as a blind to hide
> the real authorship of the disgraceful falsehoods that
> make up the sum and substance of the information
> contained in its columns, got greatly enthused, and in
> a loud tone of voice threatened to proclaim to the
> world that it was a Republican victory, while the
> imps, bottle-holders, and noisy men whose business
> has been for years to ring the changes in the policy of
> their leaders, stood in mute wonderment at the rage
> of their leaders, who had lost all control over their
> passions and prejudices....[21]

R.J. somewhat gleefully reported, as well, the messes and criminal scrapes the county officers and Madden got into. Madden was arrested on at least two occasions for misdemeanors in 1873-'74 and he, along with Robertson, Ward, Meany and others had a serious incident during their personal July 4th celebration in 1874:

TOO MUCH SIN.

> Last Saturday being the glorious Fourth of July, the
> natal day of American Independence, must
> necessarily be celebrated in a great variety of ways in
> order to do full honor to the occasion. Among other
> methods some distinguished individuals of this place

must necessarily have a blow out and show their patriotism. So coaches of four and six were obtained. Charley Peck, one of the proprietors of the new stage line, furnished the coaches and horses, had been driven down to the El Capitan Hotel where Charley Peck, Judge Robertson, Russ Ward, Jim Hicks, A.J. Meany, Ed. Madden, all loyal members of the Clique, and some other sympathizing friends jumped aboard and struck out for Plainsburg. How many drinks the party took there we do not know, but at any rate some say that many of them raised their own spirits very high, and tried to raise the spirits of the horses to a corresponding pitch by the lash, and that in consequence some of the horses were killed. That the horses were killed by the trip we think is so, but we don't think it was the whiskey or the lash that did it, but it was the immense pile of sin they had to draw on that hot day that caused them to let down. We don't know how many of the horses died, but heard of two or three horse funerals on Sunday.[22]

In July 1874, a grand jury impaneled to look into the charges of corruption and malfeasance in office by the County Supervisors, Silas March, Ion Simons and John K. Mears, that R.J. had been complaining about for years, brought an indictment, and a trial was set for August 13. At trial, the Supervisors were adjudged not guilty. March immediately resigned, and J.B. Cocanour, a favorite of the Clique, was elected to replace him. "The Clique is consequently jubilant over the result and the faithful have swallowed an enormous amount of bad whiskey."[23] Madden in the *Tribune* takes potshots at District Attorney D.M. McKenney, calling him a "pet of the ARGUS, "a lamentable failure" as District Attorney; "he has been tried and found wanting." R.J. shoots back that "Madden is not a judge of the qualifications of lawyers" and that the *Tribune* article about McKenney "was probably dictated by a 'pet' of the Tribune—a shyster, jealous of lawyers of recognized ability...." He calls the *Tribune* article "slanderous" and attributes it to "the malevolence of Madden, the Clique, and the shyster who probably dictated it." To the contrary, R.J. states, McKenney has "proved both honest and efficient. He has had the backbone to protest [the alleged corruption] and to stick to his protest. Accusations against County officers are the result."[24]

ON THE RAMPAGE.

The *Tribune* was furious last week, having gone clean daft over the verdict rendered by the jury in the case of "The People vs. the Board of Supervisors," in which the jury "agreed to give the verdict," "Not Guilty," and let off a large amount of bile and spite against the District Attorney and the Argus, replete with falsehoods and devoid of sense and decency, the editor being apparently ambitious to distinguish himself as a blackguard and subservient tool of a very dirty clique of dishonest and unprincipled men. While the Argus' columns were filled with *the facts* bearing upon the case, all of which are now on record and part of the public history of Merced county, the columns of the *Tribune* were filled with vituperative falsehoods that were as foolish as they were false, proving the utterer to be totally destitute of decency, honor, or common sense, and worthy to mingle only with the lower orders of creation, such as the monkey, the gorilla and the Hottentot of Africa. Being totally destitute of decency and human instincts, the *Tribune* managers seek only to bring others *down* to their own level, and hence the language of that sheet is characteristic of the low bar-room loafers and other worthless, wicked, dissolute characters. But the *Tribune* is a worthy representtative of the conspirators whose speculations have been somewhat interfered with by the ARGUS calling the attention of the people to them, until a Grand Jury composed of honest and intelligent citizens, advised by an honest District Attorney, brought true accusations against the conspirators and put a check upon their evil deeds, reducing the amount of spoils and convincing the spoilsmen that a continuance of their unlawful acts might soon deprive them of their official positions, if not deprive them of their personal liberty.[25]

Like night and day, in stark contrast to the political maelstrom that R.J. was weekly stirring up in the *Argus*, Rowena continued to post columns about her travels, visiting area schools, literary unions, visiting lecturers, new buildings, businesses, mills and manufactories in the County. Prominent among these articles was a particularly descriptive report on the Catholic Church's fall fundraising festival:

A GRAND SUCCESS.

——————

REPORTED BY MRS. R.G. STEELE.

The fair, festival and ball gotten up by the ladies of the Catholic Church of Merced have passed away, and are now among the things that have been. They proved a success far beyond the anticipations of the most hopeful.

THE FAIR.

opened on Saturday morning at ten o'clock and was thinly attended during the day, but when the lights were lit and the fine brass band sent forth its music in soul awakening strains, an enthusiastic crowd began to gather, and at eight o'clock Washington Hall was filled with bright eyes, smiling faces and merry voices which rose above the instrumental music. The ladies were at their respective stands looking amiably determined, a band of Amazons armed and equipped with piercing daggers made up of sweet smiles and nimble tongues. The table at which Miss Sarah Morton presided was a whole bazaar in itself, containing scores of fancy and useful articles, many of which were designed and finished by her own intelligent head and fair, white hands. Several pretty pieces of delicate leaf and framework contributed by Mrs. Ames added much to the beauty and variety displayed at this table. Next in beauty and interest was the table presided over by Mrs. C.C. Smith and Mrs. C.E. Fleming. Some of the articles upon this table were magnificent, and the large number of parlor and bedroom ornaments showed that the ladies must have been industriously engaged for many weeks. Mrs. Kate Keogh, the genius of the ice cream stand, drew a constant crowd about her, and by the jingling of glasses, spoons and coin one would naturally judge that it was a good night for ice cream. Mrs. M.A. Stanton was actively engaged in the piscatorial sports, and by the constant shouts of jovial laughter it was evident that those who patronized her cast their lines in pleasant places. Droves of young sports followed the grab bag and staked their quarters quite reckless of the consequences. Several ladies engaged in selling tickets for the ball and supper, and many others soliciting purchasers for the raffling of a variety of articles, which would take place on the following Monday [*sic*, Tuesday] evening. Father McNamara looked on the

busy scene and smiled approvingly at the grand
success. At ten o'clock the lights were extinguished
and the hall was closed.

FAIR CONTINUED.

On Monday morning the managers were again
actively engaged and continued to entertain visitors
throughout the entire day, and as daylight faded and
the sun sank out of sight, the lamps were relit, the
music began its discourse of sweet and heavenly
strains in national airs complimentary to Old Ireland
and Young America. There was a perfect rush of
youth and beauty—

> "And fairy forms, now here, now there,
> Hovered like children in the air."

For a while these pleasure seekers submitted to the
trade and traffic in the light, fancy wares and
patronized the different stands quite liberally. But it
was decided that the music was too sweet to be lost
altogether upon the ear. The tables and other
obstacles were hastily put aside, the hall put in proper
shape and the music struck up afresh,

> "Soft eyes looked love
> To eyes that spoke again."

And at the signal hundreds of manly forms and fairy-
like figures were whirling in the intricate mazes of the
infatuating dance. Simplicity seemed to preside on
this particular occasion, both in custom and manners.

> "The butcher, the baker,
> And the jolly shoemaker,
> The lawyer, the doctor
> And fat millionaire,
> Danced with Rosie and Lizzy
> Till all heads grew dizzy,
> On the night of the Catholic Fair.

THE SUPPER.

At twelve o'clock supper was announced. And permit us to ask right here, can no arrangement be thought of by which the jam and cram and general growl can be done away with? This happens on all occasions at our ball suppers. Well-bred people seem to become lost to every rule of courtesy and politeness, and rush pell-mell like a set of half-famished wolves to see who can get there first. Ladies who would blush with shame and confusion at such uncouth conduct in their own homes seem the most faulty and ill mannerly on such occasions. This not only makes it very disagreeable to those seeking seats at the table, but also disconcerts and disgusts the manager of the supper and everyone who has anything to do with the table. We move that a committee of four, composed of two intelligent men and two women, meet for the purpose of trying to establish some rule or regulation in regard to supper tickets. Excuse us for digressing, but we have thought seriously upon this subject for several years, and have come to the conclusion that this particular breach of common politeness should and must be taken into consideration and acted upon by our ball-going citizens. We will be caught in this ill-mannerly conduct some evening by a New York reporter, and the empire city of the North will open wide its eyes in astonishment, while its mouth will exclaim in the language of Milton:

> "Swinish gluttony
>   Ne'er looks to heaven
> Amidst her gorgeous feast,
>   But crams, and blasphemes the feeder."

The supper was excellent in quality and bountiful in supply—basketfuls of chickens, turkeys and other meats being left over. Those waiting upon the tables did admirably considering the immense crowd—there being over one hundred and fifty couples present; fifty-seven couples were comfortably seated at one time. After supper, dancing was resumed and was kept up till rosy morn peeped in and smiled at the artificial light.

THE RAFFLE.

On Tuesday evening there was quite a gathering of anxious ticket-holders in the various articles to be raffled off on that occasion. Following is a list of the most valuable winnings and the lucky winners: A ring, W. Healy; cow, Mrs. Cyril C. Smith; marble mantle clock, Mrs. Ivers; accordion, Wm. Fahey; piece of Irish turf, Mr. Thornton; pickle castor butter dish and finger bowl, E. Madden; a large cake containing a ring, Miss Belle Russell; two oil paintings, W. Twoomy; large shawl, Mrs. C.E. Fleming; silver watch, Mrs. M.A. Stanton; vase of wax flowers, A.J. Meany; smoking cap, Mr. Walsh; plow, Mr. Matthews; large silver urn, Mrs. McInerney; small silver urn, Miss Janie Morton; bride doll, Miss Janie Morton.

It would fill a column to describe all of the beautiful articles on exhibition and which were disposed of at good round prices.

THE PROCEEDS.

which are supposed to be at present writing about $1,000, will be given in next weeks' issue. Take it all in all, it was a grand affair, and will be long remembered with pleasure by those who joined in the festivities.[26]

Apparently something in this column provoked the anger of Madden who published a "spiteful article" in the *Tribune* about Rowena. She replied facetiously:

THAT NICE YOUNG MAN.

———

MERCED, Nov. 5th, 1874.

MR. EDITOR:—That last dishwater article must have contained a little mustard or some other ingredient of stinging quality which made the amiable young man of the *Tribune* out of sorts. That "Madam" sounded very much like a growl from behind the throne instead of the throne direct—as if coming from a husband who is in the habit of snubbing his wife occasionally. But I suppose he had bowed to the power until the old maxim, "Like master like man," has become second nature. I really did not mean the handsome young editor when I spoke of county pomposities. I guess I must have been thinking of those sleek, fat fellows who loaf around the county hospital, or some other necessary evil. And as for the School Fund, why I thought his tender sympathy reached out among the school marms. I thought he would be pleased at the idea of high salaries and constant pay to that intelligent class. But la! it's hard to please cross children, they will sometimes snap and snarl at the prettiest toys held out to please them. Perhaps he caught cold and feels a little fretful. He ought to put on nice warm flannel, take a dose of paregoric, pennyroyal and catnip, and be put into his little bed and sung to sleep by nineteen school marms. If that treatment fails, go to the gurgling

stream and pluck a *May* blossom and *Tack-it*[xi] to the
lapel of his coat and perhaps sweet smiles may take
the place of that ugly frown which darkens his pretty
face while penning the spiteful article about
VACUNA.[27]

She had finally been goaded and dragged into the fray. Little did
she realize this flippant response would lead to the most dire
consequences imaginable.

In November 1874, Rowena published her novel *Dell
Dart; Or, Within The Meshes*, based on a true story, about a young
girl who is seduced, essentially kidnapped, by a gambler, gets
caught up in his criminal activities, and spends her final days in a
brothel. In the Preface, she writes:

> From my earliest childhood my sympathies have
> gone out for the unfortunate. Some of my "high-
> toned" friends have been very much shocked and
> have even cut my acquaintance on account of the
> interest I have taken in the unfortunates. It may be a
> weakness, but it is one, nevertheless, for which I
> thank God.
>
> Many of the old residents of California will
> doubtless recognize my heroine—DELL DART. The
> story being founded entirely upon facts of course the
> names of the hero and heroine have been changed.
> The man known to the reader as Cheeney Dart, was
> a member of the California Legislature somewhere
> between the years of '54 and '64. He is dead now.
> Peace to his ashes!

[xi] This is obviously a reference to Miss Mary 'May' Tackett, teacher and niece
of Judge Robertson, to whom Rowena perceived Madden was attracted or
attached.

On November 18, 1874, Rowena left on a fortnight trip to Northern California cities and towns to promote the book, penning on her way out an "*au revoir*, with kind wishes to the Mercedites"—a description of the beautiful gardens of her neighbors against the backdrop of the "snow-capped, cloud curtained Sierra Nevadas," businesses and stores along Front street, and the new courthouse being erected "loom[ing] skyward."[28]

R.J. continued the hostility with Madden and the *Tribune* in a column about an assault "by Cliquers" on a "young gentleman upon our streets."

> It was not only an outrage against the young man upon whom the assault was made, but was an outrage also upon the whole people of Merced. And, strange as it may appear, the reputed editor of the Clique organ was thoroughly posed upon what was to be done and familiar with the whole arrangement; eager for the enjoyment of the fun, and promptly stationed himself at a point where he and several of his friends would witness the "assault" and see the young man wallowed in the mud by a burly ruffian in disguise. The act was ostensibly committed by a single individual, but the circumstances show that it was a conspiracy by which the young man was decoyed to that particular part of town at that particular hour, and, at that time the street where the assault was made was pretty well crowded with people, almost all of whom were looking out eagerly for what was to happen; and no one enjoyed the joke with greater zest than did the reputed editor of the Clique organ and his most intimate friends and supporters.[29]

Chapter IX

"[W]e know not, nor can we conceive of any offence, short of an attempt to destroy the life or honor of an individual or his family, that could be offered as a justification for thus taking the life of a human being in cold blood[1]

Avenging a Mother's Honor; Or, The Fatal Slander

'Twas slander vile, young Harry saw upon the printed page;
His mother dear, the victim, which caused the fires to rage;
His cheeks grew pale with anguish, his heart could know no fear;
He only thought of days gone by, and mother's name so dear.[2]

Rowena was in Northern California, most recently at Vallejo, on December 7, 1874, when the teletypes and telegrams suddenly started flying out of Merced to all corners of the state with the terrible news:

A TRAGEDY AT MERCED.

Rival Editors Indulge in Most Unwarrantable Attacks—Madden, of the "Tribune," Killed by the Son of Mrs. Rowena Granice Steele, of the "Argus."

A dispatch received from Merced, by Mr. James Schram, dated December 7th, stated that Edward Madden, editor of the *Merced Tribune*, was shot and instantly killed in that town, on Monday, by Harry Granice, step-son of Robert J. Steele, editor of the

San Joaquin Valley Argus. The *Bulletin* contained the following in relation to the affair:

About half-past seven o'clock this morning, as Edward Madden, editor of the *Merced Tribune*, was going to his office, he was shot and killed by Harry Granice, step-son of Robert J. Steele, editor of the *San Joaquin Argus*. It appears that the *Argus* and *Tribune* had for some time been in constant war against each other, but nothing serious was expected to come from it, until about two weeks ago, when an article appeared in the *Argus* reflecting upon a young lady to whom Madden was deeply attached. Madden made no reply until his issue of the 5th, when the following article appeared in the *Tribune*:

> "The *Vallejo Chronicle* notices the advent in that town of Mrs. R.G. Steele, who is canvassing for a book entitled "Dell Dart." If any family desires to be posted in the life of a female in a house of ill fame they can ascertain all the knowledge in that line they desire by a perusal of the publication referred to. The authoress evidently knows whereof she speaks."

At the time of his death Madden was in company with a friend, who remarked that Granice was looking for him. In reply, Madden said he supposed Granice knew where to find him. He had hardly ceased speaking when Granice, who lay in wait, stepped out of Simon, Jacob & Co.'s store behind Madden, shooting him in the back. Madden fell forward, and was about to rise when Granice fired four more shots, one lodging in the right breast, another in the left, another in the face (a little left of

the nose) and the other in the thigh, killing him
instantly. Granice gave himself up. The whole
transpired so quickly that those who witnessed the
shooting had no power to warn Madden or stop the
firing until it was too late. Madden has always been
known and respected as an upright gentleman. In
appearance he was about twenty-three years of age,
of the medium height and rather good looking, and
had frank and pleasing manners which will render his
untimely death a sad blow to his numerous friends
and acquaintances, both in Merced and Stockton,
where his mother and brother have long resided.

LYNCHING ATTEMPTED.

MERCED, December 7th—9 P.M.—The excitement
over the shooting of Madden is intense. An attempt
to lynch Granice was expected. A rope was
purchased and everything prepared; but, on going to
the jail after dark, it appeared that the prisoner had
been spirited away by the Sheriff—no one knows
where. The party, on the discovery of the prisoner's
absence, went to the office of the *San Joaquin Argus*
and mobbed it, smashing the forms, mixing the type,
etc. Steele, the editor, has disappeared. The
excitement still continues, but it is hoped that young
Granice has been taken out of reach.[3]

It would have probably been at least a day before Rowena learned
of the tragic, shocking events, and a day or two more before she
could get back home to Merced. By that time, Harry was on the
run somewhere out in the countryside, having escaped the lynch
mob, and R.J. was gone, whereabouts unknown, after the mob
ransacked the *Argus* office and threatened his life, presumably
taking 11-year-old Lee with him or securing his safety with
neighbors. George was living fifteen miles out of town at the time

and had not been involved in any of the political wrangling. Many of the state's papers were already casting the blame on Rowena "owing to the false course of tutelage imposed upon the young Granice by a too chivalrous mother, who, perhaps fails, even now, to recognize in this calamity the error of her earlier teaching,"[4] and on R.J. Steele:

> The *Argus*, edited by R.J. Steele, has been vindictive and bitter in its course toward the TRIBUNE. This spleen appears to have been carried so far as to place Steele in the attitude of reflecting upon one to whom young Madden was attached[xii] by what every lover of the pure, the bright, the beautiful will recognized as a hallowed tie. It would be difficult to conceive of a provocation more likely to drive a high-minded man to frenzy.[5]

Finally, on December 12, after five days on the run with little food, water or sleep, sick with the "bloody flux" (dysentery), Harry presented himself to the sheriff in Modesto where he was reasonably assured he would be safe from the Merced mob. He later described his harrowing ordeal in the pamphlet *Hunted Down: Or, Five Days in the Fog* written while sitting in jail awaiting trial. In it he relates that he learned his mother was on the afternoon train to Merced on December 11 that had passed by him as he lay in hiding in a barn:

> [S]ome one had whispered in her ear, your son is thus far safe. This was a great relief to me, for I had feared for her safety; I knew that rumors must have reached her of my being hunted down, and of the

---

[xii] It was actually Rowena who teasingly mentioned Mary Tackett in her "Vacuna" column.

uncertainty of my escape from the mob, and I knew that her agony must be terrible.[6]

Rowena immediately sent out a dispatch with a sketch of Harry's life, apparently hoping to garner sympathy and support for him.

Sketch of H. H. Granice.

Mrs. Rowena Granice Steele, mother of the young man who killed Mr. Madden, editor of the *Tribune*, at Merced, has contributed a sketch of the life of her son, from which some facts of general interest are gleaned.

Harry Hale Granice Claughly was born in the city of New York, December 3d, 1849, on Ninth Avenue, between 18th and 19th streets. His father, Thomas N. Claughly, was for a number of years proprietor of Extension Furniture Warerooms, on the corner of Bowery and Bond streets, New York. He came to California in '52, and died in San Francisco in '59 and was buried in Lone Mountain. Harry has but one brother, G. Law Granice Claughly. Both brothers dropped their father's name and adopted their mother's maiden name in consequence of domestic troubles. Harry, with his brother G. Law, came to California in March, 1857, to join their mother, who had preceded them just one year. In 1861 the mother was married to Robert J. Steele, and Harry, at the age of 12, entered Mr. Steele's printing office. A few years since he worked a few days on the Tuolumne *Tribune*, in which Mr. Steele had an interest. For the last six years he has acted as foreman in the office of his step-father, with the exception of nine months, six of which he spent at the Pacific Business College of San Francisco. He has been a resident of Merced county for nearly thirteen years.[7]

The *Merced Tribune* immediately renamed itself the *Merced Weekly Express*, stating that it was "an entirely new enterprise," "an independent Democratic journal" that, "[p]rofiting by the experience of others, it hopes to avoid the breakers upon which they were wrecked, and to present, each week, to its patrons, an unexceptionable paper, filled with original and selected articles offensive neither to good morals, nor good taste."[8] From that time, there was no more mention of the *Argus* or the Steeles or Harry Granice except to report on the trials and official County business.

When R.J. finally got the *Argus* office in order and the presses repaired in March 1875, the reappearance of the paper "as a candidate for public favor, shorn somewhat of its former fair proportions," was announced. The only reference to the murder and aftermath was a few lines:

> Of the causes which led to the cessation of its publication in December last the people of Merced county are familiar, and therefore need no recapitulation at this time by us. The main facts are matters of history, to us painfully unpleasant remembrances of the immediate past, but which are to be met as sad realities, which all good people should sincerely hope never again to witness a recurrence of in a land inhabited by civilized, Christian people.[9]

and promising:

> We shall endeavor to make the paper a truthful medium for reporting passing and past events of greatest interest to the reading public, a conservator of the people's rights and interests, an advocate of reforms where reformation is necessary in the

control and management of public affairs, national,
State and local, and a vehicle for the dissemination of
the general news of the day.[10]

In the next week's issue, the "Sketch of the Life of
H.H. Granice" was reprinted, adding some more details
about Harry's life and character:

He was as a child considered extremely brave in
anything he undertook—never was known to invite a
quarrel, but was ever ready to resent an insult. He has
been noted among his friends and those who knew
him for his strictly industrious habits. He never spent
an idle hour from the time he understood the
meaning of the word "work." He attended the public
schools of San Francisco for two years after his
arrival in California. His mother then moved to
Sacramento, and being engaged a part of the time in
giving parlor entertainments through the country, she
placed her boys in a private boarding school on
Seventh street, never remaining away from them
more than six or eight weeks at a time. During the
Fall and Winter months the mother resided in her
small, humble, but neat home on N street, employing
her time in writing sketches and domestic stories for
literary papers and magazines. She was known to the
public as Miss Rowena Granice, and this name
became a household word in California, through the
Golden Era and many of the mountain papers. The
first two numbers of the San Francisco *Spirit of the
Times* contain a story of fourteen columns written by
her, entitled, "Dora Fielding; or, The Actress'
Debut." She published also some little books entitled
"The Family Gem," "The Victims of Fate," and
"Leonnie St. James," and was often seen with her

two little boys, Harry and George Law, passing from door to door in the mountain towns disposing of her own original productions. Being so constantly with their mother they became her constant companions and confidants and shared with her her joys and her griefs. There ever was a deep, tender and affectionate love binding these three together. In 1861 the mother was married to Robert J. Steele, and Harry at the age of twelve entered Mr. Steele's printing office. At the age of fourteen he was an expert typesetter and could be trusted to make up the forms of a weekly paper and run the press. At the age of fifteen he was employed in the office of the Mariposa *Free Press*, which was conducted then by Mr. James Lawrence. While working there the foreman was taken ill, and Master Harry succeeded in getting out the paper for two weeks without the least assistance from older or wiser heads. A few years since he worked several days on the *Tuolumne News*, in which Mr. Steele had an interest. For the last six years he has acted as foreman in the office of his stepfather with the exception of nine months, six of which were spent at the Pacific Business College in San Francisco, from which he graduated with honor to himself and credit to his teachers. After finishing his business education, having a small capital he concluded to try journalism, and became editor and proprietor of a neat little paper called the *Merced People*, in Merced City, then in its infancy. With the help of a youth sixteen years of age, he succeeded in bringing out every Saturday morning for three months a neat paper of which the oldest [illegible] might be proud, and which was well received by a large portion of the business houses and families of Merced county, and

no doubt it would have been a success pecuniarily
had not the county officials of Merced established a
county official paper. Seeing that it would be
impossible to go on against the combined capital of
the officials without injury to himself and others, he
very wisely gave it up, and again accepted the
situation of foreman in the ARGUS office. He has
been a resident of Merced County for nearly thirteen
years, and his character for honesty, integrity and
industry is without a blemish. He possesses a larger
share of individuality than is generally found in one
man out of ten. He has never associated himself with
crowds, and has generally sought the society of those
of a quiet turn of mind. At balls and parties or public
gatherings, he was generally the escort of his mother,
of whom he was very proud. Being naturally of a
private, independent nature, he became extremely
sensitive and his devotion to his mother and his
desire to be near her prevented him from seeking a
wider field in which to display his natural gifts. He
has devoted much of his time to solid reading, and is
as well versed in the political history of this and other
countries as any man in Merced County. He is also a
forcible and argumentative political writer, and had
not this unfortunate affair occurred, he would have
no doubt made his mark as a journalist. He has
hundreds of true friends and sympathizers in this his
dark hour....[11]

Rowena wrote sporadic columns about social causes, the
weather, and her "pleasant journeyings" to Stockton, Snelling,
Yosemite, and LaGrange, visiting with old friends, but never
again under the authorship of "Vacuna." That pseudonym appears
to have ceased as of December 7, 1874, with the death of Edward

Madden. Gone, too, from the pages of the *Argus* were Rowena's weekly reports of parties, balls, festivals, and other happy social gatherings, certainly because none of those activities would be appealing for a mother whose son was soon to go on trial for capital murder and possibly face the hangman's noose, and also, no doubt, since invitations were not extended; the presence of the Steeles was not welcome in Merced society.

The Trial

The trial of Harry Hale Granice for the killing of Edward Madden on December 7, 1874, was commenced in District Court at Fresno on July 7, 1875, Judge Alexander Deering presiding.

> The prisoner, when brought before the Bar, looked a little worn from confinement, but appeared cheerful. He was accompanied by his father, mother and brothers. The prosecution was represented by District Attorney Sayle, W.L. Dudley and R.H. Ward. The defence by [General] Jo. Hamilton, [Judge] D.S. Terry[xiii] and General Chamberlain. Seventy-five jurors and thirty witnesses were summoned. The jury was impaneled with little trouble, sworn and charged by the Judge.[12]

Witness testimony began on July 8th. As reported by the *Daily Alta California*:

> E.J. Hamilton was the first witness. He testified as follows: I am County Clerk of Merced county and am acquainted with Granice; knew Madden, and have been acquainted with him two and a half years; I roomed with Madden; I saw defendant and deceased

---

xiii This is former California Supreme Court Chief Justice David S. Terry who killed Senator David C. Broderick in a duel on September 13, 1859.

the day of the killing; I breakfasted with Madden, and we went up Front street together on the way to our offices; I was inside; just as we passed the second door of Simon, Jacob's store I heard a pistol shot, and Madden fell on his hands and knees; I jumped back paralyzed; Madden tried to rise, and lifting up his hands, exclaimed, "Oh God!" At that instant Granice ran out from the store, after firing his pistol into Madden, firing four shots.

A diagram of the scene was presented to the witness and recognized by him as correct.

The witness continued: The sidewalk is fourteen feet wide; we were walking near the center when Madden fell; several boxes, etc., stood against the wall between the doors; after the shooting Granice walked down the street, and was arrested by George Kleinlin; Madden fell at the first shot; it took effect in the middle of his back, the second in his hip, the third in his face, the fourth in his breast, etc.... Madden died where he fell; the pistol was a dragoon six-shooter; Granice held the pistol in both hands.

The coat of the deceased was shown and identified by witness to corroborate the statement of the effect of the shots.

Cross-examination by the defense—Madden was a stout, robust man, and weighed about 170; witness entertains the best of feeling toward defendant; I assisted to carry Madden to a room; a six-shooter was found in the hip-pocket of the deceased; he usually carried a pistol; I don't know whether it was loaded.

Henry Levi Amar, upholsterer, the next witness, stated he was working in a furniture store on the 7th of December; I know defendant and knew the deceased; Granice came in the door and said "Good

morning," and remained two or three minutes near
the door; I saw Madden and Hamilton pass the first
door, and heard three shots fired; I tried to run, and
looked out and saw Madden as if falling; after I
reached the door I saw Madden on the sidewalk
dead; five or six shots were fired.

George Kleinlin testified as follows: I am porter at
Simon, Jacob's store—I was in front of the store
greasing a wagon when I heard a shot; I turned and
saw Madden lying on the sidewalk; Granice came out
firing and shot in the face; Granice started off; I ran
to the sidewalk and caught him, and took the pistol
away; he said "Let go," and then gave himself up;
Granice took off his belt and pistol-scabbard and
gave them to me; I turned the defendant over to the
Sheriff.

E.A. Packer saw Madden lying on the sidewalk after
he was killed; I helped to undress him afterward, and
to take him to his room at Garibaldi's building; I saw
the wounds, in the back, in the breast, in the chest,
and two in the thigh; the shot in the back did not
pass through the body.

        * * *

Here the prosecution rested.[13]

Rowena was the first witness for the defense. She related
the background of Harry's life and work and revealed an
astonishing fact: Harry was deaf. She stated that he had always
been physically "weakly" and she thought at the time of the killing
he must have been temporarily insane because of his anguish and
illness. Additional reference to Harry's deafness and how that
might have precipitated the murder as perceived self-defense on
Harry's part was related by attorney for the defense Hamilton,

who argued that the jury should be able to consider it in their deliberations.

> Madden had been grossly indiscreet and at fault in his actions. He sent messages that Granice was a "bastard," a reflection on the young man and his mother. This Granice did not notice. Madden, who published a paper, made many scandalous attacks on defendant's mother and made damaging, untrue and uncalled for remarks on her chastity when she was trying to make a living by selling books.... On December 5th the last article appeared, and Granice met Madden with tears in his eyes and begged a retraction. He was deaf and could not hear correctly, leading to a great misunderstanding. His frame shook with emotion, his strength gave way; Granice was frail, Madden robust and could break defendant's head with one hand. Madden refused to retract, calling him a bastard, and Madden drew his pistol, pointing it at Granice's face. The effect of the refusal on defendant caused him to go to bed sick for two days. Granice then unexpectedly met Madden and the deceased made a remark to a companion and put his hand back as if reaching for a weapon. Being deaf, Granice understood that an assault was intended and ran back and made fight the best he could and stayed.[14]

There was some legal wrangling about poems that had been circulated in newspapers, one a tribute to Edward Madden's mother and the other Mrs. Drake's "The Fatal Slander; or, Harry's Defense," claimed by both the prosecution and defense as calculated to prejudice the jury, as well as the self-defense and temporary insanity assertions. Finally, Harry took the stand.

He said he was 25 years of age; he knew the deceased for two years; he had lived at Merced two years; Madden was editor of the *Tribune*; he (defendant) knew no other editor or publisher; he simply knew him; their relations were not friendly; he (defendant) did not like him because he published articles derogatory to his mother; an article appeared December 5th, charging his mother with having been an inmate of a house of ill fame; he saw Madden the same evening at the El Capitan Hotel, and asked a retraction; deceased said he would make no retraction; Madden drew a pistol and presented it at defendant, and said he was a d—d bastard; that was all the retraction he would make; defendant was taken down immediately after with a flux until the day of the homicide; from that occurrence and what he heard he was led to believe that his life was in danger.

* * *

Defendant had heard that Madden wanted to clean out the d—d *Argus* and wished that some of them would take it up so that he could shoot them.

* * *

On Monday morning I left the *Argus* office and was taken with a pain in the bowels; I went to Simon, Jacob's store, and was coming out the door of the furniture store when Madden and Hamilton came up; Madden was outside and Hamilton inside; Hamilton's eye caught mine, and I saw him nudge Madden and speak to him; at that time Madden put his hand behind his back; I jumped and drew a pistol and leveled it at the head of the deceased; I kept on shooting until I emptied the pistol; when I first fired

Hamilton stepped back, and at the second shot he stepped back further; I saw Madden lying on the sidewalk; after the shooting I walked to the corner and gave myself up to the German, and handed him my pistol; I had fired four or five shots before I saw Madden pitch forward; I saw his hand under his coat, but I saw no pistol; I saw him have a pistol on the Saturday night before; I saw Madden on Saturday evening, near the El Capitan Hotel; he was sitting between Ed. Newman and P.H. Higgins; as I passed near him I saw him take the pistol out of his pocket and put it between his legs; did not catch his eye; I met him at the hotel the same evening and asked a retraction of the article published, and he answered as before stated.[15]

Watching the proceedings, Rowena was reported to be "overcome with emotion and burst into tears. Her little son [Lee] clasped his hands about her waist and tried to comfort her."[16]

Closing arguments were concluded on the afternoon of July 10, and Judge Deering addressed the jury:

He reviewed the different grades of crime as constituted under the law, and charged them that if they believed the deceased had made demonstrations of hostility sufficient to induce a reasonable apprehension in the mind of the defendant, or if they thought the defendant insane at the time of the killing, to find him not guilty. The Judge also instructed them to pay no attention to the rumors and threats or newspaper articles. The charge was quite lengthy. The jury retired under the charge of the Sheriff.

A few hours later, by seven o'clock, the jury returned with the verdict: Guilty. Punishment was fixed at imprisonment for life. The defense immediately motioned for a stay of judgment and for a new trial, and the court set a hearing for October 20 for arguing the motions.

The ensuing months' *Argus* were filled with responses to attacks on the veracity of Harry in the booklet *Five Days in the Fog*; the alleged behavior of Sheriff A.J. Meany in directing Deputy Nicholas Breen to take Harry from the jail to a place north of town, then deputizing and enabling the lynch mob to follow them; and Breen's halfhearted denial of his part in allowing Harry to escape, which was quickly challenged by the owner of the house where Breen and Harry had been ordered by Meany to stay in hiding, who confirmed Harry's version.

Particularly outrageous was the assertion that Rowena had attacked Judge Deering with a gun and that "his honor feared for his own safety and escaped through the window of his room from my presence." Rowena wrote that she had not spoken to Judge Deering at all since the trial, and protested, "[p]ersecution seems to be one of the strongholds of those wishing to harm me and mine, and all who make such statements as the above have been misinformed or intend to do me injury. I have no use for a revolver and never carry one. I only ask for simple justice at the hands of those who have it in their power to rob me of my rights on earth."[17]

Rowena's theater background was also called into question when she was evidently confused with her sister-in-law, Mary Stephens Claughley, prompting this rebuttal:

ANSWER TO A CORRESPONDENT.

———

Mrs. Claughly nee Mary Jane Stephens, the actress, came to California in 1851, played through all the principal towns of the state and died in San Francisco in 1864. Her husband, James Claughly, was a brother to Thomas N. Claughley, the deceased husband of Mrs. R.G. Steele; and the correspondent seems to think that Mrs. Rowena Granice Steele came to California previous to 1856; the following letter will doubtless settle the [matter].

> BRIDGEPORT, CONN., Jan. 12th, '75
>
> *To whom it may concern:*
>
> About 1853 to 1856, Rowena Granice performed in the role of "Yankee Girl" &c. in my New York Museum for about three years. She then had two children. She was an exceedingly good, modest, well-beloved woman. All who knew her respected her, and many respectable persons of both sexes were her friends. I am sure she was a highly respectable, good and conscientious lady.
>
> P.T. BARNUM.

If the correspondent is not satisfied, I can furnish many letters which I have received from ladies and gentlemen of high standing to prove when I came to California.   MRS. R.G. STEELE[18]

Bearing the full brunt of Rowena's particular hurt and anger was County Judge James W. Robertson, who had been so contentious with R.J. over County administration matters and had thereafter shifted his personal attacks to Harry and Rowena herself in the aftermath of the Madden murder.

MERCED, July 19th, 1875

MR. EDITOR:—I am informed by a number of most respectable parties that Judge Robertson, County Judge of Merced, when in Fresno during the late trial of Harry Granice was heard to call the defendant, my son, a d—d bastard in the saloons and on the public street, and use other vulgar and profane language in connection with the above. Now I should think these were very undignified terms to come from the lips of one whom the good people of Merced have honored with so high a place among them. And not only undignified, and extremely vulgar, but in very bad taste, considering that I stood bridesmaid to his present wife twelve years ago, when she was married to Mr. Pitman of Branch's Ferry; and also in consideration that his wife's mother and father, sister and brothers, have eaten at my table and slept in my beds and been entertained for weeks at a time at my house; and good, dear, old Mrs. Silman, his present wife's mother, has told me many a time that she loved me nearly as well as did her own daughter! And then, Harry Granice escorted Miss Mary Tackett, his wife's niece, to her first party (Ah! those are pleasant times to look back upon!) And I don't believe that Mrs. Clark, Mrs. Robertson's sister, forgets the many, many pleasant, happy days she spent at my cozy little home in Snelling, and how during that year we grew to love each other like sisters; how little Lee and little Dixey, our babies, lay and cooed and crowed upon the bright carpet, while we embroidered and cut and fashioned little garments; how she loved Harry and George and they in turn loved [illegible] Walter. The Judge, too, has partaken of the hospitality of the same home many a time. I repeat, it is in very bad taste for him to cast such vulgar slanders upon one who never harmed him, and who for years was such a warm friend to his wife's family. I can give as good proof of the legitimate and honorable birth of my children as it is in human power to give, and still I am told that this man makes a common practice of applying this offensive epithet to them. Now, if Judge Robertson has a spark of manhood left in him, he would at least respect my sorrow and [illegible] me in trouble, and cease his vile slanders of one who is helpless to act for herself and who too well knows that no law in [illegible] will protect her or anyone connected with her, if the law dispensers of this county have sworn vengeance against the editor of the ARGUS and every member of his family, and it seems they are not content to know that the iron jaws of the law have been most relentlessly shut down on one of its members, but they still seek their revenge in vile slander.[19]

On the encouraging, positive side, many of Rowena's friends and colleagues came forward with public and private shows of support with money, cards, letters, poetry, and gifts. On August 23, 1875, a "Grand Musical Concert" was presented for Rowena at Platt's Hall in San Francisco, "to aid her in her efforts to get a new, fair and impartial trial for her son, young Harry H. Granice, who has been convicted of Murder in the First Degree, for shooting the man who published a gross and infamous slander upon his Mother's character."[20] An impressive array of stage and musical artists volunteered their services, including Mrs. Von Linderman, pianist from the Conservatory of Paris; Miss Stella Bickle, "the young Prima Donna of the Italian Opera of the California Theatre"; sopranos Victoria Petrarchie and Rose Matthal; tenor J. Stein; and baritone C. Parish. A Steinway grand piano was offered for the occasion by Rowena's old friend music store owner Matthias Gray. When Mr. Gray died in April 1887, Rowena told the story of his generosity in her time of trouble.

Passed Away.

Matthias Gray, the well-known and very popular music dealer of San Francisco, who passed from earth a few days ago was one of the most noble and generous men on the Pacific Coast. His many charities were mostly of a private nature, and bestowed in such a manner that the receiver hardly knew whom to thank. A few years ago a lady who was in trouble concluded to get up a concert at Platt's hall, San Francisco. The lady was not personally acquainted with Mr. Gray; but that generous man had heard of her misfortune and distress, and when she called at his store to ask what he would charge for the use of a Steinway piano for the occasion, Mr. Gray very politely informed her that she could have the use of the piano free of charge. During the brief conversation he said: "Madam, I am in deep sympathy with you in your trouble and I wish to assist you; accept this little gift [twenty dollars]," and turning to the head clerk he introduced the heart-sorrowing lady and said, "I authorize you to give Mrs. — five dollars every week while she is obliged to remain in the city." The lady said, "I will not impose on your generosity by calling." But the lady through a friend received five dollars each of the four weeks she remained in the city. Such men as Matthias Gray don't die—they merely pass from this to a better land.[21]

The *Argus* appears to have been flourishing, as well. R.J. announced the seventh volume and thanked the readers for their continued patronage. "Instead of dying, as its enemies who hate independence in journalism fondly hoped, it is gradually increase-ing in circulation, and consequently improving in usefulness."[22] In February 1876, the paper was further enlarged with syndicated articles and stock magazine-type pieces.

The First Appeal

On October 22, 1875, the defendant's motion for a new trial was heard by Judge Deering in Fresno.

> MOTION FOR NEW TRIAL DENIED.—In the case of the People vs. H.H. Granice, convicted of murder in the killing of Edward Madden at the June term of the District Court in Fresno county, which came up before the District Court of Fresno, Judge Deering presiding, at 1 P.M. on Thursday last on motion for counsel for new trial, the motion was argued on the part of the prisoner by Gen. Jo. Hamilton and Judge D.S. Terry, and on the part of the People by W.L. Dudley, of Stockton. At the close of the argument by counsel the Judge set the following morning at 9 o'clock for rendering his decision.
>
> The following telegram gives the decision of the Court:
>
> > "Fresno, Oct. 22nd—10:10 A.M.— Motion for new trial denied. Indict-ment ordered to be photographed. The prisoner received the sentence with less emotion than was evinced by the Judge in giving it. The mother of prisoner present throughout the proceedings."

The case will go to the Supreme Court.[23]

Harry was ordered to prison where he had to wait only six weeks for the California Supreme Court's decision.

In this appeal, we first learn the underlying basis: Someone, probably the Merced County Attorney, had altered the Grand Jury's indictment by changing certain words and interpolating in the margins other words, including "maliciously" and "Murder." Although Harry and his attorneys were informed of the substitution and new charge, it was argued, that would not give jurisdiction to the court to try him for any other offense than that charged in the original indictment. The Supreme Court concurred, and on Monday, December 6, 1875, issued its ruling:

> By the COURT:
> During the progress of the trial of this action, the defendant offered to prove that certain words had been inserted in the indictment, and that certain other words of the indictment had been changed since it was filed and became a record of the court. Objection to such proof was made by the prosecution, on the ground that the defendant's attorney had been informed by one of the attorneys for the prosecution, before the defendant pleaded to the indictment, "that the indictment had been tampered with after it had been found by the grand jury;" and "that there were plenty of witnesses to prove that it had been tampered with." The court refused to permit the defendant to make the proof. It is the duty of either party to bring to the attention of the court any alteration of the record of a pending proceeding, promptly, and at the earliest opportunity at which it can be done, after the alteration has come to his knowledge. In this case, that duty was as

incumbent on the prosecution as on the defendant. Although the defendant did not promptly move in the matter, he is not thereby precluded from showing that alterations have been made in the indictment. The indictment, as it stood before the alleged alterations were made, only charged the defendant with the crime of manslaughter, but, as altered, it charged him with the crime of murder. The court, under that indictment, had no jurisdiction to try him for any crime other than such as was charged in the indictment when it was filed by the grand jury. Consent on the part of the defendant, whether given directly or inferred from his acts or omissions, cannot confer jurisdiction upon the court to try the defendant for any other crime than such as is charged in the indictment, as found and returned by the grand jury.

Judgment and order reversed, and cause remanded for a new trial. Remittitur forthwith.[24]

On December 19, 1875, Judge Deering, who had been in ill health for some time, died at his home in Merced. There is a moving obituary on the website Find-a-Grave that is not referenced or attributed, but, being very familiar with Rowena's writings, I have no doubt it was penned by her.

In other political news, prosecutor Russell H. Ward, who had moved to Stanislaus County to run for Senator, lost that election and was indicted by a Grand Jury there for election brokering, later found not guilty.

A Writ of *Habeas Corpus* having been filed on Harry's behalf by attorney Charles H. Marks, he was brought before Judge Gillum Bailey, County Judge of Fresno County, on Monday, January 10, 1876, and released on bail of $10,000 pending retrial. His appearance in Merced was reported on February 5.

The Second Trial – Return to Grand Jury – First Inkling of "Double Jeopardy"

Retrial commenced in Fresno on March 13, 1876 before Judge J.B. Campbell.

GRANICE MURDER TRIAL.—The case of the People vs. H.H. Granice, indicted in January, 1875, by the Grand Jury of Merced County, for the killing of Edward Madden, came up in the District Court in Fresno County on last Monday. On motion of counsel for the defense, and upon the evidence of Chas. H. Marks and R.H. Ward, words which had been added to the indictment after it was found by the Grand Jury by the then acting District Attorney of this county—L.D. Seward—were stricken out. This being done, his Honor Judge J.B. Campbell, declared the indictment valid for no crime higher than that of manslaughter. The defendant then plead "not guilty" to the indictment and the trial proceeded. After all the evidence, both for prosecution and defense had been offered, the attorneys for the prosecution moved the Court to dismiss the action, set aside the indictment and refer the case back to another Grand Jury. This motion was argued by R.H. Ward and W.L. Dudley for the State, and not opposed by the defense. The ground set forth in favor of the motion was that the evidence before the Court went to prove defendant guilty of a higher crime than that charged in the indictment, or in other words, that the evidence showed defendant guilty of murder instead of manslaughter. The Court sustained the motion and thereupon ordered

defendant into the custody of the Sheriff to await the
action of the Grand Jury of Merced County.[25]

Another Writ of *Habeas Corpus* was immediately filed with the
California Supreme Court returnable on April 10, 1876. At that
hearing, Judge Terry argued for Harry's release from jail because
the Penal Code provision which directed his incarceration pending
the Grand Jury's deliberation and possible indictment against him
for a higher offense was in direct conflict with Section 8, article I,
of the Constitution: "No person shall be subject to be twice put in
jeopardy for the same offense." The Supreme Court ruled that
because, under the Penal Code, the District Court had jurisdiction
over the defendant, the Supreme Court could not discharge Harry
under a *habeas corpus*. "'The writ of *habeas corpus*,' as well
observed here in *Ex parte McCullough*, 'has not been given for the
purpose of reviewing judgments or orders made by a court or
judge, or officer acting within their jurisdiction. To put it to such a
use would be to convert it into a writ of error,' etc. (35 Cal.
100.)."[26] Harry was ordered back into custody to Merced County
to await the Grand Jury empanelment which was scheduled for
November.

In the meantime, Rowena continued her travels around the
state to visit friends and raise support for Harry and money for
legal fees.[xiv] She attended the Country Publishers' Convention in
San Francisco in March 1876, at which it was noted four of the
representatives were women: Rowena, Laura DeForce Gordon of
Sacramento, Belle Lynch of Ukiah, and Dora Darmoore Boyer of
San Francisco. Her columns for the *Argus* were predominantly
personal news items about Mercedites and people she visited with
on her journeys, church festivals ("rumor says that each was well-
patronized, but I did not attend"[27]), Merced schools, and new
businesses and manufactories in Merced, such as the California

---

[xiv] Among other fundraising items, Rowena raffled off "a lady's fine gold watch
and chain" for $2 per ticket.

Joint Stock Glove Factory which opened in Spring 1876, and the new dancing school offered by the Downey brothers at Washington Hall.

An "entertainment" was held on May 6, 1876, at Washington Hall in Merced, admission 50 cents, with "dramatic readings selected from Shakespeare and other authors, together with comic and sentimenttal songs, recitations, declamations, dialogues, etc."[28] featuring Rowena, "Master Lee" Steele, Mr. M.G. Bennett, and Katie Keogh (Harry's future wife).

In May 1876, Rowena published "The Victim of the Reef," in which she gives an interesting perspective on human suffering and religion in general. In a conversation between the characters Mertie Green and her mother, Mrs. Modest Curtis, Mertie states:

> "I sometimes doubt the whole subject of religion as taught by our ministers, when I see those who are humble, charitable, patient and generous, suffering seemingly more a thousand times than the heartless, uncharitable and purse-proud. It seems strange that God permits such vile creatures to crush out, as it were, his humble fellows. See how many of the rich and those holding position never bow the knee to God nor ever stretch out the hand of generosity to the poor, or give a charitable thought to the unfortunate. See how they prosper, while the poor devout ones suffer in tears and poverty, trampled upon by the high-headed and hard-hearted, who seem to be proof against misfortune."
>
> "I know, my darling, that these things seem strange. But I sometimes think that those who suffer here who pass through the fiery ordeal and go all patient and submissive to their God are the ones he has selected for the ministering angels of the hereafter. Having endured the sufferings that human flesh is

heir to, they are prepared to fulfill the mission of bringing comfort to the afflicted. If you will observe closely, you will see that afflictions are always accompanied by comforts and blessings, that is, if they are brought on through the vileness and wickedness of others. For our self-imposed sufferings we find but little relief from angel hands."[29]

In preparation for the Centennial, Rowena took a camping trip to Yosemite, where she had grown to appreciate the peace and beauty of its natural splendor, and encouraged others to do the same:

TO THE READERS OF THE ARGUS.—Now in this great Centennial year, when the spirit to love and acknowledge and admire everything of American make, birth and growth is abroad in our land, aye! in every civilized land of the earth, I might say, when the grand proclamation has gone forth from the out-stretched hand of the Goddess of Liberty, "Come and see what I have accomplished in one hundred years!" every American family should seek to do something that will leave a pleasant impression upon the minds of their children and pleasant and happy recollection of this glorious year upon the tablets of their own memories during life's declining days.

While a large portion of the world are blessed with sufficient means to enable them to go to the great center of attraction, Philadelphia, there are hundreds in California who are just as patriotic in their hearts, who have not the gold in their pockets. I would say to such, don't let that small matter deter you and your children from enjoying this Centennial, the only Centennial in all probability that you or the children

will ever see on earth. Even the millionaire can have
a Centennial only once in a hundred years, so don't
mope at home brooding over your poverty. If you
can't go to Philadelphia you can go to the Yosemite
on a camping tour, and it will cost you but little more
than it will to stay at home. Join in with other
families or go alone with your own, but go, and my
word for it, you will never regret it.[30]

In June, the *Argus* reported on the lynching at Santa Rosa
when a mob of men broke into the jail, took a prisoner named
Henley and hung him. It must have caused considerable fright and
anguish for Rowena whose own son was languishing in the
Merced jail at the same time. "If there is a crime in the calendar
that outstrips the inventions of the devil, it is the black and
heinous crime of tearing a helpless man, who has done you no
injury, out of the cell where he is already in the iron jaws of the
law, and amid yells and hellish curses, to drag him to some lonely
tree and hang him."[31] George Granice subsequently penned an
article on "The Lynch Vengeance" in August.

Later that summer, there was a report of an escape for the
second time from Merced jail of a young man named Reno, who
was confined there for shooting at John Stanton. Even though they
could have easily walked out with Reno, as there was no guard on
duty that day, the remainder of the prisoners, eight in number
including Harry, stayed in their cell with the door open until the
deputy sheriff arrived at five o'clock with their dinner.

Harry's frail health continued to suffer all that summer
while confined to jail. In September, Rowena wrote her
appreciation for her friends and neighbors who brought him food
and "other delicacies":

THANKS.—To the kind-hearted and generous ladies
who during the late severe illness of my son Harry H.

Granice, in the county jail, who have so liberally
contributed chickens and other delicacies which have
been the means of restoring him to partial good
health, I tender my most sincere and heartfelt thanks.
There has been a double joy in the receiving of these
gifts, for I have felt that every article was bread
which I had cast upon the waters in my humble way
as I have traveled on through the sunshine and
shades of life's journey along the rippling stream of
time which leads to eternity. May the loaves which
you have cast, my dear friends, come back to you.
But Heaven forbid that they should return upon such
rough and turbulent waters as did mine. My prayer is
that they come floating amid sunny dreams and
realities in laughing ripples of smiles and joys and
gladness feeding your hearts with knowledge which
will bring you peace and rest and unalloyed happiness
in the great hereafter.   R.G.S.[32]

He was finally freed on bail of $10,000 guaranteed by Hon.
Harvey J. Ostrander, Dr. Joshua Griffith, Daniel Yeizer, J.J. Cook,
John A. Robinson, William H. Hartley, Eli Grimes, W.C. Fisher,
A.R. Casaccia, W.H. Lee, George Powell, William Griffith, and
W. Fitch. It seems Harry and the Steeles still had several friends
and supporters in the Valley, which must have lifted Rowena's
outlook considerably. Presumably to raise money for bail and
legal defense, R.J. advertised for sale a "large building on corner
of Front and K streets, now occupied by Jno. A. Robinson as a
dwelling and fruit store," and "a few pairs of pure breed
Aylesbury ducks. Also, English topknot and common ducks at
reasonable prices."[33]

The Third Trial

On November 21, 1876, the Grand Jury issued the new indictment for Murder in the Second Decree. Harry was arraigned before the District Court in Merced, Judge J.B. Campbell presiding, with J.K. Law, W.L. Dudley, R.H. Ward for the State, and Judge David S. Terry and Charles H. Marks, of Wigginton & Marks, for the defense. Trial was scheduled for November 29th.

THE TRIAL OF H.H. GRANICE

This case came on for trial in the District court on Wednesday last, Judge Campbell presiding, and is in progress as we go to press with our paper. The case is an interesting one and presents features of which no parallel is known to the history of criminal juris-prudence. In a few weeks after the commission of the homicide an indictment was found by a Grand Jury of the county. Someone who had access to the place where the indictment was to be found, altered the indictment for the purpose of making it so strong that conviction for murder would follow. The fact of the alteration was discovered and defendant's counsel moved the court (Judge Deering) to correct the mutilated indictment so as to make it read as it did when it was filed in the District Court Clerk's office. The motion was denied and the defendant was convicted of murder and sentenced to imprisonment for life.

An appeal was taken to the Supreme Court, which reversed the case, and the court below ordered to correct the indictment and try the accused upon the indictment for manslaughter. The case then coming on in the District Court for Fresno county for a new trial, Judge Campbell presiding, a jury was impaneled

and the formula of a regular trial gone through with
to the extent of taking the testimony of witnesses for
the prosecution and the defense, when the
prosecution moved to dismiss the indictment and
remand the accused to jail to await the action of the
Grand Jury, and the court dismissed the indictment
accordingly. At the following term of the County
Court of this county another indictment was returned
by the Grand Jury against defendant for murder
upon which indictment he is now being tried. If
conviction follows these proceedings there is no
efficacy in written constitutions for the protection of
the declared rights of individuals.[34]

The same witnesses for the prosecution were called to testify. For
the defense, R.H. Wilson, who worked and roomed at the *Argus*
office, testified that he had witnessed the interchange between
Harry and Edward Madden at the El Capitan Hotel two days
before the shooting and Harry's illness over the weekend. Harry
again testified in his own defense and this transcript reveals new
details about the meeting at the El Capitan and the shooting two
days later on December 7th:

> I met [Madden] on Saturday the 5th day of
> December. The first time in front of El Capitan Bar-
> Room. He was sitting with Peter Higgins and Henry
> [*sic*, Ed?] Newman; I was proceeding on my way
> from the office to the house and that was on my
> direct route, and as I came very near opposite to
> them, Madden put his hand behind him, this way
> (indicating) and took out a pistol and laid it on his lap
> that way (indicating) and watched me as I was
> passing by and looked at me in a very threatening
> manner. I did not catch his eyes. He had his hat

down over his eye that way (indicating) scowling and
watching. I then hurried into El Capitan Bar Room,
and in a very few seconds—a few minutes—turned
and met Lawrence Levinskey and got him in between
me and these parties and proceeded on my way to
the end of El Capitan porch and then went along off.

* * *

Between the hours of six and seven of the same
evening, right after supper, I left our house and
started back up to the office to go to bed. When I
reached El Capitan Hotel, I met Orchard Scott and
had a conversation. I stood there talking to him and
my attention was attracted to Madden standing in
front of the Postoffice talking to Hattie Hubbard. He
stood in the door with his hands upon the door sill
this way (indicating) back towards us, and we stood
talking a while and in a short time Hattie Hubbard
went away, and Madden turned and came toward
me—this young lady he was talking to went back into
the Postoffice, and Madden turned and came toward
me and I met him. I asked him to retract the slander
he published against my mother. He pulled his pistol
out, and pointed it to me and said, "This is the way I
will retract, you damned bastard." I was very sick,
and I got behind one of those large pillars and hid
behind it, and he turned and went back into the bar
room. While I was standing there young Wilson came
up, and then we proceeded to the office. I was very
sick, and he put me to bed and went and got Dr. Lee.
Dr. Lee came in that evening and attended on me
and gave me medicine.

* * *

Monday morning I left my room in the *Argus* office
about a quarter past seven o'clock to go to the

butcher shop, and then home. I left the *Argus* office
and proceeded around that way, and just before I got
opposite to Simon, Jacobs [store], I was taken with a
pain in my bowels. I had the bloody flux and was
suffering from that, and I turned into the third door
from the corner into the furniture store and went in
there about twelve or fifteen feet—some distance—
from the door, and leaned up against one of those
large bedsteads until the pain passed off, and the pain
passed off after stopping in there a short time, and I
started to go out of the door. Just as I was about
stepping out of the door my attention was attracted
up the sidewalk, and as they drew very near opposite
to me, Madden being on the outside and Hamilton
on the inside, Hamilton nudged Madden and spoke
some hurried words to him, which I could not hear,
and as they got very near opposite to me, or opposite
me; they might have been passed; Madden put his
hand behind him and looked in a very threatening
manner towards me and turned around in a very
threatening attitude and I just stepped out of the
door; I was about to step out; and I jumped right out
ahead of them, Hamilton was in between the two of
us; I was afraid Madden would shoot over his
shoulder. That left Hamilton between the two of us,
and I jumped right out ahead. They were coming this
way (indicating) and I was in that position
(indicating) and jumped out this way (indicating) and
fired. The first shot took effect on the face; the first
or second; and I kept on shooting, and about the
fourth or fifth shot Madden threw up his hands and
fell forward, and I fired again; fired again; fired
before he touched the ground; fired my last shot.[35]

After twelve hours' deliberation, the jury, consisting of William Andrade, J.F. Sumner, T.J. Simpson, G.E. Mills, Henry Russ, Robert Menzel, John Westling, George Shaffer, John Ivett, A.M. Graham, Samuel S. Stone of Snelling, and George Mowery, found Harry guilty.

MURDER IN THE SECOND DEGREE. – The trial of H. H. Granice, indicted for murder in the first [*sic*, second] degree for the shooting and killing of Edward Madden, in the year 1874, was commenced in the District Court at Merced on the 29th of November, before Judge Campbell. At the time of the shooting, which occurred two years ago this month, Madden was editor of a paper known as the Merced Tribune, and the difficulty arose out a newspaper quarrel. The first day was consumed in impaneling a jury, which was finished towards evening, and the jury sworn in. The Court then adjourned until Friday morning. At the appointed time on Friday morning the Court again convened, and during the day various witnesses on both sides were examined and cross-questioned. At about five o'clock the Court adjourned until Saturday morning, at which time the trial was again opened. During the forenoon other witnesses were examined, and in the afternoon the pleading began. R.H. Ward of Merced opening for the prosecution. He was followed by Judge Terry of Stockton for the defense, and during the evening session Wm. L. Dudley of Stockton closed the case for the prosecution, Judge Campbell then instructed the jury, the prisoner was taken in charge by the Sheriff, and the jury was locked up. After remaining out twelve hours, they brought in a verdict of "Murder in the second degree." The sentence will be pronounced today. During the time which has elapsed since the murder was committed, this case has been tried in various Courts, and it is thought that Judge Terry will appeal it to the Supreme Court as soon as sentence is pronounced.[36]

On Saturday, December 9, 1876, Judge Campbell sentenced Harry to thirty years in San Quentin Prison where he was taken by Sheriff Meany on the Monday following. R.J. and Rowena remained optimistic the verdict would be overturned. "[I]t is generally believed by the leading lawyers of the State that the judgment will be reversed and the prisoner set at liberty."[37] They did not have to wait long. The California Supreme Court heard the case on December 12, 1876, and within days issued its decision freeing Harry once and for all from the charges and convictions.

THE GRANICE CASE IN THE SUPREME COURT.

Judgment of Lower Court Reversed and Order for Release of Prisoner.

The Vindictive Prosecution Defeated by Law and Sound Reasoning.

Shysters and Quibblers Nonplussed.

Judge Robertson and Balance of the Gang Furious.

The case of The People of the State of California vs. H.H. Granice came up before the Supreme Court of this State on Tuesday last, on appeal from the District Court of the 13th Judicial Dist. for Merced county, and after hearing argument of counsel for appellant and respondent, the Court promptly reversed the judgment of the District Court, and ordered the prisoner set at liberty. This result, of course, was foregone conclusion, the vindictiveness of those charged with the prosecution having led them to commit *blunders(!)* or something worse than blunders, that proved fatal to their case, which three separate times was taken before the Supreme Court—twice on appeal and once on *habeas corpus*— the judgment of the Court below in both cases of appeal being reversed. The prosecution went into the contest clamoring for a speedy trial and swift execution to satiate their thirst for the blood of their intended victim, and made up the case to suit their own views; the indictment by the Grand Jury being deemed insufficient to warrant a conviction for murder was, after a few days from the date of filing, so *amended* as to be unrecognizable by the jurors who last saw the instrument before it was placed in the hands of the County Judge in open County Court. As to who *altered* the indictment will perhaps never be positively proven, but all know that the alteration was never made by anyone interested in the welfare of the defendant.

Thousands upon thousands of people in California and the Atlantic states will read the simple announcement of the deliverance of Harry H. Granice from prison, and from jeopardy, with emotions of real pleasure, and with thankfulness for the wisdom and purity of the Court of last resort which acquitted him and set him again at liberty. *Veritas vincit.*[38]

A gracious article in the Oakland *Morning Times* in November 1877 summed up the ordeal:

ROMANCE OF MANSLAUGHTER.

Among recent visitors of note was Mrs. Rowena Granice Steele, of the *San Joaquin Valley Argus* at Merced. She is one of the most powerful of far-western women, and part of her life has been a crushing tragedy. About three years ago, her son slew a young man, a journalist at Merced, for publishing a false and wicked article about his mother. Chivalrous and filial manhood said the manslaughter was justifiable, but the iron visaged law pronounced it murder in the first degree, and young Granice was sentenced to thirty years imprisonment.

Mrs. Steele was poor. At the conclusion of the trial she hadn't a dollar in the world; but she had a mother's heart of mighty vitality and some friends who remembered the good she had sought to do for others. One good old man at Merced came up with a check for two thousand dollars; others responded with lesser sums, until seven thousand dollars had been accumulated. With this Mrs. Steele engaged the legal services of David S. Terry, N. Greene Curtis and other powerful lawyers, who undertook the release of her son. For two years and one month the battle raged back and forth, a hand-to-hand conflict with the law. The ground was fought over and over, and when the great lawyers despaired, they were encouraged and urged to renewed exertions by the resolute and indomitable mother of the prisoner. At last, maternal love and heroism prevailed, and her son was set at liberty and restored to citizenship, to become the stay in her declining years of one of the most devoted and strong-hearted mothers that ever gave birth to mankind.

Mrs. Steele has lost the worn and anxious aspect she bore during the times of her terrible trial, and looks as young and vigorous and happy as she did twenty years ago.[39]

Chapter X

Tragedy and Loss Befall Rowena Again – Death of George Law Granice; Shutting Down of the Argus by the County Clique

Rowena lost no time in her zeal and activism with social causes. On December 14, 1876, presumably while appearing at the California Supreme Court hearing in San Francisco, she also attended the State Woman's Suffrage Society meeting and was appointed to the Board of Directors. At the same meeting, her friend Laura DeForce Gordon was elected president.[xv] Her particular attention was focused for the next several months on legitimizing and elevating the status of working women and addressing the opposition arguments to women voting, especially from the female sex and her sister newspaper editors.

WOMAN SUFFRAGE.

It would appear from a little article in the *Golden Dawn* for January, 1877, entitled—"Belle Lynch on Woman Suffrage," that [Editor] Dora Daramore has found another strong-minded, self-reliant, self-supporting woman to join her in her *feeble* cry against woman suffrage. Here is what Belle Lynch says on the subject:

> In our opinion it is the duty of every woman to leave the filthy pool of politics alone; that if she faithfully fills the station in life for which she was

---

[xv] As the California delegate, Mrs. Gordon attended the National Suffrage Congress in Rochester, New York, in July 1878, along with famous national leaders Lucretia Mott and Elizabeth Cady Stanton. She later became the second woman admitted to the California Bar.

intended by the All-wise Creator, she
would have her hands full, and no
time to spare on political purposes.
Woman's sphere is in her home, her
dress and her toilet, and her weapons
of offense and defense are many,
including the broom-stick and rolling-
pin, and to these and such other
luxuries as may come within her
grasp, she ought to confine herself.

"Filthy pool of politics!" Why, this must be a bit of
sarcasm from the pen of this pungent writer, who
spends every day throughout the whole session of
the Legislature at Sacramento. True, circumstances
may have caused a change of mind in the boss of a
political journal—she may have found it to her
interest to pull on the anti-woman suffrage wire with
the amiable, ease-loving Dora, but we don't believe
it. Belle Lynch has too much good hard sense to
work against so good and just a cause. She, as well as
every other man and woman who has given the
subject thought, knows full well that it is only a
question of time—that it will come in its regular
round; it will not be of premature birth, to die out
and be forgotten.

A gentleman expressed the opinion the other day
that the right of suffrage would be allowed to
women, but that a separate place would be provided
for the reception of their ballots. A separate place for
women! What an idea! If there is to be a separate
place provided for any, it should be for the rough,
unprincipled hoodlums who get drunk, swear and use
vile language. The separate place should be provided
for such, so that women could go and vote with their

fathers, brothers, husbands, sons, or other friends. And, I think that, with woman's suffrage will come laws to protect her, even should she go alone to the place of voting.

Justice cannot be done this great and important subject in a few hurried words. It is not only all the grand, noble and good which will spring from this inevitable change that is to be told, but also much filthy rubbish, and poisonous seeds which have been sown by the thoughtless, dress-loving women, and the rough, uncultivated men is to be removed. Every little [effort], however, helps to roll on the great ball of progress.   ROWENA G. STEELE.[1]

She wrote a few more columns in the Spring of 1877 about rather trivial and mundane things such as the nationwide search for the "handsomest man" ("Will California come out and show her handsomest man? Who is he? Where is he? Is he in Merced county?"[2]), the inequity between the rich and poor, and the benefits of hard work and trust in God to sustain us.

Then, suddenly, nothing. Silence from the Steeles. No issues of the *Argus* from March 10, 1877. Four months later the heartbreaking news was published in several California newspapers.

GRANICE—At Merced, July 17, George Law Granice, a native of New York, aged 24 years, 1 month, 17 days.[3]

DIED. At Merced, July 17th, 1877, after a long and painful illness, GEORGE LAW GRANISE [*sic*], a native of New York City, aged 24 years 2 months and 17 days. Deceased was the stepson of ROBERT J. STEELE, and the 2d son of MRS. R.G. STEELE.[4]

The cause of death was later given as dropsy, an old term for congestive heart failure.[xvi] One can only imagine the immense anguish and heartache Rowena must have been suffering during those ten months of silence. There are no obituaries or loving tributes for George from his mother extant; she was undoubtedly thereafter too overcome by grief and depression to speak about it, although she mentioned her hopeful intention of doing so several times.

> PASSED away, on the morning of the 17th day of July, 1877, George Law Granice, the beloved son of Rowena Granice Steele, aged 24 years, two months, and 17 days. We had hoped to have written a few words in memory of him, who in life was so dear to us, and who in death seems so very near that spirit communes with spirit, and we know we shall meet again. We are not equal to the task.[5]

In 1899 when recalling her part in the establishment of the Asphodel Cemetery (now part of the Merced District Cemetery), to which George's remains were transferred in 1879, Rowena described his initial interment.

> "My son died (July 17, 1877) and was buried in what was termed Potters Field with hundreds of respectable citizens. Sometime after I put up a railing, set out some shrubs, and put up a marble headstone. I had scarcely had this work finished when I discovered that the remains of my beloved son, George Granice, were buried in the middle of a street which was liable to be opened at any time."[6]

[xvi] Other sources claim it was tuberculosis.

In 1879, she acknowledged receiving for the reinterment "six magnificent bouquets and two large and beautiful garlands ... for the decking of the grave of our beloved son" presented by Mrs. VanHorn and Mrs. Samuel King in honor of George's birthday. "And we thank little Birtie VanHorn, too, for the tiny wreath and sweet bouquet twined by her baby hands 'for Mrs. Steele's boy.' God Bless her!"[7]

Later in 1879 a travelling syndicated columnist by the name of John C. McPherson, who used the pseudonym "Juanita," wrote of visiting the new gravesite and his fond remembrances of George:

Visit to the Grave of Geo. L. Granice.

EDITOR ARGUS:—On Friday afternoon of last week, we rode out to the quiet "City of the Dead," near Merced City, and slowly wandering among the graves of the silent sleepers there, we at length stood before the last resting place on earth of all that was mortal of the young poet—our lamented friend, George Law Granice. On the marble monument, which affection had caused to be erected to his sacred memory, and with deep emotion, we read this inscription:

GEORGE LAW GRANICE.

Died July 17th, 1877, Aged 24 years.

The Young Poet Rests in the Bright Spirit Land.

That was all, but as we gazed upon the sod that now wraps his silent breast, various associations connected with tender reminiscences of his young life filled our mind, and we felt very sad indeed that one so gifted and so young, just in the summer of his life, should have gone away from earth and from mortal vision forever. It was a sultry afternoon when

we stood before his grave and looking around upon
the plain as far as our eye could compass, and then
upon the hills and mountains which flank the great
valley of the San Joaquin on the west, and all now
sere and brown, we called to mind the young poet's
own beautiful lines, written but a very short time
before his death, in the dry summer of 1877:—

"A faint aroma of perfume,
Comes softly stealing through the room
From the garden's flowery bloom,
And beyond, a dreary waste,
Where the eyes so weary grow,
As the barren fields they trace,
Which no vegetation show.
Now the winds that gently blow,
Tossing the foliage to and fro,
In the sunset's golden glow,
Seem to whisper on the plain
Words of comfort and of cheer,
Saying they'll toss the golden grain
In plenitude, the coming year."

Poor George did not live to behold the golden grain
of the "coming year," for 'mid the tears and
lamentations of his fond, devoted mother, stepfather,
affectionate brothers and friends he died, as already
stated, very soon after he had written the above lines.
He was a most affectionate son and brother, and
steadfast, warm friend, and in all the relations of life
his character was worthy of emulation. We had
known him well, and now that he is gone can, in very
truth, say—

"None ever knew him but to love him,
Nor named him but to praise."

The last time we beheld him was some few years ago when we met unexpectedly on the Merced river, and as we grasped his warm hand, his eye sparkled with love-light which irradiated his intelligent features like the last flush of parting day glowing upon the earth. He was animated in conversation and looked forward to his future with bright hopes and aspirations. When at length we said "Farewell, George," and we went each his separate way, little did we think that we had parted forever!

But George sleeps well in yonder cemetery, and

Though sere and brown the sod to see,

That wraps his silent breast now be,

When Spring with dewy fingers cold,

Returns to deck his hallowed mold,

She there shall dress a sweeter sod

Than fancy's feet have ever trod.

Then, too, will come soft, vernal showers,

And wake to life the slumbering flowers,

Which thus a fragrance will exhale,

On every gentle passing gale;

And little birds upon the wing,

Will fold their pinions there and sing

A requiem, plaintive, sweet and low,

For our dear friend, who sleeps below.

There, then, in that consecrated ground, let us hope the young poet may rest undisturbed till awaked by the sound of the arch-angel's trump on the Judgment morning.   JUANITA

Merced, September 23, 1879.[8]

Just five months later, McPherson would meet his own death at age sixty in an accident, probably precipitated by intoxication, when he fell off the railroad bridge crossing the Tuolumne River one mile below Modesto.

The Argus is Revitalized With Rowena as Editor

Finally, after ten months, in January 1878, the *Argus* recommenced publication with Rowena as Editor. She explained that the hiatus happened because of petty political machinations on the part of the County Clique, still intent on the ruination of the Steeles and the *Argus* even if by nefarious means.

Why Was the "Argus Office Closed?

Why was it the *Argus* stopped in its publication, and why was the office closed? are questions which have been asked of me for the last ten months. I will now simply make a statement of how the office was closed.

On Saturday, March 10th, 1877, it was necessary for my husband, Mr. Robert J. Steele, to go to Snelling for the purpose of attending to the wants of my son George, an invalid, who had been taken over by a friend with the hope that the change would benefit the sufferer; but, becoming worse, Mr. Steele went with the intention of bringing the sick one to his home. The mailing of the *Argus* was left to me to perform; and on that morning as I was seated in the office, busily engaged at the work, Edward Packard walked into the office and handed me a paper. I glanced at the outside and read: "Justices' Court, No. —— Township, County Merced. P. Carroll, plaintiff, vs. H.J. Ostrander, defendant. Copy of writ of attachment. M.C. Gardiner, plaintiff's attorney." I then opened the document and read: "Mrs. R.G. Steele, you are hereby notified"—I read enough to learn that Mr. Patrick Carroll wanted Mr. Harry J. Ostrander to pay him $160 with costs. But what Mrs.

R.G. Steele or the *Argus* had to do with the debt or
the demand of these parties was beyond my
comprehension. The man, clothed in a little brief
authority, who served the [illegible-paper?] in
earnest and appeared to attach considerable
importance either to the business or himself. He was
big enough, and loud enough to have crushed
woman, office and all. He said that he must have
immediate possession. I told him that I would finish
making up the mail and then, if it was right and
proper that I should leave, I should do so. I
continued to work quietly and in a few moments a
second man made his appearance, and politely
informed me that he had been placed in possession
of the office and all belonging to it. After sending the
mail to the post office, I sent for a lawyer who, when
he came, laughed, and said: "It will be all right on
Monday." So I took the books and a few private
letters, and left the office with its furniture, press,
type and files. Mr. H. Ostrander took the benefit of
the bankrupt law, and a week or two after all of his
property was returned to him by the United States
Marshal. But the *Argus* office and its belongings are
still in the possession of the county officers—not for
any indebtedness of the owners and proprietors—
but to satisfy the malicious, deadly, bitter, venomous
spite of a clique against an honest man who has
dared to proclaim the rights of the people. For ten
long months the family has been deprived of the
legitimate means of procuring a living. During that
time our son, a young man twenty-four years of age,
lay confined to his bed for four months and then
passed away. My husband, whose health has been
rapidly failing for the last five months, is now

confined to his bed and has not been able to sit up a moment for several weeks.

There were five men hung in Bakersfield a few days ago for stealing. I wonder if any one of them had, without the least foundation of a legitimate right, robbed a sick and dying family and then laughed over it as a good joke. Is there no law or justice in Merced? someone not acquainted with the county government will ask. Yes; but not for the poor and honest. No money, no justice. But time brings justice. We will labor and wait.   R.G.S.[9]

This gives us yet another glimpse of the tremendous resilience, fortitude, and dogged determination that characterized Rowena throughout her life. Other California papers took notice.

Redivivus.

———

After a suspension of ten months, the San Joaquin Valley Argus comes to the front this week, under the editorial proprietorship of Mrs. Rowena Granice Steele. It is doubtless with a sad heart that she enters upon the journalistic field as a resource for the maintenance of an invalid husband and son. Her intrepidity is commendable, and while sympathizing with her in her afflictions, and bidding her a cordial God-speed in her enterprise, we cannot omit to suggest that, bitter as her experience may have been in "law and justice," Merced County does not materially differ from other localities in this respect. The Shakespearian apothegm about the strong lance of justice breaking hurtless upon a gold plating is of universal application.[10]

The revitalized *Argus* was offered to the subscribers initially as a weekly folio sheet at $3 per year, cash in advance, apparently jobbed out for printing in San Francisco. With the presses having been seized and still locked in legal limbo, the office was for the time being located in their residence on 17th Street.

Rowena began with a detailed article on public schools in New York in the 1840s, personal items about people living in and visiting Merced, acknowledgements of gifts, an account of a trip to Snelling and Merced Falls, and an article about some of the prisoners in San Quentin whom she had met during her visits with Harry, particularly Millard P. Speese, a boy of fifteen, who had been sentenced to a living hell in the tough, foreboding prison for five years for a first offense of attempted stage robbery. He left a widowed, sick, impoverished mother, "bewailing the fate of her young son, who has two years yet to serve at hard labor in our State prison. Cannot something be done to give this boy back to his mother? Surely he has suffered enough for his childish folly."[11]

> Oh, is this right? Is this just? Is this merciful? Great men of our nation, lawmakers of our land, can you stand idly by and see this inequality of justice and of right, quarreling about your silver bills, wrangling for seats in high places, disputing about who shall have the largest share of the public money? Pause, for heaven's sake. Look back over your own lives and think how often, even after you had arrived to the years of discretion, you have wronged your wives, your children, how you have gone astray, how by spending your money with gay companions you have robbed your wife and children, aye, in many ways have you transgressed and erred, and you are free, while hundreds of youths, who have been led

unconsciously into wrong, are shut out from home friends, and all chance of reform.[12]

In March 1878 the *Argus* published one of George's poems, "A Day Among the Pines," and another poem by Mrs. W.A. Duchow on the evils of backbiting and scandal-mongering, which Rowena prefaced with her thoughts on the subject: "Oh! how sad it is to feel that the only beings which God has endowed with the faculty of speech should thus misuse and degrade the beautiful gift by giving utterance to malicious slanders or innuendoes which is far more poisonous than the vilest outspoken word."[13]

Throughout the next few months, she promoted Merced's shops and other businesses, especially those belonging to proprietors who had been supportive during Harry's trials, such as Andrew Casaccia and Harvey Ostrander. Interestingly, one of those enterprises was the "White Woman's Laundry," run by Mrs. M.A. Stanton, "where none but white women will be employed,"[14] indicative of the growing resentment and racism in California and the nation at the time against the Chinese workers, hired by the thousands to build the railroads and other infrastructure, who were now trying to make a living elsewhere in new ventures such as laundries and restaurants. This was made even more obvious in July, when the Workingman's Ball was held in Merced with banners heralding "Welcome All" but "The Chinese Must Go!"[xvii]

[xvii] In February 1886 an "Anti-Chinese League" was formed among major businessmen of Merced. R.J. Steele was elected temporary president. The Native Sons of the Golden West, of which Lee Steele was an officer and prominent member was also associated with blatant anti-Chinese rhetoric and activities. Rowena has never published her personal opinion on the issue of immigration by people of color that I could find; on the other hand, she was very enthusiastic about the "Hollanders" who settled in Merced in large numbers in 1890.

The financial predicament with which Rowena and R.J. were undoubtedly struggling at this time can be deduced from an article advertising land for sale.

> OUR READERS will please direct their attention to the advertisements of land and small farms for sale by R.J. Steele. Particular attention is called to the Mountain Ranch, which can be got at a good bargain. This Ranch will produce just as well in a dry season as in a wet one, as the water is plenty the year round. This will make a pleasant home for an industrious family with a small capital.[15]

In April, Rowena began reporting on regular trips to visit Merced County farms, canals, artesian wells, etc., and the county hospital, highlighting thriving establishments and calling attention to areas that needed improvement. For example, she criticized a ditch on railroad property filled with green scum and a cesspool of stagnant water, which reveals her awareness of environmental health hazards. "While this green monster lays there silently vomiting forth virus from its secreted poison depths, our town is doomed to epidemics."[16] She also started advocating for cemetery improvement, which eventually led to the establishment of the Asphodel Cemetery, and became a member of the Merced Cemetery Association in July 1880.

An "Intention to Become a Sole Trader" was published in June 1878: "The nature of the business I propose to carry on and pursue is that of printing and publishing a newspaper entitled 'SAN JOAQUIN VALLEY ARGUS,' and that of doing the general business of job printing in all its branches."[17] It was approved by the court in August. Her mid-year status report gives additional insights into the ordeals she and the family had been enduring the previous year:

TO THE READERS OF THE ARGUS.

It is just six months today since the SAN JOAQUIN VALLEY ARGUS made its appearance under the supervision of its present editor and proprietor, Mrs. R.G. Steele; and we do not wish our readers to think we are egotistical or vainly boastful when we say that we are proud of its present position and its present promising condition.

In the dark, dark days of last December when the clouds hung black and heavy, when the bleak cold winds went moaning and howling around our little home; when strong men grew faint at heart at the prospect of a hard winter, when the wealthy and healthy complained bitterly of hard times. With no winter's wood or other necessary provision, our printing press, our only means of making a living was securely locked up in the dark cellar of the Court House Bar-room, where it had been put by the lawless, unprincipled court house clique who had stolen it some eight months previously, on a groundless pretense that they thought it belonged to another party, when in fact it was done for the purpose of suppressing editorials which they feared would defeat them in the then coming election. With our husband seemingly just on the verge of the grave, two children to clothe and feed, and the sad, sad sorrow for the death of a dearly beloved son still clinging with its tearful memory around our mother heart, we saw with the other realities the lean, lank, haggard face of the wolf at the door. Silently we looked the creature square in the face; silently with our thoughts we went over the ground beneath which lay buried our rightful belongings; silently, firmly and determinedly we resolved to strike for one woman's rights. The right to labor in the field for which she believed nature, and nature's God and an acquired self-reliance, had fitted her to win an honest living and support for her dependent family. With this resolve came hope, and trust, and vim, and energy; and thanks to the many kind and fearless friends who own themselves, who are slaves to no one, on the morning of the bright new year 1878 we found ourself in possession of the means to start our enterprise, and in spite of the opposition brought to bear against us by at least fifty of the grand lords of creation, the sneers, and a few turn-up-nosish remarks of the county fed of the fair sex, the *San Joaquin Valley Argus* made its appearance upon the streets and in the homes of Merced on the 5th of January, and it has made its appearance every Saturday morning since that time. The first three months we were compelled to have the printing done in San Francisco. Then Judge Terry managed to loosen the vice-like grip of the county clique power, and the press was brought back and laid at our door, not at our expense either, and then they paid back the costs and went quietly on their way, asking no reward only to be let alone. Well, we have let them alone, while we have worked hard and honestly and to-day, just six months from the dark days our home is clean and cozy, our garden all abloom with green vines, waving foliage and bright flowers; we are not in debt, we pay as we go, and by adhering to the principles of truth and honesty, by living upright in our dealing and prompt in honest action, we hope to gain the confidence and secure the patronage of the public; and when the pressing times are over with our farmers and merchants and mechanics, we feel certain that they will come forward and pay up old sums and give us further encouragement. We shall do all we can for the advancement and prosperity of Merced. Sixteen years ago yesterday, associated with our husband, Mr. R.J. Steele, we issued the first newspaper ever printed or published in Merced county; it was entitled the Merced *Banner*. And if life and health is spared us we may publish a paper in Merced on the 4th of July, sixteen years hence.[18]

In September, Rowena announced her plans to travel to Oakland and Sacramento to attend the agricultural and industrial fairs. "If any of our friends here have a message to send or any little business transacted, we shall be pleased to accommodate them. None but those having perfect confidence in our judgment, capacity and honesty need call upon us."[19] An amusing piece appeared in the paper a week later, obviously penned by fifteen-year-old Lee Steele who had been left in charge of the *Argus* during his mother's absence and father's illness.

WHO WANTS A PUFF[xviii]?—Well, the editor and publisher, our mother, has gone off for a rest from editorial duties and household cares. The foreman, our paternal "parent," has got the toothache in his teeth, the rheumatism in his limbs, a pain in his back, and ailments in all his joints. So the responsibility of the establishment rests on us, i.e., we, the office imp: and we would say to our patrons that it's just the time to send in good things, such as fruit, wedding cake and *other delicacies of the season*. We like raw oysters, sardines and maple sugar. We are prepared to puff and blow about fruit, wedding cake, corn cake or gingerbread. Oh! we will give you "delicious," "luscious," and we will do it in way-up style. We, us,

---

[xviii] A puffing up, as in compliment and praise.

the devil are just spoiling to give someone a puff.
Send something! we don't care what, so that it is
toothsome. We are a growing boy (you know what
that means). Just give us a chance to write a pull or
two; it may help to drive that line of the old song out
of our head. It's just been dinging in our ears for the
last two days:

> "What is home without a mother?"

Oh! do give us a chance to write a puff to keep us
from feeling homesick. We don't beg; we are anxious
to pay for what we get—in puffs![20]

The County Printing Contract Conflict Continues

Once the presses were restored, Rowena announced the
paper would be expanded starting October 12, 1878. "Our readers
after this week will get an eight page paper, filled with original
matter for the small sum of 6 cents per week. To people who love
to read, reading is a luxury, and surely the *Argus* will be a cheap
luxury."[21] Sometime early in 1879 the Rowena changed the
political affiliation of the paper to the Republican Party. We do
not know what R.J.'s feelings on that were, but by May 1879, he
had recovered in health well enough to resume editorial
responsibilities so that he would "relieve Mrs. Steele of a portion
of the arduous duties devolving upon her as publisher and editor
of the ARGUS.... Mrs. Steele will continue in future as in the past
to manage the publication department, and will endeavor to
transact all business connected therewith in a manner satisfactory
to the public and patrons of the paper; and will also aid in editing
that portion of the paper devoted to local matters and general news
not connected with politics [emphasis supplied]."[22] This is not
surprising considering Rowena's historical disdain for anything
political.

Later, in June of 1880, Rowena wrote:

The senior editor of the ARGUS has been constantly engaged during the past week in agricultural and horticultural pursuits. He has devoted more time to the hoe, rake, shovel and irrigation pipes than to the pen. He has given more attention to his potato, pea, and onion beds and strawberry patch than to news home, while the associate has been gathering society notes and facts about her patrons, although the senior has worked away digging, hoeing and watering. The associate has watched the working of his silent facial expressions, and she has detected fire in his eagle eye, and political thunder like a threatening cloud has set upon his high and hairless brow, and next week our readers may expect more of the fiery element of political thunder than of the gentle and amiable.[23]

The County printing contract continued to elude the *Argus* for several years. Despite the significantly lower bid of 25 cents per square, first insertion, and 20 cents per square, subsequent insertions, compared to the rival *Merced Express* bid of $1 and 75 cents, respectively, the award of the county printing contract was given in 1879 and again in 1880 to the *Express*. Rowena was forced to take action to right this blatant discrimination.

After reading the law providing for the letting of the county printing to the lowest bidder ... published in these columns last week, we are at a loss as to how any intelligent being could award the contract as the majority of the Board did without being conscious [of the] plainly expressed provisions of the law and their obligations as officers in and for the county of Merced. When honor, justice, reason and law are the rule of action by those in authority, it is the duty of all good citizens to submit without complaint to their acts. But, on the other hand, when all these are violated, and the burdens of the taxpayers are thereby increased, we think it is time for all free and independent citizens to rise in their majesty and, in a lawful manner, put an end to such vicious and unlawful proceedings by the legislative department of the county.[24]

Represented by Laura DeForce Gordon, a new member of the California bar, she followed up by filing a Petition for Writ of *Certiorari* on August 27, 1880. The hearing was held on October 12 before Judge Charles Marks.

> This cause came on regularly for trial on the 12th day of October, 1880, Laura DeForce Gordon appearing as counsel for the plaintiff, and Russ Ward, P.D. Wigginton, and Frank Farrar for the defendants. The cause was tried before the court sitting without a jury; whereupon the counsel for the plaintiff presented arguments in support of the petition of the plaintiff, and the counsel for the defendants presented arguments on behalf of the defendants. The cause was submitted to the court for consideration and decision, and after due deliberation thereon,
>
> Wherefore, by reason of the law it is ordered and adjudged that the action of the said defendants exceeded their jurisdiction in the matter of making the award of the county printing and the same is here declared null and void. And the plaintiff do have and recover of and from the Board of Supervisors of Merced County, the defendants, the costs and disbursements incurred in this action amounting to Forty-two dollars and five cents.

Judgment recorded October 12, 1880.

Charles H. Marks, Judge[25]

An appeal of the judgment was filed; however, Mrs. Gordon was successful in getting it quickly dismissed.

Gifts, Surprise Party, and Grand Complimentary Ball

Evidence of the many friends and admirers Rowena had gathered about her to sustain her spirit and stamina during this sad and stressful time can be garnered from several acknowledgements and appreciations printed in the *Argus*.

'Tis a sweet consolation to look upon the gifts of friendship. There are days when the heart will not be light and mirthful, when all the glad seems to have gone out. 'Tis then these little gifts of love prove a solace, a cheerful beam on life's weary pilgrimage. The stars shine, but the rays are pale and faint. There is a chillness without and within. There is an unpleasant whispering among the branches and the leaves tremble as though they fear that the icy hand of death will soon blight their lovely green, and send them all seared and withering to the damp cold earth.

To drive away these intruders we will look over the little mementoes. Here is a little vase given us nine years ago by Mrs. Rosa Myers. A rug, a Christmas gift years ago from Simon, Jacobs & Co., a log cabin chair cover, from dear Fanny Green McDougall, a crochet lamp mat by sweet Mary Ludescher, when she was full of life and the joyous hope of young maidenhood; this was the work of her nimble fingers. The fingers have perished, but the spirit liveth. Ah! these faded orange blossoms dry and faded, but still fragrant, these the last gift of my heart's best friend, kind, gentle-voiced Laura Fitzhugh. Here is a soft blond lace neck-tie, fleecy as a silver cloud, 'tis the gift of Alice Tadlock. How gracefully the young fingers twined this pretty fabric about our neck; how the gentle voice tried to soothe the woe filled heart; this was given I those sad and dark days.

This box of shells, some of them so curious in formation, they were a gift from Mary Bost—little bright-eyed Mary, tripping through the wild flowers; yes, memory goes back to those school day times. This little specimen, with dots of gold, given by our true and faithful friend, Dr. Fitzhugh. This little paper containing three faded flowers, the gift of little Addie Peck; God bless the sweet little hand that plucked them for the weary hearted mother whose burden seemed heavier than she could bear. Three bright little flowers—they are faded now—but the golden light of memory will cling to them while life lasts.

This preserved funeral wreath, sacred to the memory of our beloved George—'tis the gift of our gentle friend, Mary Arnold. She with the beautiful gift of loving all that is lovely. This light worsted vase cover, a Christmas gift from sister Hanson. These tiny daisies fashioned so artistically, a gift from Lucy Spears, the auburn tresses from which they are woven from her head—the gift from the gentle sympathizing heart. This soft little white shawl, the work of fair Amal Lapham. And here a pretty wall ornament, the work of little Onie Ostrander. That lovely oil painting, a gift from the gifted poetess, Sarah Morton. Those little hanging baskets sent to us by Mrs. Bloss. The handsome vase and bracket, the gift of our loving friend, Mrs. Long.

Ah! these splashed racks [*sic*, rocks?], the gift of
Belle Curley, and here is another pretty basket, a gift
from Mr. Leeker. These two little crosses, the work
of the Sisters of the Sacred Heart, given to us by our
friend Mrs. Barber. This beautiful inlaid cribbage
board, the gift of one who was unfortunate, but
heaven smiled and the gladness came back. This
picture painted by good, true Lydia E. Drake. The
inkstand before us, blue and bronze, with graceful elk
horns, a gift from Mrs. Pratt. This elegant wall
pocket from our little friend Nellie. And that corner
bracket with the deer head and horns a Christmas gift
from brother Spafford and the bright rag rug at the
parlor door little Lizzie Corcoran's offering.

Those large sparkling specimens sent to us from the
talented Dr. W.W. Carpenter. The framed letter up
there from P.T. Barnum, ladened with a precious gift,
a *good name*. Then all of these smiling faces on walls,
tables, brackets, from every side they smile upon us,
forty pairs of bright eyes beaming with kindness
upon us, eyes of loved ones now in the bright spirit
world; eyes of those warm, tender and affectionate,
full of life and hope and promise; eyes of infant
innocents; eyes of the old, the tempted, the tried;
eyes which have all been weary from sad watching,
and eyes that have been dimmed with tears; glad,
joyous young eyes. To-night they all cast kindly
glances and lend a cheerfulness to the little parlor.

And now our eyes rest on one of the sweetest of
the gifts—a bunch of sweet, bright flowers, culled by
the gentle hand of our mild-eyed friend of verse and
song, Georgie D. Weed. Why, all the lonely feeling
which came creeping o'er us has vanished, there is
music in the whisper of the night wind. The leaves

are prattling words of love. The angels seem near
with their snowy wings, and the tender voice of him
that left us a few short months ago comes back and
mingles with the sighing breezes, and seems to say,
Cheer up, mother! Yes, all is light and joy and
gladness, and we are happy, calmly serenely happy
amid these cherished gifts. These dear dumb faces.
To-night our dreams will be of the joys to come.[26]

A BEAUTIFUL PRESENT.—Upon the corner table of
our best room we find a lovely lamp mat, the
prettiest we ever saw. As it softly rests upon the
white marble slab, it looks like a wreath of sweet,
natural flowers, so perfect is each tiny bud and full-
blown blossom, nestling among the green mossy bed.
Blue forget-me-nots, rare shaded tulips, delicate
dahlias, darling blue daisies and cunning blue bells.
This magnificent piece of worsted work is a gift from
Mrs. Fred Gardenhire. The design is from her own
tasteful and artistic eye, the work by her busy hands.
We fully appreciate this lovely gift and the generous
giver. Mrs. Gardenhire's little home is a perfect
bower of home-made beauties. May happiness ever
dwell within its walls and peace and plenty crown the
declining years of the dwellers therein.[27]

On Thursday of this week we were surprised at
receiving a large box, some three feet square, through
Wells, Fargo & Co.'s Express, directed to Mrs. R.G.
Steele, Merced. If we were surprised at receiving the
box, what should we say of our astonishment upon
opening it to find a magnificent oil painting with a
massive gilt frame. We could scarcely believe our
senses. Such an elegant present with no line or word
to give us a clue to the name of the donor. "Who

could have sent it?" was all we could say amid our joy and admiration of being the possessor of such a grand gift. The fine oil painting with the splendid gilt frame cost at least one hundred dollars. It is not alone the possession of this costly gift that gives us such genuine pleasure, but the thought that we should have a friend or friends who hold us in such high esteem as to consider us worthy of the beautiful present. We trust that the giver will make himself or herself known. We suspect a him or a her. The subject of this work of art is a scene in the tropics. We will, when we ascertain who the artist is, give our readers a full description of the mysterious gift.[28]

Further proof of the good will of neighbors and friends that the family enjoyed was demonstrated by this report of a surprise party at the home on 17th Street in October 1878.

At an early hour on Tuesday evening as we, with our family, were seated around the center table in the dining-room of our domicile, our spouse and our senior typo [Lee Steele] deeply interested in an innocent game of cribbage, ourself busily engaged in needle work, while our thoughts were wandering to scenes of the olden time, our ears caught the sound of the strains of sweet vocal and instrumental music. We dropped our work, our companions ceased their game. What was it? Had the Heavens opened and these, the sweet songsters of the upper realms pouring forth their sweet strains to cheer our heart and little home? Quietly and on tip-toe each member of the household advanced towards the front door; nearer and nearer, sweeter and sweeter came the thrilling sounds. "Oh, Heavenly music," we exclaimed, and as we peered out into the star-lit garden we caught a glimpse of a moving body, and soon light footsteps warned us that a party of friends were awaiting an initiation to enter. Spouse flew around and lit the lamps, office imp and typo rushed for extra seats, while we received the packages, done up in snowy damask towels; four large frosted cakes, a dozen pies, boiled tongues and lots of goodies. Singing, dancing, bon-mot and a general social time followed. At 11 o'clock the extension table was spread the length of the dining-room and the collation served with hot tea and coffee, the lady guests making themselves generally useful. We enjoy these little surprise parties, and whenever the old or young, or mixed, wish to have a little frolic, our parlor, dining-room and kitchen are at their disposal, and we will always furnish the beverage.[29]

Then, later that month came the news of a Grand Complimentary Benefit Ball to be given in Rowena's honor.

MERCED, October 23, 1878

MRS. R.G. STEELE—Dear Madam: In consideration of your unfaltering efforts to please your patrons through all the struggle and opposition that have beset your path, and wishing to show a just appreciation of your literary labors, we beg leave to tender you a Complimentary Benefit Ball. Please name time and place.

With true regards,

YOUR MANY FRIENDS.

————

MERCED, October 24, 1878

LADIES, GENTLEMEN AND FRIENDS:—Your kind offer, that of tendering to me a Complimentary

Benefit Ball, is accepted, and I will name Tuesday
evening, November 19, 1878, at Washington Hall.

Yours with many thanks,

ROWENA G. STEELE

The Committee of Arrangements was an impressive list of some
of the most prominent men in Merced County: J. Frank Niles,
C.H. Marks, H. McPherson, E. Jackman, William Fahey, George
Reuter, S.S. Lapham, of Merced; A. Jacobs, W.W. Abbott, Ernest
Kahl, Andrew Lauder, James Lauder, John Morley, Daniel
Donovan, of Plainsburg; James Brady, Gordon Fitzhugh, and
George Halstead, of Snelling; E.B. Lurch, John Gillman, and
Richard Murry, of LaGrange. Floor managers were William
Quigley, Willis Ostrander, and G.L. Mallett.

> The Complimentary Benefit Ball, which has been so
> kindly and considerately tendered to us by our many
> friends, will take place at Washington Hall on the
> evening of the 19th of next month. We shall do all in
> our power to make this a pleasant party. The hall will
> be thoroughly cleaned, extra lamps and chandeliers
> will be added so that the room will be flooded with a
> clear unwavering light. The music the best and
> sweetest that can be obtained. The order of dancing,
> neat and delicate and sufficient in number for each
> and every lady to secure one, they will be attached to
> a ribbon, so as to be carried on the little finger, a
> style which is all the rage in the East. Choice flowers
> for bosom or buttonhole bouquets will be distributed
> gratuitously during the evening. The hall will also be
> decorated with sweet flowers. Everything that taste
> or [illegible] can suggest shall be done to ensure the
> pleasure of those in attendance. We hope that our
> friends all over this part of the country will try to be

present. The supper will be prepared by Mrs. Stanton
and those who attended the Workingmen's Ball last
Summer will vouch for the excellency of her
supervision over ball suppers. Several of the best
housekeepers of Merced have volunteered their
services to assist in the preparation of the supper.
Two good dressing rooms on the same floor of the
hall will be in good order for the accommodation of
ladies coming from a distance. The well-furnished
parlor of Mrs. Stanton will be open during the
evening for those who wish to rest from the
excitement of the ball room for a while. The supper
will be fifty cents and the tickets to the ball $1.00.
Good accommodations for children, and should the
weather prove stormy, carriages will be in attendance
to convey ladies to and from their homes or the
hotels.[30]

THE GRAND COMPLIMENTARY BENEFIT BALL.—
Active preparations are being made to make this one
of the most brilliant affairs of the kind which has
ever taken place in the interior of the State.... A large
number of singing birds have been kindly offered for
the occasion, and more will be acceptable. The ball
room will be filled with the odor of sweet flowers
and rare perfumes. The walls will be hung with
splendid paintings and scores of lamps will cast their
shining glare in every corner. A full band of music
has been engaged. The ball will open with a grand
march *a la militaire*, with torpedo charge. "If I had a
beau, for a soldier to go."[31]

The ball was attended by at least one hundred people; Rowena
thanked each one she knew personally in the next week's column,
naming most of the ladies and describing the gowns of each, and

thanking the men by name, except for several strangers with whom she was not personally familiar. "The music consisting of five pieces was excellent, and everyone seemed to be happy and merry. A large portion of the dancers remained until the faint streaks of day brightened the eastern sky. We are very proud of the result of the Grand Complimentary Benefit Ball. And our friends will please accept our heartfelt thanks both those who attended and those who, although it was not convenient to attend, so generously purchased tickets."[32] One of the most important who did not attend was R.J., who was, sadly, "lying ill with inflammation of the lungs."[33]

Opposition to Death Penalty

In an article in January 1879 about the trial of James Scroggins for murder in Stanislaus County comes the first indication of her position on the death penalty:

> We hope that these able and talented [attorneys] will succeed in saving Stanislaus County the disgrace of another hanging and if the prisoner is found guilty of murder in the first degree, that the sentence may be State Prison for life. We are and ever have been bitterly opposed to capital punishment, for it generally inflicts more punishment on the mothers and innocent friends than upon the culprit, viz: The circumstance of the hanging of the two young men in Sacramento some three years ago. Both the mothers died within a few weeks of broken hearts, and a sister followed in a short time, while another sister became insane. If a man is sentenced to the State Prison for life, he receives and bears the punishment, and leaves the Judge and jury and Sheriff free from what we believe to be nothing more or less than legal murder.[34]

Social Work on Behalf of Orphans and Destitute Families Begins

In February 1879, we are given the first acknowledgement of what would become a remainder-of-life passion for Rowena—the care and well-being of orphans and other misfortunate people—when three children, orphans Josephine and Lillie May Swift, then inmates of the County Farm, and a boy named Tyson who was abandoned, were placed in her custody to be taken to the Good Templars' Home for Orphans at Vallejo. She was also instrumental in setting up a home for children with severe developmental disabilities. In later years, she would try to find adoptive families for the orphans and domestic abuse victims before placing them in institutional care.

In April 1879, she wrote of her objections to the new State constitution, among other reasons, because there was no provision for orphans (as there was in place in Merced County). It was carried in May by a majority of voters in Merced of at least two hundred in favor despite the efforts of both county papers in opposition.

Rowena applauded the establishment of industries for inmates at San Quentin and other prisons around the state so that they would have skills to earn a living when they were released back into society. "I have for many years believed that prisons should, in a measure, be homes of reform, particularly for the youth and the women, and that the class subject to reform should be in separate prisons."[35]

Chapter XI

With a Few Highs and Lows, a Decade of Relative "Normalcy" Returns – Marriage of Harry and Purchase of Sonoma Index-Tribune

As Rowena's efforts continued to revitalize the *Argus*, care for her husband and son Lee, and get back on her feet financially, life for son Harry was evolving in San Francisco, where he worked at the *San Francisco Bulletin*. His rekindled relationship with Merced friend Katie Keogh, daughter of Mrs. Kate and the late Richard Keogh, who had also moved to San Francisco, led to their marriage on Sunday evening, May 4, 1879, in the parlor of St. Mary's Cathedral in San Francisco.

> The youthful bride looked charming, in a neat Princess of Lavender poplin dress, trimmed with pearl colored grosgrain silk and rich blond lace, with necklace, bracelets and other jewelry of plain gold. The white illusion veil half concealed the delicate blush which bloomed upon her modest face as she repeated in a clear voice the marriage promises of her faith. Miss Margaret Moore acted as bride's maid, and Mr. John Coshell as groomsman. After the nuptial knot was tied, the bridal party was driven to the residence of the bride's mother, 404 Eddy street, where the wedding dinner awaited them. The table, under the supervision of Miss Mary Moore, looked very tempting, and the merry guests sat down to satisfy the demands of keen appetites. Sweet, gentle Katie now our daughter, may your matrimonial path be strewn with sweet flowers of hope, happiness and prosperity. And should the bright bloom be over-

shadowed by little clouds of dissension, may the
warm showers which well up from the wounded
heart meet the tender wooing of solicited forgiveness
as they course down the cheeks and mingle with the
kiss of love, prove gentle dew drops which shall add
to the brightness of their bloom and the fragrance of
their undying beauty. Fair young bride, we would fain
fill thy cup with all that is bright, joyous, loving and
beautiful, that every draught might prove the nectar
of earthly bliss. But this is beyond the power of
mortal, and not in keeping with the all wise plan of
the Giver. The bitter must mingle with the sweet.
Tears and sobs are provided for the relief of the
overburdened heart; smiles and merry laughter to
express its joy and happiness. Fair and pure, and true,
we know you will be faithful to the holy vows which
were recorded by the angels as you stood with the
chosen of your young heart's love at the altar. May
this prove the true marriage, which, summed up, is—
    "Two souls with but a single thought,
    Two hearts beat as one."[1]

Shortly after the wedding, Harry and Katie moved to Santa
Clara County where an unnamed daughter was born on July 27,
1880[2], who apparently died young[3], then to Merced where they
welcomed daughter, Cecilia Celeste ('Celia' or 'Celie'), on July
16, 1882, and back to San Francisco where Julie Hortense was
born on July 16, 1883. Their daughter Alice 'Ramona' was born in
Sonoma on November 13, 1894, where the couple had moved
after Harry bought the *Sonoma Index-Tribune* in 1884.

THE SONOMA INDEX-TRIBUNE was received at this
office on Monday last. It is published and edited by
our son, Harry H. Granice, who has for the last

seven years been engaged on the San Francisco
"Bulletin," previous to which he acted as foreman of
the ARGUS office, and for a short time published and
edited the Merced "People" in this town. Mr.
Granice has purchased the good will and material of
the "Tribune," and with his energy and ability will
make it a live paper. We wish him success in this
enterprise.[4]

Rowena visited Harry and family in Sonoma often over the
years. She described the first leg of an early trip that she and R.J.
made by horse-and-buggy in 1885:

ON THE ROAD, June 9th

After leaving Merced yesterday morning, at ten
o'clock, we proceeded down the smooth road until
we came to the Dugan bridge which we found to be
still under the hands of the carpenters. This, when
finished, will be a strong, substantial and handsome
structure. We forded the little stream and continued
our journey. About noon we stopped at one of J.W.
Mitchell's ranches, watered our horse, drank a cup of
cool water and journeyed on for an hour or two
when we came to another of Mr. Mitchell's ranches.
This we found to be a perfect paradise of green trees,
shrubs and cool water. We were kindly received by
the tenants, Mr. and Mrs. Healy, and after a few
moments of pleasant talk and a goblet of sulphur
water from the fine artesian well, we bade these
pleasant people good day and passed on to the
garden of Mr. Crombie. From the appearance of the
vegetation we should judge that the grasshoppers had
left that green spot a little to the right. We found our
old friend busily engaged cultivating the soil. Here we

got a bowl of good tea, for which we felt thankful. After passing Dover we found but little sand, and the air being balmy and the road hard we sailed along pleasantly until we reached the Stevinson ranch and from that fine farm to Hills Ferry the drive was most delightful. We reached the hotel, which is kept by the Ross brothers, just at sunset, making the trip of thirty-five miles over, for the most part, a heavy sandy road, in just eight hours. After partaking of a good supper, being weary from the day's drive, we retired at an early hour.

June 10th.

This is a fine balmy morning. A fine shower of rain fell during the night which made the trees, shrubs and vines clean and green and settled the dust. The air is delightful as we bid our host goodbye and started for Banta, a drive of forty miles....[xix]

R.G.S.[5]

Within a few years, Harry managed to turn around the languishing paper, as Rowena proudly posted in 1887.

Truth Volume.

The Sonoma "INDEX TRIBUNE," published in the old town of Sonoma, by Harry H. Granice, entered upon the tenth year of its existence on Saturday last and is in a flourishing condition. The present publisher purchased the presses and printing material together with the goodwill of the "INDEX-TRIBUNE" establishment a little less than three years ago, the paper having suspended publication for lack of patronage, and from the first issue under the new

---

[xix] Unfortunately, I cannot locate any more columns about the 150-mile drive from Merced to Sonoma or back.

management was found to be upon paying basis and has continued to increase in prosperity and popularity ever since being a faithful representative of the interests of the people of the town and valley in which it is located. The valley of Sonoma is rich in resources, the people are thrifty, intelligent and appreciative, and hence give a willing and liberal support to their local journal and are correspondingly benefited in having their interests represented, and their resources made known to the world. Continued success to the paper, and prosperity to the people of Sonoma, is our earnest prayer.[6]

Harry was eventually able to regain his good name and esteem of the public and successfully ran the *Index-Tribune* for thirty years until his death in 1915. Since then, the paper was continuously owned and managed by Rowena's descendants for almost one hundred years.

Katie's mother, Kate, moved back to Merced, and remained close with Rowena as the two enjoyed frequent visits by their granddaughters. One of Kate's business ventures was the Magazine Brush for blacking stoves.

Something New.

One of the most useful household articles we have seen for many years is the Magazine Brush for blacking stoves. Mrs. K. Keogh is the sole agent for Merced for this neat, labor-saving article. A lady or child can polish the most neglected stove and make it look like a perfectly new one without touching the hands to the stove or preparation. Should you get on your lavender gloves and pink silk dress to make calls, and then remember that you had neglected to polish the stove, you can take this Magazine Brush, and, without removing your gloves or putting on an apron, do the work and go and make your calls. No housekeeper should be without it. Mrs. Keogh will call on ladies at their homes. She will also leave one of the brushes with instructions for using it at the store of Mrs. McInerny, so that ladies coming in from the country can see this wonderful improvement. The price is only $1.00. Who would have a gray, dusty stove or soiled hands when such an article can be had for so small a sum?[7]

She moved to San Francisco in 1887, then to Sonoma, where she died on September 3, 1912, eight years after the sudden death of her only daughter Katie Keogh Granice on August 14, 1904.

Fire! Fire!

Fires in this city of homes and buildings built mostly from wood were a constant threat. Rowena was barely home for a few months from Harry and Katie's wedding, settling back into the production of the *Argus* and writing her weekly columns, when on July 21, 1879, the dreaded cries rang out.

About five o'clock on Monday morning, 21st inst., the inhabitants of our town were aroused by the cry of "Fire! Fire!" and the next moment flames and smoke issued from the roof of Washington Hall, a large two-story wooden building. The fire bell sounded the call and a few moments later the engine, well-manned, was at work. Almost instantaneously every force-pump and hose in the neighborhood was in active motion. Next door to the burning building stood a small, two-story cottage occupied by Mrs. Maddox as a dressmaking shop. In one of the interior rooms lay a young mother with an infant five

days old. In the rush to save these two lives, everything else was left to perish in the lapping flames.
Books, pictures, old family relics faded, never to be
looked upon again. But the young mother and babe
were taken out and safely lodged at the residence of
Mrs. George Turner. The invalid was Mrs. James
Corley, daughter of Mr. and Mrs. Maddox. The
house of this family with everything beneath the roof
was destroyed.

Then came the pretty home of Mrs. Castor, who is
also a dressmaker. Upon the saving of this house the
fireman and citizens bent all their energies. Should
the flames get on the east side of this house, which
stood at the corner, the dry goods store of J.L. Reidy,
and the blacksmith shop of J.W. Spears would have
caught, and in that case the entire town would
probably have been destroyed. But through the well-
directed efforts of the firemen, assisted by the
citizens, the flames were quenched at this point; and
although the house is nothing but a charred shell, and
unfit even for repairs, still the work was well applied.
The house was insured for $1,300, which, or course,
the Insurance Company should not hesitate to pay, as
it protected many thousands of dollars' worth of
property which, if the house had been left to burn to
the ground, would certainly have been lost.

Several barns and out-houses, together with a small
cottage occupied by the family of Mr. Langbein were
totally destroyed. The buildings were very dry,
causing a rapid spread of the flames and intense heat,
rendering it impossible to save clothing or household
goods from a building when once attacked by the
fire-fiend.

In addition to the losses in the houses destroyed, we hear of losses by removal of property from houses in immediate danger but not attacked by the destroying element. Among the losers was Mrs. Lucy Spears [K St. near Cor. 17th], who lost several switches and other articles of hair work, which will probably be returned when it is ascertained to whom they belong, as we cannot think that anyone would be so mean as to retain such trifles when taken out to save them from the flames. This lady had also several dollars' worth of postage stamps in a box, which has got mis-placed. The entire losses will foot up about $12,000, and the insurance about $7,500, making the majority of the loss fall upon the Insurance Companies carrying the risks.[8]

Thereafter, most of the new commercial buildings and many homes were constructed of brick and other fire-resistant materials, but the older residences and businesses were still in constant danger, as evidenced by an article in June 1880 describing what could have been a personal catastrophe for the Steeles.

On Friday of last week, at about six P.M., the editor of this paper was at the windmill in the rear of our dwelling, when he heard a man call out—"Steele, are you trying to burn your house?" Looking up towards the house Mr. Steele saw a blaze issuing from the roof of the shed room just over the family bedroom. We were in the printing office engaged in making up the ARGUS for mails and the young members of the family were working off and folding papers, when all were startled and horrified by hearing the voice of Mr. Steele crying, "Fire! Fire!" We "stood not upon the orders of going" but flew towards the house. Oh!

The agony of the moment! Our little home on fire—one woman, one man and three children[xx]—the wind blowing a gale. Already the flames roared and the timbers cracked. Each one rushed to the tubs and water box. Our son Lee mounted the roof. The first three buckets of water did good work inside, still the boards and shingles creaked and groaned under the creeping flames, and still we rushed to and from the tubs and box. Then came the neighbors with buckets and willing hearts and hands, and in five minutes from the discovery the fire was out, and the grim, charred and blackened window, window shutters, boards and shingles and a heap of black, wet female apparel, scorched carpet, quilts, pillows, trunk and other articles told of the rapid destruction of the fire-fiend. There was an insurance of eight hundred and seventy-five dollars upon the house and furniture. But what would that small amount do towards replacing the home with all the things so dear to us made dear by association. It was this thought that urged us to fight the fire with almost superhuman strength. If, with one pulse beat we felt a thrill of despair, the next bright hope and courage. Not a thing was removed—not even the fine picture of our darling dead. Save all, save all! Was the incentive to action.

HOW IT CAUGHT

A fire had been kindled about five minutes before the first alarm and the tea-kettle put on preparatory

---

[xx] In the 1880 census, the residents of the Steele home were listed as Robert, Rowena, Lee, Robert's niece Laura H. Steele from Arkansas, printer's apprentice George M. Potter, and student Olla Wright from Ohio. An advertisement in the *Argus* in 1890 informs that Rowena opened her home to teenaged schoolgirls who "will find a pleasant home with board and room in return for such services as she can render mornings, evenings and Saturdays."

to cooking the evening meal. Although there was but little fire, a spark from the stovepipe (which is as safe and secure as any chimney, being double for some five feet above and below the roof, and over ten feet in height above the roof), the wind being high the spark was carried over the house and left among some dry leaves or other light, dry matter, and being whirled about by the draft which passed under the house caught some clothing which was on a shelf under the window. Reaching the window it divided its strength and destruction between the outside and in. The damage to the house and furniture, which was insured, can be replaced for about forty or fifty dollars. The loss of clothing probably will not exceed thirty dollars, not counting the making up of new ones. But we have a long Ulster[xxi] and don't require any great amount of clothing. We received several bodily bruises from which we have suffered and are still suffering, but our joy at saving our family roof-tree proves a panacea for all aches and pains. We are very thankful to our kind neighbors for their timely aid in helping to extinguish the fire. In the excitement we did not take note of who was on the ground, but we remember of taking a bucket of water from the hands of our neighbor, Mrs. Frank Peck, who had brought it from her own home a distance of over two hundred feet.   R.G.S.[9]

The Summer of 1886 was particularly bad for fires in Merced. In June the Arcade Block burned to the ground, with damages amounting to almost $10,000.

[xxi] A style of tweed overcoat originating in County Ulster, Ireland.

It is needless to say that the costumes in which the thousands who thronged the streets to witness the progress of the flames or fight to save their own or their neighbor's property from destruction appeared were scant, and in many instances ludicrous in the extreme, while some were driven forth from the doomed buildings with nothing upon them but their scanty night dresses, who had no place to go for shelter and knew not what to do in their bewilderment other than shiver in the keen night air and timidly watch the rapid consumption of all their worldly wealth and household goods by the destroying element. The quarter burned had long been denominated "Rotten Row" and for years its fate had been predicted, but all previous prophesies foretelling its destruction by fire had failed, though many times endangered by incipient fires or extensive conflagrations destroying contiguous buildings.[10]

In July 1886, the saloon and restaurant of McInerny and Quigley burned, with embers landing on the *Argus* office.

FIRES OF THE WEEK!
———

In and Near our Town!
———

The Huffman Warehouse and R.R. Cars, Wheat, Etc., go up in smoke.
———

McInerney & Quigley's Saloon and Chop House Burns—A Close Shaver for the "Argus" Office.
———

Farm House, Header Wagon, Standing Grain and Grain in the Sack, all go to Ashes.

---

* * *

THE ARGUS OFFICE

Had a close shave of being burned, as the roof was on fire several times but a few buckets in the hands of friends saved the pioneer paper, and right here we wish to thank all who helped us in our time of need.[11]

Again in 1886, the Steeles narrowly escaped catastrophe when an untended field fire threatened to overtake their residence.

Fields on Fire.

Yesterday afternoon just as we were going to press we discovered a dense smoke which seemed to come from something very near our residence. With all haste we rushed to the spot and saw flames traveling ahead of a stiff breeze towards the barn and fence. The loud crackle as the flames swallowed up the high, dry grass seemed to threaten danger, not only to our own property but that of Mrs. Carlton and others, as the flames were rapidly spreading and the wind blowing quite hard. After fighting the fire a few moments, R.J. Steele and Constable Leggett succeeded in subduing the fiery traveler. It is not quite safe to set fire to a stubble field and leave it to wander where it will. Had there been no one about the place, the barn and fence of both Mrs. Carlton's place and our own would doubtless have taken fire, and with the wind blowing and urging on the fiery fiend, the entire neighborhood would probably have been burned, as there is no well near enough to be of service. Persons wishing to burn stubble should make sure that it is perfectly safe to do so.[12]

By 1890, Merced had organized fire companies trained and equipped to respond immediately, and the *Argus* noted, "Merced has the best fire department of any interior city. Its members are well trained and take an interest in their work."[13]

The Argus Steadily Grows and Prospers Along With Merced

Unfortunately, there is a large break in microfilmed issues of the *Argus* from August 1880 to September 1883, so we are left to assume that Rowena was continuing to engage in her usual activities of travelling to Temperance and Women's Suffrage meetings, lecturing, writing about social events, holiday celebrations, and personal items, and promoting farms, ranches, businesses and shops in Merced County. An article in May 1881 reinforces that assumption as it concludes, "she has been an active worker in the temperance cause, and a leader in the woman's suffrage movement in the State, but, in contradiction to the popular idea on the domesticity of such women, her home at Merced, under her own personal supervision and care, is said to be an ideal of neatness, comfort, and beauty."[14]

Snippets of her extensive travels on behalf of Temperance and women's rights were found in undated, non-attributed newspaper clippings in a manila folder at the Merced County Museum:

> MRS. ROWENA G. STEELE.—This well-known lady, who is California's Pilgrim in the cause of temperance, visited Oakland a few weeks since, for the purpose of lecturing on the subject here, and the Methodist church was kindly granted to her. Her audience was large; but it is a sad commentary on the temperance societies of Oakland, when it is stated that not so much as a reception committee from these organizations could be mustered on the occasion, to introduce the popular lecturer, or even

to escort her to the lecture room, entire stranger as she was. After the hour for the lecture had expired, two local male journalists—by no manner of means teetotalers—resolved themselves into a reception committee, sought out the lecturer at the hotel, and gallantly ushered her into the presence of her auditors. After apologizing for the delay, and a brief allusion to the circumstances which occasioned it, Mrs. Steele delivered an able and eloquent lecture against the infamous liquor traffic. This lady believes firmly in moral suasion, prosecuted through the instrumentality of thoroughly organized temperance societies and the pledge, as the most effectual mode of throttling the monster. So say we all of us.

* * *

ROWENA GRANICE STEELE.

Yesterday we had a friendly visit from Mrs. Rowena Granice Steele, a lady journalist from the San Joaquin Valley Argus. She is the good and accomplished wife of R.J. Steele, the editor of that paper, and has made herself favorably known to the country as a literary writer, dramatic reader and lecturer, in all of which capacities she has been successful and popular. On Sunday night Mrs. Steele delivered a splendid address to the Temperance Legion in San Francisco, and made a great sensation, as lady-elocutionists of her magnificent powers are not often heard there. She has gone to Livermore to address the Society there, and also at Hayward, and we believe there is a movement on foot to have her speak her in Oakland on Sunday night. Mrs. Steele is a State officer of the Good Templars, and if she decides to make an address here at this particular time, some sensation will be created.

* * *

The Champions of the Red Cross, a new temperance and beneficial organization, gave a picnic and ball at Plainsburg recently, and among other exercises was a magnificent address by Mrs. Rowena Granice Steele. This good woman, in her quiet way, is doing more for the temperance reform than any other single individual in California. She is beyond all question the best lady-speaker in the country, and her great warm loving heart overflows with sympathy for the sufferers under that fearful curse.

* * *

LECTURE.—Mrs. Rowena G. Steele will deliver a lecture at Visalia, on or about the 28th or 30th instant. Subject: Women and Girls of the Past, Present and Future.

* * *

LECTURE.—The lecture delivered by Rowena G. Steele, at the M.E. Church, on Monday evening last, contained many ideas and facts well worthy of remembrance. Quite a respectable audience was present, but many more Visalians could well afford to have heard the truths presented.

* * *

PEN AND INK SKETCHES OF PEOPLE I CARE ABOUT — ROWENA GRANICE STEELE.

Straying one fine Spring evening among the beautiful foothills of the Sierras, where they are most beautiful, in the lovely little valleys of Tuolumne, I came suddenly in view of Mount Pleasant, the fine residence of my friends, Mr. and Mrs. Taylor; and as it is one of the first articles of my social creed, when this house is near, never to pass by to the other side, I turned my steps in that direction. On entering the gate I saw a light buggy standing at the front door and by it stood a lady with reins in hand ready to mount the carriage and drive away.

At the first glance I saw she was no ordinary character. Her whole presence was inspired by a power, which I could see, even at a distance, genial, sweet and attractive. And when she was presented to me as Mrs. Steele, the gifted writer, whose sweet and simple home stories I had read with so much pleasure, I was not surprised at the influence, though all persons of genius are not externally their own best representatives. We were mutually drawn together, and subsequent acquaintance has confirmed the first attraction.

In person Mrs. Steele has envious advantages. With a form and manner at once commanding and graceful, she does not appear tall, though quite above the medium height. She has a fine expression, dark gray eyes, and soft, silken, nut-brown hair. Her features are regular and harmonious, though too expressive and [illegible] to be quite classic. She is in short, aside from her superior gifts, a most attractive, amiable, and fascinating woman.

                    FANNY GREEN MCDOUGALL.

Some of her short stories published during the early 1880s include "How Dollie Dean Became a Capitalist" (1880), "Margaret Wier, an Original Christmas Story," (1883), "The Miser's Victim" (reprint) and "Jessie Vaughn's Christmas Gift" (1884). Other than the ode to her childhood home, the only other original published poetry that can be found is one she did for New Year 1886, "respectfully dedicated to the Merced Canal Company":

Twelve years ago our fair young town
Had scarcely discarded her baby gown;
So proud were the people to let it be known
A town had been started and was nearly grown
That all kinds of business had for its head
The name of the beautiful, flowing Merced!
Hotels, saloons, restaurants and stables
Had the name of this river painted on their gables;
Bakeries, breweries and secret societies,
"Merced" was distributed in a score of varieties.
"Merced" county, falls and town,
Were named after this river of great renown;
"Merced Market" and "Merced Bank,"
"Merced" windmills and "Merced" tank.
Everything at that period was known as "Merced"
Without regard to quality, age or grade.
This was quite flattering to the river, no doubt,
As she gurgled and gracefully swept on her route,
Over rocks and 'neath bluffs on her way to the plain,
For she swelled and looked grand and laughed at the rain.
"That's rather slim wetting you are giving the ground,"
Said the haughty deep river with a dash and a bound,
"I could irrigate more land in the half of a day,
Than you and the windmills with your fussy display,
Could wet a month. Aye! And six of them, too!
While you keep the people all looking so blue,
With your uncertain coming and staying away!
The grain all dies out and makes nothing but hay;
The farmers all grumble and say with a sigh,
'We will all sure be ruined, the ground is so dry.'"
After this saucy speech she passed scornfully on,
Leaving the rain and the grain and the farmer to mourn.
She basked in the sunshine and sought the cool shade,

She cooed and she hummed her sweet days to the glade,
And seemed content in her narrow retreat.
She never had sighed to go gadding the street,
But when the news reached her that her name stood so high,
And how she was worshipped, she said, with a sigh,
"If some man will come and woo me with plenty of cash
I would take a run over and give them a dash.
I will water the flowers and moisten the grain,
And give promise of wealth to the desiccated plain."
"You would?" cried a voice not far from the shore.
"I can find you a man with a million or more,
And our promise to get the stake,
To make Merced the pride of the State."
"I'll do it," said the river, with a gurgling laugh,
"But I may require a million and a half.
I'll keep my word and give you a stream
That will make glad your hearts and start up the steam.
The steam that will people your now arid plain
And fill all your fields with bright, golden grain!
I'll creep into your orchards and coax up the trees,
And bring sweet, luscious fruit among the green leaves!
I'll slip in your gardens of carrots and beans,
And turnips and cabbage and all kinds of greens!
Make flowers, shrubs and vines grow lovely and high!
Your gardens and green lawns shall never go dry!
In order to do this I must have plenty of gold,
Horses, wagons, and men that are fearless and bold!
We must dig, we must delve, go up hill and down,
Make channels and windings to get to the town."
"All these, Madam River, you shall have on demand,
And to make good the promise, I'll give you my hand!
Charles Crocker is the man who will furnish the cash,
My name is C.H. Huffman, and don't think me rash,
For I have studied for years on this great enterprise,
With my head and my heart and wide-awake eyes!

And now, gentle river, our interest is one.
We will stand by each other till the great work is done!"
All hail to Charles Crocker, Charles Huffman and Drake!
Merced, through their efforts, will be the pride of the State!
With these bright prospects before us let us keep up good cheer,
And all wish each other a HAPPY NEW YEAR!
R.G.S.

Just as she had for the past twenty years, over the next decade Rowena continued her regular personal visits to the business places and homes of hundreds of people all over California and wrote about them in detail. Her travels provide a near forty-year span chronicling the history of California and the people, famous and plain-folk, who settled here. These travelogues are worthy of a separate volume and will be a gold mine for genealogists and historians. Also, fortunate was the deceased who came to Rowena's attention. She wrote dozens, if not hundreds, of obituaries, praising and blessing decedents, young and old, rich and poor, most listing their accomplishments in life. Rowena set a new standard of writing epitaphs with her motto, "Of the absent and the dead, speak nothing but good."

The *Argus*, with Rowena titled as publisher and associate editor and R.J. as editor, announced in August 1883 the commencement of its fourteenth year of continuous publication, which was noticed by other newspapers around the state. "We note this event with especial pleasure because of the announcement by our old friends that the paper is established upon as firm a foundation as any in the country, owes no debts, and is prepared to expand its business facilities as occasion may require. May it long continue in this comfortable condition."[15] Two years later, at the inauguration of the sixteenth year, Rowena declared, "The ARGUS is devoted to no isms or cranky notions. It is simply a family and business newspaper. The principal aim of the proprietor is to make the ARGUS worthy of the patronage of an intelligent public, collect

all the money justly due her and pay all debts contracted."[16]
Accolades came from every corner of California, including a very
special tribute from son Harry, *Sonoma Index-Tribune* publisher:

> The SAN JOAQUIN VALLEY ARGUS, published at
> Merced, has entered upon a new volume. This paper
> is one of the oldest in the southern part of the State.
> It is edited and published by Mr. and Mrs. R.J. Steele,
> who for nearly a quarter of a century have been in
> the newspaper business in Merced county. The press
> they now print their paper on was brought to this
> State early in the fifties and has been in their
> possession nearly twenty-five years. The ARGUS for
> two decades has been a terror to a corrupt clique of
> politicians in Merced county and for years it
> unceasingly labored to get the management of the
> affairs of that county in honest hands. At the last
> election it had the proud satisfaction of seeing the
> backbone broken of one of the most corrupt,
> unscrupulous and depraved Court House cliques that
> ever held sway in this state. It was this gang that
> made the boast fifteen years ago that they would
> crush out the ARGUS in three months. But the paper
> still lives and flourishes while many of its old time
> enemies are groveling at its feet.[17]

Perhaps in response to an article in December 1883
condemning the dozen or so gambling halls, opium dens and
"houses of ill-repute" clustered together in the Chinese section on
the same block on Main Street in Merced (a "blot upon our
town"[18]), for the year-end of 1883, Rowena wrote a positive
outline of the tremendous progress of the past twenty years in
Merced County.

TRANSFORMATION.

***

THE PROGRESS OF TWENTY YEARS.

***

A DRY, DESOLATE PLAIN CONVERTED INTO SUNNY HOMES.

***

If the history of the progress and improvements which have been made within the limits of Merced county within the past twenty years could be printed in book form and bound in cloth and gilt and put in the hands of those who do not read the newspapers of the day, it would seem like the stories of Baron Munchausen, or the "Travels of Gulliver" and the tales of wonderful giants and Lilliputians.

Who among our old residents does not remember the smile of incredulity that overspread the face and the feelings of doubt which lingered in the mind while yielding to the delightful temptation of devouring that forbidden literary fruit? And still the strange narratives were really not more astonishing than the facts which have transpired in our day and generation.

A PICTURE OF DESOLATION.

Twenty years ago the main part of Merced county was a wild, barren, desolate waste. The only sound then heard in the unsettled portion of this now populous county was the doleful howl of the hungry coyote, the dismal lowing of wild cattle, or the hooting of the night owl, mingled with the dirge-like sound of the moaning turtle dove. No grateful shade trees; no cool, clear water to refresh the weary traveler. During the stormy season the black mud, dangerous bogs, and quicksand prevented stockmen from hunting their herds, so the cattle and horses were let to roam over the man-forsaken plains with the deer and other wild animals. At certain times during the summer of each year hundreds of men and boys, mounted upon their caballo bronchos, followed by some enterprising individual with a hotel and barroom on wheels, would spend many days and nights on the plains hunting and branding stock. This *modus operandi* was called a rodeo.

TRANSFORMATION.

At the present day these once desolate plains are, as far as the eye can see, either plowed up and being smoothed by the harrow ready for seeding, or are already covered with young grain. Eucalyptus, cypress and other evergreens stand up in their tall grandeur, attired in many shades of green, bowing gracefully to the whispering breezes and seem to be proudly defying Jack Frost, and the roaring and battling of Old Boreas. Clear, sparkling water goes gurgling and dancing through the canals and ditches, or bubbling up in bright beads from the many artesian wells. Substantial farm residences with spacious barns and other out-houses dot the land.

MERCED—ITS GROWTH AND ITS LUXURIES.

Here, in Merced, which was the very heart of a desolate waste less than twenty years ago, stands the stately El Capitan Hotel, with its hundred rooms; the seventy-five thousand dollar Court House; a twenty-thousand dollar school house; and six churches lift their spires heavenward. Magnificent private residences tower high in their architectural beauty and completeness. Soft, rich carpets cover the floors; bright, costly mirrors reflect the loveliness of the satin damask covered furniture, and the delicate lace and dainty tapestry. Enchanting music from the piano, organ, and guitar floats out upon the air mingled with the gentle cadences of well-trained voices. A well-organized brass band discourses sweet notes. Schoolhouses, presided over by competent instructors, are scattered here and there at convenient distances all over the county. It will be seen, by reference to the ARGUS, that no small number of enterprising merchants have followed in this march of progress and improvement.

SOCIETIES.

Eight or ten secret orders have been organized, while quite a number of social clubs are in a flourishing condition. Among the most successful, socially, is the Farmers' Club, which meets monthly at the home of some member, where a feast of good things is enjoyed without money and without price. This was organized four years ago, and if you would see genuine refinement mingled with domestic duties and home happiness, these gatherings present the picture in its full perfectness. There are many important facts connected with this wonderful progress which cannot be mentioned in this brief sketch.

LIBRARIES.

Fine libraries of books, newspapers from our own cities of the Pacific Coast and from the Eastern and Southern cities are received here daily, and the moving power which helped to hasten the steps of this wonderful progress,

THE RAILROAD,

Sends its steam engines puffing and rattling through the town at all hours of the day and night. Christmas Eve 1883 will be celebrated by a Christmas tree social

and a Santa Claus in four different churches in this
town. A fine large theatre will be thrown open to the
public on New Year's Day of 1884. If any one of the
old residents who has not visited this county for the
past twenty years should happen here at this time, he
would rub his eyes and, like Rip Van Winkle, exclaim,
"This is a change indeed!"[19]

Garden Parties, Ice Cream Socials at the Steele Residence

In the 1880s Rowena and R.J. began hosting several
parties at their home, an example of which is illustrated in this
1887 article:

The Good Templars Garden Party.

At an early hour last evening, the beautifully
illuminated garden at the residence of Mr. and Mrs.
Steele, began to fill with gaily dressed ladies and
gallant gentlemen. Tables and chairs had been placed
in every shady nook of the large grounds. Chinese
lanterns were suspended from the limbs of the trees,
mingling their bright red and blue lights with the pale
soft rays shed upon the scene by the Queen of night.
Merry voices and gay laughter, together with the low,
sweet notes of the organ, and the singing of songs
accompanied with the chorus of twenty voices, while
the wind tossed the branches of the tall trees and
shook the vines and bushes until it seemed that the
spirits of the wind were determined to join in and
have a jolly good time. Nearly one hundred persons
were in attendance. Ice cream and peach glacier were
served in the garden, while tea, coffee and chocolate
with cakes and doughnuts were dealt out in
plentitude in the large dining room. The parlors,
porches and halls were filled to their utmost. The real
genuine pleasure enjoyed by the large company last

night fully demonstrates the fact that wine is not necessary to happiness and good cheer, fun, frolic and enjoyment. Several fine recitations were delivered from the front porch. The singing was lovely. The Good Templars have cause to be proud of their garden party, which was gotten up under the management of Mrs. B.F. Fowler assisted by Miss Olivia Smith, Mr. Ferris and others.[20]

Inauguration of the Daily Argus

On October 2, 1886, an announcement was made of the coming publication of the *Merced Daily Argus*.

THE "DAILY ARGUS."

On Monday next, Oct 4th, will be issued from this office the DAILY ARGUS, which will be delivered to subscribers by carrier at the low price of ten cents per week, and furnished to subscribers by mail at $4.50 per annum; six months $2.50; three months $1,25; payable in advance. The daily will be one-half the size of the weekly SAN JOAQUIN VALLEY ARGUS, neatly printed and contain a synopsis of foreign and domestic news by telegraph and the local news of the town and county; also, current political news and editorial notes. This enterprise is not for the political campaign only, but designed to become a permanent and live daily newspaper, and we invite the cooperation and support of the public of Merced and adjoining counties of the valley.[21]

Over the next few years, Rowena used the *Daily Argus* to inform the community about child welfare and other domestic matters. She raised money to care for needy families and children and to call attention to issues that required immediate attention.

In 1889, the *Daily Argus* announced the enlargement of the paper to a six-column folio, and otherwise improvement, "being printed on new type." "The publishers have recently made a large outlay in cash in purchasing new presses and type, and enlarging the office building in the hope of being reimbursed by an increase of business. The growing grain crops of the county promise a fair return to farmers for their labor at the coming harvest, and it shall be the aim of the publishers of the DAILY ARGUS to keep pace with the march of progress and continue to improve the paper as business increases and complaints of dull times cease."[22]

Lee Matures, Undertakes More Responsibilities, and Marries

After attending Stockton Business College for two years, Lee returned to work at the *Argus* and, in October 1883, we learn that he went into partnership with Bailey K. Leach in the publication of the *Merced Advertiser*, when they announced the printing of two thousand eight-page papers for the week prior to Christmas to be distributed in Snelling, Merced Falls, Hopeton, Dry Creek, and the West Side. In December, he was referred to as the "foreman" of the *Argus* when he set off on horseback to solicit business in the burgeoning West Side communities. He became an active member of the Native Sons of the Golden West[xxii] and celebrated his twenty-first birthday with a party on May 19, 1884.

> A NEW VOTER.—Lee R. Steele, our youngest son and foreman of the ARGUS office, celebrated his twenty-first birthday on Monday evening last. There was quite a large number of ladies and gentlemen present, notwithstanding the severe inclemency of the weather; the rain poured in torrents for at least four hours, commencing at about 8 o'clock in the evening,

---

[xxii] This group over the years was the target of considerable scrutiny and condemnation because of their racist stances and activities, particularly anti-Chinese in the late 1800s and anti-Japanese during World War II.

and many who were dressed for the occasion looked out upon the darkness and listened to the dashing, splashing rain, their courage failed them. Those who were present enjoyed themselves and the music, the dance, and the supper within was not dampened by the pouring torrents without.[23]

In June 1884, the printing department of the *Argus* was moved to Arcade Block, L Street, where Lee was put in charge of all printing orders. "He is prepared to do job work in all its branches from a colored three-sheet poster to the delicate wedding or visiting card."[24] He became officially a "publisher" of the *Argus* in Oct 1885.

A NAME ADDED.

With this issue the name of our son, L.R. Steele, appears as publisher of the ARGUS in connection with that of Mrs. R.G. Steele. Lee R. is a native of Merced County and with the exception of two years spent at the Stockton Business College, he has always resided here and been employed in the ARGUS office, first as devil, then as typo, next as foreman, and now he steps up. We trust that the people of Merced will lend their aid in keeping him in this position by giving a goodly share of patronage to the old pioneer paper of Merced county.[25]

In 1886, the Argus office moved to the Pythian Block on Front Street near the El Capitan Hotel. Lee was elected a trustee of the Merced Cemetery Association to fill the vacancy of George Isaacs who had passed away, and in 1887 he became an officer, along with Rowena, in the Merced Lodge of Good Templars.

In October of 1887 the McCreary family took up residence in Merced, moving from their ranch on the Merced River near Merced Falls. They were longtime friends of the Steeles from the early years in Snelling. William Alec McCreary, from Conecuh County, Alabama, was an 1850s pioneer miner to California. He and his wife Nancy 'Nannie' Gibbons had four children, including daughter Lennice 'Lennie' McCreary, born April 13, 1870, at the ranch. Soon the pages of the *Argus* were filled with small blurbs about Lennie's comings and goings, appearances at balls and social events and, in June 1888, a little hint of forthcoming nuptials: "L.R. Steele is elected Marshall of I.O.G.T. and Captain of Co. B; Lennie McCreary, future wife, also an officer."[26]

The couple were married on February 14, 1889, by the Rev. G.W. Lyon of the First Presbyterian Church at the residence of her parents.

> The marriage of Miss Lennie McCreary and Mr. Lee R. Steele, junior publisher of the Merced *Argus*, took place on Thursday evening last at the residence of the bride's parents, on Main street, Merced. The ceremony was performed by the Rev. G.W. Lyon of the First Presbyterian Church — Mr. A.G. Shriver as groomsman and Miss Lizzie Peck as bridesmaid. After the congratulations the bridal party and friends proceeded in carriages to the residence of the parents of the groom, Mr. R.J. and Mrs. R.G. Steele, where the wedding reception was held.
>
> The parlors and two large supper rooms were beautifully decorated with evergreens and violets, and the whole house was so equally warmed that the atmosphere was like unto a pleasant evening in May. The extensive grounds were brilliantly illuminated with lighted and gay-colored lanterns. Over one hundred guests assembled to congratulate the happy

young couple, after which all were invited to be
seated at the bountifully spread tables. Several
talented performers entertained the company with
piano music and singing.

At 11 o'clock the guests departed amid happy good-
nights and wishes for the life-long happiness and
prosperity of the bride and groom.[27]

There followed a long listing of over sixty wedding gifts, along
with the names of the presenters, received by the couple including
"a new modern cottage" and "life-sized portraits of the father and
mother of the groom" from Rowena.[28]

Lee and Lennie welcomed daughter, Constance G.
'Connie' on November 20, 1889. Just six weeks later, in January
1890, Lee suddenly left the *Argus* and became proprietor of the
City Bakery on Main Street, formerly owned by John and Mary
Stanton. The partnership of Lee and Rowena was dissolved, and
the *Argus* became managed solely by Rowena. She was, in
public, enthusiastic and supportive of the move, but one has to
wonder what untold undercurrents were roiling within the family
unit to cause this sudden separation.

Lee R. Steele Retires from the Printing Business.

Lee R. Steele, for the past five years junior publisher
and local reporter for the Merced Daily and Weekly
ARGUS, has severed his connection with that paper
and has purchased the stock, fixtures and good will
of the City Bakery situated on Main Street, Merced.
L.R. Steele has been in a printing office from the day
he was born up to the present time with the
exception of three years of college life and one year
at the study of law under Superior Judge C.H. Marks.
He has for some time been anxious to enter into
business of a more lucrative nature than that of

junior publisher of a country newspaper as he has a
family depending upon his exertions. The City
Bakery under the management of Mrs. Stanton has
flourished for many years, and we see no reason why
it should not be a profitable investment for this
young man. The outdoor exercise of driving the
wagon will greatly benefit his rather delicate health,
make him strong and perhaps enable him after a few
years to return to his favorite study of law.

In February 1890 Lee opened a branch bakery in the Kirkman
fruit, vegetable and variety store on Front Street. "This will be an
accommodation which has long been needed in Merced by the
people living in the northwest part of the city, and we hope that
those people will take advantage of this new order in the bakery
business."[29] Later in the spring he advertised the expansion of the
bakery to include food items, "consisting in part of cold roast
mutton, roast beef, baked beans, potted ham, clam chowder,
tongue, Vienna sausage, sundries, and many other toothsome
articles of food ready for the table."[30]

Chapter XII

Summer 1889 – The Trip East

> Mrs. R.G. Steele of this paper returned from Sonoma this morning and will start for a trip East Thursday next.
>
>   * * *
>
> Mrs. R.G. Steele, of this paper, started for her old home in the East to-day at 2 P.M. While East, Mrs. Steele will be the guest of her sister, Mrs. W.K. Gray, of East Orange, N.J. She has not been home for thirty-eight years and her brother and sisters, who were then in the prime of life, have now all reached old age, but they will welcome her just the same. We hope she will induce at least one to return with her to our sunny slopes.[1]

From Merced to Salt Lake City.

A Pleasant Trip—A Jolly Crowd—And Who They Were.

ON THE TRAIN, June 21:

EDITOR ARGUS:

When I left Merced on Tuesday, I naturally felt a little lonesome at starting on this long trip, and leaving Merced, where I have spent the last twenty-seven years of my life; yes, it was just twenty-seven years the 19th of June, since I arrived in Snelling with two little boys to join my husband for the purpose of entering upon the exciting life of journalism, and with what success I have met, let those who know me best judge. Now for the trip so far. After entering the car … I was shown the seat and sleeper which I was to occupy until we reached Ogden. You will laugh when I tell you that I, an old traveler by sea and land, felt a little embarrassed when I found myself face to face with a car load of strangers. To use an old expression, I felt that every eye was upon me, but as the afternoon wore on, one after another had given me a kind word and when supper time came I was handed some nice warm tea by a lady who had her little stove with her. In return I handed her a chicken wing, and when breakfast time came there was a general exchange of good things from the many lunch baskets.

THE SLEEPER.

The sleeping arrangements are good. The lower berth is constructed of two seats drawn together by some unseen machinery. The upper is a berth which is made of slats and fastened up during the day, and let down a few feet at night. Each berth is furnished with a mattress, a pair of blankets, a pair of clean white sheets and two good sized pillows with white cases. Heavy damask curtains conceal the sleeping passenger from the gaze of passersby.

So far the trip has been a pleasant one. We have passed many large settlements. We arrived at Truckee at about 4 A.M. and remained until seven, then we journeyed on for miles through a rich timber country with clear running streams, so refreshing after the hot dusty ride of the day before. Everyone felt buoyant of spirit and at about 10 o'clock a large group gathered together and with the assistance of a fine violin the dear old song of "Home Sweet Home" was sung. I saw several present wearing little bright jewels on their cheeks, a funny place to display jewels, but it is a favorite spot for these dew drops of the heart to show their sparkle. We stopped a short time at Lovelacy[?], a pretty little settlement. I dined at Humboldt after a long hot ride over the dry desert, at about two o'clock we came to water, green trees and cool air, and the singers sang, "Oh, Ain't I Glad To Get out of the Wilderness." We arrived at Elko about six and found a good supper awaiting the passengers. Elko is a pretty green village. After supper we were on our way to Ogden where we arrived about 8 in the morning. Here we changed our roomy quarters for the narrow gauge which took the tourist to Salt Lake city. The morning was cool and delightful and we all enjoyed the trip. Of what I saw and how I enjoyed the day among the Mormons

I will give you in my next. The following is a list of those occupying No. 1 and 2.

John and Sarah Bell, Orion, Ill.; Mr. and Mrs. J.H. Claudius and son, Chicago, Ill.; O.A. Garner, Chicago, Ill.; C.G. Heimbach, Houston, Ill.; John Yettel, Chicago, Ill.; Miss Grace Cochran, Morrison, Ill.; Mrs. R.J. Goddard and son, Sparta, Ill.; Mr. C. and A. Arn, Kansas City; P.W. Hotchkiss, St. Louis, Mo.; S.S. Bottom, Sparta, Ill.; Mrs. Wm. McCarty, Chicago; W.S. Douglas, Oneonta, N.Y.; Mrs. Reno Brown, Valparaiso, Ind.; W.E. Gard, Fremont City, Ohio, and Anton Zilm, Leadville, Colo.

MRS. R.G. STEELE.[2]

LIFE AMONG THE MORMONS AS VIEWED BY OUR EDITRESS.

An Interesting Letter from Mrs. R.G. Steele, who visits the Heart of the Mormon Nation.

On the Train, June 21st.

The excursionists left Ogden at 7:45 this morning for the great Salt Lake City. Tickets for the drive around the city and dinner cost the small sum of one dollar. Arriving at eleven o'clock we were escorted in a carriage which carried with ease thirty passengers. This one being full, the remainder of the ladies and gentlemen were seated in two large carriages and away we went; the drivers of each vehicle being prepared to describe each point of interest shown.

The exterior of the Tabernacle does not impress the beholder with much admiration; it being an oblong, plain, low building of a drab color entirely without ornaments; but once within its portals a feeling of solemnity takes possession of the mind. A room with the capacity for seating 12,000 people, lighted by over one thousand gas jets and in which, at the farthest distance from the pulpit a pin dropped can be heard, strikes one with wonder. Our party was invited to take a seat in the gallery, 250 feet from the pulpit. When we were all seated and quiet, the guide said, "Now I shall drop a common dress pin, and if you are attentive you will hear it fall to the floor," and so we did. The organ, no doubt, is the finest in the world costing several hundred thousand dollars. The temple is still unfinished although the corner stone was laid in 1853.

The Assembly Hall and Amelia Palace together with the beautiful homes, the widows and children of the late Brigham Young, and the grave of the Old Saint and of his wives, and many other points of interest makes Salt Lake City a desirable place for the tourist to visit. Our party alighted at 2 P.M. at the White House and as hungry as hunters. A fine lunch was in waiting and was devoured with keen appetites. The excursion train started out at 7 P.M., and the passengers retired early and slept soundly, and on the morning of the 23d awoke to the grand eye feast which was to be presented to them during the afternoon.

Grand! Oh, for some mightier word! At about 10 A.M. the train commenced to pass through what each and all thought to be grand scenery, and all eyes were strained and every voice would, every few moments, exclaim in concert, "Oh, isn't it just perfectly magnificent!" and other words expressive of deep admiration. But the *ne plus ultra* was still in reserve. Near the hour of 2 P.M. we reached Black Canyon, a pretty, shady little place, with purling streams gurgling and whispering as they run from our gaze, perhaps never to be seen by the same eyes again. Here an observation car was attached to the train, and some fifty to seventy-five ladies and gents took seats for an eight mile ride through Black Canyon. As we passed along, looking in wonder at the rock scenery, I felt satisfied that no tongue could tell, or no pen describe, the wonderful and awful sublimity of this gigantic grandeur of the grand old rocks which for miles stood like rows of old castles of quaint, mysterious architecture, fluted columns, gabled roofs square, round, oblong, painted by nature in many colors. While these silent monuments of creation stood on their lofty eminence frowning down from their majestic height on the one side and the waters of the rapidly rolling Gunnison river, dashing, rushing and foaming in mad frolic on the other, on we sped; rounding curves stretching out on dangerous points and through narrow passes. Oh, it was a glorious ride in that open car through this gorge of wonderful sights, with great rocks hanging threateningly over our heads liable at any moment to drop, I was told by the conductor that men are there on guard night and day clearing away the debris which falls from the crumbling, time worn giants of this fearful canyon. At 4 P.M. we arrived at Gunnison and found a splendid dinner in waiting [at the] Laveta hotel kept by J. Cuenin. The table was spread with a variety of the most choice viands, among the many kinds of dessert were dishes of iced pineapple.

"All aboard" shouted the conductor, and surely a happier crowd of people never took a train, and soon we were mounting the famous Marshal grade, up, up we rolled, our train following another section of our train, each section being draw by two engines. The sight as we watched the preceding train was most exciting, the passengers of the first section shouting, and waiting handkerchiefs to those hundreds of feet below. Then came the snowsheds and for an hour it was perfect jubilee, at last we stood on the summit of the grand old Rockies 10,856 feet above the sea. The sun had gone down and by the gray misty light we watched the winding down of the grade.

At about nine o'clock we reached Pueblo where we changed cars for Denver and Chicago. Some of the excursionists took the train for Denver and others for Chicago. It was with feelings of regret that we parted from the pleasant co-travelers who had helped to make our journey a pleasant one by showing those little kindnesses so acceptable to one in poor health. Today, Sunday, we have traveled all day through the state of Kansas, most of the way has been a green stretch of plain with here and there a pretentious city or town. The scenery has been monotonous and a strong wind has moaned and whistled around the train. Still it has been a pleasant and enjoyable day upon the cars. We have not tired of looking upon the smooth green ground with an occasional grain field, potato patch and cornfield.

The evening shades are closing around us; we are running at a rapid rate and hope to arrive at Chicago on Tuesday at 11 A.M. and New York on Thursday at 6 P.M.

MRS. R.G. STEELE.

* * *

A postal from Mrs. Steele, dated June 28th, informs us that she arrived at the home of her sister, Mrs. William K. Gray, at East Orange, N.J., on the 27th ult., just one week after leaving home, safe and well. She describes the journey as being beautiful.[3]

ON EASTERN SHORES.
Patriotism in the East on the Fourth of July.

———

A Visit to Edison's Home—The Wonderful Phonograph and How it Talks.

EAST ORANGE, N.J., July 9th

EDITOR ARGUS:—The celebration of the Glorious 4th here was a strictly social private affair. Families having large lawns purchased fireworks, balloons and punks and invited their friends and relatives to join them in the sport. I will give my experience which, no doubt, was the experience of a thousand families in East Orange.

The celebration commenced the evening of the third, and guns, firecrackers and other noisy demonstrations continued throughout the night. At five, on the morning of the 4th, the bells began to ring and such a racket for one whole hour has seldom been heard in time of peace even in a large city. Ring! Ring! Bang! Bang! Snap! Snap; and then the prolonged snapping of barrels of crackers. Then came a calm and I think all went to breakfast. The noise was kept up all day, and hundreds of paper balloons went sailing through the air, notwithstanding the rain poured in torrents all day. I was invited with Dr. Wm. K. Gray and wife to dine at the home of Dr. and Mrs. R.M. Sanger. The dinner was excellent and furnished the most delightful food for mind and body, and during the hour at table we were constantly reminded of the fact that this was the natal day of Freedom by the firing of pistols and crackers on the streets. The rain continued to fall during the afternoon until sundown. Then the clouds rolled off and a clear sky and bright stars smiled down upon the celebrators as they opened fire, and for a time it seemed as though the earth was one huge fire cracker and the main part of it rested on East Orange. Dr. Sanger had invited his two brothers-in-law, Dr. R[ichardson] and T[homas] N. Gray, and their wives and children to join him in the sport, so that Dr. and Mrs. Gray had the pleasure of their six sons and daughters and eleven grandchildren on this merry night. From eight o'clock until ten the large lawn in front of Dr. Sanger's residence was a constant blaze of beautiful red, white and blue lights, while growling rockets shot heavenward and scattered their wealth of brightness in the upper air. At least twenty large balloons brilliantly illuminated were sent up from that porch.

The same scenes were enacted at every house as far as the eye could reach and I tell you it was grand beyond description. At least four hundred dollars' worth of fireworks must have been exploded in that immediate neighborhood. After the noise had ceased, the party, consisting of about twenty-five, including the children, were invited to partake of a bountiful supply of ice cream; and thus ended my first Fourth of July in the old states for thirty-three years.

On the morning of the 5th, in company with my sister, I paid a visit to Greenwood Cemetery. Forty years had passed since I had seen our sainted mother laid beneath the green sod in that grand burial ground, but memory guided my footsteps and we were soon standing beside the spot to memory dear. The plat has been kept in good order during all those years. Ah! How the past came up before me. I could see a sweet, calm face and hear a gentle voice and I knew that another in spirit was very near. As we turned to leave I knew it was the last time I would look upon that smooth green mound, marked by a white slab with the simple inscription

Julia A. Granniss

This cemetery is at Brooklyn, Long Island, and is one of the largest in the United States. My visit to Parsippany and the old haunts of my childhood I reserve for my next.

EAST ORANGE, July 14th

On Saturday, the 6th inst., seated with my sister, Mrs. Gray, in an easy comfortable carriage with a fine team and a safe, experienced driver, we [drove] about East, South, and [Orange] proper. It would be impossible in a letter to give your readers the slightest idea of the real beauty of the picturesque scenery and the lovely, magnificent homes, covering miles upon miles of this beautiful country, each and every one telling a sweet story of temperance, morality and untiring industry, where old age can rest and revel in ease and luxuriant comfort and listen to the sweet voices of grandchildren, and watch the well-clad forms of their sons and daughters flitting upon the lawns and porches. Hundreds of the occupants of these palatial, suburban homes are men doing business in New York, driven by their wives, daughters or servants to the train every morning and met at the train in the evenings. These grand residences are from one to two hundred feet from the road with green laws speckled here and there with fancy beds of bright flowers, but the crowning beauty is the great number of giant shade trees surrounding these restful homes. The vaulting ambition of the owners seems to have been in building to out vie each other in queerness and quaintness of architecture. The newest, among the many, have the appearance of being at least a hundred years old. The most of them have the large brick building on the outside, and though the buildings themselves are from three to four stories high, the balconies and porches are low and shady and the painting is done to imitate old boards and shingles. I think during our drive that we passed over five hundred of these magnificent homes and never saw two just alike.

Leaving the streets we entered Llewellyn Park, which is the private property of the heirs of the late Mr. Llewellyn. It is a beautiful cool drive, with a good road for the benefit of the public. Many acres have been sold to wealthy men who have built elegant summer residences for their families. Among the residences was that of Edison, the great inventor, and also that of the family of the late General McClellen.

On the following day Dr. Gray took me for a drive on Prospect avenue. We also visited the home of Mr. Jaffries, one of the employees of the Edison laboratory, who has a phonograph machine. I am not very well versed in this new-fangled invention and can only use my own language in writing of what I saw and heard. A box about ten feet [*sic*, inches?] square and about the same height was placed upon a table, and when it was wound up the operator placed two little tubes, which were fastened to small cords or wires, into my hands and told me to place one in each ear. I did so, and in an instant I seemed to be in a grand opera house listening to an Italian prima donna. The singing was exquisite and I seemed to see the very gestures of the singer. This had been taken on the little cylinder a few evenings previous at an opera. Then I heard "Old Black Joe" just as plain as if the singer stood before me, and several other songs and a few short speeches. Mr. Jaffries was not prepared to give as interesting an exhibition as he would have been pleased to have given had there not been illness of a serious nature in his family. It is surely a most astonishing invention and will at some time, no doubt, become a necessity like the telegraph, the telephone, the typewriter and other late improvements.

Mrs. R.G. Steele.[4]

OUR EASTERN LETTER.

Further News From Our Absent Editress.

"How Dear to our Hearts are the Scenes of our Childhood when Fond Recollections Present Them to View."

East Orange, N.J., July 9th

On Monday, the 8th inst., we took the 8:30 train from East Orange to Morris Plains where we arrived at 9:30. A fine carriage and a dashing span of sorrels were in waiting according to prearrangements which had been made by letter. The young man who held the reins informed me that he was the son of Mr. Francis Young, of Mellpardus[xxiii]. "Indeed," said I, "I knew him well when we were both young people." The morning was lovely, and the three miles to Mellpardus was soon run over. It was with feelings mingled with great pleasure and pain that I met my sister, Mrs. M.A. Keeler, whom I found an incurable invalid. Now changed from the bright, intelligent, strong, beautiful sister I had kissed good-bye thirty-five years ago. Now at the age of seventy years a helpless child. Her husband, 71 years old, I found strong and healthy and as able to write and keep books or turn his hand to anything as when forty. After an excellent dinner, Mr. Young called and again we entered the carriage for a drive over the places where I had spent the happy days of girlhood. The first call we made was at the beautiful residence of Mr. and Mrs. Eugene Quimby. Mrs. Quimby was Miss Louise Harrison. Mr. Quimby is a brother of the Hon. J.A. Quimby of San Jose, Cal., member of our Legislature in 1856 and was mayor of San Jose for eight consecutive years. Both brothers were among my young friends of the long ago. The next call was upon Mrs. Harrison, widow of the late James Harrison. Then came the lovely place where my invalid sister had reared a family and spent thirty happy years of her life. How natural everything looked, but it is now occupied by strangers so we paused but a few moments to gaze upon this place where those I loved had dwelt.

The very earliest recollections of Miss Gussie Schenck are associated with the trees and flowers and the large halls and rooms of Oakville House and grounds. With one long look of regret I passed this place where so many sad changes had occurred during my absence of over thirty years. Sad changes have taken place with regard to the loved ones I left behind, but I do not think there is a place in the United States to-day where there has been so little

---

[xxiii] Unknown what town Rowena is referring to; perhaps it is the typesetter's misunderstanding of her handwriting.

change as in this neighborhood, either by decay or improvement. The ten houses that stood there when I was a very young girl are all standing and with one exception are all in good repair. The oaken floors upon which we danced at our evening gatherings in the cottage by the brook are still good and strong, and the little stream of water running over the white pebbles seems to be singing the same happy song it sang when the world looked so fair to the happy girl who listened to its whisperings on the bright moonlight nights of the long ago.

But alas, for the dear, little, brown house on the hill around whose every piece of timber clings sweet memories. The wreck and ruin and decay of this dear, old, darling house and grounds was complete. Here it was where transient tears were shed for imaginary woes, and from the portals of which floated sweet strains of music and merry peals of laughter. The dear little gate over whose pickets the good-night kisses were given. The sweet flowers whose fragrance filled the air, the well, the old oaken bucket, the old house, the gate and just a few flowers such as Robin Run Away, Sweet William and Johnny Jump-up are there but ruin is written on all. "Who has done this?" I mentally exclaimed. The answer came. The dear old folks are sleeping beneath the sod. So are many of the youths whose voices made the walls of this little brown house ring with merriment. But death did not bring this ruin. No, not death, but RUM! Yes, this monster entered into this pretty cottage and planted his fangs into the being of one of God's most noble and gifted men, and now the gentleman, the classic scholar, the friend and companion of my childhood days, the heir and owner of these broad acres is an intoxicated sot, living among the ruins the demon has made himself, the most pitiful wreck. It made me feel sad to think of that once bright, merry, fun-loving boy, that intellectual educator of Greek, Latin and English in the after years now a perfect wreck, caring for naught but rum—burning rum.

At our approach he fled to the woods and I did not see him, so after looking around for a few moments we started for the village of

Parsippany, a drive of about one mile from Oakville. Here there had been but little change in the last fifty years in the appearance of this settlement; the same houses but not the same people. Those I had known so well were, with a few exceptions, sleeping in the beautiful cemetery. I found but little change in the town. All the old houses of fifty years ago were standing and not more than half a dozen dwellings added. I looked in vain for some familiar face, but I found the names of scores of my young companions of my girlhood days engraved on marble as I walked through the old graveyard, now a magnificent cemetery filled with magnificent monuments. With a little sadness in my heart I entered the carriage and we were driven to the depot seven miles from Parsippany. All along the road was scattered the old homes where I had received a hearty welcome in the long ago. We arrived at East Orange just as the sun was shedding his last rays upon the tops of the waving trees. This day's visit will never be forgotten while life is blessed with memory.

EAST ORANGE, July 21, 1889

A few days over a month since I left home and still I linger regretting to say good bye to the dear ones here and longing to see the loved ones at home. Every day since I left has been an enjoyable one. I could not have believed that there was so much enjoyment awaiting me in the home I left so long ago, and while there has been very many marked improvements everywhere I go, still the people and the places which were the most familiar are unchanged or nearly so. On Tuesday of this week one of the finest of an eastern summer day, in the early morning while the birds were warbling their sweetest lays and all nature was green and cool from the showers of the day previous, my niece, Miss [sic, Mrs.] Laura [Frances Grannis] Hall, assisted myself and other lady relatives to a seat in her comfortable family carriage and we were soon on our way to Livingston a small settlement lying just over the Orange Mountains, six miles from East Orange. The fine black animal seemed to know that he had a precious load of old ladies for while he sped with rapidity and the fleetness of a deer he was careful and obedient to the rein. As we climbed the smooth road of the high mountain the scenery became more and more magnificent. Cities, towns and villages arose in the distance, broad sheets of water shimmered in the sunlight, tall trees and tangled wildwood, beautiful homes and old-time country farm houses, waving corn and golden grain, well-kept gardens, hundreds of cows browsing on the green hills, light milk pans in even rows, men, women and children engaged in useful labor, all bespoke beauty combined with thrift. About ten A.M. we arrived at the farmhouse wherein dwells my aged brother John and his faithful bride of 56 years, their son and his wife and a son and daughter, of the three generations not one uses alcohol or tobacco, the second and third never have tasted of either. Here is a family indeed, not wealthy as wealth is considered in these days but with

"A farm well tilled
And a house well filled."

where peace, happiness and joy abounds. My brother and his good wife, Rachel, now each seventy years old, are as bright, intelligent and healthy as they were twenty years ago and both do as much work every day as will keep them in good health probably for several years to come. Both have bright clear eyes and rosy cheeks and love to talk and read on literary subjects. They are very proud of their only son, Mr. Daniel Grannis, and well they might be. Their grandson (an only son too) turns all his attention to experimental chemistry. He is still in his teens and is extremely modest and unassuming, but I believe he has a bright future before him. The garden of this home abounds in bright, sweet flowers, tall trees and lovely verdant lawn. At noon the family and visitors, eleven in number, sat down to a well spread table and although in a country farmhouse style and table etiquette was not lacking. Coffee and chocolate was served in china cups and saucers over one hundred years old and the set was as complete as when it was purchased by Mr. and Mrs. Quimby, grandparents of the lady who is seventy-four years old and the sugar dish was the one used by Mr. and Mrs. Grannis the first year after their marriage and is consequently 56 years old and has been in constant use. During the day's visit we were shown many relics of the olden time among them an old earthen pie platter such as were used by our grandmother in New York and New Jersey a hundred years ago. This I hope to have the good fortune to bring to Merced. This was a most pleasant dinner for in addition to the delicious viands the talk over old times and the presence of old familiar faces made "good digestion wait on appetite and health on both." After dinner the host and hostess and family accompanied their guests around the farm and through the beautiful grounds, where bloomed lovely flowers, the finest was the fine variety of dahlias of such lovely colors and such perfect form. At five o'clock tea was served then came the good byes, never to be spoken again by the same lips to the same dear ones on this earth again.

"'Tis sad to part when harrowing fears whisper we part forever."
Again and again the adieus were repeated. Then, with "Get up, Tom," the carriage moved on at a rapid rate. We did not return by the Orange Mountains but by the way of Caldwell. And as it was at the lovely hour of sunset we were met by many happy people who had been to the trains to meet husbands, mothers, nieces and friends. We also passed many beautiful homes and saw much interesting and magnificent scenery. When we passed through Caldwell we were shown the house in which Grover Cleveland and his sister Elizabeth were born, if that be the house it has been greatly improved within the past 35 years, for at that early date and for many years previous I frequently visited old Caldwell. The place is much improved and appears to be a favorite summer resort for city people. The view from the hills near this place is perfectly enchanting.

We arrived in East Orange just as daylight was kissing the earth good night and that night my sleep was sweet for I was in my dreams dwelling among the pleasant scenes and people of childhood. In my next I shall tell of my visit to the tomb of Gen. U.S. Grant.

MRS. R.G. STEELE.

    * * *

Mrs. R.G. Steele, we are informed by private letter, will start from East Orange, N.J. for California on August 1st and will arrive here about the 8th.[5]

OUR EASTERN LETTER.

___

A Visit to Gen. Grant's Tomb—Childhood Scenes.

___

EAST ORANGE, July 25.

A few days ago I visited Riverside Park, which is, as almost every American citizen knows, situated on the banks of the beautiful Hudson, a river of magnificent distances. The drives and the fine hotels, the verdant knolls. The grand view of the lovely scenery for miles up and down the banks of the river will in time make Riverside Park a place of beauty. At present the tomb of the brave soldier and Statesman and a nation's pride is the attraction. On the side or rather at the foot of a lovely knoll and beneath a clump of tall trees stands the dark gray vault which contains the iron casket wherein rest the remains of the hero. All about and completely covering the casket are green plants, among which are ferns, palms and myrtles. A very handsome sentry box stands near the tomb and two sentinels are constantly on guard. One of them informed us that there was some uncertainty as to the exact spot upon which the monument would stand. Some of the committee, he said, are in favor of it being on the knoll just back of the tomb, others would like it a short distance to the right of it on a larger and higher mound, either will be a fitting site for the monument to the noble dead.

Seeing two magnificent residences on the right side of the drive and anxious to know if they were connected with the park property, we crossed the road and as we approached the buildings we observed a lad sitting upon the steps of one of them. "Do these buildings belong to the park?" we asked. "No, ma'am," was the polite reply. There was something so prompt and manly in the tone of his voice that I felt drawn to him, and after a few moment's conversation in which he informed us that his father was the owner of one of them and also mentioned the name of the gentleman who owned the other, I felt convinced that this was no ordinary boy. In answer to my inquiry, he said, "My name is John C. Gibbon." He also informed us that it was his intention to study medicine. I think that he said he was twelve years of age. Such a gentlemanly, scholarly boy as this John C. Gibbon is seldom met with and although a stranger whom I shall never meet again I shall often call to mind his pleasant voice and bright face.

During the day we took a stroll into Central Park, but this popular place of resort is too elephantine in its proportions to be seen in one or even two days, so I contented myself with the few wonders I had gazed upon during two hours walk. We then took the cars for the city, and in the afternoon visited the neighborhood in which many years of my young womanhood were spent: Hudson, Charlton, King, Varick and Grove streets. The school house on the corner of Grove and Hudson although somewhat improved, looks much as it did sixty years ago when a five year old lisping child, I muttered the words Baker, Briar, Friar, etc. and strange as it may seem with all of the gigantic strides improvement has made in the great city of New York I found little change in the streets I have mentioned. The same houses for blocks and blocks. There stood the building in which the Hon. David C. Broderick kept his saloon for many years, looking just as it did 40 years ago, with the exception of the red curtains then fashionable for windows and glass doors of a Porter House as saloons were then called. I am informed that the cause of this standstill in the way of improvement in this part of the city is owing to the fact that the property is owned by the Trinity Church and the Astors and was leased by the owners of the buildings for one hundred years. Of course, the time has nearly expired, and the lessees do not wish to make any new improvements.

In 1830 a man by the name of Berrian put up a small one-story house on a leased lot on Varick street, near King, and opened what was then known as a Victualling House and had a large sign painted upon which was the following: "Our own house, on our own plan and I can sell as cheap as any man and my name is Sam Berrian." This was repeated daily in a loud voice by the urchins of the neighborhood as they passed by. That house with its broad sign is still standing although the lettering is obliterated either by the brush or by time.

A few days after our visit to the tomb of the late Gen. Grant, Mrs. Gray called upon and introduced me to Mrs. Cramer, a sister to the dead hero…. [W]e found Mrs. [Mary Frances Grant] Cramer, a most charming woman having resided abroad for many years in company with her husband, [Mr.] Cramer who has been Consul and Minister to several foreign countries since the administration of Andrew Jackson up to that of Grover Cleveland. She has in addition to her superior natural gifts engaged many advantages which go to make the true lady. Mrs. Cramer has been a most industrious worker, the walls of the large parlors are covered with her paintings on which great versatility of talent has been developed, finest landscapes, groups of figures and flowers. Besides these were shown dozens and dozens of pieces of chinaware of every conceivable design and shape. The house throughout is most elegantly furnished. As you enter the parlors on the right side of the street door the first object which meets the eye is a fine portrait of Gen. Grant, it stands upon an easel and rests amid the folds of the American flag. Everything about the house bespoke exquisite taste in selection and arrangement. Mrs. Cramer is a devoted Christian and a most entertaining lady. We had the pleasure of listening to a most excellent and interesting sermon delivered by her husband on last Sunday morning at the M.E. Church of which Mr. and Mrs. Cramer are members. This gentleman filled the pulpit in the absence of the regular pastor.

In my next I shall tell your readers about the far famous Coney Island.

MRS. R.G. STEELE.

* * *

Returned.

Mrs. R.G. Steele of this paper, who has been visiting her old home in New Jersey, returned to Merced today.[6]

OUR EASTERN LETTER.

———

A Visit to Coney Island—The Famous Summer Resort.

———

East Orange, July 29

Last Tuesday, a very pleasant day, I accepted an invitation from Mrs. F.A. Gray to visit the far famed pleasure grounds of Coney Island. Not caring to dare the dangers of the waves of Old Ocean we went to New York by express train. Crossing the city to the east side we took the elevated steam coach to some of the many avenues of the city of Brooklyn, then several surface cars until we arrived at Brighton Beach. This is one of the aristocrat's places of resort on the Island with a magnificent hotel, with a porch thirty feet wide extending over the entire front, which I should judge was at least five hundred feet, perhaps more; upon this porch was spread tables covered with damask cloths and each arranged to accommodate four persons. The dishes are of pure china and silver and every piece is branded (to use a California phrase) with the name of the owner of the Hotel. Everything about Brighton Beach is first-class. A very small mould of sago pudding with tea costs 35 cents. After a slight but excellent lunch we entered a street car and passed on to the famous pleasure grounds by the sea, Coney Island, which we had visited in girlhood and found but one little house where visitors who came to take free baths in their own bathing suits could get hot Clam Chowder for six cents a plate, but the air of the Island was purer and the unbound waves leaped freer and higher. Now, where the little house stood 50 years ago, can be seen blocks upon blocks of business houses and quite a number of private summer dwellings. With few exceptions the ground for a mile square appears to be occupied for the purpose of giving a certain class of pleasure seekers a good time. Not having learned the names of all the pleasure-giving machines I can only give a description of a few, and of these I can give the reader but a faint idea of the noise, racket, din and bottle-like confusion. You might gather all the pianos and organs and fiddles in Merced around Laura Park, put the Merced and Snelling brass bands in the park, then let every little boy have a tin pan and drum sticks, get several good braying donkeys and all the Hoopold boys, ring all the bells and get them all ago-ing in their loudest keys, and let this concert take place on China new year's day, all this would be but a piping squeak beside the Coney Island racket. Confusion of noises here hath made their masterpiece. This commences about 9 A.M., grows louder and louder and more loud until 10 P.M. There are on the four corners of one street a merry-go-round each with just difference enough to make the fun-loving city children of the middle and lower classes of New York who get off for a holiday to try all of them. These joy-giving machines are composed of a circular platform some ten feet wide upon which are placed three abreast, wooden or metal animals representing every animal ever found on earth. There are also chariots, ostriches and swans and fishes, all with saddles, bridles and stirrups. In the center of these magnificently decorated circular platforms is placed a large musical(?) instrument which represents a full brass band with piano and organ. These mammoth instruments are run by steam. If you can imagine four hundred boys and girls from two to eighteen years of age all yelling at the very top of their voices, the noise of these four steam instruments, and the fizz and whiz of the flying animals with the bells and whistles of the incoming and outgoing trails, the strains of music from a dozen saloons and anything else you can think of, you have about half caught the true situation.

Looming up in the air some two hundred feet is a house built in the exact form of an elephant. The whiskey found on the first floor makes the greenhorns feel that they have seen the elephant.[xxiv] Then

---

[xxiv] Experience more than one wants to, learn a hard lesson.... For example, *After the expedition lost two climbers in an avalanche, they had seen the elephant and turned back*. This slangy expression, first recorded in 1835,

there are games and amusements to suit every age of every class except the strictly moral and people of purely refined tastes. After one has paid a visit to this place they cannot help feeling that they have been shown the elephant. There are some interesting arts and industries practiced here, such as the making of wax flowers, art galleries, glass works, china painting, look stands, gentlemen's furnishing goods and many other things and places which have passed out of my memory.

About three P.M. we entered the neat cabin of a little steamer and started for a point near Brooklyn and arrived at East Orange at 5, where we found a good dinner awaiting us.

Having been invited to attend the Broadway theater on that evening by my niece and nephew, Mr. and Mrs. R.M. Sanger, I bade my aching bones be quiet, donned my very best attire and started off as though Coney Island had not been visited that day. Frank Sanger, one of the proprietors of the Broadway and a brother to my nephew, was absent from the city. But we were shown into a grand private box and oh! the dazzling beauty of the interior of that theatre with the lovely glittering scenery appropriate to the play, the magnificent costumes of the players, the artistic arrangement of everything, animate and inanimate fairly dazed my senses for a time but I was not long in coming to a full realization of the fact that I was in one of the largest, best and most safely arranged playhouses in the world and that the actors and actresses were truly gifted artists. The orchestra was grandly sublime and nearly every seat in the immense house was filled with the elite pleasure seekers of New York and surrounding cities. The play was a comic opera, entitled "Oudi," which was exceedingly interesting and amusing. Everything connected with the stage, the house and the players was perfectly gorgeous. This opera has run one hundred nights and still some of the performers, both ladies and gentlemen, were called back four and six times by the highly pleased and enthusiastic audience on that

---

alludes to having seen all the sights one can see, including that rare beast, and returning home unimpressed or disappointed. Dictionary.com

occasion. Time has brought change in theatricals as in everything else. Now every actor and actress must be an educated artist. They must sing, dance and kick gracefully, each dress must be faultless in texture and style. Now the people are satisfied with one well-presented play an evening instead of a five act tragedy and a two act farce, as in the days of Hamlin, Mrs. Shaw, Forest, Ellen Tree, Booth, Scott, and a host of others who electrified their audiences by their great powers of representation and have passed away. As I watched the sprightly antics of the young and bewitching elves on the stage that evening, the words of the song I had so often heard came to me:

'Tis thus I sail from youth to age
By toys our fancy is beguiled.

And left the theatre with a heart filled with queer, old-fashioned recollections of yore.

MRS. R.G. STEELE.[7]

OUR EASTERN LETTER.

A Visit to Mount Tabor—Rain for Seven Days

Our Welcome Among Friends and Relatives in East Orange.

EAST ORANGE, July 31.

Notwithstanding the fact that it has rained here for the past six days coming down in torrents, Mrs. Gray proposed on Monday last that we should take a trip to Mount Tabor, a distance of 26 miles from East Orange and a half mile from the railroad. At the time of starting the signs were for clear weather, but we had not been on the cars more than five minutes before down it came and continued throughout the day with an occasional sunbeam. Arriving at the depot, we found a carriage in waiting and were soon in the sunny little summer villa of my niece, Mrs. R.M. Sanger, who with one servant and her two children, Kitty and Frank, was up for a few day's recreation and change.

Mount Tabor is owned by a Methodist Association. Approaching this mountain for miles you see nothing but a round mound of green foliage, this deception is kept up until you enter the dense wood when a sight of unexpected beauty meets the eye. For the mount underneath the tall trees and heavy boughs is thickly dotted over with the most fairy-like miniature mansions ever brought to the vision, even in dreamland. The best description I can give of the hundreds of these residences is by telling your readers of Merced to take a look at the residence of Mr. and Mrs. Milton Huffman, of Merced, and then imagine a house like it with the decorations, curves and angles, windows, doors and fences; say 12x15, two stories high, the height to compare with the width and each house painted in all the most artistic colors; the little green lawns embellished with roses, lovely growing flowers and the whole over-spread by a forest of chestnut trees, and the picture is as complete as I, with my weak powers of description, can give you. Some of these houses cost as high as two and three thousand dollars and are furnished in most exquisite style. They are occupied by families living at East and South Orange for several months in the year. It is considered one of the most healthy resorts in the State. The mountain is laid out in streets graded and lit up every night with gas. Over two thousand people live there during the summer months. The association holds camp meetings here every year, commencing about the middle of August. A most appropriate place, this shady cool retreat, to worship the Creator. It is quite a curiosity to see how nicely the meals are prepared in the cute little kitchens, and how neatly they are served in the band-box of a dining room. I regretted the rain as the outdoor enjoyment had to be dispensed with. The evenings, especially those of moonlight, are said to be lovely.

"The gentle queen of night
Beams o'er yonder winding hill
As they listen to the notes
Of the lonely Whippoorwill."

What could be more lovely than a calm, clear, cool night in this grove of lofty trees, whose trunks stand thirty feet without a branch or leaf, with music from hundreds of sweet human voices and at last to be soothed to sleep by the drowsy hum of a thousand insects? The peddlers have not been slow to find out this little retreat of the wealthy and fresh fruits and vegetables, ice cream and every conceivable dainty is served at each door daily, clear or cloudy, rain or shine.

Mrs. Sanger seemed very well contented inasmuch as it is the custom and choice of the husbands and fathers to come up on the evening train and return to business in the morning. At 6 P.M. I bade good-bye to my niece at her beautiful children. The sadness of that good-bye was somewhat lightened by a promise of a visit from Mr. and Mrs. Sanger in the near future to my California home.

Still the rain pours and the clouds are blacker and blacker and this is the seventh day of the storm. East Orange is a lovely place; a township of palatial homes, shady groves, immense wealth, grand churches, kind, generous, hospitable and moral people, and my reception and entertainment has been a perfect ovation. I have been feasted and feted. My relatives have made my five weeks among them one round of unalloyed pleasure, nothing that money or influences or time could command has been left undone; kindly but loving hearts have sought constantly to make joy and gladness; willing hands have brought me flowers and other things of brightness and beauty. Twenty-two little arms have clasped my neck and with their loving, rosy lips have given their aunt from the far west many loving words. All this will cling to my memory and make the hours of the remainder of my life hours of blissful remembrance; and still with all of the present surroundings my heart is filled with untold joy at the thought that in a few days I shall be enjoying the lovely sunshine of our own lovely California. A troop of old familiar smiling faces arrive before my mind's eye and my heart sings in joyous strains

"Oh, give me these, I ask no other."

And still I shall feel very, very sad when the farewell time comes for I know that I shall never see many of the dear ones again on this earth. I am sorry that the news of the illness of my family should have reached me before my visit here was finished and my anticipated visit to Nashville had been realized. But as I am a true optimist, I must be content and practice what I preach.

MRS. R.G. STEELE.

* * *

A Narrow Escape From Death on the Rail.

Mrs. Steele Passes Through the Scenes of Desolation Around Johnstown

Merced, Aug. 10th.

On Thursday evening the 1st inst. I bade good bye to my dear relatives and friends at the Newark Station. At 6:59 I entered the train of the Pennsylvania Central line and was soon rushing on the road, every mile of which bore me nearer my home. The first hour I enjoyed the pleasant scenery of Southern Jersey and the pleasant villages, towns, and cities through which we passed. Then came the shades of night and with them deep rambling thunder, flashes of lurid lightning and dashing rain. On, on we sped; all the passengers were evidently strangers to each other as not a word was spoken save when the train stopped to let off or take on passengers. About midnight the conductor called out Philadelphia and by the electric lights which glowed on every side we could see as well as in mid-day. There was not much of the beautiful to be seen from the depot; still as we moved out I could see that many improvements had been made to the Quaker City of years past.

The passengers had been informed that the train would reach Johnstown at seven in the morning, and all were wide awake and ready to look upon the place of the dreadful calamity, but at half-past six the train stopped. What is the matter? passed from the lips of each anxious passenger after half an hour's delay, but nothing definite could be learned. The keen demands of appetite began to stir the people and soon it was learned that coffee could be obtained a few yards from the train and coffee became the order of the hour. "Have you found out why we are delayed," asked a lady to several gentlemen who were in earnest conversation on the track. "The road is out of order and has to be repaired," was the reply, and just then I discovered that there was an express passenger train behind our train and I was told that several freight trains were also behind us. We got started about eleven o'clock, five hours behind time. We had not gone over two miles before we found the cause of the delay. On the right hand side of the road and down an embankment lay several wrecked freight cars which had been thrown from the track by rocks and debris, which had fallen from the hillside during the night.

At 12 Noon, we were informed by a passenger that we were nearing the spot where the Johnstown flood commenced. We could not see the reservoir as that was in the mountains to the left. But the first glimpse of the steep hills where the turbulent waters had rushed and in their mad fury had devastated the grand [illegible] woods of trees, rocks and everything in its course caused a shudder to pass over all present. For four miles it had leaped and roared and plunged—master of man, beast and the mighty forest; howling and moaning and laughing in demonical glee at the mad work before it. The work of snatching life from mothers' babies, strong men and little children, of sweeping away the house, the roof and fireside causing weeping and wailing and bitter sorrow, destruction and ruin. No tongue can describe even the sadness of the sight of silent ruins. Then who shall tell of the agony and anguish and desolation of the terrible hour of the happening. A gentleman who got on the train at the ruined town told many sad tales. He had come upon the grounds a few hours after the flood had burst upon the fated town and his recital was blood curdling. Just the evening before our arrival a man who had been engaged in clearing off a spot of ground stepped upon a small board which sank down beneath his tread. He lifted the board and to his horror found a little babe lying beneath in some water. The finding of limbs and bodies is of almost daily occurrence. A gentleman who had spent several days in the town told us many tearful incidents of the flood. A little girl of five years was in a room on the second floor of the house with her aged grandpa, and when told by him that both must be lost, she cried, "Pray, grandpa; pray to God! He will save us." And then the little one screamed, "Oh, God, save me and grandpa! Grandpa, do pray loud so God can hear!" Then she would again call out for God to save grandpa, and although in a most perilous situation with every other member of the family lost, this little child and her grandpa were miraculously saved. I supposed the book writers will give their readers many of these touching incidents but all the readers of the *Argus* may not see the published books. The train passed slowly through the place and gave all a chance to see. But all were glad to pass on rapidly as the atmosphere seemed filled with an unpleasant smell. It was hours before I recovered from the gloomy sight. During the afternoon we passed through fields and fields and fields of green corn which waved peacefully in the wind and as it shook its silken tassels seemed to whisper pleasant tales of prosperity and happy homes, where love and peace and temperance smiled down upon honest and earnest efforts, and I soon found myself in a happy frame of mind.

The journey from New York for second-class western bound passengers to Chicago is on the first-class cars with upholstered seats, but you never know the real pleasure of the trip across the continent until you find yourself seated in the tourist sleeping car. There is such a home-like feeling connected with these pleasant carriages. I am not saying this to advertise the railroad company, for I had to pay just as much for my fare as though I had not been writing and taking up C.P.R.R. for the past dozen years. So what I now say I say for the benefit of those who wish to visit friends in the East and who feel unable to go palace fashion. A ticket bought at the El Capitan for sixty dollars and fifty cents, and three dollars for sleeper, will take you to New York just as pleasantly and comfortably as a ticket for first-class. A good, obliging colored porter in each car attends to your wants and keeps the car neat and tidy. The ice water never gives out. The tourists are all intelligent, genteel people, and the person of most delicate desires will find nothing to offend their daintiness. Two days before arriving at Sacramento I discovered that W.H.L. Barnes, of San Francisco, the talented and popular lecturer, was a fellow passenger. Brother Barnes had been on an extended tour of the states in the interests of the Ancient Order of Workmen and was returning to his home. This, said he, in a jovial, happy way, is the first that I ever took a second-class car, but it will not be the last, I assure you, for, said he, I have enjoyed the two days I have been on this train better than any train ride I ever took in all the thousands of miles I have traveled. As soon as it became known that brother Barnes possessed the talent to entertain and amuse he became a hero, every lady searched her lunch basket for delicacies. One sent a large china bowl of iced lemonade, another a dish of strawberries and a third a dish of iced bouillon, and all were anxious to entertain and strengthen him for the amusement he volunteered for the occasion, and I tell you it helped to shorten the trip amazingly. On Wednesday at 3 P.M. I arrived at Merced, at home sweet home, well pleased with my eastern visit and trip over the continent.   MRS. R.G. STEELE.[8]

Of the remaining siblings, Rowena's sister Mary Granniss Keeler, whom she had sadly found to be an invalid during this trip, died the following Spring on April 24, 1890 in Parsippany, New Jersey.

OBITUARY.

Mrs. Keeler was the mother of Dr. W.S. Keeler, of New York City and Frank Keeler, of East Orange, N.J., and sister of Mrs. Dr. W.K. Gray, of East Orange, John Granniss, of Orange, and Mrs. Rowena G. Steele, of Merced, Cal. The deceased was born in Goshen, Orange Co., N.Y., January 1ˢᵗ 1820, and was married to Thaddus Keeler in the city of New York, May, 1840, and had she lived a few weeks longer, would have welcomed in the anniversary of her

fiftieth wedding day. She had been ill for several
years, and death was a welcomed friend. Mrs. Keeler
was a poet and in her younger years was a brilliant
society woman, noted among her friends for
possessing the happy gift of entertaining large
assemblages at her home. She was a member of the
M.E. Church. She leaves a husband, and two sons
and several grandchildren. Her remains were laid in
the family plot in the Parsippany Cemetery beside her
two daughters, Virginia and Rowena, and other loved
ones who have gone before. Dear sister, farewell, till
we meet on the shore beyond.[9]

Brother John V. Granniss died on July 31, 1898, in his home in
Livingston, New Jersey; his wife Rachel died on January 18,
1899. Sister Frances Augusta 'Fanny' Granniss Gray passed on
March 3, 1902, in East Orange.

Just six months after returning home to Merced, husband
Robert Johnson Steele died.

Chapter XIII

Silver Anniversary Celebration

In June 1886, R.J. and Rowena celebrated their twenty-fifth anniversary with a large party at their home.

THE SILVER WEDDING.

—

The twenty-fifth anniversary party given by Mr. and Mrs. R.J. Steele at their residence on Monday afternoon and evening last was in pleasantness and enjoyment all that could be desired. There had been no effort on the part of the aged couple to make this a grand or extravagant affair. The pleasant little home was beautifully decorated with cape jasmines. This beautiful little white flower nestling among the delicate green leaves was entwined in a wreath of over two hundred feet in length and gracefully festooned on the walls of the parlors, supper rooms, and dancing hall. Flowers were banked on the mantle pieces and a large bell composed of cape jasmines and oleanders. For these beautiful and artistic decorations Mr. and Mrs. Steele are indebted to Mrs. Helen W. Brown, of Alameda, Mrs. J.F. Lewis of Monticello, Minn., Mrs. H.H. Granice, of Sonoma, and Miss Lizzie Seaman, of Alameda. About one hundred guests were received during the day and evening. The weather was delightful and Luna lent her silvery beams in addition to the many beautiful gifts in silver from friends and relatives. Among the gifts are many beautiful and useful articles for household use, hand needlework in great variety, also hand painting and many different kinds of material, which will be kept as mementoes and in memory of the dear hands, heads and hearts of the givers.

Among the numerous gifts we will mention especially a lovely three-jarred silver pickle castor, the jars are of colored cut glass, and the gift of Mr. Sohlke; a silver individual syrup pitcher, Mr. and Mrs. N.H. Wilson; heavy silver pickle dish, Mr. H.H. Granice; half dozen individual silver butter dishes, Mrs. H.H. Granice; half dozen silver teaspoons, Mrs. J.W. Bost; half dozen silver knives in beautiful plush, satin-lined case, Mr. and Mrs. J.H. Simonson; pickle dish and fork, Mr. and Mrs. Clark Ralston; elegant library lamp, Mr. and Mrs. I.H. Jacobs; heavy silver sugar dish, with the following beautifully engraved on one side, "From Mr. and Mrs. Wm. Fahey to Mr. and Mrs. R.J. Steele." Many pretty articles in etching, knitting, crocheting and needlework were from the deft fingers of Mrs. H.W. Brown, Mrs. J.F. Lewis and Miss Lizzie Seaman. The following were among the guests present: Mr. and Mrs. Steele [R.J. and Rowena], Mr. and Mrs. Granice [Harry and Katie], Mrs. Brown, Mrs. Lewis, Mrs. [Kate] Keogh, Mr. and Mrs. Ralston, Mr. and Mrs. Atwater, Mr. and Mrs. Barclay, Mr. and Mrs. Simonson, Mr. and Mrs. DeWitt Jones, Mr. and Mrs. Jacobs, Mr. and Mrs. Fahey, Mr. and Mrs. Ordway, Mr. and Mrs. Manchester, Mr. and Mrs. Reid, Mr. and Mrs. Wilson, Mr. and Mrs. J.M. Schofield, Mrs. Frazier, Mrs. Blackburn, Mrs. Deering, Miss Estelle Jacobs, Miss Snediker, Mrs. Allen, Mrs. Bost, Mrs. Kahl, Miss Julia Manchester, Miss Julia Mensing, Miss Carrie Mensing, Miss Hallie Bost, Miss Luella Ralston, Miss Grace Deering, Miss Lizzie Seaman, Miss Annie Coakley, Miss Lizzie Coakley, Miss Eliza

Atwater, Miss Rose Tinney, Miss Russie Ward, Mr.
Jake Blackburn, Mr. L.G. Crocker, Mr. Geo. Scott,
Mr. C. Clough, Mr. L.R. Steele [Lee], Mr. A.C. Bean,
Mr. Geo. Brown, Mr. Frank Ralston, Mr. C. Walker,
Jas. Dugan, Judge C.H. Marks, Mrs. C.C. Smith, Miss
Kellett, Mr. and Mrs. J.A. Norvell, J.A. Sohlke, Celie
Granice, Julie Granice, Edith Coakley.[1]

R.J.'s Decade of Decline and the Final Farewell

We learn from mentions in the *Argus* that R.J. suffered
with his health for several years from at least two illnesses, asthma
and a general heart condition. He was spending less time at the
Argus, when he was not confined to home and in bed as was
reported often. He had turned over the *Argus* officially to Rowena
in the summer of 1885, went into partnership with J.O. Blackburn
in the real estate business, and in 1887 added disability insurance
through the Home Accident Association to the portfolio. In April
1886 he enjoyed an extended visit from his sister, Martha Ann
(Mrs. Josiah Flint) Lewis, who travelled out by train from
Minnesota, and he was able to make the trip to visit Harry and
Katie in Sonoma at least three times, once in July 1886 when
Harry was so ill R.J. had to undertake management of the *Sonoma
Index-Tribune* for a few weeks.

The real estate business seems to have thrived. An 1886
advertisement in the *Argus* touted "We offer for sale some of the
Finest Property in the County—ELEGANT HOMES, SMALL FARMS,
NEAT COTTAGES, and Several Houses and Lots in the Town of
Merced," including a "cottage which contains nine rooms,
pantries, porches, closets, ... a good windmill, two good barns and
a fence in good repair" for the price of $1,200.[2] In April 1888, he
commenced a new business in partnership with James Schofield—
the "double-acting force pump ... the easiest working, most
durable and cheap well pump ever yet offered to the public."[3]
Another business enterprise he briefly conducted was acting as

sole agent in Merced for "Dr. Spencer's Carbolic Smoke Ball and Debillator [*sic*]," which claimed to be a cure for influenza and a number of other diseases. No other information can be gleaned on whether they were financially successful endeavors.

News of the death of his sister Martha, on June 1, 1888, at her home in Monticello, Minnesota, arrived by telegram on June 9. R.J. was well enough to take the arduous month's-long journey to Minnesota and return by way of Nashville, Tennessee, where he visited his sister Mary Victoria (Mrs. Benjamin Fielding) Brooks.

Heard From.

R.J. Steele, ye big editor, has been heard from, he is enjoying the summer suns of Minnesota. He says California is a paradise and he will return in about four weeks.

* * *

AN EASTERN LETTER.

———

NASHVILLE, Aug. 1, 1888

DEAR WIFE AND SONS—I arrived here on Saturday last, completely worn out and have been resting and recuperating as well as possible in this sultry climate. I have traveled near Nashville considerable, visited the factories and noted places. J.K. Polk's tomb at the residence of the widow and many notable places—and will visit the "Hermitage," and the tomb of General Jackson before I take my departure, which will take me several days yet to do, putting off the time of my starting homeward bound, until next week. Nashville is a city of from 125,000 to 150,000 population, in most parts of which the blacks and whites are so sandwiched together that it is hard to tell which is most numerous. The cotton, woolen, iron and other factories here give employment to many thousands of the laboring classes, and as it is a railroad center the commercial advantages of the place are very great. As an agricultural country it is as fine as any in the highlands of the south. The farms are generally small, the railroads tap every important town, village and settlement, and a perfect network of turnpikes, [illegible] and roads supply the entire country with good avenues to drive through by which to reach railroad depots, steamboat landings and all local markets with the products of the country, and all appear prosperous. I am charmed with Nashville, although I cannot commend the climate to a Californian the heat being oppressive and not a puff of air to fan one, and the perspiration continually keeps one's clothes wringing wet throughout the day from sunrise to a late hour at night, rendering sleep, even with open doors and windows, out of the question until near morning. In fact, this is the case in all parts of the Atlantic states even those the farthest north is my experience in Minnesota, Wisconsin, Illinois, Indiana, and Kentucky prove, and I am anxious to get back to California for a sniff of cool air from the Golden Gate and the bracing breezes from the snow-clad Sierras. Thunder showers are frequent here as in Minnesota and no one ventures out a mile from home, in fair or foul weather, without an umbrella— wraps being too hot to be tolerated, however hard the shower, and anyone would take a wetting rather than be enveloped with overcoats or shawls.

I think that I will return by the Southern Pacific or some other southern line of road, as it will be quicker than to return by any northern route.

ROBT. J. STEELE.[4]

That year, in R.J.'s absence, Rowena held the Merced County Fourth of July Celebration at their home, since no one else in the community had stepped up to do the planning and management. Ticket proceeds were donated for the Mexican War veterans monument, another of her many causes.

The next Spring, shortly after Lee and Lennie's marriage and just months before Rowena went on her extended trip to the East, R.J. began a somewhat peripatetic search for a healthier clime in an effort to ease his asthma. On May 25, 1889, a blurb was printed in the *Argus* announcing that "R.J. Steele, editor of this paper, started this morning for the mountains of Fresno county. He goes for a three week trip. He took gun, blankets and 'grub' and he expects he will have a fine trip." The next week the *Argus* noted the first knowledge of his location or welfare.

> **Heard From.**
> One day last week our editor left here all dressed up in a "plug" hat and light britches and up to Saturday next we had not heard of his whereabouts. On Saturday we received the Madera "Mercury" and from that we discovered his whereabouts from the following notice: "R.J. Steele, the veteran editor of the Merced Argus, was shaking hands with his many Madera friends this week. Mr. Steele is the pioneer journalist of Merced county, and he has grown gray in the editorial business."[5]

Apparently he was back home in Merced by mid-June when he advertised a mountain farm for sale in Fresno County, and Rowena left for Sonoma to spend a week with Harry and Katie. In early August he hosted an old friend, fellow Mexican War veteran John M. Denny. On August 17, it was noted that R.J. was "still sick." "R.J. Steele, senior editor of the Argus, who has been ill for several weeks, although seen upon the streets occasionally, is still in critical condition. He will go to the mountains in a few days with the hope of being benefited by the cool air."[6] It seems a wave of sickness swept generally over Merced that summer, as Lee, Lennie, and several other citizens were also reported to be confined by a severe, unnamed illness.

In September, while Rowena went to San Francisco to deliver the three abandoned Bosco children to a foster home, R.J. headed out again for the mountains.

> Robert J. Steele, senior editor of this paper, who started for the mountains on Sunday, the 13th inst. and who has not been heard from since he started, was heard from yesterday. Mrs. C.S. Peck saw him at Fresno on Wednesday last. He was suffering from asthma and told our informant that he should return to the mountains as he found the mountain air quite beneficial to him in health. We hope to hear in a few days of his recovery from that troublesome disease.[7]

He stayed away throughout October, reporting that he had "taken up a piece of land and says in his last letter that he will in a few years have a nice farm. He will indeed then be able to tell what he knows about farming."[8] On November 2 it was noted "Mr. R.J. Steele is still in the mountains. Last we heard of him he was building a cabin. The next time we hear we should expect to learn he is putting up a sleigh and inventing snow shoes." Rowena also reported he was expected back in Merced soon and that his health had much improved, however, by November 30, just days after granddaughter Constance was born, R.J. was again confined to bed at his home on Main Street from a severe attack of asthma. It was just a few weeks later that Lee left the paper and bought the City Bakery.

R.J. finally succumbed to his illnesses on January 28, 1890. The condolences and tributes immediately began coming in from New York, New Jersey, Nebraska, Oregon, Tennessee, and all parts of California.

Robert Johnson Steele.

Robert Johnson Steele died at his residence last Tuesday morning. He was born in Rockingham, N.C., October 22, 1822. He joined Company E, State Fencibles, at Jackson, Miss., in May, 1846, under Captain Louis McManus and was mustered into service at Vicksburg in the First Mississippi Rifles, commanded by Jefferson Davis, June 6, 1846. He sailed with his regiment from New Orleans to Brazos, Santiago, and saw active service at the battles of Monterey and Buena Vista. In 1849 he crossed the plains to California, and commenced his first mining venture in El Dorado County in 1850. He went to Columbia and started a newspaper; he also edited the Placer Courier, and has been the proprietor of several newspapers in northern mining towns. In 1861 he married Mrs. Rowena Granice. He leaves a widow and one son, Lee R. Steele. His step-son, H.H. Granice, is a proprietor of the Sonoma Index-Tribune. For the past twenty-nine years Mr. Steele has edited papers in Merced County. He was a pioneer journalist, and for the last ten years was a correspondent for the California Associated Press.—S.F. Call.

———

MERCED, Cal., Jan. 28, 1890
Mrs. Steele, My Dear Madam:—

It is with sentiments of deep regret that I learn of the death of Mr. Steele. Yours, very truly, JAS. A. NORVELL.[xxv]

> SAN FRANCISCO, Cal., Jan 28.
> 4:30 o'clock P.M.

To Lee R. Steele: Accept our condolences for your family in your bereavement.

> A. RICHARDSON,
> Manager, Cal. Ass'ed. Press.

* * *

R.J. Steele, editor of the Merced Argus, died at his home in Merced on Tuesday morning last after an illness of several months. Deceased was a writer of much ability and had been engaged in the newspaper business for the past twenty-eight years in this county, was a Mexican War Veteran and a pioneer of California. The funeral took place yesterday at 2 p.m. from his late residence on North Main Street.—Merced Star.

* * *

Robert J. Steele, editor of the Merced Argus, and husband of Rowena Granice Steele, died at his residence in Merced yesterday at the age of 67 years. Deceased was a veteran of the Mexican War, he having seen active service at the battles of Monterey and Buena Vista. In 1849 he crossed the plains to California and commenced his first mining venture in El Dorado County. In 1850 he went to Columbia and started a newspaper. He also edited the Placer Courier, and has been proprietor of several

---

[xxv] James A. Norvell was the new proprietor of the *Merced Express* and County Superintendent of Schools, also a close neighbor of Rowena and R.J.

newspapers in the northern mines. In 1861 he married Mrs. Rowena Granice, who with a son, Lee R. Steele, survives him. Harry H. Granice of the Sonoma Index-Tribune is his step-son. Mr. Steele was an able journalist, and his writings were always of a vigorous and convincing style. For twenty-nine years he has been identified with the press of Merced County, and for several years has been a trusted and able correspondent for the California Associated Press. His widow is a gifted and talented writer, her literary achievements having won for her considerable distinction in the world of letters. Her liberality and sympathetic and generous impulses have made for her a host of warm, personal friends, who will console with her in her sad bereavement.— San Francisco Daily Cricket, January 29.[9]

MERCED.— Jan. 28. Robert Johnson STEELE died at his residence to-day. He was born in Rockingham, N.C. Oct 22, 1822. He joined Company E, State Fencibles, at Jackson, Miss., in May 1846, under Captain Louis McMANUS, and was mustered into service at Vicksburg in the First Mississippi Rifles Regiment, commanded by Jefferson DAVIS, June 6, 1846. He sailed with his regiment from New Orleans to Brazos, Santiago, and saw active service at the battles of Monterey and Buena Vista. In 1849 he crossed the plains to California, and commenced his first mining venture in El Dorado county in 1850. He went to Columbia and started a newspaper. He also edited the Placer Courier, and has been the proprietor of several newspapers in the northern mines. In 1861 he married Mrs. Rowena GRANICE. He leaves a widow and one son, Lee R. STEELE, and one stepson, H. H. GRANICE of the Sonoma

Index-Tribune. For the past 29 years, he has edited papers in Merced county. He was a pioneer journalist and for the last ten years has been a reporter for the California Associated Press.[10]

A sad twist of fate, especially for Lennie Steele, was that her own father, William A. McCreary, died within hours of R.J.

A Sad Coincidence.

A sad coincidence occurred this week with Mr. and Mrs. L.R. Steele. Wednesday Mr. Steele was called upon to attend the funeral of his father, Robt. J. Steele, and on the next day Mrs. Steele attended the funeral of her father, William A. McCreary. This is a coincidence that will never be forgotten by Mr. and Mrs. Lee Steele and their relatives.

The remains of W.A. McCreary which were taken to Snelling on Thursday last for interment, were escorted to the grade by the Odd Fellows of Merced in a body.[11]

Another Pioneer Gone.

That dreadful disease, pneumonia, this week has carried away another victim in the person of William A. McCreary, a pioneer citizen of this county, whose death occurred at his residence on Main street Wednesday morning last at 8 o'clock, after a week's illness. He had been failing in health for some years and when the disease took hold of his shattered system he was not able to stand the severe shock which it received, and he passed peacefully away. He was a native of Conecuh County, Alabama, and was born January 28th, 1828. He came to California in 1850, via the Isthmus of Panama, and was engaged in mining at Mariposa and Stanislaus counties. At the expiration of three years he gave up mining and settled with his brother, L.I. McCreary on a stock ranch near Chowchilla flat, below what is known as Old Middleton road, in which business he continued until 1868 when he was married to Miss Nannie Gibbons, who survives him. After his marriage he gave up stock raising and bought a farm on the Merced river, near Snelling, where he resided until about two years ago, when his health failed himself and family and they rented out the farm and moved to Merced. The deceased commanded the respect and esteem of all who knew him, and leaves a widow and four children, three girls and one boy about 8 years old. His eldest daughter, Lennie, is now Mrs. Lee Steele, and his second daughter, Miss Leota, is a pupil at the Normal School, San Jose, and his third daughter, Miss Etta, resides with her mother in Merced. The remains were taken by the family to Snelling Thursday morning, where the funeral and interment took place under the auspices of Willow Lodge No. 121, I.O.O.F., of which the deceased has been a member in good standing for twenty years.[12]

Rowena noted with gratitude that the flag on the *Merced Express* building was flown at half-mast for two days in respect to the memory of these two pioneer citizens.

Mr. Jas. A. Norvell, superintendent of the Public Schools of Merced and proprietor and editor of the Merced *Express* will please accept my heartfelt thanks for many Kind acts of true friendship in respect to the memory of my late husband Robert J. Steele. For two days previous to the funeral, the American flag waved at half-mast over the *Express* offices. A kind letter of condolence was received by the widow and family. Mr. Norvell procured a lifelike cut of the deceased and placed it above a grandly written obituary, and had it published in the *Express*. These courtesies must be looked upon by all as the acts of an unselfish, noble and generous hearted gentleman. May heaven shower its richest blessings upon Mr. Norvell and those of his home.

MRS. R.G. STEELE.[13]

Rumors immediately started in Sonoma that Harry would be quitting the *Index-Tribune* to manage R.J.'s estate and businesses, which he quickly refuted.

A report has been started in this community by a mischievous and irresponsible person that the editor and proprietor of the INDEX-TRIBUNE contemplates removing to Merced to manage the estate of the late Robert J. Steele. There is not an atom of truth in the report. In the first place Mr. Steele left a widow fully competent to manage the affairs of the estate. In the second place we are in no wise interested in the same, not being a blood relative, and thirdly we have our hands full in minding our own business, which is more than we can say of the individual who has seen fit to circulate a report, which he knew was false, with a sinister motive in view. We are here to stay. Here it is we expect to live and here it is we expect to die and be buried. We have founded a home and a fair paying business in Sonoma, thanks to our many kind friends and patrons in Sonoma Valley who appreciate in the INDEX-TRIBUNE a fearless, clean and respectable paper ever ready to do battle for the interests of its particular section as against the whole world. We are here to stay and don't you forget it.[14]

Coping With Widowhood and Advancing Old Age

Rowena soon after made an application for R.J.'s Mexican War pension.[xxvi] Characteristic of the vigor, fortitude and determination which had been her strength for almost seven decades, she attempted to carry on publishing the *Argus* by herself and took over R.J.'s real estate business, advertising a "Tract, 125 acres, on Bear Creek, with two Flowing Wells, lying convenient to the railroad" on May 31, 1890.

She took at least three trips to San Francisco, in March, April and May, and on the April trip had quite the shock of experiencing an earthquake.

The Earthquake.

We happened to be at one of the largest hotels in San Francisco the time of the shock, on Wednesday morning. Awakened from a sound slumber, or partly awake, we at first thought we were in our own cottage home at Merced, and thought that someone was at the window of our room. This must have been during the first shock for in an instant after we were wide awake, and rocking to and fro. Everything in the room seemed waltzing around. We sprang from

---

[xxvi] Apparently this application was denied; she reapplied in February 1893 giving more personal details. "I am in my 69th year and from hard labor, both mental and physical, am entirely unfit for manual labor. I was married to R.J. Steele 1861 and lived with him 29 years, out of those years I nursed and cared for him 20 years, and [supported?] the family. I was sole trader and conducted a county newspaper. The next year after his death I broke down and had to sell it or sacrifice. We had one son and he inherits his father's ill health, and I had to assist him until the little I got for the printing office was gone and now I write a little for the paper for which I get but little pay and do not have but little to do at this."

the bed and flew to the door, and upon looking out saw many figures clad in snowy robes flitting about. We rushed back and caught up our shoes and stockings, determined to be ready for flight if another and heavier shock should come. We sat down near the door ajar and while engaged in buttoning our boots we heard the following, "Oh, wasn't it jolly?" "Why, it was a perfect daisy!" "I declare it was quite a treat!" and then followed little light ripples of laughter. "Pooh!" we exclaimed, "It was only a farce, what's the use of getting frightened at such a puny thing as a San Francisco earthquake." Then we laughed a kind of artificial stage laugh, threw our boots across the room and went back to bed with a sort of who's afraid kind of feeling.[15]

In May came the excitement and anticipation of the arrival in New York of about eighty immigrants from the Netherlands who were heading to California to settle in the Rotterdam Colony just northeast of Merced. Rowena made several trips out to witness the progress of construction.

THE HOLLANDERS.

———

They Arrive in New York Sixty-Five Strong.

———

A Small Army of Wealthy Farmers—They Come to Stay.

———

The following dispatch from New York relative to our colonists is taken from the San Francisco "Chronicle" of Saturday last:—

As quaint and picturesque an ideal reproduction of a page from Irving's

"Knickerbocker History of New York" was
the scene at the Netherlands-American pier, at
the foot of York street, Jersey City, this
morning, when the steamship Spaarndam
arrived from Amsterdam.

Clad in typical costumes and possessing all
the characteristics so inimitably portrayed by
Irving, a colony of genuine Hollanders landed
from the Spaarndam. The strangers numbered
sixty-five. They came from Rotterdam,
Amsterdam and the interior cities of Holland,
and are going to locate in Merced, Cal.

These colonists are more than the ordinary
immigrants. They came over as cabin
passengers, and a special train was chartered
this evening to carry them to their destination.
A San Francisco attorney is at the head of the
enterprise.

Four months ago he was sent abroad to
induce the Holland families to emigrate to this
country. The sixty-five persons who landed
today are the first fruits of his mission. If they
prosper and find California the El Dorado
pictured by the persuasive attorney, others will
follow and Merced will become a typical village
of Holland.

They will engage in agricultural avocations.
The combined wealth of the sixty-five is
$350,000. They carry with them a retinue of
servants. They are not transient settlers, but
each one landed with the avowed intention of
becoming an American citizen. As soon as they
reach Merced they are going to establish a
church for themselves, import an ecclesiastic

divine to give them spiritual consolation, and build a school for their children.

Thirteen Hollanders arrived here some five months ago and have been overseeing the work of fixing up the colony to receive the newcomers. When the sixty-five arrive they will be met by their friends, our local Board of Trade, the Band and our citizens generally, and escorted to their future home on the Rotterdam colony where two large hotels have been built to accommodate them until their homes are made ready for them.

* * *

TRIP TO ROTTERDAM.

One day this week we rode over the smooth grade of the county road to the Rotterdam Colony. Our pen will fail to give a just and true picture of the surprising improvements of that once dreary and apparently worthless section. It is truly wonderful to behold the change that has been wrought in a few months. One very noticeable feature about the improvement on the Rotterdam Colony is the superiority of the buildings erected to those generally built in starting a new town in California. There are no cabins, no rough board houses, every one is a neat, well-furnished modern building, some two stories, others one story cottages around which vines are already beginning to creep and climb. The two large hotels which are nearly finished will, when completed, be to Rotterdam what the El Capitan is to Merced or the Palace Hotel is to San Francisco. We noticed that white paint is used on nearly every house in the colony, giving them a neat and homelike appearance. We congratulate Messrs. Huffman and

Crocker, the original promoters of the colony, on the success of their giant undertaking in the face of the great weight of opposition they had to contend with.[16]

Determined that there should be a bigger, better Independence Day fete in 1890 than in the last few years, Rowena sent out the call in late May to the ladies of Merced to join the planning committee, chaired by Mrs. C. Ralston and with Rowena serving as secretary. "Merced has had no celebration on the natal day for several years and now that the ladies have taken the matter in hand the gentlemen should show their patriotism and generosity by giving all they can afford to make this the grandest celebration ever held in our county."[17]

According to the *Argus*, the event lived up to expectations. "The celebration yesterday was a grand and glorious success everything passed not exactly quietly but pleasantly, no accidents or anything of an unpleasant nature happened through the day or evening. It was just simply a grand, jolly, enjoyable Fourth of July...." "The day's pleasures were wound up by a grand ball in the evening at the El Capitan, and all who were present enjoyed themselves to the greatest extent. Merced may well be proud of her 4th of July celebration...."[18]

By early June 1890, all of this frenzy of travel, work and other activities had obviously taken their toll on Rowena. She suddenly announced her retirement from management of the *Argus* and passing of the baton to Lee, who also took over the real estate and insurance businesses in partnership with W.C.C. Russel, Jr.

DOWN AND OUT.

———

After having for twelve years the entire control of the business department of the ARGUS and occupying the greater portion of the time the editorial chair and acting at all times woman of all work from working the press down to the lively vocation of carrier, I find it necessary on account of age and of desire for rest to retire from active business. And this day the publication of the Daily and WEEKLY ARGUS passed into the hands of my son, Lee R. Steele. Lee is too well known in Merced County to require any eulogistic or commendatory remarks from my pen. Having been reared in a printing office, he fully understands the art of practical printing. Of his gift as Editor the public must judge. And now, in bidding goodbye to the dear old ARGUS and its patrons, I will say that in my twenty-eight years of service for the people of Merced County in Journalism that I have formed many loving and lasting friendships and I say to the people of Merced, as Ruth of old said to Neomie, "Entreat me not to leave thee. Nor return from following after thee. Thy people shall be my people, Thy God shall be my God, and where thou diest will I die and there will I be buried." Through the liberal patronage of the people I have acquired a sufficiency to keep the wolf from the door, and I hope to spend many happy days in this my chosen home. This goodbye is only to the editorial chair and the care devolving upon the publishing of a daily and weekly newspaper. Not to my many friends and beautiful Merced.

MRS. ROWENA GRANICE STEELE.[19]

Lee accepted his new managerial role as publisher and editor.

UP AND IN.

With this issue we take off our hat and salute our
friends from the high position of editor and
publisher of the Merced Daily and WEEKLY ARGUS.
Our parents have been in the business for the past
twenty-eight years in this county, and we hope the
people will give us encouragement enough to keep us
in the business the same length of time. We will
make no promise, only this: We will try to run a good
paper at all times; it will be fearless and outspoken
and yet have regard for the feelings of others. We
think we are well known in the county, having been
born and raised here, and we pride ourselves on
having quite a number of friends. The ARGUS will
pursue the same course in the future that it has in the
past, and with this we take our seat in the editorial
chair and henceforth our interests are the people's
interests and the people's interests are our interests.
LEE R. STEELE.[20]

Rowena continued over the next few months to write
extensively about her trips around the state, including in late June
a visit to Snelling with Lennie's mother, Nannie McCreary; to
Chico in early July; and in July to the Van Akin house near
Rotterdam in company with her widowed brother-in-law, Dr.
William K. Gray, who was visiting for a few days. The *Argus*
promised more travel articles in the coming months. "Mrs. R.G.
Steele, traveling correspondent for the ARGUS, will favor our
readers with a few of her communications soon. While away she
will travel nearly all over the State. She will visit Chico,
Sacramento, Sonoma, San Francisco, Santa Cruz, Los Angeles,
and in fact all the places of note in the State and our readers will
get the full benefit of her visit."[21] She was back home on August

23 in time for a meeting of the Merced City Cemetery Association.

In September, Rowena and Lennie took a day trip to the Rotterdam Colony to observe and report on the progress of development. "As it is impossible for a person to see all the improvements of this grand work in one day, I shall visit the Colony again in the near future and give the readers of the *Argus* an idea of the extensive building operations of this wonderful town of Rotterdam."[22]

There followed a trip to Los Angeles and San Diego. By late October she was back home and reported to be "quite sick"; she apparently recovered fairly quickly, attending a party at Lee and Lennie's home on November 14 in honor of Nannie's fortieth birthday. That night, there was a frightening incident where Lee and Lennie narrowly avoided what might have been a disastrous fire when toddler Constance pulled a lamp off the sewing machine and onto the floor. Fortunately, the lamp was filled with non-explosive oil.

In Quick Succession: Sale of the Argus – Investment in the Lodi Valley Review – The Lodi Weekly Budget – The Tracy Times

Just two weeks later, on December 5, 1890, Lee abruptly sold the *San Joaquin Valley Argus* and the *Merced Daily Argus* to Justus Hubbard Rogers and Charles Daniel Radcliffe, both experienced newspaper publishers and editors. By January 1891, Rogers and Radcliffe had also purchased the *Merced Journal*, and on January 19, the consolidated papers became the *Merced Evening Sun* and the *Merced County Sun*, with the volume numbers of the *Argus* continuing so that they could still claim to be the pioneer newspaper in Merced County.[23]

Suddenly, the near weekly tidbits of news and articles from Rowena ceased. Nothing more is heard from her or Lee until February 1891 when Lee was reported to be visiting family in Madera.

Lee R. Steele, who formerly conducted the *Daily
Merced Argus*, dropped in on us this week.
Accompanied by his wife, he is visiting relatives in
Madera. Lee states that he has retired forever from
Journalism and that it is his intention, as soon as he
returns to Merced, to commence the study of Law.–
Mercury[24]

In April, it was related that Rowena had been the victim of
a robbery by a tramp on whom she had taken pity and allowed into
her kitchen to eat a meal.

Mrs. Rowena G. Steele, the journalist of Merced, fed
a tramp in her kitchen April 9, and he stole a lot of
valuables before he left. Her son, L.R. Steele,
followed him to a tramp camp about a mile from
town and took him to jail. He confessed.[25]

John Sullivan, the burglar who robbed Mrs. Rowena
G. Steele's residence at Merced when she fed him
and who was caught by her son, has gone to Folsom
prison for ten months.[26]

Despite his attestations in February 1891 that he was
retiring "permanently" from journalism, in January 1892 Lee
purchased a half interest in the *Valley Review*, published by Gertie
DeForce Cluff (Laura DeForce Gordon's sister) and her son,
Frank B. Cluff, in Lodi, a town eighty miles north of Merced in
San Joaquin County (population of 1,013 in 1890).

A CHANGE.
With this issue the REVIEW makes its appearance
under a partially new management, L.R. Steele,

formerly publisher and editor of the daily and weekly Merced ARGUS, having purchased a half interest in the office. With this addition to our force it will be our pride and ambition to strive to make the REVIEW one of the best mediums of advertising the wonderful resources of the county, and the Mokelumne valley in particular, and also the best medium for the merchant and other business men to make their wants known to the public. We shall endeavor to give our readers each week all the interesting local news, such as social gatherings, court reports, real estate transactions, and matters pertaining to educational doings. In politics the Review will be independent. We shall, in local political matters, always support the one who we consider the best man for the office aspired to. We shall endeavor to give praise for all good acts but shall handle a trenchant pen in denouncing crafty and dishonest political evildoers. By fulfilling strictly to the letter the above promises we hope to receive the patronage of the people of Lodi and the surrounding country.[27]

Several other state newspapers noted with positivity the change in management and wished them well. "Lee is a typo and a newspaperman by birth and education, and he ought never to engage in any other business."[28] "Mr. Cluff is to be congratulated on securing so able an associate whose experience will greatly aid him in the conduct of the paper."[29]

Rowena immediately went up to visit Lee and Lennie in Lodi, and the next week it was announced that Gertie DeForce Cluff and Rowena, "both well-known California writers, will act as traveling correspondents for the REVIEW, and from time to time favor its readers with choice descriptions of other parts of the state."[30] Rowena presented an article about her impressions of Lodi the next month.

A GOOD TOWN.

A Stranger's Opinion of the Business of Lodi.

What a Well-known Writer has to say of the Thrift Displayed Here.

EDITOR REVIEW:—Permit me, in an humble way, to say a few words complimentary of your town and the surrounding country.

During my late brief visit, I noted, with pleasure, the vast improvements which have taken place within a few years. I found upon the ground formerly occupied by old wooden buildings, rows of fine brick business houses, with large show windows filled with merchandise of every description. The narrow, wooden sidewalks of old have disappeared and smooth flagstone walks have taken their place. As I alighted from the train, my eye rested upon the pretty park situated in the business center. Your merchants all look like business men, and substantiate the fact by being always ready and willing to wait upon customers, of which there appears to be no lack.

Your town is unlike many California towns, it has not outgrown the country around; it has modestly waited until the farming and other industries had a chance to accumulate in number, and thereby gained a population and a demand for the goods offered for sale. You have a fine settlement; for miles in all directions the country is dotted with substantial farmhouses, extensive orchards, vineyards and large grain fields, and now in this early springtime when all is in bloom how lovely!

When approaching your town a week ago and gazing upon the delightful scenes, the following lines from the pen of the gifted poet Mrs. A.B. Welby, ran through my mind as I inhaled the fresh spring air:

"What scenes of delight, what visions she brings
Of freshness, of gladness and mirth—
Of fair sunny glades where the buttercup springs
Of cool, gushing fountains of rose-tinted wings
Of birds, bees and blossoms and beautiful things
Whose brightness rejoices the earth."

On the main street I saw no idle merchants looking for customers, for the people from the country were there, and enough of them to keep all hands busy. "Thrift" was written upon all things in the business portion of the town of Lodi. As I strolled through the suburbs I was astonished at the sturdy growth of the magnificent shade trees which form a perfect grove through the private streets, the hundreds of handsome, substantial residences with their pretty gardens, so comfortable and homelike. Your fine gigantic school building and churches tell of culture and refinement and everything in and about your lively, active town gives certain and unmistakable proof of a grand and prosperous future.

MRS. ROWENA GRANICE STEELE.
Merced, March 22, 1892.[31]

Nannie McCleary immediately moved to Lodi and, on April 24, 1892, opened a stationery store in the International Order of Odd Fellows (I.O.O.F.) Building. Lee and Lennie's son Clarke Lee 'Jack' Steele was born in Lodi on June 1, 1892.

The touted Cluff & Steele partnership was short-lived—
very short, indeed. Within a week, the notice went out:

TO THE PATRONS OF THE VALLEY REVIEW AND TO
ALL WHOM IT MAY CONCERN:

Notice is hereby given that the partnership formerly
existing between F.B. Cluff and L.R. Steele, in
publishing the VALLEY REVIEW, has been dissolved
for some time past, and all payments for work done
by said office, or for advertising inserted in said
paper, from and after February 1st, must be paid to
Lee R. Steele. No other person is empowered to
collect for said work.   L.R. STEELE.

                    * * *

With this issue the REVIEW goes to its readers
somewhat reduced in size. However we give our
readers as much local news as ever, the only
difference being that we have rooted out all "dead"
and nonpaying advertisements. We are running a
paper for the money there is in it and not for the
glory. We shall at all times endeavor to give value
received to our patrons and from time to time we
propose to enlarge the REVIEW until we have it as
large, if not larger than its former size. We want it
distinctly understood that the present reduction in
size is not permanent but simply to get rid of a lot of
advertisements that have been left in the forms from
time to time to fill up space. This kind of advertising
we do not want and prefer to give our readers a small
paper, well filled with local happenings of the day
and articles benefiting the country than to give them
a large blanket sheet filled with nonpaying or trade
ads. Hoping the public will appreciate our endeavors,
we remain, respectfully.   L.R. STEELE

Then came the announcement in May that Rowena was endeavoring to set up a weekly paper in Lodi, which she had resolved to name the *Lodi Budget*.

> Mrs. R.G. Steele, who was editor and proprietor of the *San Joaquin Valley Argus* for fifteen years, and connected with the paper twenty-nine years in this county, left Merced on Wednesday for San Francisco to purchase an outfit for a weekly newspaper which she intends to establish at Lodi. The paper will be independent in local politics.[32]
>
> Mrs. R.G. Steele came up from Lodi Wednesday night but returned Thursday. She is very busy helping to get out the first issue of the *Lodi Budget*.[33]

In early June 1892, Rowena announced the commencement of the *Budget*. "Mrs. Steele has had plenty of experience in the profession, and should be able to publish a good paper."[34] No extant issues of the *Budget* can be found, so a search of general California newspapers has to be relied on for further information. On June 29, 1892, it was announced in the *Sacramento Union* that Lee had become editor and general manager of the *Weekly Budget*, and by July, possession of the *Valley Review* had been wrested away from Lee in court proceedings and relinquished back to Frank and his parents, George and Gertie Cluff who abruptly returned from San Francisco where they had intended to move.

ON DECK AGAIN.

> The Valley Review, after a short rest of several weeks, goes forth to greet its many old readers, and we hope it will be as welcome a guest as heretofore. Hereafter the Review will be published each week

under the personal supervision of Frank B. Cluff, which is a guarantee that every issue will contain an abundance of local news as well as the choicest miscellaneous reading. In the future, as in the past, the REVIEW shall ever strive to maintain the highest standard for country journalism; and it shall be our aim to excel in the production of local news. We shall retain the style of an eight-page paper, with a view of giving our advertising patrons the greatest possible returns for the least outlay of money. In this politically the REVIEW will be Democratic as it always strives for "the greatest good to the greater number." In our typographical appearance we shall strive to adhere to the most pleasing and artistical styles and keep abreast with the progressive craft. The days of the "patent outside" and "local poster" are numbered as every live, thrifty and wide-awake community needs and demands a local paper that will reflect its progress. Now that we have gained our "second wind"—excuse the term, but that expresses it exactly—we shall show the people of this neighborhood what a local newspaper is in our earnest efforts to maintain the position we have enjoyed in the past; and, also, in making the VALLEY REVIEW the favorite family journal of the great and glorious Mokelumne Valley. With the foregoing words, we shall end our salutatory.

The non-appearance of the REVIEW since May 19th was owing to a difference between Lee R. Steele, and the present publisher Frank B. Cluff, which merits no discussion here. All we have to say, however, is that we are very sorry the REVIEW failed to make its appearance for so long a period.

In an article about the dissolution published in May 1892, it was alleged that "Steele has been appropriating too much of the partnership money to his own use."[35] A blurb from Galt, California, in October 1892, quoted Rowena regarding some disparaging words she is supposed to have printed about "the editor of a disliked contemporary" (Cluff?).

> "That decayed pimple on the small toe of journalism" is what the Lodi Budget calls the editor of a disliked contemporary. As the editor of the Budget is a female sex, it would hardly be gallant in the other fellow to get back and tell her she is an innocuous desuetude bunion on the big toe of journalistic avocation. But were the she a he, he might retort by calling her that kind of a cuticular excrescence.[36]

This makes one wonder if the feud between Frank and Lee had escalated into general bad feelings between Rowena and Gertie and her large group of family and friends in Lodi. This is further supported by an article from Oakland in April 1893 where Rowena is referred to as "editress of the Lodi *Budget.*"

> Mrs. Steele ... hates a liar and isn't afraid to say so. She says: "A liar is worse than a thief, for you can guard against a thief. Lodi has several of this kind of cattle and they have been quite busy the past two weeks circulating their malicious falsehoods. This is simply to let them know that we are 'onto' them and if we hear any more we propose to give their names and prove them to be cruel, cowardly liars. We do not particularly care what they say, but for the fun of the thing we will give them some free advertising if

they persist in their folly." What in the world could
they have said to make the madam so mad?[37]

What "liars" she is referring to is unknown but can be inferred as
those spreading tales about Lee and his brief association with the
Valley Review.

Under a headline of "Legislative Chips" in January 1893,
Rowena is quoted, "Some of the Smart Aleck reporters at
Sacramento are sharply criticizing the ladies who are there
lobbying in the interest of different measures. We are acquainted
with several of these ladies, and know them to be ladies in every
sense of the word. We also know several of the drunken loafers
who are writing these criticisms, and know them to be drunken
loafers in every sense of the word."[38]

On October 28, 1893, the *Weekly Galt Gazette* reported
that "Editor Lee" had changed the format of the *Budget*.

> Editor Lee R. Steele, of the Lodi Budget, paid the
> Gazette office a friendly visit Thursday. In
> connection with his newspaper business, Mr. Steele is
> at present engaged in the publication of an official
> railroad timetable for interior small towns, with the
> hope of making money out of the scheme by the
> advertisements which he proposes to publish for
> each town on a large card surrounding his
> timetable.[39]

Sometime in late 1893, Rowena's final novel, *Weak or
Wicked, A Romance*, was published by the Steele Publishing
Company, Lodi, described as "a romance of the East and of
California, in which the writer weaves a number of incidents in
the life of the heroine, who has gone wrong, for the purpose of
demonstrating that wickedness in children, developed in after life,

is often the result of an ill-assorted marriage of a brutish man and a gentle but dissatisfied woman."[40]

On March 20, 1894, it was announced that the Lodi *Valley Review* had been purchased by George B. Broadberg, J.E. Ruggles and T.G. Spencer,[41] followed on April 21, 1894, with a notice that "[t]he *Valley Review* and Lodi *Budget* are consolidated under the name of the Lodi *Review-Budget*,"[42] revealing that Lee had also turned over their paper. One week later, Lee was reported visiting Stockton, informing of the new endeavor. "L.R. Steele of the Tracy *Times* was in town yesterday. He formerly published the Lodi *Budget*."[43]

By late 1894, Lee and Lennie were living in Tracy, San Joaquin County, where in January 1895 he made an unsuccessful attempt to be appointed Justice of the Peace. In June of 1895, Lennie was reported to have visited her sister Mrs. Herman Bigelow, at O'Neals, Madera County, her sister Mrs. Fred Frost in Fresno, and her mother-in-law, Rowena, in Merced. They were still living in Tracy in June 1897, when Clarke celebrated his fifth birthday, but, by the next year, Lee had sold the *Tracy Times* to Jacob Blumer, and Lennie was back in Merced where she obtained a divorce from Lee on October 4, 1898. Lee moved back to the family home in Merced and briefly attempted to start a new paper called the *Merced Penny Press*, but was listed as "day labour" living with Rowena in the Main Street "Coterie Cottage" in the 1900 census. Lennie married her second husband, William C. Crawford, on October 5, 1899, at her home on Main Street in Merced, nearby to Rowena and Lee.

On June 29, 1900, the *County Sun* (acknowledging the *Express*) noted that Rowena had recently celebrated a birthday. She "was 76 years of age on Wednesday and was remembered by her friends with an abundance of cake, pies and other good things."[44]

The Final Kiss Goodbye

In late January 1901, Harry was called to Merced to see his mother who had been seriously ill for two weeks. He arrived in time to kiss Rowena goodbye for the last time at 7:30 on the morning of February 7. She died "from a general breaking down of the system" according to the *Merced Express*. "She had been failing for several years and rapidly in the last few months."[45] Norvell continued in the kind and complimentary obituary,

> Mrs. Steele was a native of Goshen, Orange County, New York, and in pioneer days came to California. Some forty years ago while the widow Granice, she married Mr. R.J. Steele in Placer county and after their marriage they removed to Snelling, in this county, and established the "Merced Banner" which was afterwards merged into the San Joaquin Argus, which was published for a number of years at Snelling and at Merced. Ten years ago she retired from the newspaper business on account of failing health. Mrs. Steele during her newspaper work wrote several novels and was known in the California literary world as the pioneer novelist of the Pacific coast. She was proverbial for her many and beautiful obituary notices of departed friends, which the editor of this paper never considered were appreciated by the ungrateful public.
>
> Mrs. Steele was also proverbial for many charitable acts which the public passed by unnoticed. Her good work and kind acts are now ended and she is at rest. She leaves two sons, H.H. Granice and Lee R. Steele, to mourn her death.
>
> The funeral will take place this afternoon from her late residence on west 17th street at 3 o'clock.[46]

The *Merced Evening Sun* echoed Norvell's praise (with a few, relatively minor errors).

THE PASSING OF MRS. R.G. STEELE

———

Death Today Terminates an Eventful and Honorable Career.

———

This morning, Feb. 7th, 1901, Mrs. R.G. Steele, aged 76 years, gave up life's struggles and sank into the rest that awaits the just beyond mortal gaze.

The funeral will be held from the First Presbyterian Church at 2 o'clock p.m. tomorrow, Rev. O.S. Barnum to officiate.

The life of Mrs. Steele has been an eventful one. She was born in Orange County, N.Y., June 20, 1824. Subsequently her father removed with his family to New York City, where at the age of twenty [*sic*, twenty-five] deceased was married to her first husband.

The issue of that marriage was two sons, Harry Hale Granice, publisher of a paper at Sonoma, in this State, and George Law Granice, who died at the age of 24.

In 1856, she came to California to join her husband who had preceded her. Shortly after [*sic*, four years later], the husband sickened and died in San Francisco, leaving the widowed mother without means. For a time she supported herself and two sons by writing for periodicals and giving dramatic readings.

In 1861 the deceased was married to Robert J. Steele, who was then editing a paper at Salmon Falls, in California. The following year they removed to

Snelling and jointly commenced the publication of the "Merced Banner," the first paper published in Merced county.

Upon the removal of the county seat from Snelling in 1872, Mr. and Mrs. Steele removed to Merced and commenced the publication of the "Merced Argus," which was continued by Mrs. Steele after the death of Mr. Steele, which occurred in 1889 [*sic*, 1890], up to the year 1890 when the Argus was sold out and Mrs. Steele retired from the active duties of a publisher. The issue of the second marriage was one son, Lee R. Steele, now residing in Merced.

The deceased was a writer of no mean ability. To her was attributed the authorship of the first novel written by a lady in California. She espoused every just cause and gave to it of her time and talent. She was a true friend to the friendless and unfortunate, giving to them such counsel as only a mother can give.

Mrs. Steele will long be remembered for her zeal in behalf of charity. The homes she has secured for orphans can be counted by the score. But her active, helpful life is ended.   J.G.E.[47]

Harry's paper printed a tribute from an unnamed friend.

Gone to a Better Land.
[Written by a Friend]

Mrs. R.G. Steele has passed to silence and pathetic dust. Life's slender cord, worn out by the continual activity of seventy-six years, has been severed and the spirit of a noble life winged its flight into the mystic realm of eternity. Mrs. Steele had been ill for several months, and when the dark curtain was rung down on the final act of her earthly existence she passed away as peacefully as in infancy she slept upon her mother's bosom.

Deceased was a woman of marked ability and her entire life was devoted to literary pursuits. For thirty years she was in the newspaper business in Merced county, and in the city of Merced she died at 7:30 o'clock last Thursday morning. In her prime Mrs. Steele wielded a versatile pen, and many of her articles, printed in leading publications, were considered literary gems. As a friend she was true blue, and in her the cardinal qualities of ideal womanhood were combined. "For justice all place a temple and all season summer" was her life's motto.

Deceased was the mother of H.H. Granice, proprietor of this paper, George Granice (deceased) and Lee Steele of Merced. She was a native of New York, but came to this State many years ago.

The funeral was held at Merced yesterday.

Now, as a last tribute to one who in life was noble, honest and true, let us hope that to her death did not bring oblivious dreamless sleep, but brighter fields where she met in joy the loved ones that had gone before and will await in peace the loved ones that are left behind.[48]

Rowena is buried next to R.J. and George in the Steele plot in the Asphodel Section of the Merced Cemetery.

Epilogue

✠

Rowena's Family Legacy—Harry and Lee and Their Children

Ten years following the death of his first wife, Katie Keogh Granice, Harry married second wife, Grace J. Bonner, on September 29, 1914, at Santa Rosa. Just three months later, he died at Lane Hospital, San Francisco.

> H.H. Granice, for thirty years editor of the *Index-Tribune*, has crossed the Great Divide and in his passing Sonoma has lost one of its most valued citizens and more than one man in the community a faithful friend and splendid adviser.
>
> His passing occurred at the Lane Hospital, San Francisco, shortly after two o'clock, Saturday morning, January 2nd. Although Mr. Granice has been in failing health for many months, yet when the summons of the Death Angel reached the veteran journalist—the dean of the newspaper fraternity in Sonoma County—his death came as a profound shock to his family and friends.
>
> While suffering from a complication of disorders, these were aggravated by congestion of the lungs which followed the inhalation of large quantities of smoke at the fire which occurred at his home in the early morning hours of Sunday, December 20th.
>
> Mr. Granice is mourned by a more than ordinary circle of friends, embracing as they do men and women of every faith and creed and of every walk in life. He was a man quick to see and appreciate the virtue and possibilities of his fellows and interested himself in them in a way that made for him life-

lasting friendships. While he made countless friends, he also had his factional differences, but he ever respected his antagonists when they played fair and it was only the charlatans who suffered criticism at his hands. It was this fair, broad dealing policy that made the *Index-Tribune* a power in the community, in the county and throughout the State of California.

The upbuilding of Sonoma was his life's work, and his abiding faith in its future and citizenship never faltered.

Honest and above board in his business dealings, fair and square with his fellows, loyal in his friendships, staunch in his principles, Sonoma has lost a magnificent friend, but the newspaper he has built will endure, and be unswerving in the policies he has outlined for it—a monument to his life's work and enterprise.

No better words than those of Mr. Granice himself, taken from the issue of the *Index-Tribune* on its thirty-fifth birthday, bear out this encomium:

———

"With this issue the Sonoma Index-Tribune enters upon its thirty-fifth birthday. Established in 1878 by Ben Frank, a well-known newspaper man of those early days, the paper passed through many vicissitudes during the first five years of its publication, and during that brief period changed hands no less than a dozen times.

"In 1884 it became the property of the present owner and editor, who purchased it from ex-Congressman E.J. Livernash, then a mere boy of seventeen but a writer of ability, whose only fault was that he was too outspoken in his editorial utterances for so limited a field as Sonoma was in those days, and he thought it best to retire and devote his energies elsewhere. This he did and afterward became famous as a writer, lawyer and politician, and has never ceased to congratulate himself upon passing the buck up to us.

"Succeeding Mr. Livernash, the present management has now for a period of thirty consecutive years, without missing an issue, successfully shaped its policy and made the paper a good paying proposition. There are reasons for this success which can readily be made plain in a few counts:

"First—These columns have always been free and untrammeled and have at all times been used in the interests of the whole people regardless of petty cliques, clans and combinations which have sought in the past to shape its editorial utterances in the interests of the few as against the many.

"Second—This newspaper has always consistently worked for the development of the resources of both town and valley and endeavored the best it knew how to make the charms of this nature-favored section known to the outer world and not in vain, we know.

"Third—The Index-Tribune has never under its present management been under the domination of any one man (except its editor) or any set of men with private axes to grind, and always tried to do right and endeavored to serve the people of both town and valley faithfully and well.

"Fourth—The editorial columns of the Index-Tribune have never been conducted on a commercial basis—that is to say, they are not for sale to further the plans of schemers, mischief-makers, agitators or corrupt politicians, who have been forced to enter the newspaper field themselves in order to fool some people.

"Fifth—Last, but not least, the Index-Tribune has never repudiated a debt, but for thirty years has paid every bill promptly, has had no debts, has contributed in a modest way to charity and public enterprises, and after all these years of activity is still backed up by public opinion and confidence and the editor's private bank account."

* * *

The remains of Mr. Granice were brought to the home wherein for several decades he had resided, and from which just one week before he had departed, hopeful that he would return improved in health. Old-time friends—the associates of thirty years and the friends no less sincere and true of recent years were gathered to pay sorrowful tribute when all that was mortal of Harry Hale Granice was borne within the home portals.

* * *

In the family plot in peaceful Mountain Cemetery, by the side of beloved ones gone before, the remains were consigned to eternal rest, and his grave was covered with the most beautiful of floral offerings.

Besides his wife, to whom he was wedded but three months ago, in September, Mr. Granice is survived by three daughters: Mrs. Walter Murphy of Alameda, Mrs. Frederick Sprague of Los Banos, and Mrs. Ernest G. Lynch of Ukiah.

His Wife's Sentiments.

In some sad hour I'll hold your trembling hand,
And plead the passing moments for delay,
And one must stay.

It matters not for us which it shall be,
Who first shall tread alone the hidden ways,
But God be gentle in that lonely hour
To the one who stays.[1]

There followed a years'-long court dispute between Harry's three daughters and their stepmother wherein the latter was charged with dissipating the estate and squandering Harry's inheritance.

The *Index-Tribune* was spared from the legal wranglings, however, when ownership and active management of the *Index-Tribune* was taken over by daughter Cecilia Celeste 'Celia' Granice Murphy and her husband, Walter. Since her graduation from college in 1901, Celia had continuously worked in the business at papers in San Rafael and San Francisco and had published articles in *Life* magazine, among others. Her 1937 book *People of the Pueblo: The Story of Sonoma* is considered to be the first complete history of the area.

Celia and Walter spent the remainder of their lives in Sonoma where they lived in a unique, historic home in Sonoma, the former barracks of Mexican General Mariano Guadalupe Vallejo's troops, in which they entertained politicians, writers and other luminaries over the years.

The Murphys successfully ran the paper until their retirement in 1949, at which time the helm was turned over to their nephew, Robert Lynch, the only child of Alice 'Ramona' Granice Lynch and husband Ernest Glenn Lynch. Ramona was an accomplished singer and entertainer in her youth and had also taken an active interest in the *Index-Tribune* over the years, but suffered from health issues and died rather young at 42 in 1923.

Robert carried on the family newspaper heritage until his death in 2003, whereupon his son, William 'Bill' Lynch, became publisher and editor-in-chief until his retirement in 2012. Bill is now continuing the family literary tradition with the publication of a novel, *Mekong Belle: Love's Impossible Choice*, in 2023.

As far as I can determine, middle daughter Julie Hortense Granice Sprague was not involved in writing or publishing following in "Grandma Steele's" footsteps, although at an early age she was lauded for her singing voice and stage presence. She married Frederick Fellows Sprague, had two children, divorced, and lived in Berkeley, California until her death in 1973 at age ninety. Among her descendants will be found at least one writer/editor, and several following the professions of teacher, attorney, minister, community worker, therapist, political activist, bank manager, nurse.

Lee Steele seems to have struggled both personally and professionally following the death of his father in 1889, the divorce from Linnie, and mother's death. Galloway writes that Lee was bequeathed five city lots in Merced that Rowena had homesteaded through the years[2], but he appears to have lost or sold that land within the next five years, since in June 1907 he was reported to be living in Arroyo Grande in San Luis Obispo County and working as manager of the Recorder Publishing Company, managing company of the *Arroyo Grande Recorder*.[3] Later that year he moved to Huasna in San Obispo County.

> Lee R. Steele, manager of the Recorder Publishing Company for the last year, now that the paper has been sold, has entered into business arrangements on the Huasna, where he will go next week.—Arroyo Grande Herald[4]

Two years later, in the April 1910 census, he is listed as a printer living alone in Mariposa. He remained a bachelor until August 17 of that year, when, at 47, he married teenager Eloisa Mae Castro in Mariposa, California. Eloisa was the mother of Rowena May (February 5, 1916), Marie Alfreda (May 10, 1918),

Robert Lee (September 9, 1921), and Julia Agnes (1924), all in Mariposa.

Lee died the following year on August 25, 1925, just a month after being employed by Eugene E. Foley in the publication of the *Yosemite Tourist.*[5]

LEE RICHMOND STEELE, PASSES AWAY SUDDENLY

Lee R. Steele, who resided a short distance above Bootjack, died in the office of Dr. J.L. McDaniel in Mariposa Wednesday evening at 8:30 o'clock.

Death was caused by hemorrhage of the brain.

Mr. Steele had been in Mariposa on that day and appeared to be in his usual health. About 5 P.M. he left here on horseback for his home and had gotten as far as Big Spring Hill, where he was found lying unconscious by the roadside by Neil Hansen, a Standard Oil employee, who brought him to Mariposa for treatment, but medical assistance was of no avail.

He spent the past summer in Yosemite Valley, where he was employed by ... Foley, assisting in the publication of the "Yosemite Tourist," he being a printer by trade.

Mr. Steele was a native of Merced county, the son of the late Robert and Mrs. R.G. Steele, pioneer newspaper publishers in Merced County.

He was a veteran of the Spanish-American War.[xxvii]

Lee Richmond Steele was aged 63 years. He is survived by his wife Mrs. Eloisa Steele and four small children, one son and three daughters. Two children

---

[xxvii] Co. H, 6th California Voluntary Infantry, May 11-December 15, 1898.

by a former marriage are Clark Steele of Fresno and
Mrs. Constance [Duarte] of Delhi.

The remains were interred in the public cemetery
yesterday afternoon, the funeral being in charge of
Undertaker D.E. Johnson.

PIONEER MERCED EDITOR IS DEAD
Lee R. Steele, Once Publisher of "Argus," Known
Through State

Found lying by a roadside, Lee R. Steele, former
Merced newspaper publisher and prominent in early
press circles in the San Joaquin, died last night at
Mariposa. He was 63 years old.

An apoplectic stroke, suffered while he was riding
home from Mariposa to Bootjack, mountain village,
caused his death, according to a Mariposa physician.
Steele was found by Neal Hanson, an oil company
employee. He rushed the sick man back to Mariposa,
where he died shortly after arrival. Funeral
arrangements were to be completed today by
Coroner D.E. Johnson of Mariposa, who took the
body in charge.

Born in this county, Mr. Steele was for many years
publisher of the *San Joaquin Valley Argus*, one of
Merced's first newspapers. He later published a paper
at Tracy and occupied a most prominent position in
editorial circles here and over the entire valley. His
mother, Mrs. Rowena Steele, was also prominent in
early county history.

For the past several summers, Mr. Steele had been
engaged in publication of the "Yosemite Tourist," a
paper in the interests of Yosemite valley. He was a

conspicuous figure on his famous white horse, which he invariably rode.

Mr. Steele's death caused scores of Merced residents who remembered him in connection with his newspaper to express sorrow at his passing today.

Twice married, Mr. Steele is survived by two children by his first wife, Clark Steele of Fresno, and Mrs. Constance Duarte of Merced. A wife and four children also [survive].[6]

It does not appear that any of Lee's descendants followed in the family path of printing and publishing. Several of them had tragic lives, for example, Lee's son Clarke became permanently disabled when he was severely injured in an explosion at Kingsburg, California in 1925 while working on a bridge construction project.

Rowena's Societal Legacy

For fifty years, Rowena's views on women's rights, education for girls, women's suffrage, and women working outside the home were expressed continually through the publication of her columns in the *San Joaquin Valley Argus*, several of which were reprinted in other newspapers around the country, and in her vivid, engaging stories and novels. Hers was indeed a "voice in the wilderness" of a bygone era in a rough and uncivilized "wild west" California of the mid-19th century.

It would be more than sixty years after Rowena began writing about the right of women to vote that it would be officially recognized and enacted by the U.S. Congress. The principle of universal education for all children, boys and girls, was not widely acknowledged until the early 20th century, and, even then, for many decades after there was a wide swath of illiteracy among Americans and very few women in higher education. Likewise, the concept of women having careers outside the home would not gain widespread acceptance until the latter 20th century.

She was a prominent voice in a small chorus her whole life, but that did not deter her. With the power of the virtues that were either innate or honed through the harsh lessons of life, she persisted and never wavered in her convictions. In this, Rowena has been a paragon for me personally, and I hope her spirit will touch and inspire the readers likewise. It has been an honor and privilege bestowed on me to be her biographer and champion.

In Volume II, I will offer Rowena's short stories and novellas written from 1857 to 1873; Volume III will contain works from 1874 through her last novel in 1893. As Rowena herself described in the Introduction to *The Family Gem* in 1857:

> They are simple stories simply told, and the only merit the writer presumes to claim for them is, they are the children of fact, not fancy. This, and this alone, is the only consideration which could have induced me to put them before the world in their present form.

In Volume IV, I will present many of the dozens of columns describing her travels around 1800s California.

Priscilla Stone Sharp

April 2024

Endnotes – Chapter I

[1] Granice, Rowena, "My Childhood's Home," *The Family Gem*, Sacramento: S.H. Aspell, 1857, p. 40

[2] *San Joaquin Valley Argus*, Merced, California ["SJVA"], 15 Apr 1871

[3] Granice, op cit., "The Rag Party; Or, the First and Last Love of Aunt Debbie," *The Family Gem*

[4] SJVA, 21 Nov 1883

[5] SJVA, 15 Jan 1876

[6] Steele, Mrs. Rowena Granice, "The Old Shoe, A Christmas Story," *Merced Herald*, 26 Dec 1868; reprinted SJVA, 27 Dec 1873.

[7] SJVA, 29 Jun 1879. Rowena added the word "Dutch" to the quotation, which should read simply "Old Continentals..." thus leading some family members and historians to conclude that the family was from Holland. (*See* Galloway, R. Dean, "Talented Mrs. Steele Was Editor, Publisher, State's First Woman Novelist and Actress," *Merced, Ca. Sun-Star*, 8 Sep 1969, p. A-4.) This is possible, since there is very strong evidence that both sides of her family have been in America since the 1600s when the Dutch settled New Amsterdam.

[8] SJVA, 7 Jan 1871

[9] Grannis, Sidney S., "Genealogical History of the Grannis Family in America From 1630 to 1901," Minneapolis: The Franklin Printing Company, 1901.

[10] *Ibid.*, p. 24.

[11] Strong, Frederick Augustus, "The Descendants of Edward Grannis Who Was in New Haven, Connecticut as Early as 1649 and Died There December 10th, 1719," Bridgeport, CT, 1927, p. 36.

[12] SJVA, 17 Apr 1886

[13] SJVA, 9 Jan 1886

[14] SJVA, 10 Aug 1889

[15] SJVA, 19 Jan, 26 Jan, and 2 Feb 1878

[16] SJVA, 23 Jul 1890

[17] Steele, Rowena Granice, *Leonnie St. James; Or, The Suicide's Curse*, Auburn, CA: Union Advocate Office, 1862.

[18] *Ibid.*

[19] *Ibid.*

[20] Steele, Mrs. Rowena Granice, "The Old Shoe, A Christmas Story," *op cit.*

[21] SJVA, 9 Nov 1878

[22] Strong, *op cit.*, p. 103.

[23] Biography and Genealogical History of the City of Newark and Essex County, New Jersey, New York: Lewis Historical Publishing Co., 1898, pp. 168-9

[24] SJVA, 9 Nov 1878

[25] SJVA, 12 Jun 1886

[26] SJVA, 17 May 1890

[27] SJVA, 15 Aug 1874

[28] SJVA, 26 Nov 1887

[29] *Merced Herald*, 31 Jul 1869
[30] Strong, *op cit.*, p. 104.

Endnotes - Chapter II

[1] SJVA, 19 Jan 1878
[2] Granice, Rowena, "Blanche Blakely; Or, The Curse of Beauty," The Two Wives — A Tale of Domestic Life in California," *The Family Gem*, Sacramento: S.H. Aspell, 1857
[3] SJVA, 6 Aug 1870; though not signed, it was obviously written by Rowena from the references to her girlhood in New York.
[4] Steele, Mrs. Rowena Granice, "Eudolia Dudley; Or, Never Too Late," SJVA, 21 Sep 1872
[5] SJVA, 5 Jan 1884
[6] This name is variously spelled "Claughly," "Cloughly," "Caughley," "Clawley," etc. in the various records; however, it has never been found listed as "McClaughley," as has been suggested by some writers. *See* Cabezut-Ortiz, Delores J., *Merced County — The Golden Harvest*, Northridge, CA: Windsor Publications, 1987, pp. 73-75; *see also*, Koon, Helene Wickham, *Gold Rush Performers, A Biographical Dictionary of Actors, Singers, Dancers, Musicians, Circus Performers and Minstrel Players in America's Far West, 1848-1869*, Jefferson, NC: McFarland & Co., 1994, pp. 45-6
[7] SJVA, 20 Mar 1875
[8] *New York Post*, 29 Aug 1845
[9] Galloway, R. Dean, "Rowena Granice," *Pacific Historian*, Spring 1980, p. 105
[10] Boessenecker, John, ed., *Against the Vigilantes: The Recollections of Dutch Charley Duane*, Norman: University of Oklahoma Press, 1999, pp. 4-7.
[11] Granice, op cit., "The Two Wives — A Tale of Domestic Life in California," *The Family Gem*
[12] SJVA, 20 Mar 1875
[13] 1850 Federal Census, 16th Ward, New York City, New York Co., p. 231, House No. 283, Visit No. 835
[14] Granice, *op cit.*, "The Two Wives"
[15] *Ibid.* In all fairness, Thomas may not have had much choice as to the timing of his departure. Dates for traveling in the mid-1800s, especially on the ocean, were restricted by weather and contingent on the seasons. Also, there were a great number of people going to California; berths on all steamships were booked up well in advance, and it may have been that he was able to obtain passage only on a particular date.
[16] *Ibid.*, p. 10.
[17] *Ibid.*
[18] Fabian, Ann, "The Lost Museum," City Univ. of New York, http://chnm.gmu.edu/lostmuseum/lm/180/.
[19] *Ibid.*
[20] SJVA, 12 Nov 1887

[21] SJVA, 31 Aug 1878; apparently Mr. Logan, an Irish Catholic, was referring to the Vatican in that remark.

[22] SJVA, 30 Sep 1876, describing Merced's El Capitan Hotel, comparing it favorably with other grand hotels she had visited.

[23] SJVA, 23 Mar 1878

[24] New York Daily Times, 8 Nov 1853

[25] New York Daily Times, 17 Nov 1853

[26] *New York Sun Times*, Feb 1856, reprinted *Daily Alta California*, San Francisco 16 Mar 1856

Endnotes – Chapter III

[1] *Hutchings California Magazine*, Jan 1858

[2] Steele, Rowena Granice, "Columbia Louden; Or, Why She Loved Him," SJVA, 12 Mar 1870

[3] Soulé, Frank, John H. Gihon, M.D., and James Nisbet, *The Annals of San Francisco*, Part Second, Chapter XXVIII (1853), San Francisco: D. Appleton & Co., 1855.

[4] SJVA, 10 Dec 1870.

[5] Jolly, Michelle, "Sex, Vigilantism and San Francisco, 1856," *Common-Place—The Interactive Journal of Early American Life, Inc.*, www.common-place.org, Vol. 3, No. 4, July 2003.

[6] Soulé, *et al., op cit.*

[7] Jolly*, op cit.*

[8] Bancroft, Hubert Howe, *The Works of Hubert Howe Bancroft*. Volumes XXXVII, Chap. XIX, San Francisco: A. L. Bancroft and Company, 1882-88, p. 348; *The San Francisco Directory, 1852-'53*, San Francisco: James M. Parker, 1852: "Claughley, J.A., policeman, 244 Dupont." See also Boessenecker, *op cit.*

[9] The general time-line and much of the information gathered for the chronology was found at the website of the California State Military Museum (www.militarymuseum.org).

[10] Advertisement, *Fireman's Journal* (San Francisco), Apr 1856.

[11] *Alta,* 16 Mar 1856, p. 3, col. 2.

[12] *Alta*, 8 Apr 1856, p. 2, col. 6.

[13] McCabe, J.H., *McCabe's Journal (of San Francisco Theater)*, Vol. I, unpublished manuscript in collection of Sutro Library, San Francisco. See also Gaer, Joseph, ed., "The Theatre of the Gold Rush Decade in San Francisco" (Monograph no. 5, G-F), Abstract from the SERA Project 2-F2-132, 3-F2-197, California Literary Research (Mimeographed).

[14] Galloway, *Pacific Historian, op cit.*, p. 106 [Citing Writer's Program, California. "Theatrical Annals of Sacramento...." Compiled by Northern California Writer's Project, Works Program Administration from newspapers in the California State Library (Typewritten manuscript, 1939-1940), Volume 8, *Sacramento Daily Union*, 1856, March 17; May 7-16, 1856].

[15] Granice, Rowena, "The Two Wives," *op cit.*, pp. 10-11.

[16] Galloway, *Pacific Historian, op cit.*, p. 109, n. 16.

[17] Soulé, et al., *op cit.*
[18] Granice, Rowena, "The Two Wives," *op cit.*, p. 12.
[19] SJVA, 24 Jul 1875
[20] McCabe, *op cit.*
[21] Koon, *Gold Rush Performers, op cit.* See also Koon, Helene, *How Shakespeare Won the West: Players and Performances in America's Gold Rush,* 1849-1865, Jefferson, NC: McFarland, 1989, p. 138.
[22] *Alta,* 24 Mar 1856.
[23] *Fireman's Journal,* 24 May 1856
[24] *Daily Evening Bulletin,* San Francisco, 20 Jun 1856
[25] *Fireman's Journal,* 23 Jun 1856
[26] Buckbee, Edna Bryan, *The Saga of Old Tuolumne,* New York: Press of the Pioneers, 1935, pp. 370-1.
[27] *Golden Era,* 29 Nov 1863, reprinted in Walker, Franklin, ed., *The Washoe Giant in San Francisco,* George Fields, 1938, pp. 58-60.
[28] *Alta,* 23 and 24 Aug 1864; Langley, Henry G., *The San Francisco Directory; Chronological History of Principal Events.* 1864, 1865, San Francisco: Self-published, 1865.
[29] 1860 Federal Census, District 2, San Francisco, San Francisco County, California, p. 582.
[30] *Alta,* 23 Aug 1864
[31] *Shasta Courier,* 27 Aug 1864

Endnotes – Chapter IV

[1] An excerpt from a book of unknown title in a folio entitled "Lola Montez" at the Performing Arts Museum and Library in San Francisco.
[2] Steele, Rowena Granice, "Lola Montez," *Leonnie St. James, op cit.*
[3] *Fireman's Journal,* 23 Aug 1856
[4] *Nevada City Journal,* 4 Jul 1856
[5] *Trinity Times,* Weaverville, 23 Aug 1856
[6] Sioli, Paolo, *History of El Dorado County,*
[7] Koon, Helene Wickham, *Gold Rush Performers, op. cit.* See also Koon, *How Shakespeare Won the West, op cit.*
[8] McCabe, *op cit.*
[9] SJVA, 20 Mar 1875
[10] SJVA, 17 Jan 1885
[11] SJVA, 20 Mar 1875
[12] SJVA, 26 Jul 1890
[13] Steele, Rowena Granice, *Dell Dart; Or, Within the Meshes,* Merced, CA: San Joaquin Valley Argus Office, 1874, p.6.
[14] *The Daily Bee,* Sacramento, 3 Apr 1857
[15] *Chico Weekly Chronicle-Record,* 11 Apr 1857
[16] *Sacramento Bee,* 4 Jun 1857
[17] *Ibid.,* 6 Jun 1857
[18] *Chico Weekly Chronicle-Record,* 27 Jun 1857

[19] *Enterprise-Record*, Oroville, 10 Apr 1857
[20] *Sacramento Bee*, 10 Aug 1857
[21] Original playbills in the collection of the California Historical Society, 678 Mission Street, San Francisco, CA. According to Koon, *Gold Rush Performers, op cit.,* p. 60, one of the actors in the August company was Mr. "Dumpsy" Dumphries described as "good low comic"; another described with the same phrase was Frederick B. Glover (pp. 72-3) who was also in the Chapman Company in the flop farce *Lola Montez on the Fanny Major* (the FANNY MAJOR was the ship they took from Hawaii) a play that unsuccessfully sought to cash in on the gossip swirling around the death of Ms. Montez's manager, Mr. Folland.
[22] *Sonoma County Journal*, 3 Jul 1857
[23] *Sacramento Bee*, 8 Sep 1857
[24] *Ibid.*
[25] *Ibid.*, 10 Sep 1857
[26] Koon, *How Shakespeare...*, *op cit.*
[27] *San Francisco Call*, 4 May 1890
[28] Koon, *Gold Rush Performers, op cit.*
[29] *Ibid.*
[30] McCabe, *op cit.*
[31] Koon, *Gold Rush Performers, op cit.*, p. 5.
[32] McCabe, *op cit.*
[33] *Alta*, 15 Mar 1858, p. 1, col. 4 (copied from the *Sacramento Bee*, 13 Mar 1858, p. 3, col. 1).
[34] Granice, "A Chapter on Actresses," *The Family Gem, op cit.*, p. 38.
[35] Galloway, *Pacific Historian, op cit.*, p. 110.
[36] Bryant, Dolores Waldorf, "No. 77 Long Wharf—From Publishing Hall to Temple of Mirth," *California Historical Society Quarterly*, Vol. XXI, Mar 1942, pp. 75-79.
[37] *Ibid.*
[38] *Ibid.*
[39] McCabe, *op cit.*
[40] *New York Times,* 30 Jul 1867, p. 5, col. 2
[41] Kenderdine, Thaddeus S., *A California Tramp and Later Footprints; Or, Life on the Plains and in the Golden State Thirty Years Ago, with Miscellaneous Sketches in Prose and Verse*, Newtown, Pa., 1888, pp. 273-74
[42] *San Francisco Chronicle*, 1 May 1881. See also MacMinn, George R., *The Theatre of the Golden Era in California*, Caldwell, ID: The Caxton Printers, Ltd., 1941, p. 192.
[43] Jackson, Phyllis Wynn, *Golden Footlights, The Merry-Making Career of Lotta Crabtree*, Holiday House, 1949
[44] *Weekly Butte Record*, 25 Dec 1858
[45] *Pacific Commercial Advertiser*, Honolulu, 6 Jan 1859
[46] *Ibid.*, 10 Feb 1859
[47] *The Polynesian*, Honolulu, 15 Jan 1859
[48] *Pacific Commercial Advertiser*, 17 Feb 1859

[49] *Grass Valley National*, 26 Mar 1859

[50] McCabe, *op cit.*

[51] *Daily Evening Bulletin* (San Francisco) 10 Aug 1859

[52] Foster, Lois M., *Federal Theatre Project, Annals of the San Francisco Stage*, Vol. I (1850-1880), San Francisco, April 1937 (Typewritten MS at Bancroft Library, UC-Berkeley).

[53] *Marysville Daily National Democrat*, 16 Aug 1859

[54] Bryant, *op cit.*

[55] Galloway, *Pacific Historian, op cit.*, p. 111 [citing Bryant, *op cit.*, and *San Francisco Bulletin*, 24 Dec 1859, p. 1:2, which states that the benefit was held on the 24th].

[56] SJVA, fall 1889, quoting E.G. Waite, *Overland*, Oct 1889

[57] *Merced Star*, Merced, CA, 22 Jul 1880

[58] 1860 Federal Census, 2d District, San Francisco, San Francisco County, CA.

[59] *Alta*, 27 May 1860

[60] *Sacramento Bee*, 27 Jun 1860

[61] Galloway, *Pacific Historian, op cit.*

Endnotes – Chapter V

[1] Steele, Rowena Granice, "Columbia Louden; Or, Why She Loved Him," SJVA, 12 Mar 1870

[2] Mexican War Pension, Declaration of Widow for Benefits, 3 Mar 1890. The town of Salmon Falls does not exist anymore; it was covered over when Lake Folsom was built. It is interesting to note that Rowena waited the socially correct year before remarrying, even though her marriage to Thomas appears to have been a sham.

[3] *Mountain Democrat*, 5 Sep 1860

[4] *Sacramento Bee*, 15 Oct 1860

[5] SJVA, 8 Nov 1879, in an article about a five-gallon stone jar that had been in the Steele family for over eighty years, then in the possession of Mary Victoria (Mrs. B.F.C.) Brooks.

[6] SJVA, 3 Apr 1886

[7] SJVA, 31 May 1879. This is also indicative of Rowena's knack for finding something nice to say about everyone, even those she had never met.

[8] SJVA, 13 Apr 1872

[9] James, Russell D., "Possum Town Histories — Mexican War Veterans in Friendship Cemetery," http://www.rootsweb.com/~mslownde/Possumtown/Column_1.htm.

[10] *Weekly Merced Herald*, 26 Sep 1868

[11] SJVA, 11 Jan 1890

[12] Galloway, *Pacific Historian*, op cit., p. 112.

[13] *Ibid.* See also "History of Columbia's Newspapers," http://www.columbiagazette.com/paperhist.html.

[14] Galloway, R. Dean, "Merced Newspapers, A History and Checklist," unpublished mss., Stanislaus State College Library, Acquisitions List (Turlock,

Calif., January 1963); *but see* Kemble, Edward C., *A History of California Newspapers, 1856-1858*, Los Gatos: The Talisman Press, 1962, p. 381 ("leased by Duchow and Carder for six months").

[15] 1860 Federal Census, Forest Hill, Placer County, California, p. 791.

[16] Galloway, *Pacific Historian, op cit.*

[17] Constance Steele Cook, interview with R. Dean Galloway, 13 Apr 1968.

[18] *Auburn Herald*, 7 Jun 1862

[19] Steele, Rowena Granice, *Leonnie St. James; Or, The Suicide's Curse, op cit.*, Introduction.

[20] SJVA, 22 Dec 1883

[21] Outcalt, John, *History of Merced County, California*, Los Angeles: Historic Record Company, 1925, p. 98.

[22] SJVA, 18 Jun 1870

[23] *Ibid.*

[24] SJVA, 11 Jan 1872

[25] Galloway, *Pacific Historian, op cit.*, pp. 112-3; *History of Merced County, California*, San Francisco: Elliott & Moore, 1881, pp. 162-3; Outcalt, *op cit.*, p. 327 (Outcalt states that, according to Peter Fee's diary, the date was July 2).

[26] SJVA, 5 Jul 1879

[27] *Merced Express*, 10 Feb and 3 Mar 1877

[28] SJVA, 16 Feb 1878 (the obituaries were written so long after the deaths because the *Argus* office was closed for ten months by the rival newspaper and County "Clique" politicians).

[29] SJVA, 23 Feb and 5 Oct 1878

[30] *History of Merced County, California, op cit.*

[31] *Golden Era* (San Francisco), 23 May 1863; *see also* Walker, Franklin, *San Francisco's Literary Frontier*, Alfred A. Knopf, 1939; reprinted 1970, University of Washington Press, Americana Library Paperback edition, p. 111.

[32] California State Military Museum, *op cit. See also* Tinkham, George Henry, *California, Men and Events, 1769-1890*, Stockton, 1915, p. 195.

[33] Visalia *Delta*, quoted in *Merced Tribune*, 26 Dec 1874

[34] SJVA, 20 Mar 1875

[35] Galloway, R. Dean, *Rowena Granice Steele; Or, Mistress of Her Fate*, unpublished mss. circa 1969.

[36] *Weekly Merced Herald*, 1 May 1869

[37] *History of Merced County, California, op cit.*, pp. 162-3.

[38] *Ibid.*, pp. 125-6.

[39] Galloway, *Pacific Historian, op cit.*, citing U.S. War Dept., *War of the Rebellion* (Series I, Vol. 50, Part 2, Washington: U.S. Government Printing Office, 1897), pp. 204-205.

[40] California State Military Museum, *op cit.*

[41] *History of Merced County, California, op cit.*, pp. 162-3.

[42] *Mariposa Gazette*, 26 May 1917

[43] Galloway, R. Dean, *Merced Newspapers, A History and Checklist.*

Endnotes – Chapter VI

[1] *Tuolumne City News*, 6 Mar 1868, p. 2:4
[2] *Mariposa Free Press*, 5 Aug 1870, p. 3:5
[3] *Weekly Merced Herald*, 3 Jun 1865
[4] *Ibid.*, 1 Jul 1865
[5] *Ibid.*, 16 Sep 1865
[6] *Mariposa Gazette*, 21 Oct 1865
[7] Galloway, *Pacific Historian, op cit.*, p. 115
[8] *Messenger* (Woodbridge, CA), 22 Dec 1866
[9] SJVA, 20 Mar 1875
[10] Steele, Rowena Granice, *Dell Dart, op cit.*, p. 52
[11] SJVA, 6 May 1876
[12] SJVA, 23 Dec 1871
[13] Galloway, *Pacific Historian, op cit.*, p. 115, citing *Tuolumne City News*, 7 Aug 1868, p. 2:1
[14] SJVA, 28 Aug 1869
[15] Galloway, *op cit.*, p. 117
[16] *Merced Herald*, 22 Aug 1868
[17] *Ibid.*
[18] *Herald*, 23 Jan 1869
[19] *Journal of Commerce*, reprinted SJVA, 21 Apr 1888
[20] SJVA, 20 Feb 1886
[21] SJVA, 11 Sep 1875
[22] *Herald*, 10 Oct 1868
[23] *Herald*, 15 Jan 1869
[24] *Herald*, 7 Jan 1871
[25] *Union Democrat*, Sonora, Tuolumne County, 2 Oct 1869
[26] *San Francisco Examiner*, 11 Apr 1871
[27] *Herald*, 13 Feb 1869
[28] *Ibid.*
[29] SJVA, 15 Apr 1871
[30] *Herald*, 24 Apr 1869
[31] SJVA, 21 May 1870
[32] SJVA, 12 Aug 1871
[33] SJVA, 8 Jan 1870
[34] *Herald*, 22 Aug 1868
[35] SJVA, 1 Jul 1871
[36] SJVA, 14 Dec 1878
[37] *Merced Express*, 20 Dec 1879
[38] SJVA, 21 Nov 1885
[39] SJVA, 14 Jul 1888
[40] SJVA, 1 Oct 1870
[41] *Herald*, 20 Feb 1869
[42] SJVA, 24 Apr 1886

Endnotes – Chapter VII

[1] SJVA, Dec 1872
[2] SJVA, Nov 1870
[3] SJVA, 4 Mar 1871
[4] SJVA, 25 Mar 1871
[5] *Ibid.*
[6] SJVA, 18 Jun 1870
[7] SJVA, 5 Aug 1871
[8] SJVA, 29 Jul 1871
[9] SJVA, 5 Aug 1871
[10] SJVA, Feb 1870
[11] SJVA, 17 Jun 1871
[12] SJVA, 26 Aug 1871
[13] *Ibid.*
[14] SJVA, 15 Sep 1871
[15] SJVA, Sep 1872
[16] SJVA, Aug 1872
[17] SJVA, Dec 1872
[18] SJVA, 1 May 1875
[19] SJVA, 23 Sep 1871
[20] SJVA, 13 May 1871
[21] SJVA, 1 Apr 1871
[22] SJVA, 8 Apr 1871
[23] SJVA, 10 Jun 1871
[24] SJVA, 8 Jul 1871
[25] SJVA, 29 Apr 1871
[26] Undated newspaper clipping in a mementoes box in the Merced County Courthouse Museum.
[27] SJVA, 28 Jan 1871
[28] SJVA, 18 Jul 1874
[29] SJVA, 14 Sep 1878
[30] SJVA, 10 May 1879
[31] "Appendix: Chapter LIII: California," *History of Woman Suffrage, vol. 3: 1876-1885* (Privately published, Rochester, NY, 1886) 1013 pp., p. 980.
[32] SJVA, 29 Oct 1870
[33] *Sonoma Index-Tribune*, 1 Feb 1890
[34] SJVA, 26 Oct 1878
[35] SJVA, 29 Oct 1870

Endnotes – Chapter VIII

[1] SJVA, 26 Aug 1871
[2] SJVA, 27 Jan 1872
[3] SJVA, 3 Feb 1872
[4] SJVA, 24 Feb 1872
[5] SJVA, 10 Feb 1872
[6] SJVA, 30 Mar 1872

[7] *Merced People*, 23 Mar 1872
[8] SJVA, 15 Aug 1872
[9] SJVA, 14 Dec 1872
[10] *Ibid.*
[11] SJVA, 21 Dec 1872
[12] *Ibid.*
[13] *Ibid.*
[14] SJVA, 1 Apr 1873
[15] SJVA, 3 May 1873
[16] SJVA, 1 Apr 1873
[17] SJVA, 17 May 1873
[18] SJVA, 2 Aug 1873
[19] SJVA, 24 Jan 1874
[20] *Ibid.*
[21] SJVA, Oct 1873
[22] SJVA, 11 Jul 1874
[23] SJVA, 15 Aug 1874
[24] *Ibid.*
[25] SJVA, 5 Sep 1874
[26] SJVA, 10 Oct 1874
[27] SJVA, 7 Nov 1874
[28] SJVA, 21 Nov 1874
[29] SJVA, 5 Dec 1874

Endnotes - Chapter IX

[1] *Merced Herald*, 12 Jun 1869 (in an article about the murder of Judge George G. Belt by William Dennis).
[2] From a poem by Mrs. L.E. Drake
[3] *Daily Alta California*, San Francisco, 8 Dec 1874
[4] *Merced Tribune*, 26 Dec 1874
[5] *Ibid.*
[6] *Hunted Down: Or, Five Days in the Fog. A Thrilling Narrative of the Escape of Young Granice from a Drunken, Infuriated Mob; Written by himself while in jail, and respectfully dedicated to Mr. Nicholas Breen,"* January 1875, Woman's Publishing Co., San Francisco, reprinted August 1875, Southern Mines Press, La Grange, California.
[7] *Los Angeles Herald*, 19 Dec 1874
[8] *Merced Weekly Express*, 23 Jan 1875
[9] SJVA, 13 Mar 1875
[10] *Ibid.*
[11] SJVA, 20 Mar 1875
[12] *Daily Alta California*, 8 Jul 1875
[13] *Daily Alta California*, 9 Jul 1875
[14] *Merced Weekly Express*, 10 Jul 1875
[15] *Daily Alta California*, 10 Jul 1875

[16] *Merced Weekly Express*, 10 Jul 1875
[17] SJVA, 5 Sep 1875
[18] SJVA, 24 Jul 1875
[19] *Ibid.*
[20] SJVA, 21 Aug 1875
[21] SJVA, 2 Apr 1887
[22] SJVA, 20 Nov 1875
[23] SJVA,, 23 Oct 1875
[24] SJVA, 25 Dec 1875
[25] *Merced Weekly Express*, 18 Mar 1876
[26] Opinion of the California Supreme Court, No. 10,208, Mar 1876
[27] SJVA, 20 May 1876
[28] SJVA, 29 Apr 1876
[29] Steele, Rowena Granice, "The Victim of the Reef," SJVA, 6 May 1876
[30] SJVA, 27 May 1876
[31] SJVA, 24 Jun 1876
[32] SJVA, 16 Sep 1876
[33] SJVA, 11 Nov 1876
[34] SJVA, 2 Dec 1876
[35] *Merced Weekly Express*, 30 Dec 1876
[36] *Mariposa Gazette*, 9 Dec 1876
[37] SJVA, 16 Dec 1876
[38] SJVA, 13 Jan 1877
[39] *Morning Times*, Oakland, 14 Nov 1877

Endnotes – Chapter X

[1] SJVA, 17 Feb 1877
[2] SJVA, 3 Mar 1877
[3] *Daily Evening Bulletin*, 20 Jul 1877
[4] *Fresno Republican*, 28 Jul 1877
[5] SJVA, 2 Mar 1878
[6] From an undated manuscript by Rowena quoted in the *Merced Sun-Star*, 13 Mar 2004
[7] SJVA, 3 May 1879
[8] SJVA, 27 Sep 1879
[9] SJVA, 5 Jan 1878
[10] *Fresno Republican*, 12 Jan 1878
[11] SJVA, 2 Feb 1878
[12] *Ibid.*
[13] SJVA, 9 Mar 1878
[14] SJVA, 8 Jun 1878
[15] SJVA, 23 Mar 1878
[16] SJVA, 6 Apr 1878
[17] SJVA, 22 Jun 1878
[18] SJVA, 6 Jul 1878
[19] SJVA, 7 Sep 1878

[20] SJVA, 14 Sep 1878
[21] SJVA, 5 Oct 1878
[22] SJVA, 10 May 1879
[23] SJVA, 19 Jun 1880
[24] SJVA, 24 Jul 1880
[25] Ruiz, Sharon, *The Legal Career of Laura DeForce Gordon*, Student Paper, Fall 2001
[26] SJVA, 5 Oct 1878
[27] SJVA, 8 Nov 1879
[28] SJVA, 9 Aug 1879
[29] SJVA, 19 Oct 1878
[30] SJVA, 26 Oct 1878
[31] SJVA, Nov 1878
[32] SJVA, 30 Nov 1878
[33] *Ibid.*
[34] SJVA, 18 Jan 1879
[35] SJVA, 1 Aug 1885

Endnotes - Chapter XI

[1] SJVA, 10 May 1879
[2] *Mariposa Gazette*, 7 Aug 1880
[3] "Index of Vital Records for the Years 1869-1891, *San Francisco Call*
[4] SJVA, 6 Dec 1884
[5] SJVA, 13 Jun 1885
[6] SJVA, 30 Jul 1887
[7] SJVA, 31 Jan 1885
[8] SJVA, 26 Jul 1879
[9] SJVA, 5 Jun 1880
[10] SJVA, 19 Jun 1886
[11] SJVA, 17 Jul 1886
[12] SJVA, 13 Nov 1886
[13] SJVA, 28 Jun 1890
[14] *San Francisco Chronicle*, 1 May 1881
[15] *Alameda Daily Evening*, 29 Aug 1883
[16] SJVA, 5 Sep 1885
[17] SJVA, 19 Sep 1885
[18] SJVA, 1 Dec 1883
[19] SJVA, 22 Dec 1883
[20] SJVA, 30 Jul 1887
[21] SJVA, 2 Oct 1886
[22] SJVA, 20 Apr 1889
[23] SJVA, 24 May 1884
[24] SJVA, 28 Jun 1884
[25] SJVA, 24 Oct 1885
[26] SJVA, Jun 1888

[27] *San Francisco Call*, 18 Feb 1889
[28] *Ibid.*
[29] SJVA, 8 Feb 1890
[30] SJVA, 12 Apr 1890

Endnotes – Chapter XII

[1] SJVA, 22 Jun 1889
[2] SJVA, 6 Jul 1889
[3] SJVA, 13 Jul 1889
[4] SJVA, 27 Jul 1889
[5] SJVA, 3 Aug 1889
[6] SJVA, 10 Aug 1889
[7] SJVA, 17 Aug 1889
[8] SJVA, 24 Aug 1889
[9] SJVA, 17 May 1890

End Notes—Chapter XIII

[1] SJVA, 19 Jun 1886
[2] SJVA, 18 Dec 1886
[3] SJVA, 21 Apr 1888
[4] SJVA, Aug 1888
[5] SJVA, 1 Jun 1889
[6] SJVA, 17 Aug 1889
[7] SJVA, 21 Sep 1889
[8] SJVA, 19 Oct 1889
[9] SJVA, 1 Feb 1890
[10] *San Francisco Examiner*, 29 Jan 1890
[11] An undated newspaper clipping in the files of the Merced County Museum.
[12] *Ibid.*
[13] SJVA, 8 Feb 1890
[14] *Sonoma Index-Tribune*, 22 Feb 1890
[15] SJVA, 3 May 1890
[16] SJVA, 31 May 1890
[17] *Ibid.*
[18] SJVA, 12 Jul 1890
[19] SJVA, 7 Jun 1890
[20] *Ibid.*
[21] SJVA, 12 Jul 1890
[22] SJVA, 6 Sep 1890
[23] Kieta, Joseph, "The Sun-Star boasts colorful history, *Merced Sun-Star*, 29 Mar 2002, p. 61
[24] *Merced Express*, 14 Feb 1891
[25] *Mountain Democrat*, Placerville, CA, 18 Apr 1891
[26] *Mountain Democrat*, 25 Apr 1891
[27] *Valley Review*, 4 Feb 1892
[28] *Merced Express*, 6 Feb 1892

[29] *Valley Review*, 18 Feb 1892, quoting *Stockton Independent*
[30] *Valley Review*, 25 Feb 1892
[31] *Valley Review*, 24 Mar 1892
[32] *Merced Express*, 21 May 1892
[33] *Merced Express*, 4 Jun 1892
[34] *Sacramento Bee*, 8 Jun 1892
[35] *The Evening Mail*, Stockton, CA, 14 May 1892
[36] *Weekly Galt Gazette*, 1 Oct 1893
[37] *Oakland Tribune*, 28 Apr 1893
[38] *Sacramento Bee*, 30 Jan 1893
[39] *Weekly Galt Gazette*, Galt, CA, 28 Oct 1893
[40] *San Francisco Call*, 25 Mar 1894
[41] *Mendocino Coast Beacon*, 10 Mar 1894
[42] *Gonzales Tribune*, Monterey County, CA, 21 Apr 1894
[43] *Evening Mail*, Stockton, 26 Apr 1894
[44] *Merced County Sun*, 29 Jun 1900
[45] *Merced Express*, 8 Feb 1901
[46] *Ibid.*
[47] *Merced Evening Sun*, 7 Feb 1901
[48] *Sonoma Index-Tribute*, 9 Feb 1901

Endnotes—Epilogue
[1] *Sonoma Index-Tribune*, 3 Jan 1915
[2] Galloway, *Pacific Historian, op cit.*, p. 122
[3] *Morning Tribune*, San Luis Obispo, CA, 12 Mar 1907
[4] *Tribune*, San Luis Obispo, 17 Jun 1907
[5] *Merced Express*, 10 Jul 1925
[6] Undated newspaper clippings in a manila folder at the Merced County Museum

Index